1st U.S. Serial Rights

OPERATION RECOGNITION
HONORING
NEBRASKA WAR VETERANS

By

IVAN SCHOONE

COPYRIGHT PAGE

Certain historical facts and figures were obtained from notes that the author has collected over the years. Other information came directly from the veterans themselves. The exact source of all this data is unobtainable. Where known figures are used, the source will be so noted after the sentence.

OPERATION RECOGNITION
HONORING
NEBRASKA WAR VETERANS

ISBN: 0-9678442-1-5

Library of Congress Catalog Card Number: 00-90613

Published in the United States of America
by *Schoone Publishing*
Rt. 1, Box 62, Upland, Nebraska 68981
402-756-0217

Printed in the United States of America
by **Morris Publishing**
3212 East Highway 30
Kearney, Nebraska 68847
800-650-7888

DEDICATION

This book is dedicated to all those veterans who fought in our nation's wars. Without them, we would not have our freedom. They are indeed our heroes.

ACKNOWLEDGEMENTS

Without my wife Patricia, this book would never have been completed. Her expertise with the computer makes this book possible and completed in a timely fashion. She is also my main editor and chief. My son Daniel Schoone, also contributed with editing and I thank him as well.

Perhaps most of all, I want to thank all the many veterans, their spouses and families who have expressed to me their thankfulness that someone has taken the time to document the many stories that you will find in the following pages. They have lent their support with their kind words and expressions of appreciation. Without these veterans sending me their stories, there would have been nothing to write and I am very grateful to them or their contribution.

FOREWORD

GOVERNOR MIKE JOHANNS

Governor Johanns was gracious enough to have his speechwriter, Philip Jude Weitl, compose a foreword concerning the "Operation Recognition" program, which helped inspire this book. At the end of his document, there is a story about Harold Anderson who took advantage of the program "Operation Recogntion." The story of Harold Anderson is typical of many veterans who did not finish high school.

Governor Mike Johanns wrote:

Time and time again throughout the course of our nation's history, ordinary Americans, through their tremendous bravery and dedication to country on the seas, soils and sands of the world, became extraordinary heroes deserving of every accolade we as the beneficiaries of their efforts could bestow upon them.

The legacy of America's veterans, however, reaches far deeper into our lives and in fact our futures that storied of sacrifice and valor on the battlefield. In reality, the story of American's veterans is rewritten everyday with each peaceful and freedom filled moment we enjoy as Americans.

Over the years, we have become accustomed to a lot of things that we seem to assume are automatic. From the simplest things like going to work in the morning to just going to the grocery store, it is very easy to forget what tremendous privileges we as Americans enjoy. Probably more so than anything else, we as Americans are able to enjoy the blessings of freedom.

But the freedoms we enjoy have not been without a price. For more than two centuries, the tree of American liberty has been refreshed time and again by the service of so many American men and women who gave so much of themselves to preserve and protect the ideals that are woven like threads into the fabric of our country.

This is what a program such as "Operation Recognition" is all about. It allows us to do more than honor America's fighting men and women. It helps us to remember what our brave veterans were fighting for, and what their sacrifices won for our entire country. It allows us to say thank you.

"Operation Recognition" was started as a joint effort on the part of the Nebraska Department of Veterans Affairs and the Nebraska Department of Education to not only to honor the great sacrifices of Nebraska veterans, but also to reward the education of experience they received during their time in the service. All veterans who left school in the 1930's and 1940's without graduating, were called to serve their country in the armed forces, and, for whatever personal reasons, did not return to school and complete their education after the war became eligible to receive their high school diplomas under this program.

All Nebraska schools were asked to participate by encouraging students to identify relatives, neighbors, or acquaintances in their community who served in World War II but were unable to complete their high school education. Around Veterans Day last year, schools around the state held assemblies to recognize these veterans and present them with a diploma provided by the State Board of Education and Nebraska Department of Veterans' Affairs. In the end, nearly 700 veterans of WW II received high school diplomas in ceremonies held all across the state.

"Operation Recognition" exceeded all expectations in terms of participation, public acceptance, publicity and the patriotic enthusiasm it inspired. To me, however, the significance of "Operation Recognition" can be summed up, not with the number of diplomas given out, but with the individual stories you are about to read.

Without question, there is no amount of recognition that could ever adequately repay our state's veterans for their service to our country. At best, we can only try to do all we can to show you how much we appreciate their willingness to pay the highest price to preserve a future for generations of Americans to come.

Mike Johanns
Governor of Nebraska

Thank you Governor Johanns for your input. It is very much appreciated.

The following story states just one reason of many of why these veterans didn't finish high school.

ANDERSON, HAROLD E.

Anderson had joined the Nebraska National Guard in 1938. He was attending routine guard training in Little Rock, Arkansas when his Nebraska Guard unit was mobilized and prepared for World War II in 1940. He had joined the guard while still in school. "It was a way to make a few extra dollars," he said. But when his unit became mobilized, there was no opportunity to finish school. He was in the service and this required doing what they told him.

Destined for the Pacific Theatre of Operations, Anderson started his service with the 110th Army Quartermasters. Several others from the states guard units became members of this as well. A little later he merged with the 35th Division of the U.S. Army, and was sent to California. Some of these men went to serve in the European Theatre while the rest served in the Pacific. Anderson was taken to Alaska to serve for 30 months. He spent much of his time at Dutch Harbor in the Aleutian Islands, which the Japanese had been bombing there. He helped defend this island chain to prohibit the Japanese from entering North America via this route.

Anderson completed his service duty and returned home in 1945. He got a job as a mechanic and later as a maintenance engineer at Artistic Woven Labels in Holdrege and retired from there in 1983.

At a special graduation exercise in Holdrege on Armistice Day, 1999, Anderson, now nearly 79 years of age, received his diploma. His daughter Mardell, reminded him jokingly that now that he had his diploma he had to go to work as most high school graduates do today. But Anderson chose to hang the diploma on the wall of his home so he and his wife Lillian can admire it. He says that although the diploma perhaps does him little good now, "It feels good to have it." He was also the first one to graduate from a new facility at Holdrege called, "The Tassel," the Performing Arts building, which was completed just prior to the ceremony.

**Harold E. Anderson of Holdrege is on right; Senator Chuck Hagel
is on the left. This photo was taken on Armistice Day, 1999 when
Anderson received his high school diploma 55 years after WW II.
Anderson did not finish high school when he was young because he had
chosen to join the Nebraska National Guard in 1938 while still in school.
Tough times during the 1930's forced young men like Anderson to take
what jobs they could to earn a little money. Being in the Guard, made
Anderson readily available to enter WW II with no option to finish school.**
Photo is compliments of his daughter, Mardell Ritterbush, of Funk, Nebraska

TABLE OF CONTENTS
THE VETERANS

INTRODUCTION

The United States is a very young nation compared to others that are centuries old. Nearly 225 years old, America has not really witnessed the wars as those that have existed for thousands of years. The wars that we have had are easily recalled simply because of the short time frame they have taken place in. It is easy for many of us to say, "My grandfather fought in the Civil War" because it really didn't happen that long ago.

As Americans, we have done a pretty good job of remembering our war dead. Each Memorial Day we remember those who fought for freedom. On Veterans Day again, we honor our veterans. Many books have been written concerning our nations wars. We have the opportunity to remember, and remember we should!

The purpose of this book is to document stories of our veterans of the state of Nebraska. Some have already been documented in our history books. According to my research, I have not found a book compiled only of Nebraska war veterans and their stories. No where can families go to a book and look up a certain member of their family who fought when our country called. Hopefully, they can do that now, if a certain veteran felt like sharing his/her story, you will find it in this book. It is my wish that children and grandchildren of these veterans will one-day refer to this book and say, "My dad, or my grandma served this country. Look what they did! That's why I'm free!"

Many young people today have no idea what it cost to preserve freedom. They never lived during a time of war except for some of the small-scale conflicts that continue to this day. They never witnessed what it means when a nation like ours, as one unit, fights a war in a foreign land. We should thank God for that, but the fact remains our freedoms we enjoy were bought and paid for with a very high price. Precious blood of our sons and daughters was spilled so that the next generation could enjoy freedom.

Freedom is abused today, unfortunately. Perhaps the reason it is, may be the fact we have forgotten WHY we are free. In our legislative systems, for example, we can see daily the

1

many cases of the abuse of freedom and democracy. We have laws for everything, not that we don't need some, but break one and you will pay.

Our rights are being infringed upon. We are no longer allowed to discipline our children the way we were perhaps disciplined. No wonder they are shooting up the schools and whatever else they choose to do. We have allowed every other cult to be studied in our schools except Christianity. The Ten Commandments have been torn from our school walls. For a nation that prides itself as being, "Under God," the public school is the last place you will find Him. Schools, funded by the state and federal government has control simply because, if you want "our" money, you must keep the business of church and state separate.

After a recent school shooting in Colorado, an elementary student wrote a letter to God. The student inquired, "God, where were you when they came and shot those kids in our school? Why weren't you there to stop it?" God answered the question; "I wasn't allowed to come into the school!" Though the synopsis of this letter provokes some thought, it is however, true. God is not allowed in the public school today. It's against the law! The very Constitution and Bill of Rights in its entirety, upon which this nation was founded on, cannot be taught in our public school systems.

The school children are allowed to pierce their ears, noses or anywhere on their bodies for that matter. They can color their hair purple, pink or blue and it doesn't matter. They can curse and swear without any serious penalty, with little concern if it may "offend" someone. They can elect a pregnant girl to be the senior queen and the unwed daddy to be their king. They are taught birth control to no avail and condoms and other birth control devices are readily accepted. If a student is shot, schools are quick to offer "counseling," when they should have been counseled long before and instructed how they should morally conduct themselves. When a school shooting takes place, gun control advocates are quick to point out the need for more gun control when nearly two dozen gun control laws were already broken in the case of the school in Colorado. Gun control laws by the hundreds don't stop our kids from being killed. It is only when respect, self control, love your neighbor and the list goes on, is taught to our kids in public school, will it stop.

2

Perhaps what has happened to America is a gradual weakening of character. We seem to be filled with doubt concerning our leadership and their ability to lead. We see those whom we should be looking up to and see their infirmities. Instead of striving to be like that certain someone who leads, we become a follower; degrading ourselves and weakening the nation. We must stand up for what is right, pure and ethical. Like a recent parent who attended a school board meeting inquiring if the Pledge of Allegiance was still recited in the school system. The answer was, yes, up to the fifth grade. Schools are often reluctant to push the Pledge of Allegiance. They are afraid the phrase, "Under God," will bring about retaliation by those who fight for continued separation of church and state. The nation as a whole, doesn't seem to want to admit this nation is still "under God!"

As our freedoms are diminished one by one, I think of the tobacco user of today for another example. Where once smoking was a common practice and was allowed in every building in the state, today it is prohibited in nearly every one. I do not stand in defense of use of tobacco nor am I against it. I just feel we have the right to choose. Until the government makes tobacco an illegal substance, which may happen yet, it should be our choice. The government shouldn't have to mandate that smoking be allowed in certain places, which also may soon mean outdoors if the environmentalists get their way. Wealthy insurance companies lobbying for what the end result will be, more profits should not install our laws. Money in this country talks; we can prove that very easily. Our laws are often purchased under the disguise it's to "our" best interest. Personally, I have never seen our nation so concerned about its citizen's health and welfare. Look at the complete picture closely, and you will see the motive behind it all.

This book is written to be a reminder to the reader that he/she must very often fight to preserve that freedom one enjoys. It's the American way. This is part of our identity. It's who we are. We fight for freedom and will do everything we can to preserve it.

When I began interviewing veterans, gathering information to put in this book, I soon discovered that many of these individuals perhaps did little or no fighting. While the stories of battles are more illustrious to the reader's eyes; it's important to note that the men who are known as "Combat

3

Vets" could not have succeeded without a wealth of support from other men and women who provided them with weapons, ammunition, food, fuel for their tanks, trucks and jeeps; just to name a few. One veteran informed me that it takes nine people in the military to support one combat vet. Planes needed an enormous amount of ground support to keep them in the air. Ships of all kinds needed their support teams as well to keep them contributing to the battles at hand. On the land, sea and in the air, those who helped support our fighting men and women will also be noted in these writings. Without them, the wars would have been lost. And, as some combat vets have informed me, sometimes the battles were so long and intense, supplies were unable to be dropped or carried in. Those in charge wanted to, but simply could not.

Perhaps I should mention just how this book, "Operation Recognition," had its beginnings. My wife, Patricia, is the Regional Customer Service Coordinator for **hastings** Books, Music & Video stores in Nebraska. She heard about a program that would give WW II veterans their high school diploma; in the event they didn't finish high school for various reasons. Patricia obtained these forms from the Nebraska Department of Veteran's Affairs and placed them in all the **hasting's** stores in the state and many veterans picked up the forms and later graduated from their respective schools.

When Patricia learned that Governor Mike Johanns was going to make this event possible in Nebraska, I wondered where it all began. I learned that the entire concept began in the Commonwealth of Massachusetts when Robert C. McKean of the Massachusetts Department of Veterans' Services evidently came up with the idea. He took action to make his idea a reality with Gardner High School in Massachusetts being the first to give those veterans their high school diploma. McKean, himself a 1967 graduate of Gardner High School and a Vietnam veteran, was present when this first graduation ceremony involving the WW II veterans took place. Thirty-nine veterans were honored at this ceremony on May 20, 1999 and given their high school diplomas. All those present who had quit school during the war ranging from 1941 to 1947 went home with their diploma. For many, it was an emotional event because after all these years, they finally could say they graduated from high school.

4

This concept of offering diplomas to those WW II veterans soon caught on in other states as it did in Nebraska. The name of this book "Operation Recognition" is used by permission by Robert C. McKean and I thank him for this appropriate title to honor our Nebraska veterans.

During my interviews I first asked questions like their name, address, phone number, etc. If the veteran was a WW II veteran, I would ask them if they had a high school diploma. I had some of these applications with me for the veterans to fill out. The Department Of Veteran Affairs Director, Keith Fickenscher, stated that these individuals, "earned life experience credits that students in the class room could never duplicate!" I was saddened to see so many of them who are ashamed they did not have one. It is nothing to be ashamed about. The veterans did what they had to do and we are all proud of each and every one of them.

The WW II veterans learned Geography by traveling all over the world. They learned Biology when they gave medical attention to their buddies who were wounded. In the area of History, "They made history." And today we enjoy the freedoms that were guaranteed by the history they wrote" Fickenscher concluded.

Doug Christiansen, Commissioner of the Department of Education said the diplomas are limited to WW II vets at the present time. Those serving later still have time to go back to school he said. I have noted after talking to some other vets, there are a number of others who dropped out of school for whatever reason to join the military. Some simply were anxious to fight for their country like their father or grandfather perhaps.

An interesting note with reference to the diplomas; a grandson of a deceased WW II veteran came to us asking for an application. His grandfather had always wanted a high school diploma. The grandson was going to try to get him one. "He'll rest better knowing he now has one" he stated with a tear in his eye.

Continuing with my interviews, I would then ask them about their armed service connections. Every facet of which, I believe is represented. Numerous ranks of every branch of service as well as what division, unit, and other pertinent information will usually be listed if available. Dates of when they entered the service and dates discharged also are listed when the veteran knew them. Honors they received will also be noted.

When asked the question about how they felt about serving their country, the most common answer was "It was my duty, I'd do it again!" They are proud to be Americans and they should be. We, who were civilians, are very proud of them!

I received a few poems as I prepared this manuscript. I tried to find out whom to credit them to and to gain permission to use them, but I could not. So whoever wrote them, I thank you and hope you will not be alarmed to find them in this book. This one is entitled:

Just a Common Soldier

He was getting old and paunchy and his hair was falling fast, and he sat around the Legion, telling stories of the past. Of a war that he fought in and the deeds that he has done. In his exploits with his buddies, they were heroes everyone.

And tho' sometimes to his neighbors, his tales became a joke, all his Legion buddies listened, for they knew whereof he spoke. But we'll hear his tales no longer, for old Bill has passed away. And the world's a little poorer, for a soldier died today.

He will not be mourned by many, just his children and his wife, for he lived an ordinary quiet and uneventful life. Held a job and raised a family, quietly going his own way. And the world won't note his passing, tho' a soldier died today.

When politicians leave this earth, their bodies lie in state, while thousands note their passing and proclaim that they were great. Papers tell their life stories from the time they were young. But the passing of a soldier goes unnoticed and unsung.

Is the greatest contribution to the welfare of our land, a guy who breaks his promises and cons his fellow man? Or the ordinary fellow who in times of war and strife, goes off to serve his country and offer up his life?

A politician's stipend and the style, in which he lives, are sometimes disproportionate to the

6

service that he gives. While the ordinary soldier, who offered up his all is paid off with a medal, and perhaps a pension small.

It's so easy to forget them, for it was so long ago, that the old Bills of our country went to battle. But we know it was not the politicians, with their compromise and plays, who won for the Freedom that our country now enjoys.

Should you find yourself in danger with your enemies at hand, would you want a politician with his ever-shifting sand? Or would you prefer a soldier who has sworn to defend, his home, his kin and country and would fight until the end?

He was just a common soldier and his ranks are growing thin. But his presence should remind us we might need his like again. For when countries are in conflict then we find the soldiers part, is to clean up the troubles that the politicians start.

If we cannot do him honor while he's here to hear the praise. Then at least let's give him homage at the ending of his days. Perhaps just a simple headline in a paper that would say, Our Country is in mourning, for a soldier died today...

A beautiful poem and is packed with a lot of truths. One we should remember when we bury our WW II Veterans at the rate of 3200 plus a month nationally.

With all the many letters I have received, I have made every attempt to watch the accuracy of the stories. When I had questions, I would either call or write but sometimes I was unable to contact the veteran or the person that had sent me the story. I am sure I have made some inadvertent errors. For that I humbly apologize. In some cases, stories didn't always add up with reference to times and places. Nevertheless, I may have used the documentation as I received them, sent to me so graciously by the veteran. I did find discrepancies in some comparing one veteran's story with another whom might have been at the same place at the same time for example. I want the reader to know that it is not my intention to misquote the veteran or any other information. I am much too honored to have been sent the piece to mess it up.

7

One must also remember, it has been a long time ago when these stories took place. Some details may have been recalled in error and written to me as such. I would have liked to have had each and every story edited by the veteran but I would like to get this book done in my lifetime. Since I began the task of putting the book together, some of these veterans have died. Others are in nursing homes; stricken with strokes or other serious illnesses. They had one shot at documenting their stories and this is the final one. So if you find an error, please forgive me, I didn't want to and I am very sorry if I did.

Hopefully, when it's all said and done, the veterans of this great state will go down in history as those people whom the nation is deeply indebted too. A debt that can never be repaid, they gave too much in many cases. Many of whom I was unable to document because they are buried in a foreign land or here at home, unable to relate their story to me. THEY GAVE IT ALL! It is my prayer that this book will bring a renewed sense of patriotism to those who read it. It was written to honor the veterans who did what I could not.

I would urge you, if you are a veteran or a civilian, to think about this country. Always remember that freedom must continue to be preserved and it will have a price tag. Prepare yourself to pay, because if we don't we will lose it!

Someone told me recently that what this country needs is a hero! I thought about that and I realized that is probably true. As I think back over the years, we always did have a hero of some sort. Someone to look up to. He or she may have been in leadership like Presidents John Kennedy, Eisenhower, or Lincoln who some referred to as our hero during that era. Or how about those public figures that have been assassinated like Martin Luther King, truly a hero to those black Americans who live in our country. King, "had a dream," as we all should have and be willing to expose oneself to even die for it.

Whoever they may have been, it seems like we used to indeed, have a hero. Perhaps we have none today with all the scandal that is brought forth involving a public figure, we find it difficult to find someone today to look up to and admire. Just about the time we think we have a hero, they are smeared over the newsprint as undesirable, often even if it is untrue. Doubt is created and we look for another "hero." Perhaps what we need today is someone who will bring democracy back into the mainstream of life. Perhaps we need someone who will not

8

allow the American Flag to be burned in the streets of our cities. Someone who will take the proverbial "bull by the horns," and bring freedom back to America; freedom in line with our Bill of Rights that cannot and will not be tolerated to be abused. Our veterans fought for freedom, those heroes are documented in the following pages. Let us fight to preserve what they fought for so none of them will have fought, suffered or died in vain!

WW II

At the conclusion of World War I, the ink was barely dry on the Treaty of Versailles when the Germans had already began plotting ways to revenge the Allies. U.S. President Wilson truly believed the treaty would make the world safe for democracy. The Germans reluctantly signed it after some minor changes had been made in it. "The war to end all wars," as was said of WW I, was to be a far cry of what would take place within the next two decades.

In 1936 the Germans started a storm they would forever regret. They once again had the dream of becoming the world's greatest power. They sent troops into Rhineland, Germany because they knew the Treaty of Versailles had demilitarized it. In 1938, the Germans annexed Austria, which made a mockery of the Munich Pact. In the spring of 1939, they took the rest of Czechoslovakia, and France or Great Britain did nothing to stop it. In August, the Germans made a non aggressive pact with Russia that should have eliminated a war on two fronts which back fired for them.

Perhaps the proverbial straw that broke the camel's back was when the Germans marched into Poland in September of 1939. Hitler lied to his people saying the Poles had refused to settle peacefully. The Poles were in truth, never given an opportunity to negotiate.

The following years meant unmerciful acts of atrocities that were inflicted upon several different ethnic peoples. What Hitler wanted most was for the Jews to be exterminated. If my history serves me correct, he succeeded in the killing of some 6 million Jews, an atrocious and vile act. Hitler wanted an all white race consisting of the finest of humanity. Men and women became hand picked, ordered to copulate and bear children for Hitler. Hitler himself ordered that concerning Poland, all Poles were to be killed without mercy. When President Roosevelt learned of the situation, he took action. The U.S. and its allies had to put a stop to it.

England and France immediately began negotiations with Germany. Hitler would not respond. At that time, the Americans referred to it as a "European War," which was soon to change. Meanwhile, the Russians seem to have gotten into the war by invading Poland from the east, occupying a large piece of it. Then the Russians went into Finland and by January 1940, the Finns, though they fought bravely, were crushed by the Russians.

The Germans began sinking British ships of various types. The U.S. insisted on staying out of it. The U.S. had other problems, with the Japanese. In July of 1939, the U.S. and Japan were going through what was referred to as economic warfare. The Japanese had little and depended on the U.S. for its resources like oil, aviation fuels and metals like copper. Roosevelt drew up what was known as a moral embargo restraining countries from exporting war material to countries that were using them against innocent civilians, like the Poles. By December of 1939, the embargo involved Japan who was exporting aviation fuel to other countries.

It was in the spring of 1940 when Hitler began his march across Europe with more aggression. The Germans overran France. England's Prime Minister Winston Churchill began waging war against the Germans. The United States was asked to help. President Roosevelt asked Congress to appropriate money to build 50,000 warplanes a year. The Selective Service was born and aircraft was coming off the assembly lines.

Hitler was outraged and set in motion the Holocaust of 400,000 Jews in October, at Warsaw. Hitler appeared victorious causing some of Japan's leaders to want to join him. In September of 1940, they did. The United States by now was giving England all kinds of help, militarily, other than involving soldiers. We were not longer a "neutral" nation. Japan invaded southern Indochina, which resulted in Roosevelt's decision to cut them off all oil exports. This brought about Japanese leaders to overthrow their cabinet and have a new Prime Minister. The British continued fighting with the Germans and Italians who had allied with Germany.

The U.S. had based it's Pacific fleet at Pearl Harbor. It was not as many as once was because many ships by now were in the Atlantic aiding the British. By the fall of 1941, Japan's Admiral Yamamoto was training his pilots to attack Pearl Harbor. The Japanese had committed themselves to war. He thought he could accomplish his missions before the U.S. could mobilize the military, now focused in Europe. On December 7,

1941, Pearl Harbor was attacked by Japan, which caused President Roosevelt to draw up the declaration of war. Roosevelt referred to this attack as a "surprise" but many veterans do not believe that it was a surprise. They have said that he and many others new very well it would take place. It was what was needed to bring about the declaration of war. The U.S. provoked Japan long enough so they most certainly would attack, veterans have told me.

Hitler, on December 11, declared war against the United States. We were now in it with no way to get out but win it, which we did, thanks to our veterans and those at home who supported them.

At the beginning of WW II, American Industry had to be mobilized. Billions of dollars had been appropriated for rearmament but little had been done to mass-produce guns, tanks, planes, munitions and countless other tools of war. What had been produced was given to Allied nations on a lend-lease program. When President Roosevelt made the announcement that now we were in the war, American people and American industry produced like never before. The response was electric and the results spectacular.

The output of raw materials like steel and aluminum rapidly increased. A synthetic rubber industry sprang up almost overnight. We had lost our natural rubber supply from the Japanese held islands of Malaya and Indonesia. War plants were constructed all over the nation. By 1943 half of the nation's industry; had been converted to the production of war materials. The automobile industry was building tanks, planes and trucks. Radio manufacturers were building radar units. Vacuum cleaner plants were building machine guns. Shipbuilders were building ships like never before.

Two million of the nation's women went to work in these war plants. Terms like "Rosie the Riveter" became household words. Women worked manufacturing planes by riveting them together.

By 1942 our production in the U.S. equaled that of the Axis powers. By the end of the war it was more than twice as great. During the Normandy Invasion alone, 750,000 tons of supplies a month were shipped to England through 1943. By D-Day, the figure grew to two million tons a month.

The war would involve over 16 million Americans in the military. Of them, 291,000 plus would be killed. Another

671,000 who would come home wounded. Many would become Prisoners of War, POW's.

In Nebraska during WW II, 139,754 men and women served in the war. Of them, 3,839 were killed. (Nebraska History, Vol. 72. No. 4. Page 157.)

In Germany, 90,000 American men, would experience being captured. During the war with Japan, 15,000 would try to live through the atrocities performed on them by their captures. The Japanese, noted for the suicide missions, Kamikaze pilots who would deliberately fly their planes into our ships, sunk at least 25 of them and brought about 175 more that were damaged, and inflicting a casualty figure of around 35,000 of our Naval men. The Merchant Marines who helped transport war material to where it was needed lost over 800 men at sea with another nearly 5,000 missing or assumed dead.

I am told that when the invasion took place at Omaha beach primarily, we had casualties numbering to 4,900 men, THE FIRST DAY! Omaha Beach was a code name for Normandy which was assaulted by Allied troops on June 6, 1945. It was a difficult beach to hit. The tide rose and fell around 19 feet. At its lowest point, about a quarter mile of the beach would be exposed. The assault had to take place when the tide was just right for optimum accessibility.

Many battles took place in the European Theatre. Perhaps the one most remembered is the "Battle of the Bulge." You will find numerous stories in the following pages from men who were there. This battle became a turning point for the German Army. It was to be the last attempt for them for victory that failed badly. The Germans called it, "Operation Grief." Under the cover of heavy fog, 38 German Divisions set up along a 50-mile front on December 16, 1945. They thought they had the city of Bastogne in the Ardennes Forest. When German officials asked for a surrender, the 101st Airborne Divisions Brig. General McAuliffe responded by simply stating, "Nuts," and the battle waged onward giving the allies victory. The 3rd Army was able to penetrate the German lines and by January of 1945, the allies had recovered all the ground they had previously lost by the German assault. The term "Bulge" stemmed from a map that showed a bulging shape of the battleground in the Ardennes. This last attempt for victory by the Germans cost them 110,000 men who were taken prisoner and more than 100,000 casualties. Eventually, action taken in the Ruhr Valley by our Allies resulted in the capture of another 300,000 German soldiers. The Germans, fighting two fronts, ran out of men and supplies. You may recall that it was around this time when the ambitious General Patton tried to convince General Eisenhower to allow him to push onward and defeat the Russians, our allies at the time. Or else, he said, we would be fighting them for years. He was right, but Eisenhower chose to call it enough. I have been told by most of the weary soldiers that they also had enough.

The war was expensive, with not only human life and limb but financially. Internationally, the total cost of WW II was $1,600,000,000,000. Again, internationally, thirty-eight and a half million civilians were killed, over twenty-five million military were wounded, and nearly 15 million of the worlds military died in action. Think of it; add the military and civilian dead and it comes to 53 million people who died during WW II. The world lost over 53 million people because of what? I am one who believes it was because of a few power hungry individuals like Hitler and leaders of Japan.

It was alarming to some when killing thousands of the Japanese people with the dropping of the H-bombs brought about the conclusion of the war. Many veterans also had sympathy for them. It is sad when the world's leaders cannot conclude a war unless a disaster like that takes place. When Colonel Tibbets, pilot of the Enola Gay, dropped the bomb, pedestrians near the center of the bomb blast experienced for a fraction of a second, 100 million degrees of heat that vaporized them on the spot. Others who survived could look at what was a city with 90% of its buildings, gone. Seventy thousand died instantly and inside of one week, another 30,000 died. Still the Japanese wouldn't surrender. President Truman warned them of a second bomb, which went unheeded. A few days after Hiroshima, came Nagasaki, Japan went to its knees and surrendered. Sixty thousand more had been killed by a bomb that dropped three miles off its target. If it had hit its target; it would have been even more devastating. It dropped in a hilly region, which kept the casualty figure down.

We in the United States fought to preserve freedom, stop atrocities and help preserve democracy. We fought a noble war with a just cause. We can be proud!

It is important to note the importance of the American Indian during this war. I have made reference to them in later

14

chapters also. During the Pacific Campaign, the Japanese became very good at breaking our codes via radio transmissions. Someone suggested using a Navajo Indian to speak in his language. The idea was considered a fine one. Those Navajo Indians that were familiar with their native tongue were shipped to Guadacanal as Marines. Speaking in their own language from one point to the next, the Japanese never did figure out what they were saying. This highly successful way of communications, some feel may have been considered a turning point for victory in the Pacific. Eventually around 3,000 of these "Code talkers," were used. Highly secretive intelligence information was broadcast with no fear of anyone, no one, figuring it out, except those in charge. They were also used in Europe. Many officials noted that without them, many battles would have been lost.

Many men still living today and at the right age at the right time never had the privilege of serving their country in WW II. Many wanted too, but for various reasons, could not. Because of family hardships, farm deferments, sole surviving son and other reasons, these men who could not serve often felt guilty seeing their schoolmates go off to war while they were at home, safe. Many times, those who did not know the situation looked down on these people, adding to their guilt. When they discovered the truth of the matter, they would often change their feelings about the individual. Many of these guys were not the "draft dodger," that they were so often labeled as. Due to circumstances beyond their control, they had to stay home. However, I will be the first to admit there were plenty of these draft dodgers. We all know them, some in leadership in Washington today. But for many others, the timing for entering the service was just all wrong.

Craig Buescher of Deweese, Nebraska sent me a story that I feel needs to be shared. He writes a story about his Dad who could not serve his country during WW II. Buescher himself was at the right age when the Vietnam draft was in effect. He told me he was going to college at the time, married, but still felt the obligation to serve. The year was 1973; the Vietnam War was coming to a close. Buescher's draft notice was in the low numbers indicating it may be a while before he was called. When he was, he made the trip to Omaha to take his physical. Due to the timeliness of the Vietnam War, that's where it ended. He never had to go. He was prepared but he was never called.

Buescher's father, Don, experienced a much different scenerial when he was up to go to World War II. Don was raised on a farm east of Lawrence, Nebraska, and was the oldest of four children. He was the only boy. He recalls what it was like in the "dirty thirties," a time in history no one will forget if they lived through it. The cows had to be sold because there was no feed to give them. Life was a struggle on most farms in Nebraska during those years.

By 1944, Don Buescher was going to enter high school in the fall. He was helping his father grinding cobs one day for bedding for the turkeys they were raising. While the grinder was working and the elder Buescher was scooping in the cobs, Don, doing chores near by, heard the old Case tractor make a different noise. He went to check and saw the belt was off the pulley that drove the stationary grinder. Near by was his father, laying on the ground unconscious. He had gotten caught in the belt and was thrown against a nearby shed. For the next two weeks he lay in a coma with a 50/50 chance of living. He lived, but was unable to perform the duties on the farm because of his injuries. The neighbors, of course, came to render their help as neighbors do in a time of need. But, Don's father would never be well enough to continue farming.

In the spring of 1945 when WW II was escalating, Don struggled with making a decision to join the armed forces. Should he register for the draft or ask for a hardship case, of which many, he was told, could. He felt an obligation to register as all his classmates had done. He also felt it was his duty to fight for the freedom they all shared.

He went to take his physical, passed it and filled out the necessary paperwork. When officials looked over his papers he was informed, "you are more greatly needed by your permanently handicapped father and family on the farm." "Feed the soldiers," he was told, as he left the draft office. Even though he knew his moral obligation was probably at home, he felt empty knowing he would not be with his classmates fighting the war. Or perhaps it was the fact that he had played baseball under lights that had been donated as a Memorial to "Batch" Buescher, who died in WW I. He questioned himself, was he letting his country down even though he knew where his responsibility was? He wrestled with it, as did many.

16

There are indeed many Buescher's in Nebraska who could not serve. They served their country on the home front and in most cases were very respectful as with the case of Don Buescher.

World War II was everyone's war. Everyone took part in some way or another. Sacrifices were made in the form of food, fuel, rubber and many other items of our daily necessities that were needed for the war effort. Families were forced to consume less. Rationing was a common thing in the U.S. With the lack of manpower, women pitched in to made a difference. Some men, who were at home, worked longer shifts producing war materials that was needed badly. By 1944, 3.5 million women stood side by side with 6 million men on assembly lines. Farms had to produce food for a nation at war. Some, like Buescher, had to stay home and do it.

Some have labeled WW II, as well as WW I, as very similar in some respects to the Civil War fought on our own land. America is a land of immigrants. With the exception of the native Americans, we can trace our family tree to Europe, Asia or anywhere else in the world. During a world war, as WW II was, many times a brother was ordered to shoot against brother and didn't realize it.

I shall never forget one time over 30 years ago. My Dad and I were sitting in a coffee shop in Franklin with two other gentlemen, cousins, if I recall correctly. I barely knew them but my Dad knew them both well. For some reason or another these two guys began talking about WW II. One was telling about the time when he was fighting in the Battle of the Bulge, the other listening with great interest. As he related his story and told of dates, times and places he fought and how rough it was. The other pipes up and asks; "do you remember that church?" He names the town. To that, the other said, "Sure, I was on the north side of the street trying to get that sniper in the bell tower." The other then, said with a grin, "I was that sniper!" They had both been in the exact same place at the exact same time. The only difference was that one was fighting on the American side and the other on the German side.

The German had been captured later that day and taken to America to work at a POW camp near Holdrege. After the war was over, he was shipped back to Germany. In later years, he liked America and longed to come back and live here. He did, and these two guys had been the best of relatives and friends

17

ever since. Even though, they had not related their story to each other prior to that day. They both understood what they had to do back then. They had no choice but to serve their country. For more than an hour I listened to these two guys tell about their life during the war. I only wish I would have written it down then as I am sure they are both gone now.

Incidents like that were not unusual. Many families have informed me of this type of situation where relatives literally fought each other. Just like in our Civil War. While there were many people who resented Germans or Japanese living here during WW II, most simply did not understand the situation as to why they left their homeland and came to America. They were prejudiced towards them simply because we here in America were fighting those of other nationalities, forgetting, they were no different. For the most part, each and every one of them had a heritage in this area of Nebraska at least, of some European decent.

This indifference to Germans hit very close to home. My grandparents, on my mother's side were living in Hildreth at the time were Germans. My grandparents on my father's side remained in Germany. My Dad was one of them who came here from Germany after WW I. There was no life in Germany at that time unless you call eating bread mixed with sawdust to make it last longer, living. He was grateful he had an uncle living in Minnesota who sponsored him so he, too, could share in this "land of opportunity."

The war not only caused disrupted lives and took many lives; it cost a lot of money. The American people helped by buying war savings bonds to fund the war. When the tally was taken at the end of the war, the people of America had spent $157 billion buying these bonds. Hitler was even amazed. He had no idea the American people could produce as fast, as much and in so little time as we had done. Who knows, perhaps it helped bring about his suicide. Never before or perhaps never again, will the American people stand up and support their government as they did in the 1940's. Many gave some; some gave all! Some gave their lives in a foreign country fighting for FREEDOM!

18

ARENDT, WILLIAM F.

In 1998, Arendt wrote a book about his life during WW II. I have one of his books, which he addressed to me with his signature. I will treasure it and later, by my family, I am certain. His book is titled, "Midnight of the Soul," copyright 1998 by PRA, Inc., Omaha, Nebraska. I hesitate to record his story in this documentation. He has written his book so well that I will just urge you, the reader, to purchase it for yourself. If you want to know what life was like for the combat soldier, you will want to purchase his book. I don't want to take a thing away from him even though he said I could. His book is important, it's his, and he deserves 100% of the credit.

I will however give you a few quotes he used in his opening Prologue. "Combat infantrymen have felt its absolute, paralyzing horror, particularly when they realize there is no way out!" His book is packed with his feelings at the time. He tells the reader indeed, what it was like.

He goes on to say, "Few of us are allowed to live, let alone participate in what history may call, "important times,"-or those brief years when the course of civilization may be changed."

Arendt was totally involved in face-to-face violence, killing and destruction in Europe during the war. He or any of those who served during that time in our nation's history when history was indeed made will not forget the years of 1944 & 1945.

Arendt served with G Company, 116th Regiment, 29th Blue & Gray Infantry Division. He was a Platoon Leader, telling his story 55 years after the fact. He was wounded twice, once wasn't enough? After being hit the first time and treated, he had to go back because he was needed.

Some of you may remember Arendt when he worked for the Omaha World Herald at the news desk. When he left there in 1953, he started his own public relations, consulting and advertising agency firm.

To conclude this brief note about this combat soldier, I will again use one of his quotes. He has his thoughts about the war and the results that followed. "Probably the most important thing we did was come home and more or less quietly rebuild our lives, probably five years behind in our career paths but even more years ahead in living experiences. I like to think our actions in war and particularly, in peace, may have helped America become the powerful nation it is today. And what's more, even with all the misery and pain-yes, and the joy-my generation would probably do it all over again!"

My hats off to you Sir, and I for one shall be forever grateful!

BAY, JOHN J.

Bay lived in Filley, Nebraska at the time of his induction and now lives in Lincoln. This WW II veteran had attended the University of Nebraska from 1938-1943. He received a ROTC Commission and was called to duty in February of 1943. He served with two divisions in the Pacific Theatre, the 84th and the 88th, along with some other groups and school troops from Fort Sill, Oklahoma. He was given orders to report to Fort Ord, California and was made CO at the time of a company at the age of 18-year-olds. He had three other officers to help with this job.

Out in the middle of the Pacific Ocean, the news came that the Japanese had surrendered. Bay and the rest of the shipload of soldiers landed on the island of Leyte. He eventually received orders to report for duty at the Leyte Detention Center, to work with the many Japanese POW's. The POW camp started here in June of 1945.

At on time, over 14,000 Japanese and Formosan POW's were processed at this camp. Construction of their quarters seemed endless. We took better care of the Japanese than they did of us. With overcrowding, at least 10 additional camps were set up all under control of the Leyte Detention Center. Women and children were also numerous in these camps. Roads, airfields and buildings had to be constructed to house everyone. WAC's, female service people, were needed to help take care of paperwork and some of them volunteered for the job.

Few problems arose at the camps. On one occasion a Formosan murdered another because of a grievance he had with him years before. Once in while there would be an attempted suicide or on another occasion, a Filipino guard shot a Japanese prisoner when he rebelled against an order. "We all worked very hard," Bay said.

As time went on, tents were replaced with metal-sheeted buildings, streets were given a coat of crushed rock, and lights were installed. Things were made as comfortable as possible for those working there with some recreation like volleyball courts and the PX was made larger.

During November, plans were being made to ship the POW's to Japan. At that point, 28,762 prisoners peaked their POW population. Each prisoner had to be processed again and his name assigned to the ships for departure. Completion of this Exodus was scheduled for to be by the end of December 1945. It was a tremendous task he said, and various organizations were put on duty to fulfill this goal. Clothing and food was brought in by the truckloads. One night, 24 trucks hauled in 750,000 pounds of rations and one truck hauled nothing but bailed handkerchiefs.

Some prisoners were suspected of committing an atrocity during the war and were dubbed as war criminals. They had to stand trial in Manila. Six thousand of these prisoners were detained and tried. And yet, after a busy month of shipping POW's out, they still had 11,852 left. They were supposed to have the camp ready to close down by the end of the month, December.

Towards the end of their stay, three women prisoners attempted suicide by poisoning themselves. They failed and even tried strangulation, which also proved unsuccessful. One Formosan POW woke up one night and announced he had received a phone call form General MacArthur telling him all Formosans were to be home by December 15th. It was untrue, but it kept those in charge from getting bored.

After giving the New Year a hilarious reception, the month of January was one of the hardest working months they had experienced. They still had over 11,000 prisoners, and the camp had lost some staff, from 161 down to 80. Some of the service personnel had been sent home and others to Japan to help with the relocation. It was near calamity stage Bay recalls. There were not enough guards for all the prisoners, which also posed a major problem. Mechanics, cooks and a few civilians were called in to guard the prisoners. They proved to be mostly irresponsible, undependable and scared to death. One night one civilian was in tears trying to guard the Japanese POW's. It was to the point that Japanese POW's had to console him and promise they would not try to escape. In an effort to remedy the situation, the camp was remodeled so that fewer guards were needed.

One incident practically put the camp in combat status. A runner was sent down from a civilian employee camp to inform them that an armed band had attacked them. Everyone grabbed a weapon and swept the hills looking for them. It turned out that a POW by the name of Cinco; Leyte's most prominent bandit and his followers eluded their pursuers and were never heard from again.

Other escapes also took place. One time three prisoners just plain bluffed their way through the main gate guarded by civilian guards who were inexperienced and unqualified. Members of the armed services brought them back however. On another occasion, two prisoners had to go to the dentist and were taken there by ambulance. On the way back they frightened their Filipino armed guards and pushed them out of the back of the ambulance and drove off with it. They were headed for Bombay to join guerilla forces in the hills there. They too were overpowered when soldiers chased them down at high speed before they got to their destination. "We never knew what to expect next," Bay said.

One night a civilian Filipino guard heard a noise in the brush. He fired in the general direction and caused the bullet of the M 1 to come zipping through the area that Bay was in. The noise the guard heard was nothing more than a dog going through the brush. Another night, shots were heard on the side of one of the stockades. That turned out to be a private war between two guards. One guard was firing at imaginary noises and the other firing at the flash of the rifle as it fired thinking it must be an enemy. A few nights later, an intruder did try to enter the area and was shot by a guard. The guard and intruder spoke in different dialects so neither knew what the other was talking about. The intruder just simply kept coming into camp and the guard shot him. Incidents like this often upset the mind frame of the officers running the camp as well as the prisoners.

By the 5th of June 1946, the POW camp at Leyte Detention Center was deactivated. Its mission was completed.

22

During its existence of nearly one year, it processed around 30,000 POW's and either repatriated or transported over 26,000 POW's to Manila. Men like Bay believe they did their job well, warranting the existence of this particular POW camp and were glad when the war was over.

BELLOWS, ROYCE

On July 7th, 1996, Royce Bellows, of McCool Junction, was honored along with a number of other Nebraska veterans, who had anything to do with a B-17 during WW II. The ceremony took place at the Lincoln Air Base. They were all inducted as an Admiral in the Great Nebraska Navy. After the ceremony, everyone went out to the airfield to recall some of his or her experiences about the plane. Wayne Sack, a brother in law to Bellows, took some notes at the event where Bellows was present. "It was the first time he had ever said anything about the war," he said. Sack sent me the information concerning the veteran.

Sack served in WW II, with the Navy and arrived towards the end of the war. He told me he often comments to his listeners, "The Germans gave up when I entered the war," he says with a chuckle. He served in the South Pacific. He was well acquainted with a school classmate by the name of Hastings he informed me. Hastings was one of the men who raised the flag at Iwo Jima on that memorable day. "He's on the picture," he said. Hastings went to school at what is now Lincoln Northeast, the same as Sack.

Sack recalls Bellows showing them "his office," at the rear of the plane. Bellows was a tail gunner. The place was small but he says it wasn't all that uncomfortable. In cold weather, he wore electrically heated shoes, had a warm flight suit, gloves and oxygen mask. He pointed out the escape hatch that he bailed out of; a small 20x20-inch opening that had a release handle he pushed to escape.

Bellows was a member of the 14th Bomber Squadron stationed in Italy. He remembers, like most of those vets who flew the very tight formations they flew when conducting their

23

missions, that wings overlapped to create a tighter group of firepower the German fighters feared.

On his 12th mission, in a brand new B 17, model G, they made a bombing run over Austria and took out some railroad tracks, when Bellow's plane was hit by two showers of flack. "It sounded like someone pounding on the bottom of the plane with a big log chain" Bellows said. Then the plane was hit. Two of the engines began to smoke and burn. The pilot put the plane on autopilot and along with members of the cabin crew, bailed out. The problem was, those other men in the middle of the plane and Bellows, in the rear, didn't know the pilot and crew had left the plane. When the plane began to get out of trim, they discovered no one was sitting in the cockpit. The plane began to roll. At 24,000 feet, the remainder of the plane's inhabitants bailed out.

Bellows then had another problem. He got out of his hatch okay, but his chute wouldn't open. He pulled the cord a few times and nothing happened. He pulled the emergency cord, it opened, but what the armed forces failed to do is give men like Bellows training on how to operate the chute. He found himself swaying back and forth, thinking he was going faster and faster. He would swing upwards at times, even with the chute. He finally learned, by trial and error, that by pulling certain strings on the chute, he could control it. "I learned real fast," he said. As he neared the ground, he was still going backwards. When his feet hit the ground, so did his head. It knocked the wind out of him, but finally got it back. When he had composed himself, he knew the first thing he had to do was to hide the chute so the Germans wouldn't find it.

About that time, a big Austrian farmer was standing in front of him jabbering his native tongue. Bellows said, "I am American, I am American." The farmer smiled, and offered him some wild strawberries he had been picking. The farmer managed to tell Bellows and a belly gunner, Lionel Bebe, who had also joined Bellows, how to get to Switzerland. Bebe had broken bones in both of his feet when he landed too hard. However, he managed to walk and did get his feet fixed when he got back to the states.

They didn't get far when they found themselves staring into an over and under shotgun a German soldier was carrying. The Germans took them to town for people to look at. That night, the Germans handcuffed them and put them in a root cellar. The next day they were moved to Vienna. Along with other prisoners there, they were marched five or six kilometers to an encampment. They were forced to run. When one of the prisoners ran too slow to suit the Germans, he was jabbed in the rear with a bayonet. When they arrived at the encampment, one guy, Bellows recalls, had forty jab wounds in his rear and was covered with blood. The Red Cross heard about it and admonished the Germans for their ill treatment of prisoners. Prisoners had Red Cross kits to help them cope with their imprisonment. One kit included a week's ration. Usually they only received a half kit or sometimes a quarter. And sometimes, none at all, Bellows said. The Germans constantly harassed them.

One of the favorite forms of harassment was to line the prisoners up and shoot in front of them. Bullets would ricochet off the pavement or ground and would fly over their heads and they never knew when they may get hit or killed by one. In the prison barracks, the Germans would come in and dump jelly and peanut butter, out of the their Red Cross mess kits, in their beds and make them sleep in it.

Bellows was moved to Starlock 4 near Stern in the area of the Baltic Sea. The Germans used a train for the transportation of Bellows and many other POW's. The train didn't have enough room for them all. Bellows prayed he would get to ride on the train. He thanked God his parents were church going people and practiced prayer in their home. Without prayer Bellows said, he doesn't know how he would have gotten through the entire ordeal of being a prisoner of war. Bellows did get to ride on the train. But for some others, they were forced to march the 1500-mile trip. Many of those on foot, died along the way. Because of the shortage of food and the constant harassment, the trip was very bad he said. "I lost so much weight that I could put my thumb and forefinger around the biceps of my arm and have room to spare" he added.

Bellows made it through captivity and was very glad when he and his fellow prisoners were finally liberated. Prior to his release, a letter was sent to Starlock 4 which was signed by Stalin, Churchill, and Roosevelt and threatening reprisals if they did not improve living conditions for the allied POW's. The Germans soon brought in sacks of potatoes for them to eat. They found buckets to cook them in over one fire they were allowed to have. When one bucket was cooked, they set on the next bucket to cook. In a matter of two weeks, every prisoner was beginning to get "flabby fat" Bellows said.

He was captured on July 14, 1944, and was liberated April 30, 1945. For Nine and a half months he suffered it out. He remains grateful that he escaped injury, "Not even a scratch" he said.

Looking back at the situation when they were forced to bail out of the plane, he thinks that if the pilot could have cut the two engines that were on fire and feathered the props, they could have possibly made it back to base on the other two good engines. But that's hindsight, I'm sure Bellows would agree. In a situation such as this, what would you do? Quick decisions have to be made, sometimes the lessor of two evils.

BENNETT, LEONARD & GLADYS

Gladys and her husband Leonard are both veterans of WW II. They live in Elgin, Nebraska. On July 18, 1990, they were both interviewed by the Nebraska State Historical Society conducted by Lori Cox for research and historical purposes. The Bennetts forwarded that interview to me to formulate a story out of it. My thanks go to the Nebraska State Historical Society for their efforts in documenting this story and for giving me permission to use the piece for this book.

When war broke out, Gladys was attending beauty school in Hastings. She had been to church that Sunday morning when the news came that the Japanese had attacked Pearl Harbor. "I was young and it scared me," she recalls. Her husband to be was working in California at the time in the shipyards at Maywood, California.

Leonard remembers he was supposed to be sworn into the Air Force exactly one year later, December 7, 1942. He went to the induction office in Maywood thinking he could volunteer. They wouldn't take him, so he let them draft him when he was scheduled to enter the service.

War was inevitable Leonard said. Even when he was in high school, 1939 and 1940, he could see that one day Hitler would have to be stopped. He expected it and when the mandatory draft began in May of 1941, at 18, he knew he would be a prime target and enlisted.

Gladys, after her parents evidently thought it was time for her to be on her own anyway, consented that she could go to

California and join her betrothed. She had acquired her Nebraska license to be a beauty operator. California, however, wouldn't recognize it and wanted her to acquire more schooling. She thought she could not afford that so she decided to get a different job. Lockheed Aircraft was looking for laborers and she was hired. Women were being hired; they had no choice she said, as the men were all leaving for war.

She found herself having a nickname that would go down in history. "Rosie the Riveter," they were called, building airplanes for the war. She worked on the elevator tail section that controls the vertical pitch of the airplane and it's up and down movements. She worked on P-38's. The salary far surpassed what she would have been earning as a beautician anyway she said.

Leonard soon entered the Army Air Corp. and began taking the many tests to see where they could use him. He tested out well in the mechanical end of the test and tried to convince him to go into that field. He had also passed the test for flight training and was leaning in that direction. That would mean more training so he was sent to Nashville, Tennessee, where the screenings took place for pilots, navigators, bombardier and other facets of the planes expertise. Some of the tests involved the steadiness of your hands for example. They would have you hold a metal rod and told to place it in a little round hole without touching the sides. The ability of using both hands doing different things was also conducted. He was given two screws and was told to screw them into two different holes; one was threaded to the right, the other to the left. They had to be inserted at the same time.

He passed the tests and was sent to Montgomery, Alabama for flight school. He was enrolled in the 12 class of 1943. This was extensive training and his algebra and math he had learned in high school paid off. He found himself helping some of the other cadets who had forgotten some of their mathematical skills.

From there he went to Lakeland, Florida to primary training school. Civilians owned this school but it was under the guidance of the Army Air Corp. He called his first solo flight, which was flying the Pt-13, with laughter. After making about five passes over the landing strip, his instructor later told him he thought he was going to have to shoot him down. It was just a matter of using proper judgement and after that he had no problems he said.

Then it was on to Cortland, Alabama for more training in a BT-13, a single engine plane where he would need to spend another 60-70 hours flying. Then on to Selma, Alabama flying the AT 6 with a retractable landing gear for anther 70 hours. Here he learned instrument flying and how to solve many different types of navigational problems that could arise. He graduated there and got his "Wings," December 10, 1943.

Gladys went there and the post chaplain married them. They had an amusing time just prior to the wedding doing all the paper work. Gladys had a maiden name of Bennett. She was also marrying a Bennett. The chaplain had a little difficulty getting that matter straight it seems and they had a good laugh about it.

Just one more 75 hours of training was needed for Leonard at Venice, Florida where he would learn the facts about combat flying, gunnery, dive bombing and cross country flying. Gladys now followed along with him. "It was fun following him around. You would meet a lot of nice people," she said.
She also remembers the sadness when one of the other girls would learn their husband had been killed or injured overseas. They supported one another she added.

Then the waiting game had to be played. Each morning a list of names would be posted and everyone would have to look to see if they would be next to go overseas. The waiting was the worst. Finally his name came up and he found himself in Liverpool, England on April 30, 1944. It was required that airmen have a short physical when they arrived. This turned out to be a surprise to Leonard. He thought he recognized the doctor but was not sure. It was his hometown doctor from Elgin, Nebraska. The doctor didn't recognize him at first but when he did, they visited upon occasion several times after that.

Leonard was with the 10th Fighter Squadron flying 47's. Conducting more training he once had to belly land a plane because of engine troubles. The propeller was at fault. Fortunately he was not injured.

His first mission was two days prior to D-Day, June 8th. He was to do some strafing of targets like vehicles and tanks, whatever was moving behind enemy lines.

About 19 days after D-Day, he was sent to Carentan, France to another base. On his 22nd mission he had engine trouble and again had to belly-land the plane. This time he was not so lucky, he was injured and had to be in the hospital for months back in England. When he came back he went to another base in Toul, France, an airfield that was used in WW I. After flying a number of missions from there he went to another base, this time in Germany near Wurzburg. Here they had 10,000 feet runways that were nice he said. He was used to only 4,000 feet with steel matting. This one was concrete.

Eisenhower had told them to shoot anything that moved when flying the fighters. Bennett did as he was told. Some of the missions were easy, which he calls, "gravy runs," others were rather dangerous. He flew escort missions too of course. He was involved in some "dog fights," and came out of them all right but they were often a little scary. His primary job was providing ground support for the troops.

About one mission in particular he described the many planes when the bombing of St. Lo was scheduled. He, along with 144 P-47's supported 144 B-26 bombers over some town in Germany. "It seemed like there were planes all over the sky that day," he said. When the bombing of St. Lo took place, Bennett, along with many other pilots sat on the runaway all day on alert ready to fly should they be needed or if the Germans at this base would attack them. He stopped counting the bombers when he reached 1,500 and more kept coming and coming.

Bennett was leading the squadron on another mission heading for Nurenburg from his base at Toul. On the ground, the forward tank would have someone in communication with the planes. Bennett was informed that German tanks had them pinned down in this little town. "Boy, am I glad to see you," the voice from the tank stated. Taking four planes, Bennett buzzed the town and found nothing flying at roof top height. He could see our men waving at them as they flew over but no tanks could be seen. He informed the radioman in the tank of this and he insisted there were enemy tanks firing at them. Fuel was running low and if they didn't spot them soon they would have to head back to base.

Down below was a field with haystacks scattered around. They looked like ordinary haystacks when Bennett flew over them until finally, he saw one of them move. There they were, camouflaged with hay. The fighters let them have it and when the smoke cleared, 18 enemy tanks had been destroyed.

The radioman called Bennett back just as he landed his plane 250 miles back at base and expressed his appreciation. Just then, another squadron of our planes came in to provide support to our guys left near the town.

The ground forces always appreciated us Bennett said. "When we were there, they got a break," he added. Their presence would usually quiet things down for them for a while.

It was interesting to learn how enemy tanks were eliminated. Since they were armor plated, I had wondered about that. Bennett said the fighters would attack them from the side and ricocheted bullets underneath the belly of the tanks setting them on fire. They found the tanks weak spot. Trains were also on their hit list. "We destroyed a lot of trains," he said.

Bennett flew 101 missions with his P-47. He flew 80 of them after he had been injured and in the hospital that time. Incidentally, while he was in the hospital, his son was born back in the states. He was glad she didn't learn of him being injured before the baby was born. Gladys felt alone but said that if her mother had not been there with her it would have been much worse. She cried many tears in the baby's bath water. She worried about Bennett and he finally came home when the little boy was eight months old.

Bennett also commented about the "remedies" doctors would prescribe during time when pilots would become a little nervous or when anxiety could be a problem. This odd remedy was called a fifth of whiskey. He would tell you to go and get good and drunk to release the tension. It worked. Some days pilots like Bennett would have to fly as many as four missions a day. That's when you got the fifth he said. Under normal conditions, the doctor would give you two ounces of whiskey for every mission you flew. He saved the very first two ounces of scotch the doctor gave him.

On a humorous note, Bennett says it was fun when he would find a German motorcyclist going down a road. The cycles had no mufflers so the cyclists couldn't hear him coming. He would fly up right beside them, scare the daylights out of them and usually the driver would jump off and the motorcycle would crash. "Scratch one motorcycle," he said.

He stated that pilots with 20+ missions under their belt increased their chances of survival became because of their experience. Evasive action became automatic, never having to think about it, you just did it. One learned to never fly at the same altitude very long so the enemy could get a fix on you. Your head became a swivel that turned back automatically watching your rear for the enemy who liked to sneak up on you. The worst job was strafing airfields he said. Even at flying 300 miles an hour, anybody could take a shot at you because you were flying so low that the shingles on the buildings were shook loose.

When he got back home, the war was still going on. He had used up his points so had to be sent home. Bennett then entered the reserves until he retired from that in 1969 and completing another year after that with the Air National Guard. He was discharged from active duty on November 10, 1945.

For his service among his medals, he was awarded the Air Medal with 15 clusters, the Distinguished Flying Cross with a presidential citation with one oak leaf cluster and the Purple Heart. He has five battle stars because he served in all five major operations. He served in three Air Forces as well. In the 8th, 9th and for a short time the 1st Tactical Air Force Provisional supporting the French army.

He would have been eligible to fly during the Korean war but thinks that by that time in his life, he had three dependents, probably being the reason they did not call him back into active duty. A lot of his friends went and never returned home, he sadly remembers.

Sometimes he regrets not taking advantage of the GI Bill or staying in and one-day breaking the sound barrier with a high-speed plane. "I envy those guys, it must have been a lot of fun," he concluded.

BESCHEINEN, CALVIN R.

This veteran of WW II is from Lincoln. He was drafted into the Army and entered the service in February of 1945 after he finished high school. He was another farm boy sent off to serve his country. He felt it was his duty. He served with the 1479 Engineering Maintenance P.I., 2751 Heavy Shop section.

Bescheinen was sent to the Asiatic Pacific Theatre where he conducted his work as he was trained for. He worked on tank maintenance and equipment repair. At Guam, he also served as a telephone operator at the Engineers Base Depot. He says he spent a lot of time in boats and survived many storms while traveling around the Philippines, Luzon, Guam and Saipan before coming back to Oakland, California and finally back home in November of 1946.

BRANDT, EARL O.

Brandt grew up on a farm near Malcolm, Nebraska. "I was intrigued as a young man with the huge Bombers, B-17's and B-24's flying over our farm as they carried out maneuvers out of Lincoln Air Base," Brandt said. He wanted to join the Air Force, or, as it was known then, the Army Air Corps. Unfortunately he was only 17 at the time and his father would not give him permission to join because his father felt he was too young. When Brandt turned 18, he was eligible for the draft. By that time, the quota for pilots had already been filed so he elected to join the U.S. Navy.

He was drafted into the Navy at Omaha in January of 1944. He, along with several other men from Lincoln, was assigned to Farragut, Idaho, for their "boot camp" training. After eight weeks in land locked Idaho, they were assigned to their different duties. Everything from truck drivers to cooks, and all the other specialized fields.   He was assigned to Treasure Island, California, right outside of San Frisco, for training as a radio operator.   It was basically training in mastering and translating the Morse code. He studied this for three months.   Then he was assigned to permanent duty aboard a destroyer, the U.S.S. Gregory DD 802, a 2100-ton destroyer with five single turret five-inch guns. He wanted to serve with his buddies who were assigned to the U.S.S. Linsey, but to no avail.   Later, he learned,   "It was a blessing in disguise."

In August of 1944, with a full compliment of crew of 300 men, they found themselves with an overseas assignment on the brand new vessel. They spent that Christmas in Hawaii and then they went to the battle zone.   They were involved in two Iwo Jima invasions and were offshore about 100 yards, they supported ground troop landing crafts with fire from the vessel. "We kept the island lit up for several nights by shooting star shells for the benefit of the Marines on the island," he said.

32

On another occasion they picked up a radio transmission from a distressed B-29 hit by enemy aircraft over Tokyo. They were able to give the pilot instructions to land on a small airstrip used for fighter planes on Iwo Jima. It was the first B-29 to land there and later it did become quite common, Brandt said.

Brandt was also in the middle of the action on Easter Sunday, 1945 at Okinawa. Following some hair raising experiences on a radar picket station 100 miles from Tokyo, the destroyer was finally hit by a Kamikaze Pilot which damaged the ship substantially. They were able to keep it afloat and they limped along and were towed into Buckner Bay. "We were able to claim 10 Zeros shot down before one finally got us" he recalls. They could really claim 11 if they counted the one that was scattered all over their destroyer, he added.

After several attempts to repair the ship, they eventually had to head it back to San Diego for more extensive repairs. The war ended while they were waiting for the ship to become sea worthy.

As far as the U.S.S. Linsey, Brandt did have two buddies who he wanted to be with. He later learned that both of them had never left the states. One returned home because of a family hardship, and the other received a medical discharge. A Kamikaze plane also hit the Linsey. The entire forward portion of the ship was blown away from the bridge forward. The casualty count was very high Brandt said. The radio shack, where Brandt would have been had he had his way, was also blown away. "The Good Lord looked out for me," even if he did experience several narrow escapes involving torpedoes and mines on his ship too.

Brandt was discharged in April of 1946 and then went to the University of Nebraska and majored in Geology. Brandt said that the Geology class of 1950 was the largest class to ever graduate from the college. He pursued the oil industry and presently lives in Wichita, Kansas, where he serves as president of Brandt Drilling Company.

BROWN, ROBERT C.

Brown is from Chadron, Nebraska. "My friends and neighbors selected me," Brown says with a grin, to serve in the military. Or, in other words, he was drafted like thousands of other Nebraskans. After training at Fort Benning where he went to "jump school," he was a paratrooper in the European Theatre during WW II. He was attached to the 17th Airborne Division and many others he said. He also learned how to repair radios, but wound up in artillery, earning four combat stars, one arrowhead among other honors for being a part of leading the invasion in southern France.

"We were just kids, but we thought we were the toughest guys in the world," Brown reminisced. He was pretty tough because he played football at Chadron State College when the war was over in 1947-1948. That year the whole team was inducted into the hall of fame he said proudly. I would imagine that Brown got much more enjoyment out of playing football than where he had just came from.

The paratroopers Brown was with first went to Naples, Italy, then on to Rome. They trained for the big jump they were to perform into southern France. When they landed there, they held their positions and crossed into Italy heading directly to Nice, France. The troops then fought their way into Belgium and "Got the Bulge under control," as he puts it. Under heavy mortar fire by the Ruhr River, Brown was hit with shrapnel two times. One leg was hit quite badly and he couldn't walk. A medic shot him up with morphine and helped him to get to the first aid station. There were no comfortable enclosed ambulances to ride in or no helicopters to medi-vac him out. He was laid across the hood of a jeep to get there. Treated, he eventually found himself in Leige, Belgium, at a hospital. There they operated on him and took out most of the shrapnel that was embedded in his body. "It was the last day my outfit was in combat," Brown said. Others relieved them, taking their place as the fighting continued.

When able to travel he was taken to Paris, "at least I saw it through the back windows of an ambulance," he recalls. Then he went on to England by plane. Healing more, he began marching again, assuming he would have to go back into the war, but fortunately, it was back home instead going home via the same ship he had arrived, the Christobul.

Before long he was in Oklahoma, being one of the first vets to get checked out at Okmulgee Hospital. He was okay, other than frostbitten feet and toenail problems, so then he went to Fort Carson, Colorado, where he was discharged with 50% disability.

He got paid $52.50 a month while serving his country. Under the GI Bill, he got $50 a month to go back to school. He said he hesitated in getting married, with his wounds, scars and all, but he did. His wife passed away in 1995 and, at a College reunion in Chadron, in 1998, he met a lady who was also a teacher like himself. She had lost her husband. They married a little later in November of 1998.

After Brown went to college, he taught school. He was a superintendent or principal at Morrill and at Kimball. Today he is retired, and along with many other veterans, carries the scars he got a long time ago while fighting for our freedom. "I was proud to do it. I participated with some of the best guys you could ever run into," he concluded.

BROWN, WILBUR B.

This WW II veteran from Elm Creek, received seven Bronze Battle Stars and one Silver Battle Star. He was involved in aircraft in the European Theatre. He was trained as a propeller specialist but after the Normandy invasion, he became an assistant crew chief and earned the rank of sergeant in the U.S. Air Force. He served with the 435th Troop Carrier Group. He was drafted and he entered the service in September of 1942 and stayed with it until September of 1945, when he was discharged. Through it all, "I would do it again," he said.

When he left the good old USA he traveled by ship. When he came home he was on DC-3's and it took seven days to make the trip. He was accustomed to the DC-3, which was used to drop supplies into areas where the fighting was taking place. He recalls, Christmas day, 1944, he was on a DC-3 when it flew supplies into the area where the Battle of the Bulge was taking place. They flew so low; grass and leaves clogged the air vents on the plane that served as oil coolers. "There was lots of enemy fire that trip," he said.

Following is a bit of history concerning the 435th Troop Carrier Group. It was activated by the Army Air Force at Bowman Field, Louisville, Kentucky in February of 1943. Within eight months the men of the five units associated with it had completed extensive training and were sent to England to begin final training for the airborne invasion of Europe.

The training and deep sense of mission gave birth to a troop carrier combat record second to none as the men of the

435th responded to every call in the conduct and prosecution of World War II. C-47's, flown by combat crews of the 435th, flew over 575 sorties behind enemy lines, delivered more than 15,000 American and 500 airborne British troops, 1,500,000 pounds of arms, ammunition, military vehicles, medical supplies and food by parachute along with CG-4A gliders and British Horsa gliders.

During the battles of Normandy, Southern France, Rome-Arno, Northern France and Germany, the 435th hauled more than 20 million pounds of combat supplies and at the same time, evacuated thousands of wounded.

Because of the merited reputation of the 435th, it was chosen by the Commanding General of the 101st Airborne Division to deliver him to his Drop Zones in the Normandy and Holland invasions. The British selected the group to carry their airborne troops into the Southern France invasion. They towed 36 Horsa gliders from Italy, piloted by British pilots, to their landing zones in Southern France.

In December of 1944, when the American 101st Airborne and the 7th Armored Divisions were trapped by the enemy in the Bastogne, Belgium, area, the 435th parachuted over 450,000 pounds of ammunition, gasoline and food to them in 179 sorties, helping them resume their progress.

The glider pilots of the 435th were formed into a combat unit and assigned a mission by the American 17th Airborne Division at Wesel, Germany, in March of 1945, after they landed their gliders laden with troops and cargo. Their mission was to clear and hold a road intersection near Wesel, later known as "Burpgun Corner." They repulsed an attack by over 140 enemy and did accomplish their mission. It is said, this mission was "militarily unique."

The 435th was never idle. In non-combat flights, they flew over 5,000 sorties in re-supply missions delivering over 30 million pounds of top priority military supplies to forward airstrips. They evacuated 12,500 wounded to hospitals, and transported over 25,000 repatriated POW's to their homeland.

During WW II, the 435th men earned 3,000 individual combat awards. The group also earned the Presidential Citation as well as seven Battle Campaign Stars. Many of the men of this group gave their very lives for their country.

Brown is proud to having been a member of this group. After graduating from Wauneta High School in 1941, he was drafted by September of 1942. He went to an induction center at Fort Logan, Colorado and from there to Ogden, Utah, for his basic training. From there he went to the Lincoln Air Base for Airplane Mechanic School. After three months of training there he was sent to Chanute Field, Illinois to learn how to be a propeller specialist. He found it interesting to have learned that some propellers have 3,000 parts to them.

After his prop training he was sent to Windover, Utah, for his field training from March until September. At that time the base was on the Salt Flats and a filling station was all that was there. Now it has Cassinos, Resorts and Motels. The base is gone.

The men were put on a troop train, not knowing where they were going. They ended up in New Jersey in a large quonset type building. In the night they were taken by truck to a ship, which they boarded, heading for Liverpool, England. They were sea sick and homesick, but in 10 days they docked at Liverpool.

In England, the 435th was on three different bases there. They trained from October 1943 until the invasion in June of 1944. Brown recalls on June 5th, 1944, they were called out for combat readiness at dusk. Paratroopers were there by the hundreds. Between 8 and 9 a.m., General Eisenhower made an appearance. He and one of his aides drove up. He gave a short talk and offered prayer. Then he said, "Men, this is it!"

In a few short hours their planes were loaded with paratroopers and ready for the invasion. Brown's job was mechanic. Along with three others, they were sent to the coast with a truckload of parts and supplies and a truck with gasoline. They were to camouflage the trucks the best they could and stay close to the English Channel as feasible and watch for crippled or other aircraft that could make it that far and needed gas or other help.

The armada, many of them firing at the beachhead, was awesome he said. Being within easy hearing range of the ordeal, it was a fierce battle he added. There were so many planes in the air, both friendly and enemy, "It almost looked like a big flock of birds." He could see the many "dogfights" taking place among the planes.

The 435th dropped supplies, towed gliders and hauled and dropped paratroopers. In January of 1945, they set up a base close to Paris, France. Brown was there and he got to see French General Degall and General Eisenhower driving down main street.

The 435th hauled prisoners of war that were released to the hospital. They hauled the Russians from POW camps in Germany over to where the Russians could take care of them themselves. They hauled the English as well as American soldiers to England where they could be treated for their wounds.

By June of 1945, Brown was assigned to a plane and along with about 60 planes that were sent home. There were five members to a crew and thirteen planes flew together. It took seven days to get home as in those days they didn't have radar so they had to do their flying during the day and in good weather. They hopped around all the way home. First from France to French Morroco, over the Rock of Giberaltor, to South Africa then on to South America. Then he went to Brazil and then to Argentina. The last night en-route home, they were in Porto Rico. Here, their luggage was all fumigated including the plane so no lice or bugs would be brought back into the U.S. "It was quite a process," he said. On July 4, they landed in Huntersield. Georgia. Brown had a thirty-day leave coming and after that he reported back to Fort Wayne, Indiana, where he thought he was destined to go serve in the Pacific Theatre. Japan surrendered and he was discharged in September of 1945.

He recalls never having a furlough while in the states. He saw his parents one weekend while in Lincoln and never saw them again until his discharge. He did have a seven-day leave in England one time and spent that time in Scotland.

BROWNSON, JAMES E. (JIM)

As I began this book I knew deep down that some of these veterans would not be with us when the book was published. I have done my best to hurry as many of the veterans have indicated that they were very anxious to see their stories in print. I am sorry to say Jim Brownson passed away August 8, 1999. He was a well-known individual in the Lincoln area as well as known nationally. He will be missed by many.

Brownson was a graduate of the University of Nebraska, Lincoln Teacher's College. He was an art educator as well as an artist. His pottery is displayed across the U.S. Senator Mansfield's office in Washington D.C. has some on display. Brownson displayed his work in many assorted art shows nationwide.

With WW II on the horizon Jim joined the Marines in August of 1942 and began his active service in July of 1943. He served as bugler and was involved in field music. As an artist, he utilized his artistic ability in the Marines 2nd Division, Intelligence Section by drawing maps from aerial photographs. He was shifted to function as a chaplain's assistant serving under three different chaplains and found this role most rewarding. He was charged with the responsibility of distributing some Red Cross supplies to a few needy and distraught Japanese natives in Nagasaki.

Brownson was in Nagasaki a few weeks after the big bomb was dropped that killed an estimated 80,000 people. He remembers the lonely streets, with everything burned to a char. "It was hard to believe it had been a metropolitan city. It was flat and empty except for a lot of twisted ironworks," he said. It was deserted, "there was nobody there," he added.

As he reflects this experience he realizes it would have been considered very dangerous today to enter an area where so much radiation had taken place. It never bothered him he said. He is sure if he would have had a Geiger counter with him; it would have gone crazy.

Brownson had been part of a regiment that was sent to Japan as part of the U.S. occupation that swept in after the surrender of the Japanese. He was stationed next door to Nagasaki in Ishihara. He was with the 5th Marine Division at the time. "We were the first ones there after the bombing," he recalls.

Looking back he wonders if the bombing of Nagasaki was really necessary when Hiroshima had been bombed just three days before. He believes the threat alone of dropping another bomb maybe could have caused the surrender. The horror of seeing the destruction caused by the atomic bomb was etched in his mind until the day he died.

When Brownson entered the Marine Corp., he was assigned to serve as bugler because of his musical ability. Every morning at 5:30 a.m. he played Reveille, time to get up. Although this assignment may have saved his life, because he never had to serve in combat, playing the bugle at this hour of the morning brought about threats from some of his own people he said with a grin.

On a sad note, he recalls the training he had when he first entered the Marines. One was combat preparation using live ammunition. He earned the sharpshooter award in that. Secondly, he was taught to hate, hate the enemy, and in this case the Japanese. They were taught to use derogatory names referring to the enemy as if they were less than human. He never cared for that attitude.

When he was in Japan, he learned there were a lot of very nice Japanese people, very friendly. The learned hatred and antagonism soon wore off as he came to sympathize with them and appreciate their culture.

When he helped hand out Red Cross boxes, the Japanese in need turned out to be his friends. He remembers the tent cities the Japanese built. They were victims of the bomb and all developed a form of cancer and were dying he said.

Brownson developed a new vision of nuclear weaponry. He feels that no more nuclear weapons should be made and said, "we already have enough to destroy the world." Those thinking you can survive a nuclear war better guess again he said.

This marine was discharged in July of 1946 earning the rank of Field Music Corporal. In 1948 he served as drum major for the VFW Drum and Bugle Corp., marching the group for eight miles at the national convention in Miami, Florida. He was a college professor at Northern Montana College teaching art for 28 years before moving back to Lincoln. He taught much more when he returned home. When an opportunity arose, he jumped at it, doing what he enjoyed, teaching. He was very active in many other organizations by volunteering his time to help others.

BURGESS, CLYDE W.

Burgess lives in Lincoln. During WW II, he was with the 41st Replacement Battalion in the European Theatre. He trained in battle simulated training exercises in the states along with Companies A, B and C, at New Orleans, Louisiana, which began in February of 1943. When his training was completed, he boarded the Queen Mary on September 20, 1943 in New York with its final destination, Scotland. It sailed without escort, which is in itself rather unusual. Most troop ships, according to other veterans, traveled in zigzag courses with escorts in case of German attack. He arrived safely six days later. More training took place in England. In England companies A, B & C, were re-designated to, K L & I. Company M was also activated, which was a medical detachment. Later, these companies became re-designated to the 309th, 310th, 311th, and 312th Replacement Companies of the U.S. Army.

James W. Wible, Major FA, in Command of the 41st, wrote a history of the battalion of which Burgess has a copy that he gave to me. It is an account of what the 41st did while serving in the European Theatre of operations. Burgess was with this battalion for the long haul. He feels this that in account Wible tells what it was like for those like him. The following are exerts from this story.

Just one day after D-Day, the battalion boarded a ship to cross the English Channel. They waited just off Easy Red Beach on June 10, 1944, until the morning of June 12th, when they could make their landing. Here they saw the biggest collection of ships that anyone could ever imagine. As far as the eye could see were ships of every size and shape. Warships, freighters, tugboats, supply ships and landing crafts of every type. Hospital ships; the Texas and the Nevada. Burgess was aboard the USS Arthur Sewal. Just a few hundred yards from the Sewal, battleships poured shell after shell into the mainland supporting the hard fighting 2nd Division already about 10 miles inland.

When the men waded to shore they witnessed the terrible evidence of the invasion. Waters at the beach were still strewn with ship debris, sunken ships, half submerged trucks, boxes and crates of supplies dotted the beachhead. Fires were still burning at German fortifications that overlooked the beach. Thousands and thousands of discarded life preservers dotted the beach. Equipment and clothing that had been abandoned was stained with the blood of soldiers who fought for control of the beach from the D-Day invasion. Mines were also still in the water waiting to explode other ships. Mines also were active along the beach. White tape marked a route for the men to take to the top of the bluffs. Once there, they were to march six miles to a bivouac area near Formigny, France. Within an hour, the act of replacement began.

By June 14th, the battalion set up headquarters at Rubercy, France, in an old stone building surrounded by orchards and hedgerows. From June 12 to the 30th, 13,798 replacements were received; processed and delivered to ground forces replacement systems.

Now involved in the war, men began to dig their foxholes deeper. Aerial strafing and bombing attacks by the Germans were common. Men would sleep with one ear listening for the drone of the planes. They encountered one plane that they could nearly set their watches by. It flew over nightly at 11 p.m., just looking. It was assumed to be a reconnaissance plane. The men named the plane, "Bed Check Charlie." The 41st, for it's efforts in keeping replacements flowing, received an accommodation from the 1st Infantry Division and the Commanding General of the 5th Corp.

The men hungered for entertainment when they had the opportunity to rest. One day, about 2,000 gathered in an apple orchard with some musical instruments. In spite of the dangers of enemy strafing, they held their own concert. For nearly an hour everything went well, then came the enemy planes with their machine guns blazing. Everyone dove for cover. It is estimated that in less than 5 seconds the field had been cleared of all men. A few musical instruments remained on the ground where they were tossed. After the strafing, men again took up those instruments and it was announced that although they had been rudely interrupted, they resumed the entertainment.

By August, the flow of replacements still continued but vehicles to transport were in short supply. Delivery of replacement troops was conducted around the clock, 24 hours a day. Upon one occasion when bombs were exploding in the area, two soldiers, in an effort to avoid the bomb blast, dived into the latrine to avoid being hit. They later had stated, they weren't sure if a bomb blast wouldn't have been a better choice.

When the Germans finally retreated from Paris on August 25th, the battalion moved in. They were met by throngs of very happy French citizens because the Americans had liberated them. The closer they got to the city, the heavier the crowds were, almost mobbing the Americans showing their gratefulness. Buildings, once beautiful, were now bombed and ugly and bomb craters were everywhere. Men enjoyed the beautiful women who hugged and kissed them.

Snipers still existed in the area. The battalion rounded up each and every one of them. "Gay Paree," had no electricity and transportation was limited in the city. Young ladies rode their bicycles with skirts blowing nonchalantly in the breeze exposing their bronze legs. Soldiers found them to be a welcomed sight.

But the stay in Paris was limited. The goal of overtaking Germany was still being conducted with full speed. On the 13th of September they entered Noville, Belgium, and were welcomed there by the Belgium people. They moved onward to Anbleve, where the men bivouacked in a thick forest. Flying bombs from the Germans were being shot towards them. At this time, the Germans never knew for sure where their shells were going to land. They were meant for major cities and towns but often fell short of their objectives landing in the fields, forests and among the troops. Often, as each shell sailed through the air, soldiers, in complete silence, wondered if this would be the one with their name on it. The flying bombs would have motors on them that resembled an outboard motor. If one heard the motor, chances are you were okay. "Let the motor silence," meant the deadly bomb was about to drop in a short time of five seconds.

When the men arrived in Kalterherberg, Germany, they found some temporary comfort as they moved civilians out so the battalion could take over half the town. Men were able to eat off tables and sleep under a roof with a decent bed. They could also experience once again a "real bathtub," which was a most welcomed accommodation. A wine and bottling plant was there which also proved to be very welcome. But the Germans were still directing artillery fire into the town. One shell killed a Lieutenant as he checked on his men while walking from building to building. Planes flying bombs were also still being used. One day, one flew into the town injuring six soldiers and wrecking some buildings. Frequent strafing by the Germans also took its toll.

In the early part of December, the headquarters in Kalterherberg became more and more a target by the Germans. Enemy artillery created many casualties. At one point, the front lines were only about 500 yards east of the town. Grave concern was noted that the Germans would break through. The 41st was called upon to get ready to act as a reserve unit to defend the town so that all elements of the 3rd Battalion could commit themselves to the line. Machine guns were dug and made ready for "instant use," if the need would arise. A liaison officer was kept at the 396th Infantry Regiment command post and was in contact with the outpost by phone.

By December 17, enemy paratroopers had landed north of the town. Germans, disguising themselves as Americans, in American uniforms, managed to make it through the lines at several points. The enemy trained for this and was well versed in American slang words. They rode in U.S. vehicles they had stolen along with weapons and GI identification tags taken from American soldiers. As the enemy approached roadblocks manned by the 41st, they would use the English language to inquire as, "how many kids does Bing Crosby have?" They used other phrases assuring the 41st they were Americans being well trained in this tactic. But a lot of things that every GI knew were beyond the enemy's comprehension and they were taken captive.

On December 18th, it was evident the Germans were not coming through lines. The Americans would have to evacuate the town because enemy shelling became so intense that phone lines were destroyed and communications was lacking. Men began being shuttled away. The process continued on the 19th. On the 20th, a new location was established near Herbesthal, a more centrally located area. The processing of more troops, replacements, continued there. From December 16th through the 31st, around 8,000 men were processed to replace others. Four hundred and fifty stragglers, soldiers who had lost their unit in the heat of battle when the lines were broke through by the Germans, were sent to units where men were desperately needed.

At the first of the year, Major Wible, the writer of this historical paper, was made commander of the battalion. In January, 12,299 soldiers were processed and sent to new assignments without delay. By February, the battalion returned to Kalterherberg, and found the town in near complete ruin. Roads were in shambles with mud now instead of frozen snow and ice. Truck axles drug as bulldozers were stationed along the route to help pull them through. By early March, the battalion was once again on the move near the front lines. The chatter of machine guns could be heard day and night. With the speedy advance of the 1st Army, supplies, men and war materials had to be made available. The 41st found themselves becoming broken up into three parts at the same time. One would be setting up a new area; another would be holding men to replace those in the 1st Company and the final part continuing to move. They managed to furnish replacements as well as gasoline, rations, supplies, food and everything else that was needed to be at the proper place at the proper time.

The plan was that when the troops reached the Rhine River, they would regroup and prepare for a full-scale amphibious assault. Navy personnel exchanged their navy blues for army uniforms preparing for the assault 450 miles away from the sea. They had loaded their assault boats on trailers in preparation. On the 10th of March, as the troops neared the Railroad Bridge at Remegan, they found it still unblown and in good repair. It was prepared for blowing however. Several brave men ran several hundred yards along the bridge and cut wires leading to the explosive charges. The bridgehead was secure and the infantry used it to save thousands of lives. This opportunity was classified as "once in a lifetime." Men and supplies now could cross the river and push forward with the war. Other traffic continued moving eastward, night an day.

At Neiderbriest, Germany, our engineers who feverishly constructed a pontoon bridge there to cross at that location accomplished another feat. It was known as the "V Corps Bridge." The 41st now took over another mission other than replacements. They now would also see to the handling of civilians, refugees and German prisoners. By April, the 41st, in keeping up with the swift advance of the 1st Army, drew near the city of Weissenfels, Germany. It was very close to the front lines. But by now, things were moving so fast; the front line changed from hour to hour.

One day, while going down one certain road, Military Police were not stationed on roadblocks, as they normally would have been. Everything appeared peaceful with no noises of war to be heard. Germans soldiers had surrendered by the hundreds, lines of them followed down the road. Some Germans were noticed standing in a ditch near the road and no one thought much about it, just assuming they had been captured. Then someone noticed they were armed. The command jeep, leading the group, immediately turned around and headed for them. They didn't fire at them and the Germans were as surprised as the Americans who perhaps were more embarrassed than anything else because they hadn't taken notice of them. Near as I can tell, the two groups of soldiers quickly split and no action was taken.

The battalion continued moving, now with the 3rd Army, 200 miles southeast near what was a German training camp at Vilseck. It was now April 30th, and the job now was to process transient personnel. The town, heavily bombed by the Allies, was cleaned up so living conditions could be improved. More Germans were captured and taken to POW camps.

As the war drew to an end, men looked forward to going back home. When VE Day was announced, the 41st looked back on a job well done. It was noted that while the 41st was performing their duties, men of the 41st Battalion, most heading for some fighting unit processed 4,156 officers and 100,190 enlisted men. On June 10th, 1945, the battalion was officially demobilized.

The 41st participated in five major Campaigns including the Rhineland, Ardennes and Central Europe. Some men received medals for meritorious service during the Normandy Campaign. In a letter Wible wrote to the officers and men of the 41st, one sentence strikes me as unusual. "What next?" he asks, "Who knows, many of us who have enough points will go home and rough it out as civilians again." Perhaps they did have to "rough it" as civilians. To those who went home he wishes them "Good-bye" and "God-Speed." To those who stayed with the 41st, he wishes them "Good Luck."

BUSS, MELVIN J.

This WW II veteran from Hastings has a rather humorous story to tell. Buss served under General Patton in the 3rd Army in the 26th Infantry Division. Buss was with the 818 Tank Destroyer Battalion as they made there heroic way to Germany to help defeat the Germans. I am sure that Buss was another one of those veterans who saw a lot of action.

His story unfolds when they camped one night in a wooded area with a dirt road running through it. The next morning they were ordered to go down that road, which was lined with trees. About a half-mile down they encountered some

German resistance. After some exchange of gunfire, the area became rather quiet again for a short time.

Buss recalls that alcohol in many different forms was usually readily available. One individual, an older fellow, always seemed to have some alcohol on him as they fought their way towards their mission of the day. This man was picked one particular day to go forward and scout ahead along with guys like Buss. As this drunk made his way down the road he staggered a lot, Buss said. But staggering wasn't to his disadvantage. The Germans couldn't hit him in the state he was in. When he ran, he staggered and then would make it to the next tree and sit down and take a few more sips. Then he would sing a popular song at the time, "Playmates Come Out and Play With Me."

When things would quiet down again, this guy would get up, and with another staggering run and with bullets flying all around him, he would make it to the next tree, wait a few minutes and do the same thing over again. This would last several hours Buss said. He must have been running point because Buss says, when the rest of the company moved up, they would find the Germans waving their white flags wanting to be captured. What was it about this guy? Were the Germans afraid of him? Maybe the Germans figured if they couldn't stop this guy, they probably couldn't stop the rest of us either. Whatever the reason was, Buss says on this particular day that this drunk was a real hero. "He never did get hit," Buss concluded.

CARR, CHARLES D.

Carr graduated from Malcolm High School during WW II. He graduated from Lincoln Flying School where he took a sheet metal course and he then went to Buffalo, New York where he worked in an airplane factory. He then enlisted in the Canadian Air Force after Pearl Harbor had been attacked. He was sent to England as a pilot officer, 2nd Lt., and was immediately transferred to the AAF as a 1st Lt. Later he earned the rank of Captain. Today he lives at Garland, Nebraska.

Carr was a fighter plane pilot first and flew the P-47 Republic Thunderbolt and then transferred to the P-51 Mustang. He flew many missions beginning in October of 1943. But on April 5, 1944, he was reported as MIA, Missing in

47

Action.   He had been captured by the Germans and was a POW
for 13 months.

While stationed in England he flew the very first
missions over Berlin; flying as a bomber escort. Carr was with
the 4th Fighter Group, a member of three Eagle Squadrons
which held the record of those scoring the highest among the
fighters with reference to enemy aircraft they destroyed. The
total tallied up to 1,012 he said.   But his life as a fighter pilot
came to an abrupt end. "You can't dodge ground fire," he said
when flying these planes.   The morning of April 5th would be
his last mission.   Carr is an exceptional artist.   He drew
photographs depicting his story as to how he was captured.   I
will try to explain, as the old saying, "a picture is worth a
thousand words," perhaps is true in this case.

On April 5th he left his base with other planes and flew
to Gardenlegen, Germany. Their mission was to strafe an
airbase there.   The base appears to be cut out of the woods and
heavy stands of trees surround it.   The planes were flying one
behind the other flying very low, almost just clearing the
ground.   He followed another plane in along the enemy runway
firing as they flew.   Enemy armed Germans in foxholes lined the
runway firing at the pilots as they flew by.   The plane ahead of
him was smoking, no doubt severely damaged.   The time is
noted on the picture as 1535 hours.

Two minutes later Carr depicted a plane flying upside
down with the pilot ejected and the chute was prepared to open.
At 1545 hours, the plane crashed to the ground near the base
in the thick stand of trees, in the background.   Carr was
standing near the burning the plane with his arms extended.   A
German soldier was pointing his pistol at him stating, "for you
der var is over!"   He was now a POW headed for Stalag Luft I,
Barth, Germany.

Carr also related to me a story about another pilot, Doc.
Bunte who also flew escorts for bomber planes.   They were
ordered to strafe airdromes in the Berlin area.   Bunte also flew
escorts for bomber planes.   It was very cold with a 10/10 mist
at 30,000 feet.   Near the area they were to strike, Doc dropped
down to 15,000 feet and began looking for targets.

It didn't take long before an airdrome was spotted and
the fighters descended like wolves, he says.   Full bore, gun
sights on, trigger fingers flexing and drooling at the mouth.
Flying around 450 mph. he spotted a J.U. 52 on the far side of

the airfield. He dropped to down to "brussel sprout" height and began blazing away. About 10-15 seconds later he noted his fan had stopped and he could feel a hell of a lot of heat he said. Looking down in the cockpit he saw the fire coming out fast, his left boot and pants leg were already burning and his face had began to scorch.

He was only about 20 feet off the ground and he realized it would be impossible to gain enough altitude to open a chute. He looked out ahead of him and he noted he was almost immediately over a lake, "I jammed the stick forward," he said.

Bunte doesn't remember when he passed out. It was either right before or at the moment of impact. He has no recollection of hitting the water. He did, however, regain consciousness under the water. He could feel his aircraft settling down on the bottom with him still in it. As anyone would do, he panicked. Instead of unfastening his seat belt he started fighting for his chute harness thinking if he could get out of that he would be okay. It didn't take long for the "lights to begin flashing," and the bells at the gate of St. Peter's door began ringing the last assembly.

Fumbling for his chute harness, "everything went black," he said. But remarkably, he popped to the surface and came to his senses once again. He tried to pull the cord on his "Mae West," life jacket but didn't have the strength left. He started paddling and after an eternity of passing out and regaining consciousness he managed to reach a small tree only about 10 feet from shore. He hung on to it until he thought he had enough strength to make it to dry land. When he made it, he pulled himself up on his elbows toward a small shack nearby.

He saw a group of civilians approaching him. He gave up hope and resigned himself to the Gods of Fighter Pilots. They stood around him, jabbering and appeared afraid to come to close to him. He had blood on his face from cuts he had received on his forehead. His hair was matted with blood and sand.

Finally the Luftwaffe arrived and took him back to the sick quarters on the same base they had been trying to shoot to pieces. Two people dressed as female Huns, stripped him, bathed him and dressed his wounds. Bunte's story is another one, which clearly portrays what, is what like and is the reason for my adding it.

Carr and Bunte were taken to Stalag Luft 1 at Barth, Germany, about 60 miles from the Swedish border. Life here was not good as was the case for most POW's. Carr says the food was not good and there was hunger both among the allies as well as the Germans. It was the Red Cross parcels that saved them from starving to death. When he entered the camp he weighed 135 pounds and when he got out he weighed 90. Treatment was not too terribly bad. Beds were provided with little bedding consisting of straw. Harassment at this camp was not bad either, as the commander of it would not allow it. Nice guy!

Hitler towards the end of the war sent out a directive that all POW's should be killed. Hitler, by now had turned into a mad man. Fortunately his vicious order was not carried out. The president of the International Red Cross at the time, Dr. Burckhardt, had gained permission to enter the POW camps to help prevent any such type of executions to happen. The Wehrmacht had also refused to carry out the order. Here is a case again where we see the German people were more like us. Germans, for the most part, didn't want to make things any worse than they already were

However, a Colonel with the 8th AF Fighter Group had been sentenced to death at this camp for giving a pep talk to the POW's. He was saved when the Russians were about to overrun Stalagluft 1. Many Germans, fearful of the Russians, evacuated the camp. The POW's had rehearsed for just this type of situation. They quickly captured the guard towers and radio station. Scouts were dispatched in all directions and they set up fully armed skirmish and picket lines. The POW's had freed themselves and took more than 200 square miles of German territory before they linked up with the Russians. There was only one casualty. Two thousand Germans were captured by these POW's and nine thousand prisoners were liberated that day, most of them American airmen like Carr. Nine of the men were from the Lincoln area. In three days, the 8th Air Force Fortresses evacuated all of the men.

These men quickly liberated five other neighboring POW camps primarily due to these actions. Although they experienced little opposition, the Germans they encountered were quickly disarmed. Weapons of all types were seized along with vehicles and fuel. Carr left the camp flying out on a B-17.

50

Reflecting upon the ordeal he states that perhaps it was regrettable at the time that men like Eisenhower, in command of the European Theatre, didn't allow Patton to finish off Russia while they were there. It would have been quite easy to do that many vets have said, even though the Russians were our allies at the time. Also, regrettably, it would have not come without additional costs of lives and misery. Some vets I visited with said too that, "they had enough fighting!"

For his service to his country, Carr received many decorations including the Air Medal and at least three, Oak Leaf Clusters. "I wouldn't take a million dollars for the experience and I wouldn't take a million to do it again," he concluded.

CASPER, ERWIN D.

Casper entered the Army in October of 1942. This WW II veteran was stationed in Camp Crowder, Missouri, until July of 1943 when he transferred to the Army Specialized Training Program at the University of Denver. He was then assigned to Company K, 232nd Infantry, 42nd (Rainbow) Infantry Division. Due to heavy casualties to the infantry during the Battle of the Bulge, he was sent to Europe on Thanksgiving Day, 1944. By Christmas Eve, Casper found himself on the front lines. "What a wonderful Christmas present," he says. He fought as a part of Task Force Linden for the next three months, which suffered many casualties.

Here is what it was like for Casper who was decorated with seven medals and decorations for his service to his country including the Bronze Star.

The ship ride to Marseilles, France was everything but pleasant. Seasickness and other odors plagued those aboard. One officer asked a PFC as he vomited over the rail, "What's the matter, got a weak stomach?" The reply was, "No sir, I can throw it out as far as the next man." One of the men who most appreciated seeing land was their 2nd Lieutenant who spent the entire trip on his back. Although no one was happy to see France where the inevitable fighting would take place, the Lt. however was very happy to get off the boat.

As the gangplank lowered on December 8th, 1944, "We were loaded down like mules, big packs, rifles and personal items," Casper said. Lining up in columns of three they drug their way five miles along the waterfront of Marseilles. At dusk they were told that this was the bivouac area. The weather was windy and cold, already causing problems. Tents were hard to erect but most everyone was still in pretty good humor. The evening menu was Spam, a common menu for servicemen. Some of the men received passes to go the city where they enjoyed nothing other than wine, women and not Spam.

On December 19th they boarded the 40 and the 8's, train cars capable of holding 40 men or 8 horses, as they watched the towns go by, one by one. Soon cold and travel weary, they already didn't seem to care much where their destination would be. Pranks were played on the Commanding Officer of Company 1, to keep up the humor. The train was a real streamliner. They made fun of it going so fast that they couldn't count the fence posts. The joke was that it moved so slowly that you could count the blades of grass in the ditches.

They eventually unloaded in a tiny dingy village and they crammed in trucks and headed for a French Cavalry barrack. A few hours of shuteye and they left for Strasbourg and went through a beautiful French chateau where another division, the 36th was let off.

On Christmas Eve, Casper and the rest were in position along the Rhine. Immediately across the river, the Germans sat in their pillboxes with machine guns aimed at the new recruits. A very popular Sgt. in K Company met his fate quickly. Everyone was jittery Casper said.

On Christmas Day, one of the cooks had his gasoline stove explode. He wound up in the hospital at Bremen for several months. There was no Christmas turkey and the men complained.

More mishaps occurred at the start of this campaign. Two jeeps collided with both drivers ending up in the hospital and they called the ordeal a "bang up start!"

On the 31st of December, the battalion shifted to La Wantzenau. A swift canal ran through the town and it had only one bridge to cross. The machine gun guard section was to guard it. But by New Years morning, the Germans had effected a way to cross the Rhine, tanks and all. The mortar section and the 1st Platoon succeeded to cross a field into Kilstedt on the 5th. There two Sergeants were killed, one by a sniper and the other by a mortar shell. The machine gun section sweated out an artillery barrage concentrated on the bridge. The Company command post was only a few yards away, in the "basement" a round dirt hole under a house. It didn't offer much protection. One side of the building had been completely destroyed by previous shelling.

PFC, Private First Class, Neal, now a squad leader, was clipped in the head by enemy machine gunners. He managed to crawl 750 yards in open terrain to safety however. PFC Wachtler, aid man, who himself was wounded continued to save another sergeant's life.

Lt. Twombly was killed the next day by an enemy concussion grenade, the first officer to be killed in this particular battle. The 3rd platoon was battered but returned the morning of the 7th.

Some french columns of infantry and tanks passed over the bridge early in the morning cutting the communications lines with the battalion Casper was with. Sgt. Rains and Casper were sent out to fix it. As they stretched this wire along it crossed a manhole that another PFC was dug in. The wire hit him on the face scaring him half to death in the inky darkness. He thought the Germans had broken through and were trying to strangle him.

Casper was a witness to many acts of heroism and close calls. Two days later after repairing the wire, they were on patrol north of La Wantzenau. Sgt. Sullivan, after seeing a German raise his rife at him, turned sideways, which saved his life but he will forever bear the scar of the bullet that made crease on his chest. PFC Fuchs was wounded in the leg the same day but managed to make for nearly a mile to safety. PFC Peeler walked up to a German pillbox and forced them into submission with his BAR. Browning Automatic Rifle, blazing.

They marched to another part of La Wantzenau and took off for Fort Oberhoffen. They found a former platoon Sgt. of the 1st platoon on regimental guard duty. He didn't like it and wanted some action. He left his post and climbed aboard a DUK, amphibious vehicle, with the rest. He had nothing but a rifle, overcoat, a bandoleer of ammo and a quart of schnapps in his stomach. He was ready. From Oberhoffen they marched to Schirrheim until they reached a deserted house of Mueller, chief forester of the district.

Fanning out across the woods the company set up its main line of defense. The 1st platoon was on the right side of the road and the 2nd platoon on the left. Also to the left was a bridge crossing another canal, which would be vital to the King Company.

Two patrols were sent out on the bridge. They disclosed that the Germans had a sentry on the bridge and also pillboxes along a railroad track on the other side. The second patrol managed to capture a German Lt. who was making an artillery reconnaissance of the area. From his map he carried, they learned the extent of the enemy's knowledge of their positions. The commanders wondered if they should blow this bridge or not. They did not but rather decided they should possess it instead. On the morning of January 17th, they made their advance. Unknown to them, the Germans also planned their own attack on them the same day, which was to take place before dawn. "We had delayed too long," Casper said.

Bullets began to fly as the men made their advance. A trailer arrived loaded with rifle and machine gun ammo. They put the trailer in a hollow so it would be somewhat protected. They fought to within 20 yards of the railroad track. The Germans had a burp gunner on the other side of the tracks. The men in our observation post were being attacked.

An attack was made on a pillbox but it was not the Germans who conducted it. It was our own tanks. Our troops had occupied it and they didn't know it. Thanks to good radio transmissions, the firing from our tanks stopped immediately. But it was too late, the pillbox had been destroyed and the damage to the men had been done.

During the night the men ate rolls in the light of burning tanks. Shortly before daylight on the morning of January 18th, the Germans sneaked upon the observation post. Two of our men were blown apart, and an aid man was wounded. A mortar round killed another one and everyone dug in. By noon the Germans threw a continuous barrage until about 2 p.m. Then white capped enemy soldiers swarmed down the railroad embankment.

The GI's knew this would be a crisis. It was now destroy or be destroyed. They opened up with all they had but what could so few do with so many? The ammo trailer was on fire; it was impossible to get more ammunition. They had no choice but to fall back to the road. As they withdrew, fire was exchanged between the two enemies at 35 yards. They tried to get some more ammo from the burning trailer but it was halted, it was too dangerous.

Lt. Zillmer managed to reorganize the men to defend a line along the road. By now the Germans were flanking them to their left. They had to withdraw even more. Now Casper, with the King Company was face to face with the enemy across the field at the main line of defense. The fighting continued.

Later in the afternoon, the 103rd Division came to help with a counterattack providing some help for King Company. That gave Casper and the rest of the men some relief from this fierce fighting. But at dusk they underwent intense artillery fire the Germans imposed on them. Five minutes after they had crossed the field; the German artillery laid a terrific barrage on this field putting a tremendous strain on the main line of defense. They learned it was too late for a counter attack. So before dawn the company had to pull back to Schirhofen, checked their losses, and the entire battalion went by truck to Sufflenheim. Later they learned that the 10th Panzer and the 36th Volks Grenadier Division, some of Germany's best, had hit them. The Germans had fired 2,000 rounds of 88 MM. shells at them. "Those of us who survived shall never forget this first real taste of battle," Casper said.

As the Americans marched through Sufflenheim, the Germans welcomed them with another artillery barrage. The allies took refuge that night in the cellars of houses. The population all lived in fear and kept to the cellars most of the time. Through the grapevine, they seemed to know the movement of the enemy before the allies did. The next day, allied command learned that the Germans were planning to take the town that night. Since the company Casper was with had no armor of any kind, they decided they had better retreat on foot. So, at 10:45 p.m., they assembled on the outskirts of town and commenced marching. They placed the machine gun section in the rear to serve as guard. It was a march men like Casper will also never forget.

The men of King Company were carrying backboards of machine gun ammo. Being rather burdensome, they discarded the backboards and carried the belts of bullets over their shoulders. The roads were glazed and the night was bitterly cold. One Sergeant broke his ankle and was taken to a field hospital. "We had no idea where we were going or what would happen when we got there," Casper recalls. Nor did they know if the enemy was advancing behind them in their footsteps. They prayed they were marching in safety. Some of the men fell out of position only to be told by their Major, "My God men, you can't fall out, there is nothing behind you!"

By 5 a.m., somehow the men slipped and slid to their destination at a town called Haguenau. They slept until 9 a.m. that morning on stone floors of a deserted religious hospital. All the men were wet and cold. About noon, tow trucks were loaded and they made a long trip to Bossendorf. The shattered company was reorganized. King Company was now down to 90 men. Casper said some of the other company's were worse.

During the next three days, men were transferred from other company's who had could spare a few men and attached to those battered company's who were short of men. While this was taking place, the Germans attacked the 242nd Infantry near the Moder River at Ohlungen by surprise. Casper, along with the entire regiment, traveled by trucks most of the way and marched the rest. When they arrived in Ohlungen, the town was empty of civilians. Refugees did line the roadways and had no place to go. Their homes were no doubt gone. After another sleepless night they scrambled thought the woods to the river behind a heavy rolling barrage for the river. Late in the afternoon, the men of the 79th Division relieved the company Casper was with. Casper spent the night in a village. The next day they went to a town far to the rear called Gremecy where the men hoped to enjoy a chicken dinner that awaited them there. But because of the urgency of the situation to slow down the attack on Bossendorf, they had to leave without it the meal. The cooks had cold chicken for the next four days with well-frozen fruit cocktail on the menu.

After returning to Gremacy, King Company then went to Lichtenberg relieving another company of men there. A line of foxholes was dug about a mile from the town facing the Germans across the valley. Through this valley ran a stream bordered by marshy meadows on both banks, the Germans were busy mining their lines and digging in machine gun emplacements. The allied artillery forced the Germans to keep their heads down and this also removed any possibilities of counter attacks.

For the next 28 days the men of King Company sent out innumerable combat and reconnaissance patrols. They provided the company with knowledge of every German position. Hot meals were served only when they happened to be in the rest area. The Germans lobbed shells in at mealtime. The cooks were forced to wear helmets because of the shelling. At a barbershop, a private was knocked out of his chair because of the shelling. The barber found a new place to set up shop.

On the morning of March 2nd, the first platoon set out on patrol to Hill 403. They encountered a vicious cross fire that pinned them down from three sides. Some of the men were wounded, one gutshot. A Sergeant found an escape route and they all went for except seven men who stayed behind throwing phosphorus grenades and they too eventually made it back to safety.

About four days before the Big Rush, the area was explored again by Recon patrols. They brought back valuable information on the enemy positions through they had to travel through mine fields to get it. By noon, March 16th, with a total of just three "K" rations in their pockets, they pushed off to take Hill 415. Slowed down by some mine casualties, by 5:30 p.m., they had taken their objective. Through the hills and woods they kept the Germans on retreat. They entered the town of Phillipsburg where houses were searched and a command post was set up. But the Germans were not far enough away that their 88's couldn't reach the allies and continue to deal with this type of shelling.

As the men of King Company pushed forward they came to the town of Neunhoffen where German snipers got a few of our soldiers. The remaining Germans were soon cleaned out in the few houses that remained. Our artillery leveled anything else that posed a threat to the men. But the terrain in the mountains was even too rough for them. On the 24th of March they went on to Darstein and seven days of needed rest. All were footsore and weary from the constant day and night surge forward never giving the enemy a chance to recover and form a sort of line. They then continued to push, going with little or no sleep. Men walked with their eyes closed. They had the enemy where they wanted them and they were determined not to give them a chance to turn around. Engineers spanned bridges only to have the Germans blow them up behind them. After crossing the Main River, they came upon a town they rushed. A castle wall near the river had a sign painted on it that read, "Heil Hitler," which and soon read, the "42nd Rainbow Division." They had to battle for it first, which they did and won. The enemy continued with their machine guns. Sniper fire was very prominent and accurate. When one thought an area was secure, they had to watch or a sniper would shoot them in the back as they proceeded. After some firefights, they would capture some of the Germans. One occasion, 65 Germans were captured and on another occasion, 14 more. One night a private was standing outside a barn where inside some of the men were trying to sleep. He heard a column of men coming down the street. First they thought maybe it was some of their own, but no, it was a new column of Germans. Fortunately they had not spotted him and the Germans left.

The company marched on to Dittlebrom. On the way, the Germans mowed down some of the German prisoners they had with them. Casper's company had taken about 100 of them. One our men, Rizzo was his name, was wounded. Rather than have one of our litter squads carry him he insisted that the German prisoners do it. Reluctantly they did after being prompted by Rizzo's M-1. After that, the men marched on taking town after town. They were now moving very fast. More bridges were also taken or destroyed. Munich now was only 75 miles away. King Company swung into action going for this home stretch as they called it. Through rain, sleet, snow and hail, the men continued to advance, crossing the countryside. A motorized convoy of Germans would be spotted and quickly brought down under fire. The numbers of prisoners attested for their success. Onward they pushed, not stopping to eat or sleep sometimes. The Germans were now retreated much faster heading for the Danube with the hope of crossing it to its south bank and safety. But with the speed our forces were moving, few made it.

King Company soon wound up its fighting in Europe. Munich, the seat of Nazidom, had fallen. It now was just a place of starving people, Beaucoup champagne and streets of rubble. It was like a ghost town with real people playing the part of ghosts scavenging the swill buckets and garbage in search of a scrap of food. Munich became the first place the company witnessed the surrender of Germany and V-E Day. There was a sigh of relief and prayers of thanksgiving emitted as the radio announced the good tidings. The men of King Company continued their mission of occupation, at least temporarily until they could all go home.

Casper says he escaped without an injury, "I was one of the lucky ones."

CHAMBERS, FRANK

Many veterans that I have visited have told me, "My dad was a veteran too." It seems that when the first generation of Americans served their country, the siblings followed. It was expected of them, they were proud to do so. Chamber's dad served in WW I. Frank served in Europe in the Army Signal Corp, which launched balloons to observe enemy troop movement behind the lines. Although Frank was living in Illinois at the time his draft number came up, he considers himself a Nebraska veteran, living in the state for many years.

He was in college, the University of Illinois, when Pearl Harbor was attacked. He was in his third semester when he was called to duty. He got in the ROTC program, Field Artillery and he went to Fort Sill, Oklahoma for basic training. He was invited to take tests for the Army Specialized Training Program, ASTP, that should have led to a commission in the engineers. He went to school at St. Norbert's College in West DePere, Wisconsin, a suburb of Green Bay. Several months later, the ASTP program was being phased out so he took an exam for the Aviation Cadet program and passed. Then he was sent to Marshall College, which is now a University, in Huntington, West Virginia, for college and pre-flight cadet school. This program also was severely cut back and thousands of cadets were sent to infantry units.

It was a traumatic experience for him, but his original field artillery training saved him from being a rifleman. Each infantry division had a "Cannon Company," which was a version of the 105-mm howitzers that he had trained with at Fort Sill. He was assigned to the unit and immediately saw that the best place for him to be in the infantry was to be mobile. He became a truck driver for one of the gun crews. He also qualified to be a gun crew chief if it was necessary.

The 75th Infantry Division was training at Camp Breckinridte, Kentucky when he joined them. They shipped out from New York on October 20, 1944 for Europe and landed at Swansea, Wales. They made their way to Rouen, France with the intent to relieve some battle-fatigued troops who had been there for several months. On the 16th of December 1944, Hitler made a "Last grasp, desperate attempt," to drive to the English Channel through Belgium. The battle later known as the "Battle of the Bulge" was now underway. With the allied lines very thin and scattered along the German front, everyone felt that the Axis powers were nearly defeated and had no capabilities of launching any major offensive. Some of our Allied troops were caught unaware of the attack and many were captured...some shot on the spot at the Malmedy Massacre. It was a disaster for the allied troops. Hundreds were taken prisoners.

The 75th Infantry Division was rushed into Belgium to attempt to stop the German advance. Many of the foot troops did not have winter gear to cope with the deep snow and bitter cold. To add to the problem, German soldiers wore American clothes and drove around in American vehicles. They even "Whitewashed" the vehicles, which hid them in the snow. German soldiers were given identification that had been taken from American prisoners. They attempted to learn the passwords, like "Babe Ruth" and "Lou Gehrig." Chambers said they would often change their password several times in 24 hours.

Chambers said the 75th consisted of three regiments, the 289th, 290th, and 291st. He was in the 291st which was held back in reserve while the other two regiments fought and experienced high casualties. "In retrospect, I was extremely fortunate, but didn't know it at the time," he reflects. People watching the Theatre newsreels and reading newspapers knew more about what was going on with the war than those fighting he said. He was fortunate to have been a truck driver. "I had more protection than most." He spent a lot of time picking up troops with frozen feet, a common dilemma at the time.

Around Christmas day of 1944, the fog and clouds lifted so planes could come in and rescue some of the weary soldiers. Clear weather turned things around very quickly. Chambers watched paratroopers and gliders dropped into the city of Bastogne. The Germans in Bastogne were asked to surrender. The Germans asked the Allies to surrender. This is where General McAullife replied to the German's surrender demand his famous word, "NUTS." When McAullife received the terms, he stated, "Awe Nuts." When he was trying to decide what his reply should be, one soldier reminded him of what he had just said. NUTS! And McAullife wrote it on the note.

After the Bulge in Belgium and Luxembourg was erased, Chambers's division dashed down to Alsace-Lorraine to push the Germans back in the Colmar Pocket near Switzerland.

They went back north to the Ruhr industrial area where the Germans finally surrendered on May 8th, now known as V-E Day.

At this time the war in the Pacific was not yet over. Troops in Europe were being collected to go to the Far East. Everyone knew millions of troops would be needed there Chambers said.

In August, the news hit Europe concerning the dropping of the big bomb on Japan. Chambers said he recalls them describing it as being as strong as "20,000 tons of dynamite." That was his introduction to the bomb. Then after the second bomb was dropped, it was apparent that the Japanese would surrender. Although it was controversial concerning the two big bombs, Chambers, like many veterans who fought in the war, feel that millions of lives were saved, both civilian and military. The Japanese homeland would not have given up without a huge loss of life on both sides, he added.

Chambers was awarded the highly coveted Combat Infantry Badge, the Bronze Star, several sharpshooter awards, and the European Theatre Ribbon with three Bronze Battle Stars. He was discharged in January of 1946. He went back to college and bought a home under the GI bill. He considers the GI bill one of the most important and influential benefits that started the country back on the track to recovery.

He went to work for the Farm Bureau and later for the Gallup Poll where he still works now and serves as director of client and community relations.

After 55 years, Chambers went back to the Bulge and revisit the site in September of 1999. He went to the very spot where on December 16th of 1944 the Germans made their last big assault, now known as the Battle of Bulge. He recalled the surprise the allies experienced on that fateful morning. Walking on the actual battlefields, "brought back a lot of memories," he said.

Chambers says that in a year or so, he will go back and take his grandsons to Europe so they can experience where the war actually took place. "They have a strong interest," he said. It's great when grandchildren do take interest in what their fathers and grandfathers did to preserve their freedom.

Chambers shot up nine rolls of film while he was there and also took video footage of various places of interest. I'm anxious to see them.

CLARK, EUGENE

This Lincoln man had never talked much about his experiences in WWII. I heard about him and gave him a call. I was going to be in Lincoln and asked him to meet me, only if he wanted too. He did, although, I think, rather reluctantly. His wife and family wanted him to tell his story. This was one of the most touching stories that I have. When he finished, I think we were all crying I know I was. If you ever think of taking your freedom for granted, think of this man.

The couple had brought a scrapbook along to show me. His mother had made it. Clark had never looked at it before that day he and his wife visited with me. He saw the postcards he had sent, newspaper clippings and other memorabilia; it wasn't easy for him. My heart went out to him.

Clark entered the army when, "I was just a kid," as he puts it. His parents had to sign for him. He was only 17 in 1939. Little did he know at that time that he would spend his 21st birthday in a Japanese prison camp.

He was a member of "Wainwright's Warriors," a term used for men serving under General Wainwright. They were on the island of Corregidor, otherwise known as "The Rock." The island was strategically important because of its location. Anyone approaching Manila Bay of the Western shores of Luzon, Philippine Islands, could be detected from there. When the Japanese overran Luzon in 1942, the American high command had taken refuge on Corregidor. Here is where General Douglas MacArthur slipped away in a torpedo boat leaving Wainwright in charge of the troops, around 10,000 of them. They fought it out until they no longer were able to. Clark was one of 5,000 men who were captured when food and supplies ran out and there was simply nothing left to do he recalled. "We had no choice!"

At least 5000 men were left to surrender Clark said. Only 500 survived. Starvation, disease and murder killed all the rest. For two years and nine months, Clark struggled to survive himself. "I was a cook, maybe that helped, but, I don't know. There was not much for food." He went on to say that the rice they did get was full of bugs. When they had meat on rare occasions it was usually water buffalo. It was full of maggots so they had to clean it off before they could cook it.

Fish heads, were their main source of meat. They had salt and pepper but no sugar. "It was kinda tough." They slept on beds made of bamboo poles. They made what they wore out of material that they could find," he said.

One week, when he became ill, he lost 30 pounds. "We were all walking skeletons" he recalls. When they first arrived at the camp, the Japanese wanted them to make them pancakes. They had no flour to do it. This gave the enemy an excuse to "Slap us around," he said. For those who had to work, or become slaves, they had it pretty rough he added.

The name of the prison was Cabanatuan, which was about 20 miles behind the front lines. The Red Cross was not allowed into the camp like they were in most of the European Theatre. No medical supplies were available. If you got sick, or injured, it was just too bad. "Some, dug their own graves before they died." For those who survived, "We never did give up," he said.

For entertainment, they had a monkey to play with. It just wandered in one day. They made a chess game out of materials they found, he said.

It was a welcomed sight when one day, to their surprise, they heard shooting. Bullets were hitting objects everywhere. They watched a guard blown out of his shack. A squad of Army Rangers was there to rescue them. They had walked all night to spring the surprise. "There were only about six or eight of them. But they got the job done," he said with a smile. Some of the survivors had to be carried out, but they were now free. When his mother heard of the rescue she said, "It was just as a miracle happened," he said.

When they returned home at the Golden Gate Bridge, they were welcomed with a band, which played, "Don't fence me in." It was a fitting song for the occasion he said. Later, he and the rest of the POW's received a special welcome from President Franklin Roosevelt. Clark received the Bronze Star.

He regrets never seeing those brave men who rescued him and his buddies. They were like little "savior's" to them. He is yet today, most grateful. Since, he has reunited with some of those other POW's who were with him in prison and they are able to talk about a time when life wasn't the best to say the least. Unfortunately, only a few of them lived through it.

Thank you Mr. Clark!

CROMER, CHARLES R. (RAY)

Cromer now lives in Lincoln. He was drafted in July of 1942 and entered the Air Force and served as a guard at an Air Base in New Mexico. When he heard the Army was asking for volunteers for the infantry, he volunteered, and so did his twin brother Joseph J. Cromer. The $21 dollars a month wasn't a very good wage but the call to duty was. After some training at Fort Leavenworth, they boarded the Queen Mary and were off to Europe.

Cromer arrived in Europe after the Normandy invasion; he fought under General Patton with the 63rd Infantry Division. While fighting in the front lines going across Germany, he was wounded. Some where near Heidelberg, when the front was moving ahead, a German rifleman shot him in the legs.

"I laid there quite a while" he recalls, and eventually his brother and the Sergeant pulled him back into the woods where he would not be in the line of fire. Later he was taken to a tent field hospital for emergency treatment before he was forwarded on to another hospital. Eventually he ended up back in the states in a hospital in Chickasha, Oklahoma. He was hospitalized about one year from the time he was hit. His brother Joe made it though the war safely.

Like many veterans, the effects of his wounds will stay with him the rest of his life. When I visited with him in December 1999, he was walking on crutches and is nearly 80 years of age. He has always had problems with his legs but like he says, "I'm getting older." At the time of his wounds, he had to lay in dirt and that penetrated his wounds, which caused infections that go with it. He is very grateful he has legs at all. Like he says, "I'm just grateful to be alive!"

Cromer is just another example of what the price of freedom costs. Men like him did what they had to do and that was to fight for the preservation of freedom. Those who abuse this freedom have no idea what it cost.

CULVER, BOB

Bob Culver of Lincoln was a torpedo man on a destroyer in Japanese waters just prior to the dropping of the bomb on Hiroshima on August 6, 1945. He believes that his experience on a battleship was one of the last, if not the last, surface to surface actions that took place between the U.S. Navy and the Japanese.

Culver is disappointed in the government for not giving the Navy a little credit for their part in this segment of the war. No medals or anything, but he and others are still trying to get Washington to give them something to be recognized. Culver has went so far as to design and purchase medals himself and have them available for his fellow comrades who served on the nine ship Destroyer Squadron 61 mission directed to perform an anti shipping sweep in Japanese waters. The medal that was designed for their services is a bronze round medal depicting a fleet of destroyers in Tokyo Bay. The medal, written around the edge states, "U.S. Navy Destroyer Squadron 61 Mission. Tokyo Bay, July 22, 1945."

"We don't even expect a medal from the government. A simple piece of paper would be nice," he said, concerning the fact they have not received any recognition for their efforts.

Culver signed up in the Navy when he was just 17. They called it a "Kiddie Cruise" he said. If you signed up prior to your 18th birthday, you could expect to get out before you were 21. "We were just a bunch of snot nosed kids, not fully realizing the seriousness of war," he said.

When he returned home he worked for a telephone company 44 years before retiring. He also helped his son in Omaha who is in the advertising business.

Culver was very kind to send me his story that was written by him in detail. You will note that being on a ship was not the most desirable place to be during a war. Many sailors are and still remain buried at sea.

Culver was on the USS Samuel N. Moore, DD 747. Based on action reports of Captain T.H. Hederman, Commanding Officer of Destroyer Squadron 61 and the input of all nine ships Captains. Culver's story is taken from radio transmissions, ships' logs, oral statements of participants and translated Japanese documents. While many articles have been written about this mission, few tell the whole truth about what really happened. Most stories are just based on speculation of what "might" have occurred. It was a dark night with only radar indications and the inability to actually see close up the events that took place within the convoy so many conflicting reports have developed Culver said.

Culver, in his story, provides only facts. For example, one document, not written by him, states there were aircraft involved. Fact was, there was no air cover planned or provided for that mission. In another instance, some action reports state that two or three ships of the Japanese convoy were sunk. Fact was, only one was actually sunk, as is confirmed by Japanese records.

The decision to make an anti-shipping sweep into Japanese home waters was made at the CINCPAC level sometime in July of 1945. With the impending invasion of Japan being inevitable, information on the enemy's defenses urgently needed to be upgraded. The orders came down the chain of command to the Commanding Officer, Admiral Bull Halsey, of the 3rd Fleet, Carrier Task Force 38 on the flagship USS Hornet. The importance of this mission was underlined in a radio message that stated, "On contact or commencement bombardment, report to CINCPAC ADV and originator, the progress of the situation by urgent dispatch."

The Task Group Commander selected Destroyer Squadron 61 to perform this responsibility. The squadron consisted of nine Sumner class destroyers, the most modern and equipped with the latest air/surface radar and radar controlled gun directors. Their armament consisted of 40 mm., 20 mm. anti-aircraft guns, a main battery of six 5 inch guns, as well as two torpedo mounts each loaded with five Mark 15 torpedoes.

The sweeping group Destroyer Squadron 61 consisted of two Divisions. Destroyer Division 121 included the USS DeHaven DD 727, USS Mansfield DD 728, USS Swenson DD 729, USS Collett DD 730 and USS Maddox DD 731. Destroyer Division 122 was made up of USS Blue DD 744, USS Brush DD 745, USS Taussig DD 746, and the USS Samuel N. Moore DD 747. The Commanding officer of the squadron was Captain T.H. Hederman, USN, on the flagship USS DeHaven.

Among Hederman's orders he sent to the squadron included that all boilers should be online. Lines should be made ready to be towed, energize degaussing equipment, rig the available life nets, open fire on shipping targets only if directed, and the Maddox was to spot jam shore battery radar if the squadron was under fire. Other orders were to test smoke screen generators, conduct abandon ship drills and if damage occurs, exert every effort to save personnel at all costs. If some were forced to abandon ship they were to swim toward the open sea to be picked up.

The crews were made aware of conditions that prevailed at the time the raid was to be performed. A typhoon was passing through the target area, which would have a notable bearing on ship speed. The attack area was to be cleared by dawn. The area was heavily mined by the Japanese andd they had numerous free-floating mines that were encountered. Fixed mine fields protected the coast. There would be no air support. Enemy submarines patrolled the area and suicide PT boats could also be encountered. The coastline along the southern end of Honshu and the eastern shore of O Shima were heavily fortified with 16-inch guns.

The following radio message had a direct bearing on the planned activity of the squadron: "The following is secret and is passed to you on a 'need to know basis.' Callaghan, DD 792 was sunk and Pritchett, DD 561 were damaged in suicide attacks on a bright moonlight night. Several wheels down flimsy planes, built of wood and fabric, attacked simultaneously. They were very maneuverable with expert pilots, but a maximum speed of only 90 miles per hour. These planes were not picked up by any ship within 13 miles, although they only flew at an estimated altitude of 1,000 feet."

The Squadron left the main task force at 0543 on the morning of July 21st heading for Sagami Nada, north of O Shima on course 290 degrees at 12 knots. The typhoon was moving at a speed of about 20 miles per hour from the Nansei Shoto area east-northeast towards the Tokyo area. This typhoon could easily affect the whole operation because high speed was needed to complete the sweep and be out of the area by dawn. The storm followed the predicted track, passing through the target area at 2100 during the evening of July 21st. The Squadron missed the main force of the typhoon but the storm made the seas very rough with wave heights as much as 15 feet. The wind increased to as high as 36 knots but later leveled off to 12-18 knots. Surface visibility was 4-8 miles, sky overcast with openings of clear blue. At 0957, the Moore left formation to stabilize the ship by heading into the weather to make it easier for the ship's physician to perform an emergency appendectomy. By 1337, the Moore rejoined the group with the surgery being successful.

The Brush was directed to test conditions at high speed and reported that at 23-26 knots caused no abnormal effects on the ship. By July 22nd, 1600 hours, the Squadron's speed was at 17 knots on a course of 300 degrees. At 1600 hours, a Japanese cargo ship also moved out of Yokohama and joined a convoy of four other ships in the darkness of night at Tateyama Bay. They were destined for Hakodate. The convoy consisted of two cargo ships and two escort vessels. One cargo ship was carrying 7,264 tons of military equipment and 8 Army Landing Craft according to records provided by Retired Captain Noritaka Kitazawa of the Japanese Military History Department. One of the escort ships was a minesweeper and the other a submarine chaser. The Japanese convoy made it safely through the minefields by Uraga in the middle of the night.

At 1737 on July 22nd, Destroyer Squadron 61 had formed a column of their normal order. The DeHaven in the lead, followed by the Mansfield, Maddox, Swenson, Collett, Taussig, Blue, Moore and Brush. The distance between the ships was about 500 yards traveling at a speed of 27 knots for its final approach to Sagami Nada. At 2120 O Shima was picked up on radar 50 miles away. At 2305, the DeHaven picked up an unidentified target bearing about 350 degrees at a distance of 19 miles. At first it was believed to be part of the landmass but the Flagship's radar picked up the four Japanese ships that had formed a convoy at 2316. The Squadron changed course to 300 degrees at 2321, increased speed to 27 knots at 2327. At 2338 the Squadron prepared their torpedoes. At 2351 the Squadron altered its direction to 120 degrees to avoid the possibility of torpedoes that may have been fired from one of the Japanese ships that were closing in on the Squadron. At 2351, the order was given to each destroyer to fire two torpedoes. Within three minutes, all had fired at a mean range of 11,000 yards. At 2353, the order was given to open fire with all main batteries.

At 2353, the Squadron could see a sharp light on the horizon towards the south. The Japanese cargo ship, Enbunmara had been hit. The ship had been damaged to a point it was unable to steer itself. Shells kept coming into her, one in the food locker, sailors panicked and climbed aboard a landing craft, located on the main deck, with the intent of heading directly out to sea in case of shipwreck. This proved to be a bad decision as they were the first to be killed. The aim of the

Squadrons next shell was deadly as it obliterated everything on its main deck. Pieces of equipment were destroyed, one after another. Another ship, the Hakutetsu-maro was engulfed in fire, lighting up the other, Enbun-maru in the dark. It could not have been a better target. The bridge and chart house had received direct hits completing destroying all steering and navigational capabilities. The escort ships hid behind the Enbun-maru, not wanting to give their position away by firing back blindly. The smaller cargo ship, Hakutetsu-maro, sunk.

At 0400, July 23rd, sound operators on the Brush heard two muffled explosions, which indicated that at least two torpedoes had found their mark. At 0900, the cease-fire was ordered and the Squadron retired on a course of 140 degrees at 27 knots. A total of 3,291 5-inch shells had been fired and the Squadron had launched 18 torpedoes during the attack on the convoy.

Members of the Squadron also sustained minor damage. The Brush and the Taussig were hit by shelling from shore defense guns on Nojima Saki. The Brush sustained a steering mechanism problem which left the ship at right full rudder. To avoid collision, the Brush had to stop twice and back up. One of the ship crewmembers quickly repaired the problem by replacing a pin that had become dislodged from the rudder assembly. The Brush, now behind the rest of the convoy, didn't waste any time leaving the attack area at flank speed.

The Japanese ship, Enbun-maru, though badly damaged with all fires extinguished, was able to sail under its own power using manual steering back to Okinoshima in Tateyama Bay. It carried 5 dead and 7 wounded. The ship's Captain was one of the casualties. The two escort ships helped them remove their wounded.

As a result of the Squadron's attack, 7,264 tons of military equipment and 8 Army Landing Craft were successfully prevented from being used against invasion forces. The attack was termed, "very successful," Culver said.

At 1729, the late afternoon of July 23rd, the Squadron rejoined the screen of Task Force 38 and resumed normal duties.

Captain Hederman in his action report stated; "the most gratifying consequence of this anti-shipping sweep has been the effect on morale. The Navy has reached a critical morale stage in this war. With announcements by the army that approximately two million men are being returned to civilian life following the defeat of Germany, there is a feeling that these dischargees will get the pick of the jobs in the post-war industry. To have actually fired torpedoes and guns at an enemy surface target has bolstered the spirit of our personnel, causing them to feel that each man individually is contributing his personal offensive and that his retention in the Navy is necessary in the defeat of Japan."

The Commander of the 3rd fleet, Admiral Halsey, congratulated the sound judgement, initiative and aggressive spirit displayed in "beating the weather" to drive this attack home at the very door of Japan.

Concerning awards that were never received by the Squadron, there was confusion among some of the ship Captains. One Officer with the high command was undecided as which ship should be recommended for the Bronze Star. "I am at a loss to decide who on my ship should be recommended for the Bronze Star. We just followed the leader and shot when told to. What do you think? Which officers are those ships recommending?"

As Culver, feels, "every man should have received one. They earned it and deserved it."

The importance of the sweep was emphasized by the fact that Captain Hederman's Staff was required to go aboard the USS Hornet and personally report the details of the sweep to Admiral Halsey.

According to Captain Hederman's report, there was no assigned division commander in Destroyer Division 122, which affected his plans considerably he said. He notes that the Commanding Officer of a 2200-ton destroyer has all he can do to maneuver and fight his ship without being given the added duties of a division commander in a tactical setup. Therefore, he said, everything he did was in the effort of keeping the Division together and to be maneuvered by the Squadron Commander. Earlier, the Commander of Destroyer Division 122 had been transferred to a staff that already had about ten Captains attached to it. After four weeks elapsed and no replacement had been provided by the time of their embarking on this anti-shipping sweep, Hederman stated the following in his report. "It is difficult to fully understand such a system."

Perhaps the action of Destroyer Squadron 61 will forever go unrecognized by the US Government. They do not stand-alone. Many, many individuals who fought vicious battles also have gone without notice as this author discovered in writing their stories. As in the above story, it appears as if they couldn't decide whom to give Bronze Stars to and did not consider the fact that everyone involved should have been awarded with them.

In many cases of this type, some perhaps got lost in the bureaucratic red tape. Other records, in the fury of battle and what took place later, were simply lost. One veteran told me, "what we did, by the time it reached the Command Center, was indeed lost." The Lieutenant who was supposed to deliver the report was killed before he got to the Headquarters. All his paperwork disappeared.

I am extremely honored that Bob Culver, Coordinator of Destroyer Squadron 61, has bestowed on me the honor of a "Special Honorary Member" of Destroyer Squadron 61, an integral part of Admiral Halsey's 3rd Fleet. Culver sent me a certificate and bronze medal with ribbon given to those who served in the surface action just off Outer Tokyo Bay on July 22, 1945. I repeat, I am very grateful and I thank the Squadron from the bottom of my heart.

DAVIS, CHARLES H.

Davis served in the South Pacific Theatre during WW II. He was with the U.S. Air Force, combat division associated with the 396th Svc. Squadron, 12th Service Group and the 308th Service Group. He joined the service right out of high school in July of 1937 and completed his service in December of 1945. He was discharged in 1940 but he joined the reserves and was recalled when his country needed him. He was sent to China and was stationed at various air bases there.

Davis was in on it when all those men of valor hit the beaches at Okinawa and the Philippines. He flew in the planes that "softened" these beaches so the men on foot who had to land there would have it a little easier. He was a pilot in B-24 bombers, which provided air support for the men on the ground. He also flew P-40's from China to the Philippines. "I did see a lot of action," this humble veteran who lives in the Veterans Home in Grand Island said.

When he joined the Air Force, his friends encouraged him to go to pilot school, which he did, at Randolph Field,

Texas. He later took advanced training at Sacramento, California. He probably knew then that one-day he might be shot down over some foreign land not know if he might live or die.

The day soon came when he was flying over Burma, close to Tibet. He was hit over Hanoi and lost his ability to steer the plane. With a rudder damaged, he could only fly the plane to the right because left turns were impossible. He was flying in big circles and his fuel was running low so he decided he had to bail out. He thought the best place to bail out would be over the Himalayan Mountains in China because China was our ally. The crew bailed out and it took the entire next day for them to find each other in the thick jungle. "It was my first jump and the last," he recalls.

They walked 30 days; some of the men walked with sprained ankles, which occurred during the landing. "We never lost a man though," he proudly remembers. Each man was prepared for living in the jungle. They had their survival kits, pistol, malaria pills and Chinese money, equivalent to $10,000, to buy food from villages that they would come across on their way back to an air base. Some Chinese soldiers found them, however, eager to take them back to an American base. Chinese soldiers would receive $10,000, American money, each for each downed airmen they found in their land. The U.S. government had invested quite a bit in these guys and found that it was worth it to offer a "bounty" more or less to have them safely returned to fly again.

When he was discharged he was honored with the Chinese Defense Medal and the Good Conduct Medal and several Campaign ribbons. Like many veterans I have interviewed, when asked how they feel about serving their country, Davis replied, "I'd do it again!"

DAY, DUANE C.

Day was a farmer before he was drafted. He joined the Navy and served on the U.S.S. Washington, BB 56. He served from September of 1942 until December of 1945 in the Asiatic Pacific Campaign.

Day spent three years on the Washington Battleship, as a signalman. He recalls it was the only ship that sunk a Japanese battleship, "Krisimia." It also had a collision with the

U.S.S. Indinnia, which took off a third of the Washington's bow where his commanding officer was and was killed.

As many veterans, Day was also wounded and has a 20% disability. He came home with 15 Battle Stars which is a reminder that he served his country well.

DUNN, ROBERT J. JR.

Dunn considers himself an "Army brat," as he says. His dad was a WW I veteran. "I grew up in the service," he says with a proud smile. His dad, Robert Sr. joined the Army in 1906 and retired in 1936. He knew Patton and Eisenhower very well. It's not unusual to find a son who wants to follow in his father's footsteps.

Robert Jr. spent a lot of time serving his country in the Pacific Campaign of WW II. He was a crewmember on B-17 bombers with the 88th Reconnaissance Squadron. His story is very interesting. His plane was among a squadron of planes, that left an airbase in California on December 6th, 1941 which was headed for Hawaii. His plane was the last to leave.

It takes several hours to make the trip and the closer they got to the airfield near Pearl Harbor, they were unable to raise anybody on the their radio. They thought the radio had maybe all went haywire. They would have liked to had clearance from the tower to land but no one answered their calls. Soon the base was in sight of squadron. They could see a lot of smoke, still no one was on the radio. They wondered what was happening. It didn't take long and they found out. They had arrived in between waves of attacks when the Japanese hit Pearl harbor. They had no idea that they had until they found themselves being attacked by Japanese planes. Not only that, but our own people suspected them of being with the Japanese and fired on them, too.

The question was what to do. It was obvious they could not land at the airfield. The tower was gone at Hickom Field. With flak and bullets piercing their planes, they had to set them down somewhere. The pilot flying the plane Dunn was in chose a golf course. Others landed wherever they could and remarkably, all ten B-17's landed safely. "We were pretty well shot full of holes," he recalls.

73

Today, I doubt that would ever happen because communications are better, but back then, it wasn't that great. But imagine, flying into something like that, a major enemy attack was taking place and you knew nothing about it until you got there. Surviving enemy fire as well as our own, and survive, was remarkable.

Dunn went on to do some island-hopping for 10 months in the Philippines. He was with the squadron who brought General MacArthur out of the Philippines to Alice Springs, Australia.

He became a part of the 19th Bomb Group. The unit was replaced and he came home in 1946.

In March of 1943, he earned the rank of 2nd Lt. and was transferred to Kearney Army Air Base. He was a member of SAC, Strategic Air Command. He went to Korea where he was a staff maintenance officer. In 1956, he was transferred to Morocco.

During the cold war, B-47 bombers were constantly kept on alert in Morocco. Twenty planes were ready to fly at a moment's notice. He was there for two years as Base Maintenance officer.

His last station was as a member of the 98th Bomb Wing at Lincoln Army Air Base and retired there in 1960, settling in Kearney where he now resides. My hats off to him as another veteran who served his country for many years making sure our freedom was preserved.

EGGER, GENE D.

This Navy veteran of WW II lives in Kearney. He joined the military in April of 1944 and was discharged in 1947. He said the reason he joined the military is because, "I wanted to serve my country!" Like many veterans, he didn't finish high school but chose to serve his country instead.

He served in the South Pacific Campaign. He was an important man on a Destroyer, Escorte, DE 796. I would imagine he caught plenty of guff from time to time from what I hear from other veterans. Egger was a cook, 3rd class, and participated in the escorting of convoys over the high seas. He had experience in the meat cutting business in a Safeway store before he left for the service, which may or may not have helped him acquire this job.

I wanted to visit with Egger when I was in the process of entering his story into the computer. His wife answered the phone. I asked for Gene. Her reply was one that I have heard more than once since beginning this book. "He died in October," she said. I was very sorry to hear that and I expressed my sympathy. He won't get to see his name in print like perhaps he had hoped. He can rest assured that he will be recognized for his part in WW II.

Egger doesn't say much about his experiences, but he noted one thing that I wish to elaborate on somewhat. In my questionnaire that I had put at various locations throughout the state I asked how these veterans felt about serving their country. Egger said, "At the time it was great, but today, I'm not sure, what they are doing to the veterans!"

Egger makes a good point. What are "they" doing to the veterans? Are those who fought bitter battles getting the benefits they were promised? Some tell me they do not. Are they getting the honor they so richly deserve? Again, in many cases they do not. Numerous veterans I have visited with, both on and off the record, inform me that they never even received a medal, citation or anything from the U.S. Government for their heroic actions. They were forgotten. A few have, after fifty years, finally received them.

I have heard many concerns about health care. Are our veteran's health care facilities receiving enough funding to care for these heroes? Is the quality of care as good in a vet's hospital as it is elsewhere? If it is, that's great, but if not, that's terrible. What is wrong with a nation that does not provide the best care to those who made it possible for all of us to be free?

After fifty some years, a World War II memorial is going to be constructed in Washington D.C., at the time of this writing. Several other memorials are being constructed in our own state. Vets all over tell me, "It's about time!" I agree. In most cases it is the veterans of a certain war who bring about the erection of a memorial. Not that they want to blow their horn but they just want something there so they will not be forgotten, to be recognized for what they did, the sole purpose of this book, "Operation Recognition."

ENNINGA, HERMAN

Eldon Enninga of Kenesaw helped get this story from his Uncle Herman Enninga. Eldon informed me of important facts that took place after his Great Grandfather Enninga came to settle in an area to the north of Glenvil. I feel they are very noteworthy, because this family of Enninga's lost their land due to the fact the government wanted it. The land they owned was to be part of the Naval Ammunition Depot east and south of Hastings. The Enninga family had 400 acres in the area. Eldon was a two-year-old boy at the time.

The year was 1942 when work began constructing this monstrosity of a place to make and house various forms of ammunition for WW II. It was to be located in the heartland of the U.S.A., miles from the coasts where the danger of enemy invasion would be lessened. As to why prime farmland was taken out of production for this plant, no one knows and people still question it today. At the time people told the government they should choose a site near Red Cloud where the land is rougher and primarily grassland. But the government told them Hastings was more suitable for rail traffic and the city of Hastings wanted very much to have them nearby. It would boost their local economy, was the argument. The plant proved to be short lived and later also proved to be full of contaminates and other undesirable facets that still linger with the site to this day, Enninga said.

Eldon told me that he was almost run over by bulldozers and huge trucks that were working around their farmyard before the family could even move out. When the land was appraised and condemned by the government, landowners had 60 days to move out. After 30 days, Eldon's parents hadn't found a place to go yet and heavy equipment already had started bumping into their house. Landowners were offered around $80 an acre and ordered to "GET OUT!" Simple as that. The government could and did carry out this undertaking of taking control of the land they wanted. The takeover of their land proved to be fatal to Eldon's grandfather. He only lived a year after that and died at the age of 64. He was heartbroken because the land that had been in his family was gone. After the war, the family still wanted to have an opportunity to get their land back but it was impossible, Enninga said. Today an igloo still stands on the site where the family homestead once was.

Herman Enninga told the following story about his experiences in the Pacific Theatre during WW II. Because of his poor eyesight, he had one of his neighbors, Al Renzelman, writes the story down for him. Enninga was born in Clay County, Nebraska, in 1916. He was inducted into the army, along with 2,000 others he recalls, in April of 1941. He was sent to Marshall Field Armory in Chicago. He was living near Rockford, Illinois at the time because he had gone there to find work in the 1930's. Since there were five boys in the family, not all of them could stay around home during those hard times. So he worked for the National Lock Company, a manufacturing plant in Illinois.

He considers himself a Nebraska veteran because he was born here and I gather he considers Nebraska his roots. He looks forward every year to coming "home" to Nebraska to visit old friends and relatives. Today he resides in Haxton, Colorado where, many years ago, he married a young lady who knew a friend who had land for him to farm. Since he wanted to farm and there was no longer an opportunity like this in Nebraska, he took the opportunity. Enninga later retired there.

He was sent to Louisiana for training and also to Springfield, Illinois to participate in a four mile Armistice Parade. December 8, 1941, after the Japanese bombed Pearl Harbor, he was quickly sent to Childers, Alabama to guard a munition plant. There wasn't much duty he says and living conditions there weren't the best. He served 4 hours on duty and 4 hours off and became tired because of the lack of a good night's sleep. Half of the men got pneumonia but were still required to work unless they had a temperature of over 102 degrees F. They had to sleep on concrete floors with only two blankets. Not too comfortable, he said.

After being at the munition depot for about six weeks, he was sent to Elkola, Tennessee to break up, or prevent a strike at an aluminum plant there. Their orders were to not allow over two men to congregate and visit. If three were seen together they were to break them up. On one occasion one of the strikers stated, "you tin heads don't have the guts to shoot us," as he resisted the order to disperse. With that statement, one of the soldiers chambered a bullet into his Springfield rifle and asked him, "now what were you about to say?" The group immediately scattered. The strike never took place. The men still had to sleep on concrete floors. They begged the officers to give them 6 or 8 hour shifts so they could sleep better but it wasn't approved.

He then went back to Camp Forest, Tennessee, where he helped train recruits until the spring of 1942. Then he was moved to Fort Lewis, Washington before being moved again to Camp Clipper, California. The men trained in the desert where he thought every bit of sagebrush had either a scorpion or rattlesnake under it. From there they were shipped to Camp Stoneham and then to Hawaii. He was there about eight months serving duties as Sgt.-of-the-guard at the radar station. The guys at the station were still very upset with the officers at the base. When the attack was made on Pearl Harbor, they knew planes were coming in but didn't know for sure who they were. The officers did nothing about it or didn't bother to check it out. If the officers would have listened to them, they felt they might have gotten their planes and ships out of the harbor before the air strike was made. They had noted the planes coming in an hour and a half before they arrived. Who is to blame the officers didn't pay any attention to these men? Enninga says he isn't sure.

Enninga performed his guard duties at the bomber-training base where pilots of B-25 bombers were based. He remembers the "hot rodders," as they were called, who were young pilots flying planes like stunt pilots. The General would reprimand them but it would do little good. They would continue to fly at high speed over the base in an upside down position or whatever else they could think of. They were sent on bombing missions first simply because they were as Enninga puts it, "out of control."

Enninga would often have a chance to ride with a "responsible" pilot. The military made good use out of those who conducted themselves in a more or less reckless manner. They wanted those "daring" pilots, and often turned out to be the very best.

From Hawaii he was sent to New Guinea in the summer of 1943 and stayed there until the spring of 1944. He recalls seeing the biggest snakes there he has ever seen, often 8 inches across and up to 35 feet long. And lizards were not uncommon to be five feet long. "They were about the size of a 150 pound hog," he said. "Big monsters!" The reptiles seldom bothered anyone he added.

78

His first base was set up at the northeast corner of New Guinea at Finschhafen. His main job now was to patrol the hills and mountainsides for straggler Japanese. One time one of these Japanese surrendered to the men. While interviewing him, they learned he spoke very good English. The men asked him why he was on the Japanese side. He said he had gone to school in the U.S. and had returned home to his parents in 1940. He was met with a bayonet and ordered, "Either you go into the army or you'll be shot!" Needless to say, he went into the Japanese army. The first question he asked of the Americans was who had won the Rosebowl in 1940? He had attended school in Southern California and knew the quarterback personally. The MP's later took him away and Enninga never saw him again.

Also while at Finschhafen, Enninga and his group re-captured a group of missionaries. They were from many denominations and had been captured by the Japanese. One of them, coincidentally, was from his hometown of Glenvil. All of them were tired, weak and starved. Enninga and the missionary from Glenvil enjoyed their time visiting but the missionary was so weak, it didn't last very long he said.

The Japanese were still trying to sneak up on the camp. Everyone was told not to wonder too far away from the base. Besides the Japanese soldiers, cannibals and headhunters were still prominent in the mountains of New Guinea.

From there they were moved to the Watzie River where they had pillboxes lining the coast to keep the Japanese from getting to the coast. The army didn't want the Japanese to escape. If a Japanese POW slipped away from camp, it would be the last anyone saw of them. Enninga says he was very fortunate one night. He was manning one of these pillboxes guarding the coast. The very next night, the Japanese had slipped in behind and threw a hand grenade into the pillbox. Three of our guys never made it out. The fourth was wounded so badly that he never recovered either.

Shortly after that Enninga was moved farther west to Hilandes, on the north side of New Guinea. From there they went to the Philippines at Subic Bay and the next day General MacArthur landed there. His job now was to keep the Philippinos from fighting each other. One village would often fight the other saying the other had spied on them and got the Japanese after them. "We had to settle them down," he said.

79

From there Enninga went up the mountainside to perform his duties. The enemy too heavily fortified roads in the area so the Americans had to go in the "back way," he said. He added that the mountains were so steep even a mountain goat would not have gone that way. In many places, the men had to use ropes and lift each other up the cliffs. Clothing and even vines were used to pull each other up these mountains.

The men were able to slip behind the pillboxes the Japanese had on the main road. "One whiff from the flame throwers and that was all for the Japanese. Those who didn't burn to death, suffocated because of lack of oxygen," he said.

After scaling the mountains for several days, they finally got to the top. From there they could see Bajuio, the summer vacation home of the more wealthy Philippinos. It got very chilly there but never froze, he said.

As they neared the mountaintop, some Japanese were laying there waiting for them. Here is the first "hit" Enninga received. The Japanese got him and his buddy took the Japanese and his flag. Enninga still has the flag in his possession. Just before he was hit, one of the fellows saw some leaves moving in the bushes. He shot into the area killing one Japanese right there.

After he was wounded, the Company Commander came to him. He said, "I have one of two things you can do, either stay here, or lead the casualties and wounded out of here." Enninga said, "give me a carbine, and I'm on my way." The Commander stated, "I have plenty of Philippine Gooks who can carry the others, but you'll have to lead them. You're on your own," he concluded.

The Company HQ knew they were coming and met them in the dark, "or we never would have made it," he said. Immediately they put Enninga into a jeep and sent him to an aid station. They gave him medicine and he heaved and heaved and then heaved some more. An orderly informed him he was full of gangrene. "My whole insides were full of it," he said. The medicine he was given had brought it all out of him. The next morning he was sent to Morotai Island Hospital. The same day, one of his buddies was hit and sent to Leyte to another hospital there. Both were later sent back to their unit, again on the same day. Their time at the hospitals was nearly the same.

They were loaded on a train. It was towards evening and Enninga and his buddy found a spot to lay underneath the seats of the train to sleep. It proved to save their lives. The Japanese had sabotaged the train. The engine and the first coach behind the engine got by, but the remaining cars went off the track. The cars crumpled up into "kindling wood." "I saw people with timbers run clear through their bodies. It was a horrible, horrible mess," he said. Enninga was wounded now for the second time.

He was taken to a hospital close to Clark Field for five days and then he went back to the Company. At the hospital he was told he could leave but there was no transportation available. He was on his own to get back. As luck would have it, a Chaplain and his driver came along. They knew exactly where he wanted to go so they took him there. They were part of the 33rd Division, which was Enninga's old infantry Division.

This concluded his action in the military. The CO told him, "you're not going out anymore. You're the only one who has hard earned points," he said. Hard-earned points were with reference to him not having any children and family at home and for other reasons. He was now in charge of the quarters and other details.

He was sent to Manila at a debarkation camp. There he and about 300 other men waited to be shipped to the United States. Prior to his being shipped, the Colonel paid them a visit. He stated, "fellows, you're the cream of the crop. I need you. I need you badly. If anyone of you will step forward I'll give you an extra stripe and also a bonus." No one stepped forward, Enninga said.

When they arrived at Division Headquarters, about a thousand men were there. This time it was the General who said the same thing as the Colonel had. "You're the cream of the crop. You're all Sergeants and I need you." Again, no one stepped forward.

While they continued to wait for a ship to take them home, we dropped the bombs on Hiroshima and Nagasaki. MacArthur stopped all transportation. Nothing moved except those scheduled to go to Japan, which included Enninga's 33rd Division. They waited at Manila for two weeks, staying in quarters. No one went anywhere. Finally, they boarded a ship similar to the "slow boat to China," that took 30 days to reach the U.S., at San Diego. The men were told they could have anything they wanted to eat and drink. Some over did this and since they were not used to eating that much food, they got very sick. Enninga said he was aware of this problem and had limited his food intake and got along pretty well. Everyone craved fresh cow's milk, he said.

Soon he arrived back in at Fort Logan, Colorado. It took about two weeks for his papers to catch up with him. When the officer handed them to him, "I felt sorry for him later. I nearly shook his arm off," Enninga said.

When he finally got on a train headed for Hastings, he sat by older gentlemen whom he quickly informed; "This is the happiest day of my life." At Hastings, his family, his wife Helen and her family met him. One of his nieces who was ten years old when he left was now a nice fifteen-year-old young lady. He didn't recognize her. To this day, she teases Enninga about not knowing her.

Helen and Enninga had been married when he had been in the service already for about a year and a half. They now have been married for 57 years. He continues to have contact with old army buddies and attends reunions with them. Most are now gone, he said, and he carries emotional scars in his life. The men he knew, who suffered so much, "have left their scars," he said. They have done a lot of bonding over the years and have a good trusting relationship between members of the group. He has the highest regard for the Veteran's Administration who has treated him very well. "I am nearly blind, and the VA has treated me very well," he stated.

Enninga earned the rank of Staff Sgt. and was awarded two Purple Hearts and two Bronze Stars for being wounded and bravery in combat on the battlefield.

"I am proud to serve my country. I hope and pray there will always be those willing to do the same should the need arise," he concluded.

I hope so too, Herman.

ESCHLMAN, ART

Eschlman is a veteran of WW II and lives in the Veterans Home in Grand Island. When he was discharged from the service in 1945 he moved to his home in the David City area. He had enlisted in the Navy in 1942 and served in the European Theatre and spent his time aboard destroyers. Destroyers were ships that were very important during the war but also were a dangerous place to be. They bobbed around the ocean and they were sitting ducks for enemy aircraft as well as other vessels of war.

Upon at least one occasion, the destroyer Eschlman was on was hit by enemy fire when a bomb was dropped on it in the Mediterranean Sea. It didn't sink however, but made it back to the harbor for about a month's worth of repairs.

Eschlman's job was to load the 40-mm anti-aircraft guns on the vessel. When the ship was hit, so was Eschlman. He experienced powder burns on his eyes but in time they both healed quite well. He was up for the Purple Heart but it was cancelled when his eyes healed, which took about two months.

He recalls that when people did become wounded on the ship they didn't always leave the ship to go to some hospital nearby. If someone needed surgery, they just cleared off the tables in the mess hall on board and performed the operation there.

Although he was wounded, "It was still a pleasure to have served my country," he said. He is dismayed over the movies that are made today with reference to war. "Movies make it look like sports, its not that way at all," he concluded.

FISHER, LAVERNE D.

Fisher was a young farm boy from McCook, Nebraska, when he enlisted in the U.S. Air Force. Fisher was the oldest of eight children. His dad was partially disabled after he was thrown from a horse. "I thought I would join the service and send money home to help out," he said. Because droughts had drained the family's finances, he felt an obligation to help. As most vets will tell you, starting pay was around $21 a month, not big money by any standards. Of that, Fisher would send home $5 of it. As he rose in the ranks, he was able to send home more. He served in the Pacific Theatre during WW II. After being trained to be an airplane mechanic, they shipped him off to the Aleutian Islands where he served one year in aircraft maintenance.

Mechanics generally bunked with the entire flight crew and often in tents. He remembers the loneliness he felt when the flight crew would leave to go on a mission. He would wonder if he would ever see them again. He recalls one of the B-24 bomber Fisher had worked on, was shot down in the Pacific. Their mission was to bomb Japanese destroyers, headed for the United States. The crew, like so many others, was listed as missing in action. Since he was close to the men, "It made me feel very lonely and sad," he stated.

Fishers wife, Virginia, also contributed to the war effort by working as a telephone operator at the McCook Air Base during the war years. She was proud to be the first high school Northwestern Bell Employee of McCook ever hired to work for them.

Virginia's maiden name was Hanke. She told me about her brother, Kenneth Eugene Hanke, who gave the supreme sacrifice for his country. Virginia had written up a tribute to him in 1996. Hanke was a crew member on the U.S.S. Johnston DD-557, when it was sunk October 25, 1944 by a Japanese Center Force, in a battle off Samar, now known as the Battle of the Leyte Gulf. The Japanese fleet consisted of 4 battleships, 7 cruisers and at least 12 destroyer's history records. The Johnstons gunnery officer had stated, "We felt like little David with a slingshot."

The Johnston, along with a few other units of an Escort Carrier Task Group, made a tremendous effort to withstand the shelling. At around 7:00 a.m. that morning, the Johnston was the first to start firing at the enemy, the first to launch torpedo's, and the first to make smoke. In five furious minutes, the Johnston fired 200 rounds at the enemy plus 10 torpedo's. It sank the Japanese cruiser, Kumano. But the Johnston took three 14-inch shell hits from a battleship followed closely with three 6-inch shells from a light cruiser. By 9:30 a.m. the Johnston was dead in the water, unable to move, a sitting duck. The Japanese vessels circled the Johnston in a similar fashion Indians would circle a prairie schooner depicted in the movies. The order to abandon ship came at 9:45 a.m. At 1,000 yards, a Japanese destroyer pumped a final round into her to assure it would go down.

Of the 327 men that complimented the Johnston, 141 of them were saved. Of the 186 men lost, about 50 were killed by enemy action. Hanke was one of them that were killed.

FREESE, HERMAN E. H.

The Beatrice Daily Sun on June 6, 1994, featured Herman Freese of Plymouth, Nebraska, in a large article complete with photographs and story. He served in the U.S.

Army Air Corps with the 8th Air Force, 379th Bomb Group, and 97th Service Squadron in the European Theatre. When I asked him why he joined the armed services, his reply was, "to help defeat the aggressors of Japan and Germany who started WW II." An admirable reason I felt. He continued by saying, "I'm proud to be an American, to have served my country in helping to defeat the regimes of Japan and Germany."

As I interviewed veterans, I noted that many are of German decent. Their parents or grandparents were immigrants to this country, years before, looking for a new life. Freese is one of these, a full-blooded German who fought against his own ancestry. It was not uncommon at all, because many citizens of the U.S. can trace their roots to European countries.

Freese was a farmer prior to entering the war and went back to farming when he returned home. He graduated from high school and took an extension course of German at the University of Nebraska. In July of 1942 he went to serve his country. He was sworn in at Fort Crook, Omaha, with the Army Air Force and completed a course as a propeller and governor specialist on the Boeing B17 Bomber engines.

By May of 1943 he found himself at New York Harbor boarding a ship called the "Aquitania" with 7,000 other soldiers and headed out to sea. With full naval escort they sailed a zigzag course which changed every six minutes to avoid any enemy submarine torpedo attacks--a ship full of seasick soldiers who, as a whole had never been on a ship in their young lives. The floors in the bathrooms sloshed with vomit sometimes 2-3 inches deep. "If you weren't sick when you entered the bathroom, you probably were when you left" Freese said.

Freese didn't trust the food on the ship so he had purchased $30 worth of peaches from the PX before the left and lived mostly on them at sea. After being tossed about at sea about 8 days they arrived in the Harbor of Gourock, Scotland and finally were able to set foot on soil again. From there he went on a train to Kimbolton, England, Station 117 where he was assigned to the 8th Air Force, 379th Heavy Bombardment Group, and the 97th Service Squadron. This Airdrome was built up specifically for an American Bomber base for missions to be flown against Nazi occupied Europe. It had been bombed by the Germans prior to Freese's arrival.

Now that they knew what their duties were, Freese and the other men like him quickly began revising the building that would be the propeller-governor shop. An overhead 'A' frame and track was built out of heavy I-beam, welded together by the men. They had to be constructed to support the propellers while servicing them. Freese went back to the site in 1989; the building was still standing and was being used as an electrical shop.

By the end of May 1943, a steady stream of B-17's from the States was arriving at the new base. On the 29th of May, the first bombing missions left to a destination at St. Nazaire, France to bomb the U-boat Pens.

In the meantime, the Germans were also flying night missions to London. Freese's base was on alert every time the Germans flew overhead. The base always lived under blackout conditions because they were under constant threat by the German planes.

For nearly two years Freese lived and worked at the base. He remembers well the many bombing missions flown over the Normandy beaches in advance of the invasion. He recalls that on August 17th, the 8th Air Force, and the 379th Bomb Group, bombed a ball bearing plant at Schweinfurt, Germany, they lost 60 bombers. Soldiers died in the sky at 27,000 feet as well as on the ground. Freese said the 8th Air Force alone lost 20,000 airmen in the European Theatre.

When one looks at the magnitude of air power, it is hard to imagine, as Freese said, a thousand American bombers in the air at one time with fighter escort to bomb targets in Europe. "It was a sight to behold with vapor trails all over England," he said.

Freese spent most of his time repairing propellers and governors. They disassembled, cleaned and inspected them at regular intervals. Often props were shot up or damaged by flack and needed to be repaired. When bombers returned from a mission, damaged props had to be removed and made ready for the next mission, ASAP. "It was hectic," he said.

If the flack damage wasn't too deep, it was sanded and buffered to a smooth finish. If there was a hole in a prop blade, he ground the hole out in a circular pattern to the point where there were not cracks after magna-fluxing it. Then they had to be totally rebalanced by adding or removing weights inside the propeller hub. If not in perfect balance, the prop could vibrate an engine off it's mounting bolts.

With the war coming to an end on May 8, 1945, Freese was delighted that for one whole day, he and other ground support members were taken up in the B-17's to view the damage the war had caused. Upon return, they dressed in class A-uniforms and paraded down the runway at the base. They stood at attention for a few minutes as a tribute to their fallen comrades and wars end in Europe.

Because Freese was fluent in the German language, he was called upon to fly to St. Germain, France on May 18, 1945, with Air Technical Intelligence. His job was to microfilm a series of German documents.

On June 2, he was sent to Stuggart Germany and asked to fly as an interpreter and armed escort with two German pilots to deliver a German V14 Focke Twin Rotar 1,000 horsepower helicopter to Cherbourg, France. The Americans wanted it for research and Freese volunteered to do so. When they left on June 15, the Germans surprisingly, helped Freese with his parachute. He seated himself behind the pilots armed with his 30-caliber carbine. After a couple fuel stops, they arrived at Cherbourg. They were to land on a carrier but there was none in port that day so they landed on a nearby airfield. The German pilots were always under tight security. Upon arrival at his destination, Freese handed his orders over to the commanding officer at the airfield. Later, one of the pilots wrote to Freese telling him they had been ordered to fly to England to give an exhibition flight when they crashed. No one was killed they informed him.

Freese was then picked up by an American escort plane and flown back to Stuggart, Germany. The plane experienced engine trouble and was forced to land near Brussels. After a few days of waiting for parts, Freese and the pilot repaired the plane and started off again.

He was then sent to Berchtesgaden, Germany where the German high command was being held prisoners for interrogation purposes. Freese served as contact personnel and became acquainted with many of them. One General, humbled himself and gave Freese a portion of Turkish blend cigarettes. He still has them today. The General had told him, "Keep these for remembrance."

One General, who Freese got to know quite well, asked Freese to check on his wife. He did, and brought back a letter from her to give to her husband.

Before Freese was to be shipped home, he was able to acquire a leave and visit some of his relatives in Germany. Uncles, aunts and cousins had been waiting hoping he would visit them. At Wiesbaden, where a plane had taken him, he traveled by jeep and a driver was provided to drive over bombed out roads to a town where his mother came from, Nieder Oflieden. He didn't know where to have the driver stop so at random they stopped. He asked a lady if she knew of a Mr. Heinrich Cloos, my uncle. She took a few steps back, called Heinrich, and from around a building, he came forth with outstretched hands Freese recalls.

Freese, of course, didn't recognize him but his Uncle, walked up to him and spoke in German, "Herman, I've been looking for you for a long time." He took him to his home and because he wanted to assure him that he was who he said he was, they showed him pictures of his family that Freese could relate to. They showed him pictures of his mother, father, sisters, and Freese himself. As word was passed around that Freese was there, Freese's mother's friends came to offer their best wishes. "It was a very emotional time, there were tears and hugs of joy," Freese said, "Katharina's son Herman, was in town," the townsfolk told one another.

One of his cousins arrived home from an American prison camp just two days prior to his arrival. I would imagine that was a time when the proverbial "Blood is thicker than water" would hold true. Family usually understands what other family members have to do.

Staff Sergeant Freese returned home via the ship "Colby Victory" and landed in New York harbor where he had left at the beginning of his enlistment. He returned home at Plymouth on December 23, 1945.

He had been involved in 330 missions from May of 43 to April of 45. It was not until July 9, 1991, the Air Force belatedly informed him that he had been awarded the Presidential Unit Citation with two oak leaf clusters. He had received earlier the good conduct medal, European-African Middle Eastern Campaign and the WW II Victory Medal. Yes, he's proud to be an American veteran!

HAASE, ERVIN

Haase gave me his story in writing and I also had the privilege of interviewing him when I was in Lincoln. He entered the military in December of 1940, in the National Guard. "I figured I would know better where I would end up," he said. Hoping, after a year of active duty, he would be headquartered in Lincoln. He married in 1941 after one year of active duty. Still based in the states, his wife was able to join him from time to time. Unfortunately, he was not around when his two children were born. I sensed he felt badly about that. But that is the life of many servicemen. They can't always be home when they want to be. He was with the 134th Infantry Regiment of the 35th Division when he began with the service. He was discharged in August of 1945. He rose in rank from Private to Captain.

Haase remembers the training at Camp Robinson, Arkansas where he spent one year. Long marches, rifle training and maneuvers will never be forgotten he said. When Pearl Harbor was suddenly bombed by the Japanese, December 7, 1941, "It changed everything" he recalled. His Division was sent to the West Coast to guard the U.S. against a possible invasion by the Japanese there. Haase was assigned to an outpost to watch for enemy submarines.

He applied for permission to go to Fort Benning, Georgia, to be trained as an infantry officer in the O.T.S. Program. He was accepted and soon promoted to 2nd Lieutenant and assigned to go to Camp Croft, South Carolina. From there he was sent to Michigan to guard the Soo Locks. Then back to Fort Benning with the duty of training new O.T.S. candidates. This was supposed to be his permanent assignment. It didn't work out that way. He found himself, after a few months, shipped to Arizona and assigned to the 104th Timberwolf Infantry Division. And then there was more training. Desert maneuvers in California. After that was over, it was off to Camp Carson, Colorado to prepare the Division for assignment in the European Theatre operation, at Camp Kilmer, New Jersey. By now, Haase knew, he was going to see Europe.

He and many others boarded a ship destined to land on the Cherbourg Peninsula of France. His was the first Division to land there. Then they went to Holland and joined forces with the First Canadian Army with a mission that was clear. They were now to go to the northern approaches of Antwerp, a port vital to supply the troops in that sector and also the western front. After a month of combat, the Division was ordered to move to Aachen, Germany, to positions west of the Siegfried Line, preparing for the big push that was yet to come. He was relieved of his duties as a transportation officer and assigned as S-2 of the 3rd Battalion, 415th Infantry Regiment.

From October of 1944 to May 8th, of 1945, Haase said, "It was constant fighting. Upon one occasion, Haase was reported MIA, missing in action. He was not however; he was just unable to report to headquarters. The Germans had them pinned down and they had "hole up" and stay put until the area was secure. While they continued trying to push the Germans out, "H-hour", time of departure, on the Siegfried Line, was set for Nov. 1944 with the first objective to be the Roer River, in March of 1945. They were to then push into the Ruhr Valley. They had to cross the Erft River with their assault boats and then to the city of Cologne on the Rhine River, where fighting was severe until it finally fell in March of 1945. The center of town was a mass of rubble, Haase recalls, with one exception. A cathedral was left intact during the bombing. The gothic spires were very impressive, as they stood out surrounded by rubble, he said. On March 11th, a flag raising ceremony was held in the sports palace where Hitler had glorified his Nazi war machine.

After securing Cologne, they crossed the Rhine River at the Remagan Bridge Head, and pursued the Nazi's into the Ruhr pocket. The division completed the 193-mile advance from the Rhine River to Paderbourn. Eventually they ended up with the Russian Torau at the Elbe River where they would stay until the end of the war.

Haase says his most memorable and unforgettable memory of the war was in the city of Nordhausen and the underground factories there. It was here that the Germans manufactured V-1 and V-2 bombs. There, they found masses of corpses everywhere with living skeletons lying among the dead. In the Nordhausen concentration camp was row after row of skin covered skeletons as men lay there starving in the most incredible human filth imaginable. More than 25,000 slave laborers had been forced to work in these underground factories and were never permitted outside. They virtually died of starvation, physical abuse and disease.

The German SS, Elite Guard, was in charge when Haase and his division arrived. He was an intelligence officer in charge of POW's at the time. When they turned the prisoners of war over to him, one of them asked Haase if he could beat up one of the SS guards who had beaten him many times. Haase said, yes, turned his back and let him go ahead. "The soldier was so weak he could barely throw a punch", but I let him try he said. "I'll never forget it," he concluded.

He was awarded the Bronze Star as well as other medals and accommodations. He is another veteran who is not sorry he served his country. He stated, "we will always need to maintain and protect our country!"

When Haase returned home he began a life connected with sales. Later he and two other partners bought a bowling alley. He is also a building consultant for Schwisow Construction Inc. of Lincoln.

HAMILTON, CHARLES M.

This is a WW II veteran with a sense of humor to say the least. While telling his experiences he had to laugh, while looking back on it now. He jokes about things that happened during a time when his life was interrupted due to war. Some things were a little ridiculous, I will agree, while others perhaps; one might as well laugh, because it would do no good to cry.

Hamilton notes an old saying by an author unknown who states, "War is a few moments of intense fear and hours-days-weeks-months of boredom." He agrees with that statement saying it is very true.

Hamilton was a married man when the Japanese attacked Pearl Harbor on December 7th, 1941. He had a baby on the way and worked at a Safeway store in Lincoln. He also lives in Lincoln now. He was 23 years old and hoped he would perhaps be deferred. The way it turned out he received his induction greetings about 3-4 months after the baby was born.

Early in 1942 he recalled that while working at the store, the rationing of sugar, gas, and meat. Many other items became scarce in the store. They also sold War Bonds for $18.75 and issued a bond worth $25 at maturity. Stores were also collection points for books that would be sent to all the many training camps. Old kitchen fat and grease were also saved and made available for the war effort. As more and more young single men left the community, the store began to hire older men and for the first time, female checkers.

Before he was inducted, he attended Civilian Defense Volunteer meetings hoping to impress his draft board he says with a laugh but "It didn't."

At the store several young men left to serve their country. Some never came home. Others became prisoners of war, some of them for years in the Pacific Theatre. War bond slogans became popular almost making one feel guilty if you didn't buy one. One read, "Bet you'll buy war bonds when the Nazis are marching down your street!"

The last few months of 1942 and early in 1943 he was driving a taxi to supplement his family's income. With the baby now born the income from the store, $28 a week working 54 hours didn't cut it. While driving the taxi, he drove many service men around the city. Several asked him where his uniform was? Soon his draft notice arrived. He and his family went to the draft board asking for an extension. They were kind, he said, and granted him 30 more days before he would have to go.

After taking his physical in Omaha, he reported to the Des Moines, Iowa, induction center where he received his uniform and everything else he needed. He chuckled about the way the uniforms fit. They were cut for the average man but they really didn't fit anyone all that good he thinks. He was average and it didn't fit.

When he entered the service he would receive $21 a month. His wife and family were to get $50 a month allotment. However, this did not start until he was in the army for two months. They went to the Red Cross, which kindly gave them $50 for the first month so, his wife and son could survive. To this day, Hamilton said he is grateful to the Red Cross and all they did and supports them gladly. While going overseas, he says he probably ate $10 worth of doughnuts also provided by the Red Cross.

Before he left to go overseas he was in front of a Sergeant who was trying to determine from his papers where to place him. Hamilton reminded him he had been in the grocery business. "So, he assigned me to the Anti Aircraft Command," he said with a burst of laughter.

He remembered that while he traveled on the train heading west to California, a Sergeant was taking roll call in each car. Hamilton's name did not come up. Finally the Sergeant asked if anyone's name wasn't called they should step out in the isle. He smartly did so and found out he was in the wrong car. But because he stepped out very smartly, the Sergeant appreciated that and he made him acting Corporal. Hamilton still laughs about that. It really bothered him when they traveled right through Lincoln and he was not allowed to get off and at least call his wife.

If you happened to be in the last car on the train, your time for a meal would take a while. The food car was towards the front. You would have to take your mess kit all the way up to the front, wait in line, and then return to your car in the rear. A process that took about two hours he said. Again, with a laugh, "we had nothing else to do."

"It wasn't too bad," he said referring to the training camp other than the usual harassment by the Sergeant in charge just to let you know he was the boss. They could shower every day and they were given their 1x2 boards, play rifles. They were told these boards would "simulate" rifles. "Simulate" became a new word in the vocabulary of most. They were given gas masks and put in chambers where mustard gas would be turned on. They were told to crack open the mask a little so they could smell the gas so they could identify it. Very few did, they just pretended to he said.

While at Camp Hahn, Marsh Field Air Force base was nearby. One day he witnessed three B-24 bombers crash on takeoff in a 15-minute period of time. He never did hear the particulars; nothing was ever in the papers about it he said.

Men like Hamilton often became frustrated. One night, he and some buddies had a few beers at the local PX. He realizes now that there was no excuse for his actions but in the latrine, he had put his fist through a wall. Maybe he did it because he was lonely for his family and homesick, who knows what may have inspired this action. The next morning at reveille the 1st Sgt. tried to find out who did it but no one squealed on him he said.

After basic training he was moved to Camp Irwin, CAMA, California and to desert maneuvers. Now this "entrepreneur" saw an opportunity to make a few bucks. He would buy 3-4 boxes of candy bars at the base for a nickel each. Out on the desert, men would gladly buy them for a dime. His wife would send him wire clothes hangers because there were not too many of them at the base and he would sell them to the guys for a dime each. "Not too bad," he said.

By this time he was promoted to a Sergeant himself. He had 15 men, 2 two and a half ton trucks, a 40 mm. cannon with a director and a trailer with 4-50 caliber machine guns. Soon he was given a 10-day furlough to go home, where he wanted to be. Trains were overloaded and he often had to sit on the floor but who cared, he was going home, at least for a short time.

The 10 days at home seemed to Hamilton more like 10 minutes and it was time to leave again; this time for New Jersey. He remembers traveling through Chicago. Older men would stand beside the moving troop trains and hand the men whose arms were outstretched out of the windows, a pint of booze. "I was proud of those old guys," he said.

Before he knew it he was on the Queen Elizabeth along with 30,000 other troops, headed for Europe. No one was laughing.

Because he was with an Anti-aircraft unit, his unit manned the ships 40 mm. guns, four hours on, eight hours off during the trip. They enjoyed the freedom of being on this three block long vessel. Everyone else was restricted. He noted the ship's zigzag pattern of travel. He learned that by doing this, changing course every 45 seconds, they could out run any enemy submarine that happened to be in the area.

In five and half days they arrived at their destination in Glasgow. They were given their rations of candy and chewing gum. When they were on a train, children lined the tracks wanting the gum. "We tossed them all the candy and gum," he said.

Arriving at Stafford, England, they slept that night in a schoolhouse. It was cold, but because they were sleeping head to foot with the next guy, it became quite warm. Hamilton and a buddy were billeted to a private home after that. The government paid the family two cents a day for taking in soldiers. They had a bed with straw mattresses. In England, they had very long days because the sun didn't go down until nearly midnight. People would work 10-12 hour days in the airplane factories and come home and work their "Victory

Gardens" after that. Horses were used yet extensively. Manure that was deposited on the street by the horses was quickly collected by the townsfolk to put on their gardens. They almost fought over it he said.

Hamilton and others were later moved to an 8th Airforce glider base, waiting for D-Day. He was a part of the counter invasion forces. England was expecting to be counter attacked once the invasion had begun. All road, street and town name signs were removed so the enemy didn't know for sure where they were at or where they should go following the signs. It seemed odd for Hamilton driving through these "no-name" towns on the wrong side of the street as they still do there.

For the next two weeks he trained men as part of the English army, to fire the 50-caliber machine guns. He says he became quite good at field stripping a machine gun and putting it back together, blindfolded, in less than two minutes. The English made him look pretty bad when it came to their dart playing games he said.

The 6th of June had arrived, D-Day. Everyone cheered as they watched all the many planes heading for France with their brand new black and white stripes freshly painted on them. Question was, would there be a counter invasion.

Everyone was prepared but at this point, only the V-2, the pilotless planes the Germans had, were launched towards London. They sounded like motor boats as they passed overhead.

Hamilton and the men uneventfully crossed the English Channel. Near the shore they were transferred into smaller boats and they waded ashore without incident. Here now at Normandy, Omaha beach, they drove their trucks through a few small towns like St. Lo, which already had been taken. The men waited for a "breakout." Anticipating combat, wondering when, wanting to, yet fearing it.

On August 1st, General Patton's 3rd Army's breakout had officially began. Hamilton followed along with the 4th Armored Division through more little towns and the countryside. He saw hundreds of dead Germans. The stench of death was everywhere. "I will never forget it," he said.

Nor will he forget August the 8th when he had his gun dug in on a hillside where German planes were dropping flares at around midnight. They lit up the whole countryside, he said.

Terror barely describes how they felt, not yet hardened for combat.

As the 3rd Army raced across France, Hamilton's group was assigned to guard Patton's headquarters, leapfrogging along behind the front. Patton soon went so fast that he outran his supplies. He was running out of gas. Five-gallon gas cans were used to refill. C-47's brought it along with other supplies. The gas shortage and the winter weather caused Patton's army to stop. Through Christmas day, Hamilton and his outfit stayed in Nancy where they stayed for nearly a month. They were on an airfield and used scraps of junk building themselves little two man homes.

One night as C-47's were coming in bringing supplies, the men poured gas along the runway and lit it so they could see where to land. A few days after Christmas they were ordered to go to Belgium and Luxembourg to the famous Battle of the Bulge. The ground was covered with snow and it was very cold. By the time they arrived the battle was over. Hamilton and his 15 men drew back to Metz and found a basement to seek shelter from the cold. They found bread and butter in the house. "What a treat," he said.

They continued on back into Germany and on that day President Roosevelt died. Some of the men had the opportunity to see Dachau, where the ovens were that had brought death to many Jews.

The war ended in Europe May 8th, 1945. On V-E Day, he was in Lintz, Austria where they had been ordered to protect a bridge. After that he was ordered to check identifications of the thousands of displaced persons traveling about, most of them walking which was a sad sight to see.

A little later he was sent to northern France, LeHavre, to board a ship and head for the good old USA. When he arrived back in Lincoln he told his wife, "I don't care how high taxes get. It's worth every penny to be able to live in America and be an American."

In the spring of 1946 he was presented the Bronze Star. He often thought if he would have received it in September of 1944, he could have gotten home "20 points sooner," he said again, with a laugh.

Gladys had saved up $500 while he was gone, believe or not, he says. It was enough to qualify for a GI home loan and they bought a home at 3613 Garfield, in Lincoln. Then their daughter Barbara was born. He became store manager and was an American, of which he is most thankful. He was in heaven, as he referred to it then "sitting on top of the world. He concluded, "if heaven is any better than this, it must be truly wonderful!"

HANLEY, OCTAVE FRANCIS HAROLD

Hanley was a corporal in the United States Air Force during WW II. He served with the 29th Tactical Air Command interrupting his ranch life near Marsland, Nebraska in January of 1943. He was drafted and was with the war from the time of the invasion, on into Germany, to the finale, VE Day.

He was older than most, being born in 1918. Even today, he states, when he refers to joining the service, "I'd do it again, if I was called, but not at my age."

Hanley especially remembers the trip to Europe aboard the Queen Mary. It was a very large ship in it's time, but not immune to storms at sea. Loaded with 22,000 troops, 3-4 regiments of black troops included, the big ship encountered a high gale in the North Sea near Glasgow, Scotland. The Queen Mary rolled to a 45-degree angle during the height of the storm. Several of the big life rafts were lost overboard and a six-inch gun was torn loose from its station. "We didn't lose it however," Hanley recalls. No one was injured except one nurse who was tossed out of her upper berth and broke her arm when she hit the floor.

When they finally arrived in Glasgow, they were fed and were loaded in boxcars and were on their way to England. There they waited until the invasion was to take place. Hanley remembers how the sky was lit up with bombers and planes. "The sky was lit up like a Christmas tree with the green and red lights flashing from the bombers overhead." They were on their way to France when the invasion was to begin.

Hanley did not leave until the third day of the invasion. He was assigned to six officers in a command vehicle to set up an outpost for their unit at Utah Beach. "I spent the night underneath my command car behind a hedge" he said. German snipers were trying their best to pick off as many as they could. Two military police were shot and killed that night. Hanley did eventually make it to a big French Chateau near St. Mary's Glees.

They advanced from one place to another while following the infantry as they took over German strongholds. Hanley spent some time in Maastricht, Holland where his outfit was headquartered during the Battle of the Bulge. Then he was sent to Munich, Germany, where another air base had been set up.

On the way, Hanley remembers a truck driver who somehow had run a 2x4 through his radiator. The driver had not stopped because the radiator was out of water and burned the motor up. Hanley had been working in the motor pool keeping vehicles in top running order for use in the front. He was left behind to put a new motor in the truck. After the engine was installed the truck driver had to get his load to Munich. The truck driver left not wanting to wait for Hanley to pick up his equipment. Hanley was alone, and he didn't know for sure how to get back to his outfit. They had moved and he spent three days looking for them.

He spent one night in French army quarters. The next day he drove through the Forest of Bastion, where the Battle of the Bulge had taken place. He was alone in a single vehicle and he didn't know for sure where he was, but one thing was in his favor, the Germans didn't know where he was either. He continued on following the 9th Army football insignia as a guide to the new location of his outfit.

This story, sent to me by Corporal Hanley, is another example of what it took to win the war in Europe. Without the support of those who repaired military vehicles, the war would have been lost. Supplies of all types would not have been delivered. In other stories, in other chapters, you will read of cases where these vehicles were not able to lend their support and it was disastrous.

Hanley, after VE Day, prepared shop equipment to be loaded on ships so they could be shipped to Japan to continue the war there. However, with the dropping of the Big Bomb that ended the war, Hanley came home the same way he had gone to Europe, on the Queen Mary. He was discharged at Fort Leavenworth, Kansas, October 25, 1945.

HENDRICKS, VAUGHN

Hendricks, when I was a very little boy, was fighting for our country probably before I even knew him. He lived less than a mile from where I was born in 1943, on a farm southwest of Upland. Over the years, I have come to know and respect this man, I like to refer to him as my friend. I recall when I graduated in 1960, he volunteered to drive a car for our senior class on our "Sneak day." We went to Colorado. A trip I will never forget. Vaughn knew where to take us and what we should see. It was delightful having him as our guide.

Vaughn never talked too much about his war days serving in the European Theatre. It was rough, I always knew that, and I was interested in what he went through over there. By bits and pieces, he would tell me of different experiences he encountered. He has given me much information concerning the WW II in general, and some I will use in an attempt to relate to you, the reader, what men like Hendricks lived through, and some still live with today.

Hendricks was with the 68th Armored Infantry Battalion, entering the service in August of 1942. He fought his way through five major Campaigns from Utah Beach, Normandy, to east of Munich. The 68th Armored Division Battalion and the 14th Armored Division, experienced heavy losses from beginning to end. They traveled 550 miles, much of it with track vehicles, through enemy territory without rest or vehicle maintenance. Concerning D-Day, when the invasion of France took place, Hendricks said it could have been very easily been lost. Our numbers is what saved it. "We just kept coming and coming," he said. Hitting these heavily fortified beachheads would have been next to impossible with a limited number of soldiers. But for the Allies, men and equipment seemed endless to the Germans.

He remembers the cold. Always keeping a dry pair of socks handy so as to change when his he was wearing became wet. "You had to take care of your feet, you had to walk," he said. Frostbitten feet were an all too common problem when trudging through snow and sub zero temperatures day in and day out.

On April 29, 1945, Hendrick's outfit was involved in the liberation of an allied POW camp located at Moosburg, Germany. The 47th Tank Battalion is eight miles southeast of an allied command post located in Puttenhausen, Germany. The 68th Armored Infantry Division is three miles north of the command post. The night before they had run into hard resistance late that day, and were ordered to stay in Mainburg to avoid running into a known night ambush. Reports were coming in that the battalions were starting to move. Guns of the 500th Armored Field Artillery Battalion should be heard at any minute. The assault was to begin at 0600, but at one minute till, a strange event took place. A German Major and other Germans, strode into the camp of Combat Command A, to meet with Brig. Gen. C. H. Karlstad. The German major commanded the Moosburg Allied POW camp. Allied soldiers, including Generals, commanders and all kinds of officers were imprisoned there along with many other allied soldiers. The German Major, had, in writing a proposal that would create a neutral zone around the allied POW camp. All Allied movement of troops would have to stop where they were while German and Allied officials worked out an agreement for the release of the Allied POW's.

The proposal was rejected and the Germans were given until 0900 to surrender, or receive the American attack at that hour. German SS troops moved outside the camp to form a defense perimeter, and began to fight. By 1030, the SS were lying dead in the fields and along the roads, gray-white faces and open mouths, twisted and staring sightlessly at the cold, blue sky above, while American medium tanks roared through the cobblestone streets of the ancient city. The 47th split up into two columns. One going directly into the city and the other headed for the prison camp. Gen. Karlstad picked up a German officer as a guide through the city. The other column, as they entered the camp, many German armed guards met them. Looking into the bore of a 30-caliber machine gun, the Germans were quick to surrender. Other Americans arrived shortly and the American flag was raised in the camp at Moosburg.

Moosburg had 110,000 Allied prisoners, including 30,000 Americans, officers and men. Besides liberating the prisoners, they were also able to capture an entire German garrison at Moosburg numbering 6,000 Germans.

Once the sharp German defense by the SS was over, the German defenses crumbled. The POW's, when set free, displayed a scene of wild rejoicing as tanks ran through 10-foot high wire fences. There were virtually men from every nation in the world being held there. War correspondents, and some Russian women doctors were also being held there as well. Around the city were thousands of slave laborers, men and women. Those who liberated the camp received the grandest welcome anyone could ever bestow. POW's shouted and patted the tanks as they went slowly through the streets. A six foot four Australian soldier threw his arms around a driver and stated, "You damned bloody Yanks, I love you!"

A weary bearded American paratrooper climbed on a tank and kissed the tank commander, tears streamed down his face. Women threw flowers, Italians and Serbs crowded around the vehicles just to have the privilege of touching it as they wept. An American Air Corp lieutenant kissed a tank. "Goddamn, do I love the ground forces," he said. "This is the happiest day of my life," he added.

There were no words to express the feelings of these men, Hendricks said. As the German guards were formed in columns and marched away, each man carrying two or three loaves of black bread, some of the tankers took it away from them, tossing it over the fence to the Allied prisoners. One older American soldier freed his own son.

The 47th and the 68th continued securing the town, uncovering scores of arms of all types. Moosburg was not all the troops they were after. A bridge was next on their mission; the bridge across Isar. The bridge was blown when a tank fired at his first span.

German prisoners included boys of age nine and up, fully armed and uniformed. Girls, ages 17-18, fully armed and uniformed also.

By night, the Division was established along the Isar. There were unbelievable scenes of mile long columns of German prisoners were marching in columns. In front of the Germans, was a light tank and a light tank in the rear and each tank had its lights on full blast. Fields with Germans in a bunch were being guarded under lights, while among them lay the burned out German vehicles caught in the fight that morning. German soldiers, lying dead in grotesque positions as Graves Registration Officers moved among them preparing for burial among the bloody litter of a battlefield.

In the streets roamed a multitude of Allied newly freed POW's, wanting to do something, but didn't know exactly what. They broke into wine and liquor shops and took whatever they could. They took food from pantries, kitchens, living rooms and stores. They found clothes, shoes, shirts and pants from closets, trunks and suitcases.

Allied ex-POW's, ex-slave laborers, ex-concentration camp inmates, soldiers, and civilians, men and women, young and old, from every nation in Europe, drunk or sober, crying or laughing, roamed the streets that night and reeled along the sidewalks, singing, shouting, kissing, wearing tall silk hats, where they found them, God only knows where, carrying bootie from the city. There was rape that night, pillage and robbery. German civilians hid indoors.

Up through this wild scene, the commanders of the 68th were trying to move tanks and a long line of silent infantry men, like Hendricks. Their faces were set and hardly saw the rivalry that was going on about them. These combat hardened men had their eyes set straight ahead, showing no emotion as they trudged on. The next day the 47th and the 68th established a bridgehead across the Isar at Moosburg, still encountering small arms fire as well as tank and mortar fire. The next mission would be the next river.

Hendricks was also involved in the freeing of Jews destined to become part of the great holocaust. They, like all people being set free, never forgot it. In April of 1979, these people, who later organized and calling themselves, a "Society of Survivors, of the Holocaust," expressed their appreciation to men like Hendricks. They invited them to the Grand Ballroom at the Omaha Hilton Hotel to honor them at an appreciation dinner. They provided them with an evening of entertainment with all costs absorbed by the society. Even their parking spaces were paid for. They appreciated these brave men. The headline on the program that night reads, "Those whose sacrifices and valor enabled us to live-the American servicemen who liberated Hitler's death camps."

Hendricks remembers many instances during the war that he shall never forget. Once, while checking out a village they had taken over, they were checking out individual buildings as part of the security. While rummaging through these items they found a coat on the floor. Wondering what may be under it, he picked up the bloody coat. To his surprise, it still had an arm inside one sleeve. "You don't forget things like that," he said.

Hendricks says he was supposed to be awarded the prestigious Silver Star for his personal achievements, by his platoon commander but the commander was killed and he never heard anymore about it.

He remembers crossing the Siegfried line. It was heavily fortified with obstacles designed to tear the tracks off of their tanks. He remembers soldiers with their helmet chinstraps buckled up tight. When a shell exploded nearby, the concussion would cause their helmet to want to fly straight in the air. A fastened chinstrap could break a neck but he never saw it happen.

He remembers that days and nights just blended together, never really knowing the difference at times. He would eat and sleep whenever he had the opportunity to do so. "There was no set time for anything," he said.

Tanks were often driven by recruits that had received only one and a half hour's training. There simply was not the men or the time to train them in much detail.

A Continental R 975-C1 9 Cylinder Tank engine used in the M4-A1 "Sherman" and also the M 31 Tank Recovery Vehicle. Developing 360 horsepower, it was capable of driving a 66,500 pound vehicle at 25 miles per hour. It would get .8 miles to a gallon. Later this engine was discarded and the tanks had a Ford V-16 engine in them. The Navy used this engine as a diesel engine while the Army used gasoline. Many veterans have remarked that it should have been the other way around because of the extreme flammability of the gasoline engine in combat. *The photo was taken at the Heartland Museum of Military Vehicles, Lexington, Nebraska*

The morale among the infantrymen was always quite good he said. Unlike the Air Force men who would see empty beds in their huts, the infantry soldier never saw that. More men were sent to replace those, which were lost.

Hendricks said some men liked to keep diaries of what took place each day. Some did, but the practice was quite illegal because if the soldiers had been captured, the Germans would obtain secured information from the diaries; so the American soldiers were not allowed to keep one while in combat.

At the end of the war, Hendricks thought he would be heading for the Pacific Theatre to help fight the Japanese. When President Truman ended the war by dropping the atomic bomb, "I shall be forever grateful, because that ended the war, we had enough," he stated.

Upon his return trip home, he notes the ship, the Aquitania, a British passenger ship that was under construction the time the Titanic sank. The Aquitania had crossed the Atlantic 600 times during both wars. It was scraped in 1950. The ship was larger and better built than the Titanic and had enough lifeboats for everyone aboard. The ship was built by Cunard White Star Lines.

Hendricks said that many people feel the Vietnam veterans were treated poorly when they returned from the war. Totally unappreciative of what they did to preserve freedom. It is true, he added, but veterans like himself were often not treated any better. Veterans like himself who had spent 3-4-5 years in Europe, and discharged with near nothing in the winter of 1945-46. "We had nothing," he said. When they returned home some local people resented the fact that the veterans were receiving unemployment payments of $20 a week for a limited time. With their lives totally disrupted, some scarred forever, then to return home to an ungrateful society, was totally unacceptable he said.

Kids today, Hendricks said, will never be able to realize what it took to win WW II. If it had not been for the bombing of Japan, though it killed many innocent people no doubt, he is grateful the mission was accomplished. "It had to happen," he said.

Hendricks now lives in Hildreth, where he moved upon retiring as rural mail carrier in the Upland area for many years. He is one veteran who is disheartened to see the way the country is conducting itself. It's as if no one knows what freedom costs the way some people abuse it. Hendricks has been there, he lived through it and witnessed what takes place when freedom is fought for. Today he remains active in helping restore historical sites pertaining to the nation's wars. He writes his congressmen and senators when he sees something that is not right. He continues to fight for what he feels is right, but now it's with words, not a rifle. Thanks Vaughn!

DILL, MAYNARD V.

Dill is from Hastings and served in the United States Marine Corps in WW II. He joined the service by choice in May of 1943. He worked with intelligence as a NCO, Non Commissioned Officer. Prior to joining the military he worked as an electrician.

Dill went to San Diego for his boot training. From there, he hopped aboard the Carrier U.S.S. Chenango, headed for the South Pacific campaign. In three weeks they landed at New Hebredes and went into immediate action. He worked with Intelligence and found himself performing in several operations, including Munda, Bougainville, Green Island, Emiru and Palaus. He served with both the 1st and the 3rd Marine Divisions.

At Bourgainville, he experienced thirteen days and nights of heavy shelling. At the last invasion at Peliliu, he recalls another veteran from Hastings who had made commanding officer just prior to that invasion. His name was Russell Riley.

Dill came home in May of 1945 and completed his tour of duty at Cherry Point, North Carolina. In October of 1945 he received his honorable discharge. He had the honor of folding the flag for a memorial service in 1970.

When asked how he feels about the time he spent serving his country? His reply was: "It was priceless!"

DILL, GRAYDON AUSTIN

There were three Dill brothers from Hastings who served in the Armed Forces. Graydon, Maynard and Harry had their lives interrupted for the cause of freedom. Their sister's husband, George Kaufman, also served in the Armed Forces. Serve their country, it was the thing to do.

Graydon attended Hastings College until he joined the service in July of 1943. He said he wanted to be a part of the war effort, which is very commendable. He joined the Army Air

Corps and became an aircraft pre-flightier and line crewman. He conducted training during WW II with the 3rd Air Force.

Dill began his career in the service conducting his basic training at Jefferson Barracks, Missouri. His classification and pre-flight was at San Antonio, Texas. He flew PT-19's at Sikeston, Missouri and had more basic flying of BT 13's and 14's at Independence, Kansas. His advanced flying was conducted at Mission, Texas with the AT-6. At Matagorda Island, Texas he was with a fixed gunnery school. From there he went to Perry, Florida, to the P-51 fighter school and later discharged at Tallahassee, Florida.

He was discharged from active duty in October of 1945 and was with the Air Force Reserves and worked his way up to flight officer. When he retired in January of 1985 he had worked his way up to a Lt. Colonel.

"Freedom is worth the price of serving your country," he concludes.

HOEFT, LORAN

Hoeft is a WW II veteran from Ulysses, Nebraska. He entered the service while living in the Garrison area. He entered the service January 26, 1942. Uncle Sam sent him to Camp Haan, California, near Riverside, for basic training. Soon after that he was assigned to Battery "D" of the 546th Anti-Aircraft Division of the Third Army, and was trained by General Patton.

His gun crew consisted of one 40-millimeter and four 50-caliber machine guns on tripods and a trailer. His job was "fun pointer;" he sat on the left side of the gun and his buddy sat on the right side. They had scopes to better view their target. Hoeft would raise the barrel of the gun to get on the scope while his buddy moved the barrel. Most of their training was done in the Mojave Desert. They would practice when a plane would pull a dummy plane some distance behind it and they would fire away at it.

By October of 1943, they received their orders to go overseas. They took a troop train, Challenger U.P., to New York, and boarded the Queen Elizabeth which was destined for London, England.

The seas were rough. At times the big ship would almost be engulfed by huge waves. "It was pretty scary," he said. Lots of boys got seasick and stayed in their rooms. Hoeft and his buddy learned that if they stayed on the top deck as much as they could they wouldn't get as sick.

When Hoeft arrived in London he had to have an emergency appendectomy. From his hospital bed he could see the planes leaving for the D-Day invasion. He healed up and caught up with his outfit in France by traveling on a train to get there.

In France they set up in an alfalfa field for about a week. They waited behind enemy lines for a while. The Red Cross brought them snacks and drinks. Entertainers like Bob Hope visited them.

Soon they went to Germany. Hoeft noted that the civilian people were very glad to see them there. While in the process of taking over a town along the way, he opened a door to a large building. It was full of women and children. They held their arms up and smiled at him. Hoeft motioned to them to put their arms down and they stated "Danke shayne," or Thank you.

Patton was a fast moving General, Hoeft said. As soon as a town was secure they moved on to the next mission. "Things got pretty rough after that," he recalls. They held gun positions in Scharding, Austria; Munich, Germany; Berne, Switzerland and Berlin, Germany. He commented that the German people were very intelligent because they built their bunkers with cement underground and then covered the whole thing with dirt. They had lookouts on the bunkers.

On one occasion when Hoeft and the rest of the guys had their guns dug in across the Rhine River they noticed that there were several buildings about a half-mile away. They shot into them to assure themselves they would be secure and off to the right was a thick heavy forest with a lot of artillery fire coming out of it. The Sergeant gave the order to move quickly. They hooked the guns up to their trucks and started moving out. Moments later an artillery shell hit the gun position they had been in. "That was one lucky moment for us," he said.

Hoeft mentioned that the food was pretty good because they were lucky to have a very good cook. Some guys hated the powdered eggs but Hoeft said he didn't mind them that much.

After the war was over, they visited concentration camps where the Germans kept prisoners and they learned how they were treated and killed. They were burned in fiery furnaces like so many of the Jewish race which Hitler wanted to exterminate. They were in places like Buchenwald and Dakawu where the sadness still is present today.

Later Hoeft got a job driving a jeep for an officer. He said the Autobahn was quite a highway even back then. There were no speed limits and you could drive 100 miles per hour if you wanted to.

Hoeft comments on Hitler saying he had set out to win the war but towards the end of the war he ran out of supplies, men, tanks, fuel and then he just gave up. He got to see Berchesgarden, which was called Hitler's nest.

The outfit that Hoeft was with was credited for 27 German planes shot down. He has a picture of 27 swastikas on their 50-caliber machine gun. He made it back home on December 27, 1945.

HOUSE, RICHARD A.

House is a WW II veteran and joined the United States Navy in October of 1942. He thought the war would soon be over, "how wrong I was," he stated. I think House is perhaps a unique veteran to some extent. Not that he is any better than any other veteran, I'm sure he will attest to that, but his is the only story I have about a veteran who served in the depths of the sea, in a submarine. He is an individual who was a member of what is referred to as, "The Silent Service."

When I asked him why he chose the submarine, where to my thinking was a place where in the event of a conflict with the enemy would almost always mean certain death. His answer was also unique when he stated, "I wanted to serve my country but I didn't want to come back maimed or disabled. I figured the subs were a place I could serve and I knew two opportunities existed. I would either come back whole, in one piece, or not come back at all!"

While our armed forces boast of serving the nation on "land, sea and in the air," the subs were indeed at sea. Drifting around "beneath" the sea surface seems to me as another place entirely different to fight a war. Few men were able to withstand the stringent training required for submarines because few could overcome the "phobia" of being cramped up in tight quarters for days on end. Claustrophobia eliminated a lot of men who tried out for the subs, House told me.

House trained in several different places prior to entering the combat zones of the Pacific Ocean. He began at the Great Lakes for training before moving on to Treasure Island in the San Francisco Bay. He thought he might be interested in airplanes and aircraft carriers and trained at an air base for a while. Given an option, carriers or the subs, he made the decision to go for the submarines. He was sent to London, New Hampshire for 16 weeks of training. From there he went to Key West, Florida, for training on old WW I, R Boats, then on to Portsmouth where new subs were being built. He was assigned to the U.S.S. 381, Sand Lance. They left Portsmouth in November of 1943. They passed through the Panama Canal on their destination to Pearl Harbor for more training.

By February of 1944, they left for the northern most part of all the Japanese islands for patrol duty. They encountered two typhoons en-route. Vast fields of slush ice and patches of drift ice were floating around in the waters. The sub became a victim of heavy icing. They had to get to warmer waters. They spotted an enemy troop carrier, zeroed in on it with torpedoes and sank it on the spot. With no more action to follow they made it to waters that were 70 degrees instead of the freezing temps like they had been in.

On the night of March 12th, 1944, they were forced to dive because an enemy aircraft had been spotted. A sub can dive down to 600 feet House said. They are tested to that point withstanding the pressures of the deep. Sometimes, however, they were forced to dive below that level keeping their fingers crossed. About 2 hours after noting the aircraft, they heard the noise of ships. They came up to periscope height, 60 feet, and looked around. They found themselves right in the middle of an enemy convoy of cargo ships with 4 destroyers and a light cruiser escort ship. Two torpedoes went to a cargo ship, two more went to the light cruiser and two more went to another cargo ship. "They all sunk in a very short time before all hell broke loose," as he puts it. The four destroyers kept the sub pinned down beneath the surface at around 450-500 feet for 16 hours. The enemy dropped between 150-200 depth charges down at them. It seemed relentless. While running silent, House and a bunch of guys in the sub were in the control room. The Skipper inquired, "Dick, what do you think?" In a humorous reply, House said he thought they ought to put a note in a bottle and let it go to the top reminding the Japanese

109

that they should quit dropping depth charges. "They were going to run short."

The statement "broke the tension," House said as word spread what House had recommended. Fortunately, a storm at sea forced the Japanese to loose contact with the sub. At around 3 a.m. they surfaced and replenished their air supply and headed for Australia for some R & R and to repair the sub.

On their second patrol, they sank three more cargo ships and a passenger cargo ship, which was carrying enemy troops and supplies to the various islands in the Pacific.

On the third patrol, they were making a run on more cargo ships running at 60 feet in depth. An enemy plane spotted their periscope and dropped two bombs on them, which landed very close and caused major damage. One propeller had to be secured and they had to dive to 500 feet to escape more depth charges. Then they discovered more trouble. A torpedo was running inside its tube. Torpedoes are released by air pressure and the standard pressure didn't do the trick. The torpedo was running and caused it to heat up and it had lodged itself inside the tube. The next maneuver was to come up to 100 feet and put more air pressure on it to get rid of it. At 3,000 pounds of air pressure they were fortunate with it releasing but it was almost too late. Eight seconds later the torpedo exploded doing more damage to the rear of the sub. Seeing the explosion beneath the water the Japanese must have thought they had hit the sub and left the area. After dark they surfaced and headed back to Australia for more repairs. The repairs couldn't be done there so the sub had to go back to San Francisco Bay for major work.

With the sub in the shop, about 50% of the crew were put on relief which was called a relief crew. Their purpose was to replace a certain number of crews coming in for repairs on their ships. Relief crews help make other subs ready for another patrol. House was one of the relief crew when the sub called the sub called "Batfish" came in. Its skipper was Capt. Fyfe, who had been the executive officer on the Sand Lance with House. The Batfish was about to go on its 5th patrol. Fyfe, because he knew House, asked him if he would like to go along. Fyfe needed to replace some men in the engine room and he knew House was familiar there. House agreed and went on a 5th and 6th patrol on the Batfish before it too had to go back to the states for major overhaul.

During the time the Batfish was to go on its 6th patrol was when General MacArthur had returned to the Philippines. The Japanese were trying to evacuate their much-needed aviators from some of these islands.   U.S. subs were called in to eliminate the troublesome Japanese subs. The Batfish was stationed between Luzon in the Philippines and Formosa. Three other subs joined the Batfish and formed a scouting line. Subs, on this type of a mission were referred to as a Wolf Pack.

On February 9th, the Batfish made contact with a Japanese submarine about 6 miles away and closed the distance to 1,850 yards. Fyfe had three torpedoes released. They all missed. At 1,000 yards, he ordered three more to be fired.   The second one hit the sub and sent it to the bottom. The explosion lit up the whole sky.   The enemy sub had no escorts so there were no depth charges House recalls.   In the morning they surfaced to charge the batteries. Fyfe intended to be surfaced for quite some time looking for Japanese submarines. He spotted friendly aircraft, which proved to be unfriendly. Because the pilot mistook the sub to be Japanese, he launched a torpedo from the plane. Fyfe ordered the sub below very quickly. Fortunately the torpedo passed over the sub and missed it.

Again, on February 11th, another enemy sub was spotted by radar in the early hours of the morning at 1,200 yards. Fyfe was almost ready to order a torpedo fired when the Japanese sub made a dive.   About a half-hour later to their surprise the sub surfaced again. Fyfe had four torpedoes ready and ordered them fired at nearly point blank range of 880 yards.   It literally blew the sub apart sending it immediately to the bottom with no survivors.

On   February   13th,   contact was   made   again   at 3 a.m. with   another   enemy   sub at five miles. It joined the rest, at the bottom of the sea using only one torpedo.   The Japanese   gave   up   trying   to   evacuate   their aviators by submarine.

They arrived back in the United States in March of 1945. Before the Batfish was once again ready for sea duty, the war ended.   House went home on a 30-day leave, came back and was put on Shore Patrol duty in Frisco. He spent some time in the hospital there after an incident with some rowdy soldiers one night when he sustained some knife wounds while acting as a Military Policeman.

House said the Batfish was given credit as the only sub to ever sink three enemy submarines. They were awarded many awards and also the Presidential Citation.

Today the Batfish is on display in a memorial park in Muskogee, Oklahoma and is open to the public. House has visited his old ship three times for reunions where the crew of the mighty sub gathers to reminisce about their time spent on the sub. House remembers those who didn't make it home to have an opportunity to reunite with their buddies. He states, "God bless the 3,507 men who are still on patrol!"

Fifty-two subs were lost in WW II, mostly in the Pacific. Among them was the "Wahoo" named after the Nebraska town. Once a year in November, House attends a memorial for these men. The Wahoo was credited for sinking 20 ships, over 60,000 tons of enemy steel, before going down itself by 3 depth charges and bombs dropped by the Japanese. It was lost as of October 11, 1943. Aboard this vessel was another man with the same last name as Richard House. His name was V. A. House but was no relation Richard said.

The 52 subs that were lost were later named for every state in the union. The Wahoo naturally was designated for Nebraska. Nebraska can be proud to have commemorated this sub. It was second only to the submarine, Tang, which sunk 24 vessels before it was sunk. Most subs sank few enemy ships and some sank none before they perished themselves.

Subs were usually named after a fish. For example the Batfish, there is a fish with the same name. This sub was credited for sinking 13 ships. If my research is correct, it appears as if the submarine Bowfin holds the record for the most ships sunk at 34. Because of the efforts of the Bowfin, 179,900 tons of enemy vessels lay at the bottom of the sea. On two missions alone, it sank 9 ships on each mission racking up a total of 18.

House is proud to have served in the submarine division of the war effort. He told me the size of these great ships. Subs like the Batfish, were 311 feet long, 25 feet in diameter and weighed 1,600 tons. The crew consisted of 70 men and though most feel they were cramped to live in, House feels it wasn't that bad. They had 7 watertight compartments. If bombs damaged one, the entire ship would not waterlog. When the enemy was spotted, the compartments were secured. If you happened to be in a compartment that was damaged, "It was just tough luck," House said.

House has become quite a historian on submarines. If I were to write a history book about subs, I certainly would want him to contribute. He informed me that during the war, 290 American subs made over 1680 patrols with most of them being in the Pacific. The devastation they created was measured in tons. Each ship weighed - so many tons. So by using tonnage, House says that the subs sank ships totaling at least 5 million tons of merchant and navel shipping vessels. But it was not without the cost and the price of our 52 subs that were lost along with their precious cargo, the crewmembers.

Death in a submarine often came quite quickly. Often there was no chance to send a final message. Some of these subs were lost without knowledge of where they are even located in the depths of the seas. The term, "Silent Service," would often describe their end.

House feels that when the Japanese attacked Pearl Harbor, it was fortunate for the United States that all the aircraft carriers were out on training missions. If they had been lost the war would have extended itself a lot longer or the outcome of the war could have been quite different.

JOHNS, CLARENCE

Johns is from Elgin and relates his story in the form of a poem written by a WW II veteran 50 some years ago. Johns was with Co. I, the 378th Infantry, 95th Division of the U.S. Army. His experiences in the European Theatre are portrayed in this poem written by Staff/Sgt. Raymond D. Breesley, Co. M. 3rd Battalion, 378th Infantry. At the beginning of the poem the abbreviations, H.L.T. refer to Harry L. Twattle, Commander of the 95th *Division at the time. It reads as follows...*

From H.L.T. and his winning smile,
To the lowest buck in rank and file.
We are proud the work we have done,
Of the battles fought and the victories won.

The road to Metz was a little rough,
And the Moselle River was plenty tough.
Now Altforweiler was no kids game,

And of Saurlauten we can say the same.

Lisdorf next-and then the Sarr,
This is the worst I'd say by far.
Until we hit the other side,
Where many fell and many died.

Back to France for a needed rest,
Then Fraulauten-the acid test.
But we came through and not to badly,
And rested again very gladly.

We then hit Belgium-Holland too,
Though we didn't have much to do.
But the time was coming, bet your life,
When we were due for a little strife.

Up to Krefield but not for long,
Into Gladbaek-resistance strong.
Rheinhausen fell-and we drew praises.
For taking the area in the first four days.

Across the Rhine, which we dreaded so,
Without a shot-and on we go
On to Dalsberg-attack each day.
We remembered then what it meant to pray.

Hostelde, Derne and Dortumund fell.
It wasn't fun-it was a living hell,
But our record still remained on top.
And you can bet it will never drop.

So I come to the end of the story,
Not seeking praise nor asking glory.
It's just to show why I'll be proud to wear
the old 9-V patch,
Of a unit hurrying Hitler's decision,
Symbol of the 95th Division.

Thank you Mr. Johns for submitting that poem. I am sure it tells your story very well.

JOHNSON, DELWIN

Johnson lives today in the assisted living facilities at Methodist Memorial Homes at Holdrege, Nebraska. He is a veteran of WW II and was a farmer when he entered the service. He was a Corporal in the 3rd Army, European Theatre, from 1942 until the end in 1945.

His duties consisted of being a gunner and loader in an artillery unit. He doesn't recall where he was when he was wounded but he still has shrapnel in his knee. When asked how he felt about serving his country, his reply was a good one. He realizes the importance of fighting a war when guys like him areasked to serve. If they had refused, "we wouldn't have anything today. I'd do it again!" he stated.

KENNEDY, DOYLE E.

Kennedy was born in Lincoln in 1927 and was raised in South Bend, Nebraska. He had completed 11 years at Ashland High School when he enlisted into the armed services. His sister, Mary Fleming of Ravenna is very proud of her brother. Doyle now lives in Palmdale, California but considers himself a Nebraska veteran.

In November of 1944, after training off of the West Coast he loaded with the rest of the soldiers on a ship headed for the South Pacific Theatre. He was on a convoy destined for Pearl Harbor and arrived there 12 days after departure on November 23rd. He then went to more gunnery training and participated in various simulated war situations.

Kennedy wrote a personal account of his experience during WW II aboard the Destroyer USS Little, DD 803. On January 22, 1945, the Little left the port and provided fire support for the invasion of Iwo Jima between February 19 and early March of 1945. She then returned to Ulithi to prepare for the invasion on Okinawa.

On March 17 she was ready along with some 300 sailors aboard. The 2,050 ton vessel with 60,000-horse power was assigned to a task of feigning troop landings on the north end of the island, the opposite end that the actual assault took place. After completing the troop diversion on April 2, she screened transports and escorted LST's to the assault beaches. By April

115

19th, the Little and its crew was assigned radar picket duties southwest of Okinawa and charged with the task of monitoring aircraft approaching from the direction of the island of Formosa.

On May 2, 1945, the ship was on picket duty with another destroyer, the USS Aaron Ward. Four other vessels were also among them. One LSMR and three LCS's, support ships, acting as pallbearers in the event of attack picking up survivors.

The duties of the Little were to track aircraft approaching from the island of Formosa and identify them as friend or foe. If the incoming aircraft were identified as Japanese, they were to notify the U.S. Navy combat air patrol aircraft and vector them for an intercept. There was a total of 16 radar picket stations surrounding Okinawa.

Kennedy was on the "graveyard" shift until about 4 a.m., the morning of May 3rd. His watch station was a 40 mm. anti-aircraft gun between the number 3 and 4 main gun mounts on the aft part of the ship. Watch stations during war were manned 24 a day, around the clock. Men would conduct 4-hour shifts.

When he got off watch he went to bed about 4:30 a.m. By 6 a.m. he was awakened by the alarm sound of "general quarters," which meant enemy aircraft had been spotted. This time however, it was uneventful.

At 4 p.m. he was again sitting at his station with the 40-millimeter gun. At 5 p.m., the alarm for general quarters sounded again. Enemy planes had been spotted by radar and they were getting closer. Around 25 Japanese planes were closing in on them. The speed of the Little was stepped up from 15 knots to around 25 knots, which was done in battle situations for better maneuvering. The Little and Ward would change off following each other when their course would be reversed. The "pallbearer" vessels stayed well off to the side of the destroyers. They knew that if the enemy came, they weren't interested in them. They wanted the destroyers.

The big gunners began firing at the planes at 5 miles of their ship with their 5-inch guns. He observed one was shot down. He was told later that more than one was shot down but Kennedy said he was in a position to see it all and he didn't see more than one. When the planes came within 2-3 miles away, Kennedy began firing his gun. When the planes got within about 1,000 yards, the 20-mm. guns opened up on them too.

Searching the skies, Kennedy looked up and saw an enemy "Tojo" fighter plane. It was carrying two auxiliary fuel tanks diving towards the ship. While firing at the plane, he noted that the enemy was not firing back. "As I am firing, I see that I am hitting it in and around the engine cowling because I see parts flying off the plane," he said.

Just before it got to the ship where it would have done major damage, it went over on its left wing and plunged in the water next to the ship. One of its fuel tanks caught on fire and was burning next to the Little but caused no harm.

Looking starboard, Kennedy noted two 'Val' dive-bombers coming toward them, very low in the water, no more than 300 feet above the sea. All guns on that side of the ship were firing at them. The planes hit the ship. The first ended up in between the two stacks in the forward engine room and was obviously carrying a bomb as there was a huge explosion, fire and shrapnel flew all over he said.

The second aircraft, coming in behind the first, hit a little aft from where the first one had hit. It struck the after boiler room and possibly the after engine room. All power aboard the ship was gone. "Everything went dead," he stated.

Because the 5-inch guns were electrically operated, they could no longer be used. The 40 mm. was also electric in part but could be fired manually so they were still operating. But without the electric sights, no one was very accurate. The 20-mm. guns were manually sighted and were still doing their work.

Kennedy glanced over to the Aaron Ward just as two planes hit her, right in the superstructure of the ship, taking that and almost all of her stack completely off. Except for her 5-inch guns, barely anything was left on the deck.

Nearby he saw another Kamikaze hit the LSMR. It must have hit directly in the ship's magazine as that ship blew up. "It was the eeriest thing I have ever seen in my life," he commented. It was like a black light that literally hurt your eyes. When the smoke cleared, the LSMR was gone.

Immediately following that, Kennedy spotted another plane what he refers to as a "Betty" twin engine aircraft in a gliding dive an instant before it too hit their hip right behind the number two stack. The explosion blew the ship in half.

In the instant the bomb had exploded, one of its engines ended up back in the gun tub by Kennedy. Now he was pinned with a hot airplane engine against his legs. He was unable to exit the tub. Some of his shipmates saw the predicament he was in and came and freed him. He could not do it alone he said, because of severe burns. Soon Kennedy witnessed the bow section of the Little coming around almost parallel with the stern section. It then rose straight up and down and it went to the bottom of the sea. In about 10 minutes or so later, the stern section started settling, but not as rapid as the bow did. Kennedy and the other sailors around him were not sure what they should be doing. There was no one around to take command. They decided they probably better abandon ship because the seawater was gradually engulfing the stern. The sea would soon claim this mighty 376-foot long destroyer. One of his shipmates was severely burnt from head to toe. Kennedy helped him slip into the water off the starboard side. He assured him that everything would be okay. Within five minutes the stern joined the bow. Shortly after, something exploded under the water, which Kennedy assumes must have been depth charges they had with them. Whatever, "It was the darndest enema I ever got in my life," he said.

Shortly after the ship sank, a medical corpsman that had been on the ship swam over to render aid to the guy who was badly burnt. Kennedy was holding on to him. The corpsman informed Kennedy to let go of him and that he was dead. He probably died when he hit the water the corpsman had said.

Kennedy's back was also burnt and blood from shrapnel covered his body. A big piece stuck out from his wrist. Later, when he was rescued, doctors told him the salt water had no doubt saved his life because it had aided in stopping the bleeding.

By now it was getting dark but they could see the outline of ships coming to pickup survivors. Most of the sailors were picked up in groups of four or five. Kennedy, unfortunately, was not amongst a group to get picked up that night. The "pallbearer" ships were not able to use their lights in their search because it would expose them to Japanese subs or other aircraft in the area. The only way they could pick anyone up was to listen for their yells and head for the direction they had heard a yell. During the night he became concerned about getting rescued but kept the faith knowing that eventually he would be. Finally at 6 a.m. he and the others were picked up after spending 12 hours in the water. Kennedy was lifted aboard the ship via a litter because of his many injuries and was too weak to climb aboard. Those seriously injured, about six of them, were taken to a hospital in Kamaretta where the hospital ship, USS solace was moored. Doctors treated their wound and the ship departed for Saipan with a full load of wounded on May 5, 1945. On the island of Saipan Kennedy and the others were placed in tents surrounding a field hospital for further treatment. Here he had some minor skin grafts. From Saipan he was transported to Letterman Hospital in Pearl Harbor, Hawaii where he underwent more extensive skin grafting. He was flown to San Francisco and placed in a hospital there. Sometime in June of 1945, he was released and went home on survivor's leave.

Kennedy chose to stay in the US Navy and retired after 20 years of service. He had also served during the Korean War during the 1950's. He has served his country well and hopefully he can enjoy his retirement.

KINNEY, EARL

Kinney lived at Campbell, Nebraska at the time he was drafted. Today, he and his wife Louisa reside in Franklin. He remembers well that day in June of 1944 when he entered the service. Like most GI's, his life was disrupted and there was no choice but to answer his country's call.

He trained for combat at Fort McAllen, Alabama, for 17 weeks. He recalls an incident that I would refer to as a close call. It happened during training exercises. They would hike for 10 miles a day, take a 10-minute break to catch their breath. Usually finding a spot to sit down for a few minutes. A cloud came up one day just as they were going to a huge tree to sit in the shade. Out of this little cloud came a lightning bolt which hit the tree. The whole company was under it but no one was injured. Two days later they passed the tree again and it was completely brown from being struck by the lighting.

On December 8th, he was put on a ship at Boston heading for the European Theatre. Rough seas caused many of the men to get seasick. One morning, out of 1,500 men, only 32 showed up for breakfast. These huge luxury liners converted into troop ships would even bob around in the water to such an extent the prop would come out of the water. When it did, the entire ship would vibrate. If you were eating, you better hang on to your plate.

Once, while in the English Channel on a British ship, he noted that each day there would be a new and different dog on deck and then, never saw it again. He also noted the meat they ate was a deep red color. It was obvious what they were eating.

"They gave me a rifle for Christmas," he commented, as perhaps the only one he had ever gotten for Christmas. After landing in France they were put on amphibious vehicles and they were to land on a beachhead along the coast near LeHaurve, France. It was cold, the water was frigid, but they had to wade in it to get to dry land. The French had a very good fortress built here at LeHaurve at one time.

He had been assigned to the 106th Division, the 424th Infantry who replaced those men of valor who had either been killed or taken prisoner in the Battle of the Bulge. "We were sent in to clean up," he said. He served as squad leader as a Sergeant. The men of the 422nd and 423rd had it much worse he said, who were in the front lines in the main part of the battle. After this horrendous battle, only a few survived from these two units who were still able to fight.

After walking inland from the beachhead they were put on a train, one of those, 40 & 8's, 40 men or 8 horses, and nearly froze to death riding in one of the cars. It had been shelled, boards missing, no place to sit down and no place to warm up. The slow moving train seemed to endlessly travel along passing town after town. Finally they came to their destination, God only knows where, and placed on trucks to the battle zone. On his first night out in the field, they were told to "dig in," or dig a foxhole and crawl in it. The ground was frozen solid and it took most of the night to dig it. The darkness was so black they couldn't see their hand in front of their face. About the time they had the hole dug, 4 a.m., they were told to move out.

One of his first days out, he experienced his first mortar attack. He and the men with him sought refuge in an old church that had been bombed. The roof was gone, cold, and the pews were covered with thick ice. It was now night and they looked for a place to lay down. They knocked the ice off the pews and tried to get comfortable. A little later they were told that they had found a better, warmer place to sleep. A house with a sort of basement with a straw covered floor which had been used by German soldiers not long before. That was his bed for the night. Kinney was very tired. He had waded through waist deep snow for days. They were all cold and wet. As mortars came in, you had to hit the ground, or snow in this case. He had been carrying ammunition for 30 caliber machine guns. He had been trained to use them well. He could disassemble or assemble the gun blindfolded. His arms ached and he wasn't able to raise his arms above his head for three days he said. He was with the 4th Platoon, company B at this time. "It was not a good place to be, but there was no choice," he said.

One time, Kinney said, he was on a truck heading closer to the front lines. The truck died and wouldn't run. Was that an act of fate? The convoy he was with came back to assist. In the meanwhile, another convoy that was behind them went around them and was leading now. The Germans who were waiting in ambush destroyed the entire convoy. Had not the truck Kinney had been on died, his entire convoy would have been the one that was wiped out. "We would have been them," he stated.

Bravery didn't always account for much Kinney said. Among his squad was a little guy who liked to talk tough. "He was going to wipe out all the Germans," he had announced. As he got in the open a sniper picked him off instantly. "That was the end of him," he added.

One time a General was with them who also was wounded. He had shrapnel fragments stuck in his rear. The men enjoyed pulling out these little pieces Kinney said.

Later this same day, Kinney and his squad of 10 men were working their way through the woods, which consisted of Aspen trees. They were very tall and of course leafless, in the dead of winter. The men were on a hillside among these trees when the Germans opened up on them. It grew into a fierce firefight. When the shooting was over, only 4 of the ten returned to camp. Kinney was one of them.

One buddy of his, Davis, was just four steps from Kinney when the buddy was hit directly by a mortar round in the stomach. He died. Kinney later wrote a letter to his parents after he returned home informing them of how he had died and that he was with him. "That was tough," Kinney said, but he knew they were wondering. They answered his letter and expressed their appreciation and perhaps now they were able to put closure on the death of their son.

The army did some things that Kinney to this day, doesn't understand. At one time they were to remain at their position for 30 days. No one told them why. Just stay put and "don't fire if fired upon," was the order. Yeah, Germans could shoot at them, but they were not allowed to shoot back, what kind of a deal was that Kinney asks? It was true that the army didn't want to know their position but he thinks they knew it anyway. One day, Kinney happened to find himself in the open and the Germans machine guns cut loose on him. Luckily for Kinney, there was a tree nearby which he quickly laid down behind. The Germans nearly cut the tree down with bullets trying to get him.

When the order came to shoot back at the position they knew the Germans were in, they had already left three days prior to that Kinney said, shaking his head.

Bored with something to do at this time, Kinney and some of the men constructed their own little log cabin out of trees in the area. When "open fire" was ordered, their own big artillery behind them fired a little too short and hit the cabin blowing it to thunder. Fortunately no one was in it at the time.

On another trip they walked through a village that had been pretty well destroyed. They had nothing to eat. They noted a few chickens and a few hogs running around. They decided they should eat one of those hogs, but no one knew how to butcher it except Kinney. He killed a hog with his bayonet and slaughtered it while the other soldiers built a fire to roast it on. It was pretty good he said but they paid for that. Not being used to such "rich" food, they all became quite sick. Soon orders came down that there would be no more of that!

Water canteens were filled wherever there was water that appeared drinkable. One time they filled them at a stock tank where wounded livestock had been drinking. Some had puss dripping into the tank from wounds around the head. But it was water and they needed it. A purification tablet was added to kill the bugs that might be in it. Cold, the water wasn't too bad. Warm, it was real bitter Kinney said.

Kinney remembers the buzz bombs the Germans used to hurt moral. They did a good job of that but that's about all the damage they did Kinney said. Yes, they were explosives, but rarely did much damage.

Then there has always been the question in Kinney's mind as to how the black population got by with driving trucks to a certain point and refusing to go any farther. Seems when they knew they were getting in the "hot" zone; they would refuse to drive in it. "They got by with it, when no one else could" he said.

Furthermore, Kinney has never figured out either how the British made the U.S. pay $15 per soldier to come over there and help them fight a war.

After many battles, Kinney was transferred to guard German POW's. They had so many scattered around they needed more guards. The camp where Kinney was didn't have a fence around it. Just four corner posts and a tower on each corner. At this camp, 75,000 POW's were there. But, Kinney said, the POW's had it pretty good and seldom tried to escape. They knew there was no place to go.

Kinney spent 25 months in the service and not all of it was overseas. German POW's by the thousands were taken to the United States. When he returned back to this country they sent him to Iowa to guard prisoners there. The prisoners dug onions in Iowa. He would have like to have stayed there but in about a week he was sent to an area around Greeley, Colorado to guard other POW's. Here the prisoners were "hired" at 40 cents a day to dig sugar beets. Kinney said he got along well with them. When he could see one needed help, he would set his rifle down and do just that. They didn't want to escape either.

While at Greeley he had an appendicitis attack. It was bad because gangrene had set in. The doctors who performed the surgery couldn't find his appendix. They left the wound open for a time, which invited the infection. "I think they went out to lunch," he said, as the surgery took four hours to complete. They didn't think he was going to make it, he didn't think so either. He had dreams or visions of heaven, literally like being in heaven, he said. But he made it and was discharged from the service in July of 1946 and went home, even though he was still sick. He was unable to work and there was no help from the government he served. "It was a rough time," he said.

Kinney remains active conversing with his war time friends. Each year, the 16th of December, the 424th reunites. He invited me along in 1999 to a reunion Lincoln that I really enjoyed. More stories were born out of that day from some of the other guys there. The 16th of the December is the date that the Battle of the Bulge began and the men honor that date to meet. One of them commented at the meeting, "it was a day much like today, 20 degrees, dreary weather," he said. The battle began that fateful day at 5 a.m. he recalled.

This story like all the others, is just another reminder of what freedom really has cost. Don't take it for granted! Thanks Earl!

KORTHALS, ELMER J.

From Fairbury, Nebraska, Staff Sergeant Korthals served in the U.S. Army with the combat engineers and amphibious units that served in the European Theatre. "If you saw the movie, "Saving Private Ryan," that was about the closest to the real thing as it gets," he says about his time spent in combat. He also was involved with the building of floating bridges to cross the many rivers in Europe after the original bridges had been blown up. He served with the 348th Engineer Combat Battalion from the time the allies landed on Omaha Beach to the last river that had to be crossed in Germany. He spent 3 years, 2 months and 18 days serving his country.

It all began when he was drafted off the farm and entered the service in August of 1942. He did not finish high school. He trained at Camp Crowder, Missouri, Mojave Desert in California; Camp Young, California; Fort Pierce, Florida; Camp Picket, Virginia and Camp Bradford, Virginia. He then arrived in Halifax, Nova Scotia and boarded the 3rd largest ocean going vessel of the era; the name of it was the HMS Mauritania, which was an English ship that brought him to England. When he arrived in Swansea, South Wales; he was trained for amphibious landings and other maneuvers that were going to be needed to make the landing at Omaha Beach, June 6, 1944, and later.

Korthals doesn't elaborate much on what he went through on this heroic act of WW II. He spent a lot of time picking up mines, not a real safe job, and building roads and bridges. And as he said earlier, "if you saw the movie---that is what it was like." He mentions helping build a bridge at Heidelberg, his favorite city, that stretched 280 feet across 3 spans of concrete structures the Germans had demolished so the allies could not cross it. The old bridge was known as the Karl Theodore Bridge and was built in the 18th century just below the town of Castle. The men built this bridge in just eight days. He also was involved in clearing 50 miles of the Neckar River from Heilbronn to Mannheim on the Rhine River demolishing existing bridges.

The last town he was in was Burstadt, Germany. His battalion ferried the 82nd Airborne across the Elb River where they met the Russians coming from the other direction. Germany had been conquered but he will never forget the concentration camps he encountered along the way. The camps were a horrifying site.

The destruction of very old bridges and buildings was common in the war. Though some existed for hundreds of years, they were in a matter of seconds totally destroyed during times of war. Many veterans have mentioned sadly, the destruction of historical sites was common during the time.

Korthals was discharged in October of 1945 at Leavenworth, Kansas. He recalls that he figures he had traveled 11,000 miles and heard the command, "pick up and move out," at least 36 times while in war. An average of almost once a month he moved as the soldiers constantly moved forward. Also from the time he joined the service, he was in 23 states and 5 foreign countries he concluded.

KOTTAS, WILLIAM JAMES

Kottas is from Crete and was born near Tobias, Nebraska where he lived until the time he was drafted in February of 1941. He was 21 years old and was among the first to be drafted from Saline County. When he was inducted into the U.S. Army, he was assigned to the 134th Infantry, 35th Division and spent two and a half years in training. He became an expert Riflemen. He also spent brief periods with other outfits and he was later transferred into Cadet Training at Canyon City, Texas. He studied there at the West Texas Teachers College and then went to Santa Ana, California for more training.

He was close to graduating as a certified pilot when he became ill and needed major surgery. When he was well, he was placed in a new group. Since he had infantry training, his superiors placed him with the 77th Infantry Division which was heading for the South Pacific Theatre of Operations.   This took place in November of 1944.

He and the other soldiers landed on the island of Leyte alongside the 96th Infantry Division.   He was armed with a BAR, Browning Automatic Rifle.   The two Divisions then invaded Leyte Island and were met with machine gun fire along with the enemy support with their Air Force.   Kottas says they were very fortunate to take the island with not too many casualties.   They moved on to prepare for the Ryukyu Island Campaign which included Okinawa.

The convoy consisted of 1,200 ships.   Tanks, guns and other supplies were loaded on LST's, Landing Ship Tanks, and hit the beaches.   Kottas said his LST was number 888.

It was March 26, 1944 when he experienced his first landing.   With fixed bayonets on their rifles, the men were moving forward from the beachhead into the jungle.   A Japanese soldier jumped on top of Kottas from where he had been hiding in a tree.   "It was horrifying," Kottas said, but he managed to turn quickly enough and thrust his bayonet into the enemy's chest before he was injured or killed.   At the same moment a fellow soldier shouted at him to "hit the dirt," as his buddy shot two Japanese soldiers that were about to kill Kottas. After that experience, he walked about another 20 feet and had to sit down.   He said he became so shaky, he couldn't stand up. The near death experience which he had not yet become accustomed to, drained him of his strength.   But after about 10 minutes, Kottas said he got his strength back and was able to proceed.   This particular little island was secured the first day and they moved on to the next island.

The next island was not good for Kottas either.   He was wounded by artillery shrapnel and was taken to the Hospital ship, Solas, where he spent the next three days.   Then he was moved to a field hospital to recuperate for about another week.

Then he went back to his unit where things were really getting hot on the front lines he said.   Now on the island of Ie Shima, he dug himself a foxhole while under artillery fire.   He no more than jumped in the fox hole with all his gear when something like the spirit, as he says, something told him to get out and dig another about 30 feet away.   He obeyed what this "spirit" told him.   He no more than had jumped into his new foxhole when a mortar shell landed right smack into the foxhole he had been in.   He had not yet taken his gear and belongings out of this hole. They were totally destroyed. "God and my Guardian Angel were truly with me," he stated.

After securing Ie Shima, the men were shipped off to Okinawa where they expected to get some rest and train for the invasion of Japan. But the 96th Infantry had encountered many casualties in Okinawa so the 77th Division was called up to relieve them. He was in the 306th Infantry, Company C, 77th Division, so guess where he was going.

On May 5th, the 306th was ordered to clean out a town called Koche, which led to the main ridge of the island. For the next several days, Kottas and his buddies spent their time blowing up caves, pill boxes and shaft opening that led into the hills. "After several days of fighting, we were able to give several hundred Japanese their final resting place," he said.

On May 14th, 1945, his Regiment fought another battle on Okinawa, the largest island of the Ryukuy chain of islands. The Japanese counter attacked them after mid-night. Kottas and the men were thankful they had grenades because their vision of fire was not good. When daylight finally came, they were surprised to see so many dead Japanese soldiers lying around them. Some were only a few yards from their front line. They also discovered that many others had dug into their immediate front. Tanks were brought in to blast them out. Several hundred Japanese bodies were left behind.

On May 19th, the unit attacked the high ground that was well fortified. They lost many of their tanks and Kottas and the rest of the 306th were caught in a crossfire. The first Battalion of the 306th, was reduced to half its size. Many of Kottas's buddies were killed as they tried to run down from this hill. Three of his top officers were either killed or wounded. As Kottas was moving back, a young soldier lay wounded on the ground and begged Kottas not to leave him. "Lead was flying thicker than ever," Kottas said, and "all I wanted to do was to get the hell out of there." Kottas found himself a little hollow spot to lay in and contemplated the wounded comrade. He admits, he shed a few tears, but couldn't leave this wounded man lay there. He raced to him and he noticed the wounds on this soldier were quite severe. He was afraid to move him and he told the wounded soldier so. But again he begged, "Please don't leave me!" Knowing that if the shoe were on the other foot, he wouldn't like to be left either. He took his belt and his and put them together and tied him to his back, got up and raced for cover. He was able to get him to where the Medics could take over. "I'll never forget the smile he gave me," Kottas said. He never got his name but Kottas will never forget his face.

Still under fire, he grabbed his rifle and battle gear to help the rest of the men. By this time, out of a company of 182 soldiers, only 15 were left. Kottas was one of them. They had to hold about a fourth of a mile of ground that night. The next day, HQ pulled them back and they were ordered to a rest area. But instead of resting, the unit received replacements and then they were sent back to the front.

On May 30, 1945, they were ordered to follow a rolling artillery barrage with bayonets fixed ready for hand to hand combat. As they began their forward movement, the new replacements held back. They were scared and didn't know what to expect. Kottas remembered how he felt when he experienced his first encounter with the enemy. But now things were different, Kottas was their leader and it was up to him to get them moving. He motioned for them to follow him and then moved ahead. Kottas was unaware that apparently the enemy had him in their gun sight. A bullet ripped through his lower abdomen exiting out his back. Naturally, he fell to the ground but managed to crawl back where the medics found him. Four men placed him on a stretcher and carried him behind the lines. While they were doing that, a mortar shell hit and killed two of these men. The rest of them, including Kottas got some shrapnel. Kottas, of course was dropped and forced to crawl on his own until a First Aid Truck picked him up. He was given blood plasma and Father Heaney, a chaplain, gave him the Sacrament of the Last Rites. Kottas then lost consciousness. He later found out he was placed in C-54 Hospital Plane and flown to Guam Fleet Hospital III. He stayed there and recuperated for two and a half months. That was his last battle. Later he was flown to Saipan to the Army Hospital there.

Kottas recalls that at the time he was wounded and rescued, it was the first time he had a shave or bath in six long weeks or more. "We were all bearded, dirty and buggy on the front lines," he stated. Living only on C-Rations and tablets to place in water they could find to purify it. Biscuits were among the rations and when they drank water the biscuit would expand in their stomachs, which made them feel full. Helmets were used to cover their heads of course, but were also used for dipping water out of streams or ditches he said.

Battle records and many other men's records were lost at sea Kottas said. The command ship was hit by a suicide enemy plane, which sunk it. Consequently, Kottas, and the others who had records on this ship, never received their Battle Field Commission for which men like Kottas had been recommended for. He remained a PFC. He was awarded the Combat Infantryman's Badge, a Purple Heart with two Oak Leaf Clusters and the Bronze Star among several other medals.

Kottas was flown from Saipan to Portland, Oregon where he boarded a train and headed for Fort Logan, Colorado where he would be discharged. He found him a bus heading for Nebraska. Incidentally, there was no fanfare along the way. "I was just thankful to be back home with my wife and family," Kottas concluded.

LADD, COLONEL AVERY JACKSON

In his prime, Ladd was one of the Air Force's most prolific pilots. Now, at 92, he is still "Sharp as a tack," as his nephew Robb Rocky of Lincoln says. Rocky goes on to say, "He is probably one of Nebraska's best kept secrets." Ladd piloted bombers in WW II and flew over thirty different aircraft. He served in the Pacific Theatre and China.

If you ever had the opportunity to watch any war recruitment movies with Clark Gable, Ladd was with him, and was trying to get Gable to fit into the ball turret of Ladd's B-17.

The retired Air Force Colonel now lives in Omaha. As a young man, he was very interested in auto racing, which was contrary of his mothers' wishes. In 1928, Ladd had a wreck with his car while racing and for his mother, that was the last straw. His mother told him that if he really wanted to fly, she wouldn't object. She became convinced flying planes would be safer. At the time, Midwest Aviation of Omaha had a branch in Des Moines, Iowa that was offering flying lessons. Ladd took them and after taking only eight hours of lessons, flew solo. He was ready.

Ladd soon acquired a job with Midwest Aviation flying passengers. In 1931, he worked for the USDA and flew weather observation planes. He was a corporate pilot for General

Motors. Then in 1939, he was contacted by a friend of his that the British Canadian Airlines needed instructors to train pilots to replace their more experienced aviators who were leaving for England to fight in the Battle of Britain.

Ladd accepted the offer, but shortly after that in 1941 when the Japanese attacked Pearl Harbor, the U.S. was calling on American pilots to serve in Canada. Ladd soon found himself in a train car taking a physical for service in the Army Air Corps.

He went to Sebring, Florida, to a B-17 outfit that was headed for England. Ladd had never flown a B-17 at this time. The commander at the base told him he would be of much more value to stay in Florida as a squadron commander and instructor and he did stay there, until 1943.

They then sent Ladd to Salina, Kansas, to be trained to fly the B-29 bomber. Not long after that he was sent overseas. He first hauled supplies, bombs, gasoline, ammunition and everything else that could be loaded on a plane to a forward base in China. They overloaded the planes often around 10,000 pounds over the maximum weight limit of the aircraft. Day after day he hauled support for the troops on the ground. In July of 1944, he was ordered to fly his first air strike to an iron works plant in Mukden, Manchuria. It was a successful run and he then led other attacks on Japanese targets in the area that included a raid on Bangkok, Thailand. He made 25 trips in all what he refers too as, "Over the hump" missions. Flying over Mt. Everest was a routine experience. He had to fly at 33,000 feet to clear the mountain range.

It was Ladd who flew a C-54 aircraft in support of the 1st atomic bomb tests in the Pacific which was called, "Operation Cross Roads," which some of you veterans may recall.

At the end of 1944, while flying with the 20th Air Force back from a mission, he discovered shrapnel had damaged his planes right landing gear. It could not be lowered. He could not land on both front wheels but the plane had to come down regardless of the problem. He landed it on one wheel, with little damage to the plane. General Curtis Lemay, watched the entire effort and was standing at the nose of the plane when it came to a stop on the runway. He stated, "Ladd, that was a damn fine landing."

Lemay and Ladd had their paths cross again in 1950 when Lemay called Ladd on the phone asking him to sit on the board of Douglas Aircraft. Douglas, at the time, was building a large aircraft. The kind the general wanted and was looking for. Ladd was told that when he got down there, to tell the officials at Douglas, "You're speaking for me. If there's any questions, call me."

The plane was a C-124 and was big enough to carry an assembled atomic bomb in its fuselage. Later, Ladd was put in command of 60 of these planes at the air base at Roswell, New Mexico. He stayed there until 1961, when he retired after 30 years in the Air Force.

Ladd also commanded the 1st Transport Unit for SAC after it was formed.

In the book, Early Midwest Aviation," by Earl C. Reed, Colonel Ladd is listed as one of the Midwest's pioneer airmen. Ladd was inducted into the Iowa Aviation Hall of Fame in 1998. Ladd was born in Brooklyn, Iowa.

During his flying career, he flew 23 types of Canadian planes, 25 USAF models, and 32 different varieties of commercial airliners. He once held a record for flight time with U.S. Air Force, logging 24,272 hours in the cockpit. When one uses a little math, that amounts to 1011.33 days behind the wheel of a plane. Or we could elaborate a little more and say; Ladd was up in the sky piloting for the USAF alone, 2.77 years. That is a long time. He is truly, one of Nebraska's finest aviators.

LAMBERT, STANLEY

Lambert wrote his "Memoirs" concerning his time spent in WW II as a POW in the European Theatre. As many of the stories I have received, I have had to condense them somewhat. It is my wish that I will be able to give his detailed account of what took place the space it deserves.

Lambert says he was a victim of the Governments cancellation of the Air Cadet training program. He was a transfer from that program. In the closing weeks of December, 1944, he was with Company I, 275th Infantry Regiment of the 70th Infantry Division, a fresh unit from America, that took positions along the Rhine River near Strasbourg, France. He spent nights sleeping in barns or warehouses, he was accustomed to life in a foxhole although at this point he had not yet tasted the strife of battle. That would all change, and very soon.

In the late afternoon of January 1, 1945, his company moved forward at a point beyond Phlippsbourg, in the Alsace Region. The Germans in this offensive thrust below the Bulge area were desperately trying to salvage an offensive. Their main effort in the Ardennes was bogging down. Hitler had called this offensive, "Norwind." They had broken through portions of several other American divisions at this time, he later learned.

Lambert was considered a "green" scout with a great sense of pride mixed with apprehension now with the 3rd Battalion of the 275th Infantry rapidly approaching enemy lines. The roadway passed through narrow open valleys, clusters of farmhouses and wooded hills. The men were picking there way forward in the darkness of night barely able to see where they were going. "Had we known the proximity of the established German positions we would have been shaken," he said as he, with innocent courage, as he refers to it as, moved ahead. They had advanced further than their planned objective that night.

Men like Lambert trusted the judgment of their officers, which later irritated them sorely. He realizes too that due to rapidly changing events, things do often get confusing.

The column behind Lambert froze in the darkness, as did he when the command from a German shouted the word, "Halt!" If he had been more experienced perhaps he and men like him would have plunged into the ditch for cover. When a sudden burst from a German "brrrp" gun filled the air, everyone then dived for cover. After a moment of shock they too returned fire with their M-1's and BAR's. The BAR, Browning Automatic Rifle, was firing at least 40 yards behind Lambert. Four men between the BAR were silent and Lambert assumed they must have been hit. The sound of the BAR seemed to make the Germans pause for a moment. But then they opened up again perhaps focusing on their position a little closer. Tracer bullets lodged in the asphalt only a few feet from his nose as he peered out from underneath his helmet rim.

The Germans, he could tell, were located on a murderous angle above them. Some of the column had to move back clear to the where the second platoon was located. Yet, there were acts of heroism. One Sergeant continued to fire at possible German positions holding them back so other men could withdraw. But he soon drew too much enemy fire and he was cut down. A soldier with his BAR kept up its methodical, bang-bang-bang-bang. A Lt. from Georgia is his southern drawl coolly ordered the men to withdraw as they could yet maintain fire.

But for Lambert, withdrawal seemed impossible. He was in a slight depression, which was no more than 20 yards from where a German machine gun was doing its thing. He lay on some scattered broken pieces of tile from a roof of a shed, which took shape behind him. The slightest movement would tend to rattle the broken tiles alerting the Germans of his nearby location. Lying there in near zero temperatures in inch deep snow, he noted the moon was beginning to show itself behind a hill where the Germans were situated. He could make out objects now in the darkness. He began to feel destined to die. He thought of the shock his family back home in Ewing, Nebraska, would have to go through. "I was certain to have to face my Maker before the night ended," he stated.

Eventually, still laying there motionless, no buddies around either, he heard the German commander above him call the roll of his men. He thinks most of them answered. An hour had passed as he lay there, his right arm over his rifle, his chin against the snow and his eyes peering out under the brim of his helmet. A military vehicle stopped within 10 feet of him. Two Germans walked forward and stopped, their boots only inches from his helmet. He fully expected to be shot then and there but they undoubtedly thought he was already dead.

The vehicle eventually moved on up the road. Silence followed for at least another half-hour. He convinced himself he had to make a break. On his first attempt he fell back down rattling the tiles underneath him. His legs had temporarily become paralyzed from lying in one position so long. At the second try, he managed to get to the small shed behind him and he ran full force into a woven wire fence at least six feet high. That threw him to the ground again, but quickly sprang back to his feet and either went over the fence or around it, he isn't sure. No shots were fired so he made a run for it across an open field west of the road to a lonely out-building where he paused again.

He knows now that he should have stayed by this building until morning so he had gotten his bearings a little better and learned where the German positions were. He chose to move back to where there was another building he had passed earlier when darkness was approaching. There he came across three more disillusioned men from the 2nd platoon. They quickly informed him the Germans were swarming all over the area. He suggested they run farther west to where there was a railroad embankment that would perhaps make a safer withdrawal but he was outvoted. He realized later that would have been a mistake because the Germans could have cut them down in the now well lit moonlight snow covered field. It didn't matter as they were soon discovered and flushed out by a squad of Germans with a couple of threatening grenade blasts.

Soon after capturing them, the Germans were getting uneasy. Our heavy artillery was zeroing in on their newly won position. They were quickly marched back about a half-mile to where he had been before when the encounter took place originally. "There along the road, lay a number of my comrades," he said. Bill Shafer, his second scout, lay in a pool of blood. Lambert was certain he was dead but Shafer miraculously, was taken prisoner and treated for his wounds and survived. He now lives in Tulsa, Oklahoma.

They arrived at a command post the Germans had set up and the interrogation began. Name, rank and serial number was all they got. The Germans appeared to be nonchalant about it an offered them some hard tack biscuits which they accepted. They might have been okay except they had the flavor of gasoline on them he said. The now, POW's, four of them, related their ages to one another. He appeared to be the oldest at 22 and two of the other three were just 19 having been in the U.S. Army less than a year.

At daylight they were moved another mile or so toward the rear of the German front. They were placed in a lightly wooded area with a guard along with about 125 other prisoners. Most of them were stragglers from other infantry divisions through which the Germans had managed to progress with their drive.

The men realized the Germans had outguessed them. They had taken advantage of the darkness and had advanced on the company. It was not consoling to Lambert at the time but in the weeks to come the company that had been forced to withdraw would once again push through the same area with the retaking of the Bulge in the Ardennes.

Throughout the afternoon they could hear artillery shells exploding to the east of them. By mid afternoon they were taken back further to a large bunker of either the Maginot or the Siegfried Line. The men were interrogated again in a small office one by one by a Nazi officer. Afterwards several loaves of warm bread were sent to the bunker and divided by the men. By the time Lambert received his crust, he had almost fallen asleep in the warmth of the enclosure.

As the prisoners were moved again and again, it was always encouraging to them to hear the sound of our men not all that far away. The hope of rescue gave them a will to cheer. Seeing American planes by day and the British at night would lend encouragement. The sound of Russian artillery far to the east also helped the men.

As they were forced to march onward for five to six days, the feeling that accompany hunger became very real. Unfortunately, that feeling was to stick with the men the remainder of the war. Rations were skimpy to say the least. When they weren't marching they were also loaded in rail cars and occasionally trucks. At one stop they could sleep in a two story stone building. If you needed a drink of water you had to go to the first floor by permission. If you had to relieve your stressed bowels, or wanted a light for a cigarette, you needed permission asking the guards in German, which they soon caught on to.

At the end of the first week as a POW, they were loaded onto railcars, the 40 X 8's, known for hauling 40 people or 8 horses, except nearly 90 men were crammed into one of these little box cars. It was to the point of being intolerable he said.

There was no way one could sit down although some did and before long they took turns. Fortunately, the men were still in fairly good physical condition but diarrhea was an up-and-coming problem. No restrooms were available. They figured out they could use a couple of helmet liners to serve as a chamberpot to dispose of defecation. They were passed, overhead, to a corner of the car that had a small ventilator window at the top of the corner. The "pots" were emptied there only to run down the side of the car. When they had to urinate, the men took turns going to a crack at the bottom of the side door of the car. The train they were on they estimated had transported over a thousand of POW's already. It had been strafed by bullets and holes were visible in the cars. They sang spirituals to pass the time but nerves were becoming taut.

By the third day in this situation, those who weren't sick were desperately hungry or thirsty. By late afternoon the train came to a stop. The door was opened and some of the men were ordered out to assume duty on a bread carrying detail. The fresh air and the walk felt good but when they returned to the car, no one was enthused over the bread. All the men were dehydrated. While the guards weren't watching they obtained a large block of ice from a wagon and brought into the car. It was quickly broken into chunks and divided among 86 thirsty mouths.

The train soon moved on again but stopped before evening at Ludwigsburg, the site of a large prison camp. It was named Stalag V-A. Although they were only here for two days, the men appreciated the chance to shower and sleep in relatively clean quarters. They could also dispose of their wastes in a much more sanitary way and get all the water they could drink. They were given some cheese the first evening, the next day, some of the thinnest soup Lambert said he had ever seen. It was scarcely edible with a taste resembling alfalfa leaves. The soup was soon labeled, "dishwater" soup and the black bread labeled, "sawdust" bread but the bread soon became appreciated in spite of it's strong taste.

At this camp they saw familiar faces associated with the same company they were in. They heard what had happened to them only two days after Lambert and the others had been captured.

The international Red Cross was here and provided them with post cards providing them a way to get the message out that they were alive and not MIA. It was a terrific moral booster Lambert said. Whether the cards would reach home or not was not known, but now they at least had hope.

Lambert was impressed with the way they were treated as prisoners, "with a measure of civility," he said. Unlike the treatment of those soldiers in Japan who were captured he had heard about who were treated often with brutality. Here they did have a shower, the post cards, and at some camps even deloused. Although their treatment as livestock on the trains was nothing to brag about, at least the Germans revealed the rudiments of a civilized society. Lambert added that at this time they had only heard little of Hitler's brutality in the concentration camps.

Next they were moved to Stalag IV-B, some 85 miles south of Berlin, associated with the town of Muhlberg. The trip was long and cold with food and water. There were many delays and some close bombardments by Allied planes. One blast rocked the car with debris from it thrown up against. Another blast, from a German anti-aircraft gun position near where the train was stalled, blew out the ventilator window in the car. One condition had improved however. The number of men was not as many as in the beginning, which provided them a little more room.

For the next two weeks this camp would be his home along with thousands of other American, British and Russian POW's. Barracks were crowded and without heat. The men lay in groups of three to preserve warmth and arranged outer garments and old German shelter halves over and under them. Cold feet, if one bedded down near the door, often fell victim to stampeding dysentery victims. Lambert said the pain one would suffer for 10 minutes after someone stomped across your frozen feet would almost be unbearable.

The POW's here enjoyed the hot showers for a change. The warm water trickling over their blue frost bitten feet felt good. Their clothes, wrapped in bundles were sent through a steam delouser. Waiting for them to return was not always comfortable as you sat or stood there completely disrobed waiting for your garments.

The weather was drab very seldom even seeing the sun in this what seemed to be perpetual Baltic grayness. Endless rows of barracks filled the landscape. A field could be seen, which was assumed to be a rye field. Every day a workman would come with a horse-drawn wagon and hand pump the liquid from a big open urinal on the grounds. It was spread on the fields and used as nitrogen for fertilizing their fields.

Processing of the POW's seemed to take days. They were photographed and numbered much like a convict. They were issued a POW tag bearing the number they wore like a dog tag. British prisoners were given charge of administering typhus shots and supervising the filling out of forms.

Lambert was raised to attend church on the Sabbath. Looking for a church on Sunday seemed the automated natural thing to do. One Sunday in late January of 1945 he looked for a chapel on the grounds. Sure enough, he found one located in a building behind some British barracks. A bony British padre was conducting services to a small despondent congregation. He reminded them that their striving would not be wasted. He picked up a worn thin knit rug off the floor near the pulpit. He held it up and said, "We are like this rug, God can see right through us." Lambert commented that it was hard to forget truth spoken in a place like that.

The Red Cross was there. If possible, they would deliver a parcel delivery once a week. If a prisoner was given that, he could live tolerably well. Lambert says they no doubt saved thousands of lives. He realizes that the parcels were often seized by the Germans and the Japanese in the Pacific. He never did receive a complete parcel but shared among four to five others the contents. During the four and a half months he was there, he only received four Red Cross boxes that had to be shared. The Russian prisoners, who were not treated well by the Germans, did not receive anything from the Red Cross. The death rate in the German as well as the Russian POW camps in each others clutches, was very high, history records, he said.

One night he saw a very sick man in need of medical attention. He and a buddy helped him to the "hospital." It was very inadequate, dimly lit full of wheezing patients. Medicine was scarce, the place was cold and was nothing more than a brief visit before entering the grave yard.

Lambert worked in work camps on several occasions. This one was located on about three acres of ground, fenced with high barbwires and located at a place that may have been Lilienstein he recalls. Here waterlines were being dug to the camp and the construction of the camp continued. Lambert said he was amazed that the ground wasn't frozen solid at this time in February. The month turned out to be wet and the trenches dug for the water lines would often cave in. By late March the line was in and the men were moved to another task.

Upon arrival, they were told to clean up and shave. This was done by plucking out the whiskers; one by one. Some of the guys had not "shaved" for a month he said.

They were issued a blanket, a bowl, and a bowl of soup at night. Each evening they were given a ticket for the bowl of soup. The "sawdust" bread was measured in chunks no more than an inch thick. A smear of margarine could sometimes be seen along with marmalade, slimy cheese or once; a bit of blood sausage. Bread, once a day, and soup at night, that was it. Each morning a roll count was made by the Germans. The men quickly found out that if one would sneak in and out of their huts, the count would take longer thus making their work day shorter.

When they were digging in water lines, they noted piles of stored vegetables. Potatoes, onion and rutabagas were common. When the guard wasn't looking, one or two would sneak over to them and fill their pant legs with them. If they were seen by the guards, sometimes a bullet would whiz over their heads or they would be searched exposing their stolen treats. An American Indian, Hummingbird, soon became the camps most accomplished poacher of the vegetables. He could slip into the location easy than most before the guards missed him. In spite of getting a little something extra to eat at times, they noticed they were losing weight and also their strength was diminishing.

Food, to hungry men, became a topic of conversation. Men would talk of delicious foods they had eaten at home. They could imagine the smell of it. They promised each other that when they got home they would exchange the recipes they had talked so much about. For example, a cured ham for a box of dried fruit would hit the spot. Lambert doesn't know if that type of conversation did any good or not but it certainly helped to pass the time.

Anyone caught stealing from another would be subject to a severe beating. Some of which, no doubt, Lambert said, were falsely accused and mistreated by their fellow prisoners.

As the group became more depressed, impromptu worship services would occur. One man, a Catholic, gathered a group of men for services a night or two before Easter. Scriptures were read, they prayed and sang hymns in a untied call for Higher help. Some would promise to serve as clergy if they were to survive. Others would ask what purpose this imprisonment had in their lives. But even to question or pray for help had a cleansing and strengthening effect on the men Lambert said.

By the first part of April the work gang Lambert was with moved everything to a new location, including the work shack. It was all loaded on a wagon and the men had to pull it. Now weak, they wondered how they could but plodding along they managed. Downhill there was concern if they could hold it back and not have it run over them. How they managed, they will never know he recalled. Loading on a ferry to cross the Elbe River, they made it to their destination just on the other side. A day or two of work would prove the last they would carry out as prisoners of war.

From then on they remained in camp except to work on small details. One was to go to a nearby village and pick up a dead horse for the kitchen. He commented the soup for a while after that was the best they had encountered all winter.

Malnutrition had taken its toll. Many of the men became inflicted with a yellow jaundice condition. Their skin and eyeballs were turning yellow and feeling always nauseated. Some were put in the so-called, hospital. Through the winter and spring, many men died. A funeral was conducted in respect the best way they could. A graveyard was located a couple kilometers from the camp. A rough coffin provided the corpse with a place to rest, at least to the cemetery. There, he was taken out and the coffin brought back to the camp for the next victim.

Body lice became their closest "friends," living with them constantly, night and day. It was not uncommon to see men strip down and pick lice eggs off their bodies. Bed bugs and fleas also plagued them. Fleas would run up and down their arms. They would try to catch but one had to be quick he said. The bloodsucking insects aided and abetted to the weakness of the men. One morning in April they were marched to a place about 5-6 miles away that had a steam delousing facility. In their weakened condition the trip seemed farther than that but they were anxious to get rid of these pests. The shower didn't hurt them any either he said. When they returned to camp they took their straw mattresses outside and aired them out, pounded dust out of them and tried to curse or frighten the bugs out. They weren't successful however and they were infested with bugs again. For men like Lambert, they never were rid of these creatures until they were issued new clothing and a can of louse powder from the U.S. Army in France.

In April they began to hear the faint rumblings of the allies closing in. Waves of B-17s were seen flying over delivering their payloads. They watched one fall when it was shot down. P-51's flew over as they made their turns strafing another location. The Germans were getting nervous. Russian forces had by this time shelled and taken Dresden just 25 miles away.

The guards preferred to be captured by Americans so they began to move out.

On May 7, 1945, after several hours of confusion, they left the gates of their captivity. They picked up anything they could carry with them that had any value; most being clothing. Their now bony frames needed lots of clothing for warmth. Lambert went from 170 pounds to 120 while he was captive.

By midday they were several miles from camp. The guards tried to keep everyone in formation but it was impossible. Along the way were fields of produce and the men would try to take some of. Those with dysentery would have to stop and everyone was searching for something to eat. Irate farmers would curse and shake their smoking pistols at them as they clawed newly planted potatoes out of the ground. The procession of POW's strung out for two miles, 900 Americans, 200 British trudged along. About a quarter mile ahead, a loud explosion occurred, leaving men wounded, writhing in pain along the road. Shrapnel fatally wounded one and others badly injured. Frantic German guards stopped an ambulance and loaded a man who had a badly mangled leg while others piled in too. An empty horse drawn wagon was detained and ordered to transport some of the other wounded. The Germans began to run away, fleeing the rapidly approaching Russian advance. The once prisoners, were now on their own.

Late in the afternoon a little village appeared around the bend. Surprisingly civilians treated them well providing them with the care some needed. They took the soldiers in, fed them and homes in the town provided them with sleeping quarters for the night.

When morning came, the Russians entered the village, shattering the quietness with rifle and machine gun fire. They were celebrating the victory. Russian soldiers raped some teenage daughters of the villagers. Everyone was in fear and excitement concerning the Russians. One girl tried hanging herself because of the shame but her parents stopped her. She was hysterical. A rope burn was clearly visible on her neck. By mid morning the village pastor was making his rounds trying to comfort the natives. The people Lambert had stayed with took their daughter and fled for the countryside. They told him he could use their house as long as he wanted too. He did again the following evening.

141

Early in the night there was a knock on the door. Lambert answered it finding three young Russian soldiers looking for women and schnapps. He let them in and they searched for both. Learning he was an American they were delighted, nearly shaking his arms out of the sockets. The next morning the owners of the home returned without their daughter. They thanked him for protecting their home.

Later in the day, more Russian soldiers came to the house. Most looking for more schnapps. The women of the house slipped her watch off her wrist and gave it to one of them, which he took. Later Lambert learned that by having a lot of watches on the wrists it was badge of conquest.

After that the family in the house, Saupes was their last name, left. A neighbor later informed Lambert that the couple had shot themselves in the head, taking their own lives. Later he learned when he returned to Europe in 1993, the family had committed a triple suicide. Townsfolk recalled the incident when four shots were fired. It took two to kill their daughter who had been raped, and one each for the parents.

The next afternoon another young Russian came to the house already intoxicated. He searched the house looking as the others had. Lambert had some difficulty making him understand he was not German. The Russian found a shiny bicycle upstairs in the home, with a bell on it. He proceeded to maneuver it down the stairs and out the front door. The tires were flat but he didn't seem to care. He rode off ringing the bell.

Meanwhile one of his wounded buddies had died. A German pastor conducted the service. The men saluted another fallen comrade.

Back at the house where Lambert had been staying he was disturbed one afternoon when a Russian WAC appeared at his front door. She indicated an interest in his watch. Not thinking, he took it off just to show it to her. She took it and dropped it in her blouse. He tried to argue with her but knew that if he tried to take it from her, one scream would bring on the drunken Russian men. The watch had been a Christmas gift from his family and he hated to part with it. Later, he was offered a place by a British gent to come and stay with them, which he gladly did.

In the following days he tried to regain some strength. Perhaps he would ride a bicycle to the American lines. He pondered as to what the reunion with the U.S. Army would be like. He thought of his Parents back in Nebraska, wondering if they had received word of him being alive.

On this day, which was Mother's Day, May 13, 1945, he and the rest had just finished their midday meal when they heard a commotion outside. One of the men said, "GI's" to which Lambert quickly grabbed his knapsack and headed to the street. It was the Americans, waiting by their ambulances. "God bless them," he stated.

The Americans quickly gathered around their troops. Ambulances were loaded and took off with some of the men sitting on the fenders or whatever to get a ride. On their way to Dresden, they met a convoy of trucks. Only the sick and wounded then remained with the ambulances. The rest climbed aboard the 6X6 trucks and moved through Dresden. No tarps were on the big trucks so now they could see all the devastation the war had brought about. Leveled towns, not a whole building in site as they journeyed through them. The stench of death was still in the air. Westward they continued through the remainder of the night and into the next morning finally unloading at a large air base in central Germany.

Here they were dusted for lice, cleaned up, given new clothes and enjoyed a nice meal at the base. Tomorrow they would fly to France on C-47's.

Lambert had a craving for fresh milk. Powdered milk was all they had at the base kitchen. At this new location he spotted a herd of dairy cattle and saw a farmstead in the distance. He walked to and was met at the door by a two year old little girl. He had brought two empty wine bottles hoping to get them filled with milk. The little girl wanted chewing gum. Her mother appeared and Lambert tried to tell her in a broken French language what he wanted. Finally she said, "Milk?" She filled his bottles and he paid her in French paper money. He returned there often each time remembering to bring along some gum or candy for the little girl.

On June 1, he boarded a ship and left for Boston. From there he boarded a train for Fort Leavenworth, Kansas. By late June, he had his papers for a long leave home to north central Nebraska. By bus he continued his journey and was left off about a mile and a half from his home. As he entered the driveway of his home he stopped to reminisce the surroundings. Most everything looked the same. He trusted his folks had heard that he was alive and well. He could hear his mother playing the piano and there by lamplight he could see his Dad reading the Saturday Evening Post. He was home at last.

Lambert has returned to the area where once a war was fought with him in the middle of it. He and his friends he met during the war have retraced their steps. It all comes back, all the horrors of war. He gathers with others from his outfit across the United States to reunite exchanging stories of the many incidents that took place. Things he will never forget.

LELAND, KENNETH

This WW II veteran from Fremont has been classified by numerous writings as a hero. As you read his story, you will agree. An article in the Fremont Tribune, November 11, 1998, Salute to Veterans, refers to Leland as "Combat Hardened Soldier," by age 19, who made his way across France with a grenade launcher on his rifle. And yes, he has the scars to prove it. After being wounded, three times, he received the Purple Heart and two clusters. "He should have received the Silver Star," wrote one of his superiors and friend, James "Buck" Sheppard. "That young man was one hell of a soldier and I'm amazed he lived through all the action he saw" Sheppard said.

The Fighting 36th Historical Quarterly magazine, also ran an article about Leland. He was like most men when they entered the war. Just a kid, as writers noted when they wrote stories about him. He looked like a kid, referring to him as "Baby Faced," looking even younger than he was. He was a replacement soldier in the 142nd Infantry, 3rd Battalion, and 36th Division. He received his three months of training at Camp Walters, Texas, home of the "T-Patchers." They wore a patch on their sleeve with a "T" for Texas, Leland informed me.

His first job was to help in defending the lower slopes of the Camino-Maggiore hill mass, a 3,000-foot bastion guarding Mignano Gap in Italy. It was a tough day for the seasoned veterans, let alone new recruits like Leland. It had started raining soon after they arrived and did not let up for 17 days. German troops were well "Dug in" and shelled the men of Company L and other T Patchers, 24 hours a day. Both the Germans and the Americans knew the "Big Push" was not far away. It was in December now, 1943.

On December 2nd, Allied guns began a massive bombardment. Six hundred guns used up a million dollars worth of shells, earning Mt. Maggiore the title of the Million-Dollar Mountain. Before daylight on the 3rd of December, the 3rd Battalion crossed the line of departure halfway up on the eastern ridge and quickly seized their objective.

The 115-pound soldier, who carried his 40 pounds of gear across mountains, considered many times of never returning home. "We were walking over dead bodies all the time" he recalls. Mules were used to carry the dead down from the mountain. They came lying belly down across wooden packsaddles used to carry supplies. Their heads hung down on the left side of the mule. Their stiffened legs were sticking out awkwardly from the other side, bobbing up and down as the mule walked. Leland's Captain, Henry T. Waskow, from Texas, was one who was brought down from the mountain by mule. Everyone liked him; he looked after his men. News correspondent Ernie Pyle was with the 36th when the mountain was taken. He wrote a well-known story about Waskow and the 36th. He informed the American public what was taking place. Pyle later was killed in the Pacific. Leland knew him well.

"I didn't figure on getting home alive," he said. One mail call, the sergeant informed them that it would, "be the last one for a lot of you!"

Leland served as Scout, the first to draw enemy fire. He was a scout for Homer Wise, his squad leader. A man who later won the Congressional Medal of Honor. Wise had often boasted that he was going to get it, and he made good on his boast.

After taking the mountain, the 142nd spent the rest of the winter on Mt. Sammucro in the vicinity of Casico. It was said of this, "The physical discomforts of Washington's Army at Valley Forge could not have been compared to those suffered by the foot soldier in the Italian Mountains." Supplies were short and the men didn't have proper overcoats and blankets. Many men were carried down the mountain with frozen feet. Leland still has little feeling in his feet.

Other soldiers fared worse Leland said. One buddy from Philadelphia stepped on a land mine as they crossed a dry riverbed. He asked Leland, "would you reach down and get my foot?" But, he had no foot left Leland said. In late February of 1944, the 36th was relieved for a period of rest while the 142nd was in R & R the Allies established a beachhead at Anzio. The 36th Division was thrown into the struggle and they hit the 10 square-square mile beachhead on May 25th after traveling all night on flat-bottomed vehicle carrier boats. The night of the 27th, Leland and the other T Patchers started their big push.

More than 1400 artillery pieces fired at one time. The 36th pushed through the front line defense on up into the hills behind Velletri, cutting it off from escape. Then they went to the Alban hills and Rome lied just ahead.

The German Fieldmarshal Kesselring saw that defending Rome was a lost cause. It was soon declared an open city.

Buck Sheppard, a soldier from Texas recalls one incident concerning Leland. Sheppard earned himself two silver stars for his actions. Although he was not in the same company as Leland, they run into each other quite frequently Leland said.

On the way to Rome, trucks belonging to Company L were stopped at a big house near the city. The house was surrounded by an eight-foot high brick wall, which enclosed an olive orchard of about 10 acres. Leland and some others went over to the house and visited Sheppard and other members of the unit. They spotted a bunch of Germans coming towards the house with machine guns. It was obvious they were trying to mount them on the brick wall. The alarm was sounded and Sheppard, Leland and some others formed a semi-circle and began firing. When the battle was over, 16 Germans were dead and 10 more were wounded and taken prisoner. About 6 escaped.

"Leland fought like a tiger," Sheppard said. "I wished he was in my outfit."

Leland was with Sgt. Homer Wise on June 14, 1944 when Wise won the nations highest honor. As a scout for Wise, Leland had often overcome great odds. The average life span of a scout on the front lines is six hours. Yet Leland made it through the Italian Campaign and the Invasion of France.

Wise was credited with evacuating a buddy 100 yards to safety, killing two German officers and a number of enlisted men. He used his rifle grenades and an automatic rifle to get the job done when his men were pinned down. Then, in order to knock out a German machine gun placement, he mounted a tank destroyer, un-jammed its machine gun, and fired 750 rounds into the enemy clearing the way for his men to advance.

From Italy to France, the 36th and members of the 142nd joined in the D-Day assault. The 142nd intended to land on Red Beach but at the last minute the Navy Commander decided it would be suicide so he moved them to land on Green Beach instead. They swung an arc north and west over the mountains between the 143rd and 141st to attack Frejus from the rear. Both Frejus and San Raphael were cleared in a flurry of fighting in the early morning hours of August 14, 1944.

On the night of the 16th, the 142nd broke the last German block before Le May in the Argens valley. The next day, the unit, joined with paratroopers and entered Draguignan. The 36th Division raced across France extending its lines 100 miles in a single day.

Sgt. Sheppard recalls another meeting with Leland in France. Near Remiremont, in September, Leland and Sgt. Bill Gerrard were with Sheppards outfit. Why, he doesn't remember. A senior officer asked for a scout and Leland, although he wasn't attached to this unit of Sheppards, insisted on going.

So with a grenade launcher on his rifle, Leland worked his way across a field to determine enemy strength. When he got almost to some nearby trees, he spotted an anti-tank gun. The Germans, who had been manning the gun, were asleep. Leland fired a grenade into the gun placement and totally destroyed it.

"That woke the Germans up" Sheppard said, "and all hell broke loose." Leland was able to get back to the squad in spite of the Germans opening up with everything they had. They used 20 mm. anti aircraft guns with shells that burst on contact and inflicting heavy casualties on the unit. Men who were close to the action crawled back across a field to cover and the rest of the battalion pulled back to where they were about 450 yards behind Leland and the rest of the squad. Mortar fire with phosphorus shells, machine guns and the anti-aircraft gunfire wiped out most of the unit and some were captured. Heavy artillery from his fellow T-Patchers probably saved Leland's life that day, along with his buddies. The Germans were forced to retreat once the artillery barrage began.

Leland was wounded three times during the war, which earned him the Purple Heart and two clusters. Shrapnel hit his thigh in January of 1944 and surgeons grafted skin from his arm to that portion of his leg to heal it up. On another occasion, Leland's squad lost communications with the rest. Suddenly, they found themselves being a target by their own people when a tank spotted them, mistook them for Germans, and fired white phosphorus on them. Leland was burned quite badly before communications were restored. Lelands hands and one eye was damaged before his sergeant finally found a radio and called them off.

The other incident happened when Leland and a group of men came upon some Germans and Russian Mongolians cooking soup. Gunfire broke out and Leland ducked behind a small tree and the tree wasn't big enough. A bullet went through the edge of the tree and into his right shoulder. He was sent to the 46th General Hospital in Besacson, France where his brother Don was a mess sergeant. While Leland was there, he came down with jaundice too yet. He worked in the bakery at the hospital until he returned home in November of 1945.

After returning home he went to work as an engineer for a railroad company and retired after 41 years. The city of Fremont honored him as he stepped off his locomotive for the last time. He and his wife, Jean, have four children and continue to reside in Fremont.

Leland says he doesn't watch war movies, "There's not a lot of truth in them" he said. Moviemakers tend to glorify the war and there's not much glory to it he feels.

"There is no victor, because all it does is kill a lot of people" he concludes.

Leland was instrumental in the construction of a monument in front of the Dodge County Courthouse. It is called the, Dodge County Veterans Memorial and was erected in 1998 and was funded through donations and fund-raising efforts of the Dodge County Veterans Committee. It honors all veterans who have served their country. It simply and firmly reads, "All Gave Some-Some Gave All;" a lasting and honorable tribute to the veterans of Dodge County.

MONTGOMERY, EVERETT

Montgomery is a 20 year veteran that served in WW II in the European Theatre. He was with the 91st Bomb Group, 8th

Air Force and retired as a Major. He joined the Air Force in May of 1942 enlisting in the Air Cadet program. After his training he went to Lincoln where he was assigned to a crew. He then went to Sioux City, which was then nicknamed "Suicide City," because so many planes had crashed there during training.

Men serving their country also often had nicknames and his was "Smokey," because he always smoked a pipe. "Everyone had a nickname," he added.

Since 1961 he worked for the Hastings Tribune and retired from there in 1988 and continued living in the area. He had gone to college and majored in journalism. He worked primarily with sports in other newspapers but worked as city editor and news and wire editor at Hastings. Presently he resides in a nursing home in Kenesaw.

While in the Air Force, he was a radioman in B-17 bombers, flying missions to Germany. "You didn't know from one day to the next if you would live or die," he recalls.

His plane he flew in primarily was called the "Yankee Gal." He shared with me how planes were given names during the war. When the plane was brand new, the first pilot to fly one on a mission had the honor of bestowing a name to the ship.

He remembers the "Nine O Nine," a plane named using the last three digits of the plane number. Most planes were named with a lady in mind. Some pretty fine art work also appeared along with the name. But the Nine O Nine, Montgomery says, had the reputation of flying the most missions, which totaled 146 before the war ended. It went through 21 engines, 15 fuel tanks and was up in the skies 1129 hours.

When the B-17's first came to England where he was stationed, the early ones didn't have gun turret at the bottom part of the nose of the aircraft. Officials discovered that when the planes met fighters it was most vulnerable spot so later gun turrets were added. "With head on fighter attacks, you needed it," he stated.

Montgomery didn't get to fly a full 35 missions, which was required for this type of airmen. He only flew 30 and the war ended. He remembers when the war ended the bomber crew took the ground crew over the areas they had bombed to "show them what we had done with their help." At Cologne, the city was leveled by allied forces but a big cathedral was untouched. "It was a miracle it was still standing," he said.

Montgomery knows his planes. He noted the importance of the P-51 fighters, which escorted them on missions. Bomber crews call them, "Little Brother." When they were flying next to them, they appreciated them. P-51's with a top speed of 450 miles per hour, could climb 16,000 feet in four minutes, "We didn't need to worry about enemy fighters if they were nearby," he added.

When on missions, other planes from other squadrons would often join in formations to secure a safer trip back to the base. They thought nothing of it. On one occasion, a B-17 flew in formation with them. When they reached the border flying back home it suddenly dropped out of formation. Later they found out the plane had been captured by the Germans and they were flying it snooping around with the squadron.

Montgomery was happy to meet Colonel Jimmy Stewart, the actor who also flew planes during the war. "He was a common a man as I've ever met wanting no special treatment." The first time he met him, Montgomery addressed him as "Colonel," to that Stewart quickly stated, "Just call me Jimmy."

Flying missions was often dangerous and for many, unforgiving. Fortunately, men like Montgomery were lucky. He recalls once seeing a large hole in another plane directly into the radio room. "I was glad I wasn't in that plane," he said.

Montgomery was among those who partied when the war was over. He said he and a bunch of GI's lit a bon fire in the middle of Main Street in a little town. They didn't stop to think that the street "pavement" consisted of wooden blocks. "We were burning up the street," he said with a chuckle. A fire truck was called to extinguish the blaze he concluded.

NELSON, GILBERT

This farm boy from Kearney County enlisted in the armed services hoping to get into the Air Corp. That's when he found out he was color blind and not eligible to enter that type of service. But the army could use him and use him they did. Twice he came close to giving his life and has two Purple Hearts to show for it. He joined the army in September of 1942.

He took his basic training at Camp Robinson, Arkansas. From there he went to Camp Buttner, North Carolina and then went on to Fort Ord, California where he joined the 7th Infantry Division.

Nelson spent his entire service hitch in the Pacific Campaign. He more or less was island hopping cleaning out the Japanese that dominated them. The men of the 7th Infantry Division first took the island of Attu, in the Aleutian Island.

Much was learned at Attu concerning the war. The 7th experienced heavy casualties, wounds and sore feet. The fact is that they became so foot conscious that on the island of Leyte, soldiers demanded and received 46,000 pairs of new shoes. They learned that "bad shoes mean poor fighting," and they never forgot it.

The men had to carry supplies at Attu because there was no way they could be trucked over the mountains from the beaches. They learned to "palletize" supplies, dragging them to the front on sleds.

The wounded had to all be hand carried back to field hospitals. The men cried out because of their weariness but continued going back to the battleground for more wounded. Later, this division became equipped with what they referred to as "Weasels," which was the newest member of the jeep family capable of climbing mountains and crossing rivers with a design similar to that of a caterpillar.

After Attu, the war in the Pacific became recognized more as a science with better planning and better specific training. They learned what it was like to fight a war in the bitter cold with all the ill effects of it on the icy mountains. They learned what it was like to fight in extreme heat and humidity in the jungles as well. Adjustments had to be made and the men had to be equipped accordingly.

From there they were supposed to go to the island of Yap, but plans changed and they were sent to Leyte Island instead, in the Philippines. The island was destined to be taken by the fighting 7th Infantry Division.

After a little over a month of fighting, Nelson was wounded. Hit by shrapnel from a hand grenade. "We heard the Japanese coming, we were shooting at them," says the hardened veteran who was given the Carbine Shooters Badge with the 30 caliber rifle with a high score of 172. But the Japanese were persistent and were great in number. They

151

managed to move forward into hand grenade throwing range and lobbed one to where Nelson was manning his 50-caliber machine gun. The grenade exploded as most do, lobbing bits of steel to wherever, hitting anyone who is nearby. Nelson carries with him to this day, one piece of steel in his knee and another near the bridge of his nose. After he was given time to heal, he was again at the front where he continued to fight.

Gilbert Nelson of Upland as he poses by his 50 caliber machine gun While he was island hopping the South Pacific during WW II.
Photo is compliments of Gilbert Nelson.

On Easter morning, the 7th Infantry Division with Nelson aboard landed on the notorious island of Okinawa. Little did Nelson know at the time that this would be his last fighting experience. It took about six weeks and Nelson found himself again in harm's way. He happened to be a little too close to a Japanese gasoline dump when it was shelled and ignited the fuel. Nelson was seriously burned where the skin is exposed around his head and hands. His head was the worst he said.

He was taken to a hospital in Guam where he stayed for three and a half months. From there he was sent to a casualty camp at Saipan. It was there that a Chaplain came around spreading the news that they all had been waiting for, the war was over. Eventually, four months later, he completed his healing at Letterman General Hospital in California. On December 7, 1945, he was discharged at Fort Carson, Colorado.

Nelson recalls visiting his brother, Harlan, who was stationed in Hawaii with the 40th Infantry during the war. Harlan told Gilbert about a soldier who claimed he was an atheist, one who doesn't believe in God. When Harlan's outfit landed at Guadacanal the fighting was intense. Everyone was in a foxhole. Harlan happened to be with in earshot of this atheist who was also alone in his foxhole. With bullets whizzing overhead and shelling wherever you looked, it looked hopeless. All at once he heard this guy in the next foxhole. "He was talking to someone," he said and it wasn't to any of his buddies.

Perhaps this story is where the saying came from; "there are no atheists in foxholes." When things look pretty bleak, everyone, even the atheist, looks for someone who will perhaps provide a means of escape.

As Nelson looks back on the war days, he says, "It was a good experience. Then in his usual humorous nature ads, "It was important, at least it must have been, everybody was going,"

In a statement to the men of the 7th Infantry, Major General A.V. Arnold commended them for their efforts at Okinawa. The fighting lasted 82 days, all tough fighting and took one hill after another. Later the 96th Division took over when the 7th needed a rest for ten days before continuing fighting. The 7th then returned to participate in at least sixteen more battles to win the island. In the final nine days of the Campaign, 7,925 Japanese were killed. During the entire Campaign, 24,166 Japanese were killed and 880 taken prisoner.

A radio broadcaster at the time noted that, "the 7th Division was the fightingest, toughest, wisest and all round best Division in the army today." Arnold stated that it was indeed one of the finest and smoothest working teams. Nelson is proud to have been a part of it.

NICHOLAS, BILL

This veteran, from Norfolk, served with the 5th Marine Division during the South Pacific Campaign during WW II. He dropped out of high school in 1943, joined the Marines and fought the battle for Iwo Jima in 1945. He was wounded twice.

Nicholas doesn't say any more in his letter about his experiences. He informs me that the biggest reason he has for writing was to tell about the National Hall of Honor he is associated with at Norfolk. The project began in 1998. Two men, King Spittler of Norfolk and Gerald Kane of Wisner, donated the building, which is located at 711 Michigan Avenue. They gave it rent-free for the purpose of honoring veterans. It contains a museum, a fund-raising office, conference room and a storage room. The building will be the headquarters of what he hopes will be a national attraction. By naming it "National" he hopes that it will appeal to people all across the nation when they are approached for fundraisers. Also, they welcome anyone who wants to donate or loan them their military memorabilia, to do so. "Everyone will know they are welcome," he said.

The next goal was to find land to construct the National Hall of Honor on. They found it, seven miles south of Omaha Avenue in Norfolk. It now consists of 426 acres with an opportunity to increase it to 600 acres. An architect has been hired to design a building and professional fundraisers have also been hired to assist in this local, statewide and national fund raising Campaign.

The National Veterans Hall of Honor that honors all five branches of service has grown so large already that it is believed to be the largest five-branch service museum in the United States. The military has incorporated the use of the "Star" in just about everything. The new building will be 500,000 square feet and built in the shape of a star. Each point will represent a branch of the armed service.

A large playroom for children will also be a part of the building. The building will include a library, video rooms, gift shop, concessions, and very detailed murals from the Revolutionary War to the present date. It will also have WW II home front displays, an I-MAX theater, large dance floor/convention room, military technology center and more. Outside will be a motor pool building. On the agenda is the purchase of 20 to 30 restored vehicles from WW I to the present, including U.S., German and Japanese tanks. Other foreign vehicles will also be found there. Vehicles will be used in parades and reenactments, as well as giving rides around the grounds.

The 202 veterans represented are the main focus of the Hall of Honor, Nicholas says. They want to re-create some of the situations they were in while in the war. Civil War battlefield reenactments will take place as well as WW I trenches with a no man's land detailed to 1918. A WW II bomber base from England will be reconstructed complete with a 6,000-foot runway to accommodate the only B-29 bomber still flying. At least a quarter of a mile of a Japanese beachhead will be constructed with Japanese bunkers on one end with Omaha beach at Normandy at the other along with German bunkers and everything else that was present at the time. A WW II era house with a victory garden will be on the grounds. There will also be a Korean War yearlong winter display with defensive positions, artillery, etc. A Vietnam fire base with sandbags, gun emplacements, bunkers, artillery etc. will also be there. Desert Storm Iraqi defensive bunkers, trenches etc. will also be reconstructed. "These attractions will be outside and give the visitor a feeling of conditions and obstacles our Veterans had to overcome to maintain our freedom," Nicholas said.

As of May 1, 1999, the 18 member board of directors includes members of the American Legion, VFW, mayor of Norfolk, a Madison County Veterans Service officer, and the architect, to name a few. For questions and to see how you can help, call 402-379-1011; or email, hallofhonor@conpoint.com. Or visit their website, www.hallofhonor.org. The websites were donated by Connecting Point Computer Store at Norfolk.

Wow! What a project to honor veterans.

NIDER, BERNARD W.

A veteran from Lincoln was very kind in sending me a step by step account of what took place on June 6, 1944, D-Day, the invasion of Normandy by American, Canadian and British forces. This individual, a Nebraskan, was one of the first to hit the beaches when the historic invasion took place. This is his story, one he wrote in remembrance of the 50th anniversary of D-Day, June 6, 1994. It is lengthy but I feel it important to print it in its entirety so the reader can picture from the story what the invasion was like. What it took so freedom could be preserved.

For those who do not know for sure what D-Day stands for, Bernard W. Nider explains it. It was a designated day that time was measured from. For example, D-3, meaning 3 days before or D+3, signifying days after the day. All schedules at the time were set around that designated day, 6-June-1944.

Nider was born and raised on a farm near Plymouth Nebraska. He was attending the University of Nebraska in the spring of 1943 when the war was beginning to really get going. It was announced that if he would join the Army Reserves he would have a better chance of staying in school. He was only 18 at the time. He felt that his chances of staying in school were good so he joined. He was called up in 30 days.

Off he went to basic training in Camp Robinson, Arkansas. Then transferred to Camp Fannin, Texas. After 13 weeks of training, he was sent to Camp Sharks in New York. He boarded the Lle de France and then was off to Glasgow Scotland. He was then put on a train to go to the southern part of England near a town called Plymouth, which probably reminded him of his own hometown.

It was around midnight when the troops were called to gather in a large building. Their names were called and they were assigned to a unit. Nider met his Company Commander now for the first time. His name was Captain James Madill. Commander Major Howie and the Regimental Commander Col. Canham also greeted the new troop. About 115 of the guys Nider was with went to the 2nd Bn, 116th Infantry Regiment. The Colonel told them, "You men have a lot going for you because you are young and that is what is needed for the operation that you will be training for." They were loaded on trucks and transported to barracks at Bristol, England.

Training was rigorous with camping out on moors, lots of forced marches of 25 miles and amphibious training. Aboard the U.S.S. Thomas Jefferson, they would climb down the cargo net with pack and M-1 rifle, onto a landing craft with the exercises conducted at Slapton Sands, a beach in England similar to the one they would land on in France all too soon. They made their first landing on Slapton Sands the day Operation Tiger took place when German U-boats sank many of the landing craft of the 4th Infantry Division killing about 800 men.

It was around mid May of 1944 that the men in Niders company were issued their battle gear. They wore impregnated clothing to aid to protect the wearer from gas attacks. Combat field jackets were issued that held pockets for hand grenades, ammo, satchel charges and medical packets. A new M-1 rifle was also offered but few took a new one because they preferred the one they were used too. As Nider refers to as "Old Faithful,"

It was time now to find yourself a buddy. Nider found an older guy by the name of Fred Bitsig, a veteran who had already made two landings in Italy. "I learned a lot from him" Nider recalls. Bitsig instructed Nider how to assemble his pack. "Don't put anything in there that you will need" Bitsig told him. He would leave it in the landing craft anyway because of the need to be as mobile as possible. "There will be plenty of stuff laying around that you can pick up" Bitsig assured him.

May 25, 1944, at reveille, Capt. Madill announced they would be moving out at 9 a.m. He told them they could plan to be gone for 30 days so pack up for it and they would be leaving as soon as the trucks arrived. Sure enough, 9 a.m. sharp, the trucks arrived and they found themselves on their way to the Marshalling area at Weymouth. With so many troops and equipment in this area, it took Nider and his buddy hours to get where they were suppose to go. When they finally arrived, tents were set up with an open mess outside. Then the rains began. It poured, tents collapsed, "It was a real mess" Nider said. This phase was referred to as "Operation Overlord."

June 1, began with chow at 8 a.m. Then they marched over to the U.S.S. Thomas Jefferson and went aboard. "That was a gift from God to get out of that mud hole" Nider recalls. After doing some calisthenics, having lunch, receiving instructions from officers, more equipment was issued. Bunches of belly life preservers were to be fastened to ammo bandoleer shells of all kinds, bangalore torpedoes, and everything was waterproofed so it could float ashore because they would be landing during low tide.

After four days on the ship, it became crowded. Everyone became edgy because the ship was appearing to get smaller by each passing day. There was trouble at the dice games with many hot heads getting into fights.

Nider said they had a great group of officers with about one half being West Point graduates. At this time they had become attached to the 16th Infantry Regiment Combat team

157

and were the 116th Regt. Combat Team taking orders from the "Big Red One." Their officers worked very closely with them and they respected their officers.

The weather simply would not cooperate and caused the invasion to be delayed. But on the 5th of June they saw a little sunshine but the winds were still quite severe. That night, Nider went to bed about 11 p.m. He could feel the ship moving but had not received any orders at this time other than the exception of being sent to their quarters because of all the fights that had broken out.

On June 6, at 2 a.m., the Navy boatsmen blew a whistle and shouted to all Navy hands, "Man your battle stations!" He blew his whistle again and told all assault teams to gather at the mess. Unlike normal gatherings at the mess they were allowed to "buck the line."

After mess, the assault teams were instructed to go board the landing craft. But the sea was very rough. As the landing crafts were lowered into the water, they bobbed around like corks. The cargo nets, which the men were to climb down the ship on, were whipping out and back against the ship. They were ordered to climb down in spite of the roughness of the sea and winds. The first five guys got about half way down when the cargo net swung out away from the ship causing the men to have their feet become knocked out from the net. Hanging by their hands on the net, they were slammed against the ship smashing their fists forcing them to let go, falling to their death.

Capt. Madill said, "No more of this, we are going to top load." Navy men argued that the winches and cables would not be strong enough to lower both the craft and men. Madill reminded them they would do it anyway and they did. Now, Nider says, "We were all bobbing around like corks in the landing craft."

Aboard landing craft, LCVP 13, Nider's craft was blessed with a good Coxswain. He and his assistant knew how to maneuver the craft in spite of the waters. They had made landings before. "They were a real asset to our landing section" Nider writes.

Their landing craft circled until all landing crafts were in the water. They were to meet at a given rendezvous point and then head toward their destination. But the sea was so rough that water kept coming over the top of the craft's ramp and sides. Pumps aboard were not able to pump it off fast enough so the men used their helmets to bail so the craft wouldn't sink.

It may have been somewhat of a blessing they had to bail because, as Nider said, "it kept our minds off what was coming up."

The Navy was shelling the beach heavily. The Battleship Texas and the Arkansas combined with destroyers and cruisers, "Were getting with it" Nider remembers. As they looked toward the beach, they also noted air support with the 8th Air Force giving it all they had.

Problems continued to plague the combat team. A LCM ship was on duty that was converted to fire missiles from its deck. This was a new era in weaponry, the use of missiles. The missiles could have been a real asset if they would have had a guidance system that worked. They wiped out a company of the 116th Regimental Combat Team, with only a few surviving. "I am sure we killed a lot of our own people but with an operation as large as that, it could be expected" Nider concludes.

As they continued heading toward the beach, winds caused them to drift about 2 miles off course, off to the left. They were to land on the beach code named, "Easy Green" but they ended up in the 16th Regimental area of the Big Red One which they were attached to. By this time they were all about deaf from the noise, but when they were ready to land it seemed like the noise stopped Nider said, as the Coxswain stated, "I will put you on the sand even if I never get off again." He gave it full throttle, he did hit the sand as fire began from German pillboxes and their 88's.

Nider and his buddy Bitsig were located at the rear of the craft when it hit the beach. The Coxswain told them to jump in the water and they did just before the craft was hit again by crossfire in the middle of the craft. Nider and Bitsig were now the only ones who remained healthy as Nider puts it. Using the protection of the remaining portion of the landing craft, the two contemplated what their next move should be.

"What are we going to do" Nider inquired of Bitsig. Bitsig told Nider to look at their firing pattern. Whenever a shell or mortar shell explodes and the sand flies in the air, they would change to a different area.   There was also a lot of other landing craft getting close to the same area now. Bitsig advised that when a shell hits and creates a hole in the sand, head for it while the sand was still in the air. They did that a couple of times and then they got the idea that if they would throw their own satchel charges and blow the sand in the air they could make even more headway. "By God it worked" Nider stated.

The two made it to the sea wall, among the first ones to make it. Nider still wonders how they missed all that lead that was flying through the air that horrible day. "It was a real slaughter" he said.

Within the next 30 minutes, more troops were attempting to land on the beaches. More were killed or wounded, and a lot of them were about to give up because of their wounds. "It was looking real bad" he said.

The sea wall was about 20 feet high. The Germans could not hit them with their machine guns now but were throwing sledgehammer grenades at them below the sea wall. The second wave of landing crafts were now on their way in and "they were really getting hammered" Nider said. The tide by now had come farther in and the landing crafts were now hitting obstacles on the beach that were mined by the enemy. "They were blowing the hell out of them, unloading troops in 10 feet of water with all their gear. They were just sitting ducks" Nider said.

At about 10 a.m. they were becoming a little better organized although the shock was tough on everyone. They had succumbed to the fact that, "We just have to push them back before they kill all of us" Nider said.

Nider and Bitsig walked up the beach looking for leadership. They had none, they were all gone. They ran across a navy man leaning up against the sea wall. Bitsig asked him if he had any good ideas. The navy man informed them that a blue box that had a radio in it was slowly washing ashore. If it didn't get blown to kingdom come before it made it, they could contact the Ancon, the ship command for the invasion. They decided to go for it. Bitsig warned the others that if the Germans spotted them and the box, they would destroy it.

The Navy did a good job of painting it. It blended in with the color of the sea. They found a rope with a grapple hook on it and tossed it at the box but missed it. Another guy came over and said, "Let me lasso it" cutting off the grapple hook and he got the box the first throw. "Talk about a morale builder" Nider states.

They set up the radio, it worked and they contacted the Ancon, which was the very first message that Ancon had received from the beach. The Navy man told them to send some ships to knock out the pillboxes. "If you do not, it will be a *Mayday*'" he reminded them. Soon two or three ships came to their area and took out the pillboxes that had been firing on them when they came to shore. Nider and his friends fired tracers at others in the ravines to show the ships their location. The Germans seemed to become even more active now.

Machine guns by now had been set up but barbwire had to be blown up in order to get something going as Nider puts it. They couldn't move forward. Some officers were also now on scene and instructed the mortar crews to put some shells in the trenches to pin the Germans down long enough to get at the barbwire.

A soldier on the mortar crew told an officer they didn't have enough ammo. The officer quickly reminded him to send what they had because they wouldn't need it where they were located anyway. With the help of the Navy, and the mortar fire, they finally made it to the last of the barb wire entanglements.

"You cannot imagine the slaughter," Nider said. "I have to give credit to the officers, the main one being Major Bingham. "He did a good job! We had to either fight or die!" he added.

When they got to the top they started gaining control. The beachhead was being established and the Germans were not prepared for ground battle even though they still had the advantage.

At 4 p.m., the officers told their men they "Had to either fight and kick the hell out of them or we are dead." Nider said they did just that but not without the cost of many of their own.

There was not much humor that day but Nider mentions a young GI coming up to Major Bringham in the trenches tapping him on the shoulder and inquiring. "Do you know where such and such Glider Bn is?" With each officer scrambling for troops due to the huge losses, Bringham told the GI to stay with them. "We will take care of you and we do not want you to go out there and get lost. Your outfit isn't due here until tomorrow." The kid laughed and said, "I think I will stay here!" He stayed with them all the way to St. Lo.

Nider concludes his story with a fact that he feels was never written down in any history books about D-Day. "I think it was one of the turning points on Omaha beach" he says.

It was about 4 p.m. when a one star general, about 45 years old, appeared on the front line and gave an order. Nider had never seen him before or ever again. His order was that if any Germans wanted to surrender they would have, at that moment, time to do so. The shelling stopped and the Germans were assured that if they did surrender, they would live. It worked, as 35 Germans surrendered and Nider was one of the American soldier's that led the German prisoners down to the beach. Spaced about 75 feet apart, the remaining Germans did not want to risk shooting any of their own so they also ceased fire. Nider said he has been trying to locate this General and has been unsuccessful thus far. Unfortunately, he did not find out his name in the midst of turmoil of D-day.

Even in spite of the fact that the thing that happened on Omaha beach was disorganized the beachhead was taken. Bear in mind it was done by young people that played a large part in the victory that day. "We confused the Germans. They couldn't figure out our line of attack. The first thing they knew that afternoon is that we were everywhere" Nider states.

The invasion was the biggest day of Nider's life and wonders to himself why he is even able to talk about it 50 some odd years later. "I am very proud to be an American with the freedom we have. We must never let that be taken away from us" Nider said.

For a bit of history about the Normandy invasion, it consisted of a 50-mile stretch of coast where the attack took place. The Allied armada of 700 warships and 2,700 support ships with 2,500 landing craft closed in on the beaches. In the first six days, 326,000 men, 54,000 vehicles and 104,000 tons of stores were landed.

A member of the 29th Division wrote a book named "Hedgerow Hell." His closing statement was, "War is hell" and this, "Was a hell of a war!" Nider concluded.

OSTERBERG, MYRON

This veteran from Kearney served in the Navy during WW II, in the Pacific Campaign. He was with the USS Oglethorpe AKA 100, as a Yeoman 2nd joining the military in October of 1944 and was discharged in July of 1946, still under age 20. He was just out of high school when he went off to serve his country, like many of those who fought for the red, white and blue.

162

Osterberg was also one of those, unknowingly, joined the service when the war was just about over. When he was enroute to Pearl Harbor, the big bombs were dropped on Japan, ending the war. But transportation of many different materials and men was still very much needed.

His duties on the ship were with the Captain and Executive officers in the ship office. He was, what they call, a Captains Talker on the bridge.

His story is interesting. He related it to me via a letter. Here are the contents.

Osterberg grew up on a farm in southeastern South Dakota. He recalls a little train consisting of an engine, a passenger car and caboose sounding its whistle at 10 minutes before midnight. "You could set your watch by it," he said. The train had a nickname, "The Galloping Goose." As he boy, he never dreamt that this same little train would one day, whisk him off to Omaha one late November night as he entered the service.

He took his Navy boot camp at Great Lakes, Illinois. After the first 10 weeks, he took another 16 weeks of service school and assigned to a new AKA, an attack cargo vessel on the East Coast. The AKA 100, USS Oglethorpe, had just finished its shakedown cruise in the Atlantic. He was put in the ship office as both, Captain and Executive Officer's yeoman. As a kid of 18, "It was a tremendous responsibility." At the time, he didn't think much about it, just doing his job.

When they left Norfolk, Virginia, through the Panama Canal and half way to Hawaii, was when they received the news about Japan being bombed. The crew never got into combat but there was also no place to go to celebrate VJ Day either he said.

Though the war was over, there were still many mines floating beneath the surface of the ocean. Two kinds, Osterberg said, were prevalent. One was a magnetic variety, which looked like a smooth huge steel ball with a can shaped type figure at the top. They would explode upon contact with a ships outer surface. They encountered some of these on their voyage. Seeing them in time, the ship gunners shot them so full of holes in finally sank.

When they came across the other type mine, a contact mine, about the same size as the magnetic mine, it had steel spikes sticking out it. They were designed to explode when a ship hit one hard enough to depress the spikes and then explode. Again, gunners kept shooting at it until they hit one of these spikes. It then exploded. "I've had never seen such a geyser of water before or since" he said.

Osterberg had plenty of ocean travel. I guess when the service boasts of joining them and "Seeing the world," they aren't kidding. He traveled the entire Pacific Ocean from New Caledonia, off the east coast of Australia to the Philippines, and back and forth several times. They were at Guam, Saipan, Kwajalein, Eniwetok, Ellice Islands and at Guadalcanal where he incidentally spent the hottest days in his life; one hundred twenty eight in the shade. They hauled troops and equipment back to Pearl Harbor or the U.S.

Christmas of 1944 he found himself singing in Great Lakes with the Blue Jackets Choir, a 1,000 man singing group. They were broadcast over NBC radio that night. It was a live show; the directors allowed no mistakes. Five, three hour rehearsals each week eliminated errors. "It was a great experience," he said.

Christmas of 1945 he was able to visit his uncle and aunt at Bremerton, Washington, where his ship was dry-docked. After another trip to the Philippines, he was discharged July 29, 1946. "I seen a heck of a lot of territory in 212 months," he had concluded.

Arriving home, the Galloping Goose, no longer existed. He missed it.

Osterberg went to college, received his degrees and married Eva Spencer, who was also in the military. For the 29 years he was at the University of Nebraska, Kearney, where he taught vocal music. He retired in 1992 and resides in Kearney. . Both he and his wife are active in the American Legion and Veterans of Foreign Wars. They will host the WW II reunion at Kearney this year, 1999. They participate on the color guard, firing squad at funerals of fellow veterans and parades and flag presentations.

OSTERBUHR, LEROY

Osterbuhr was drafted into the U.S. Army in September of 1942. He was farming at the time. The day he received his draft notice, his father died. The draft board gave him a 30-day deferment to help the family make arrangements and to help decide the future of the farm. An auction was held and he left to serve his country.

He received his basic training at Fort Leavenworth, Kansas, as did many of these WW II veterans. Then he spent six weeks at Camp Barkely, Abilene, Texas for more training. He was to be a medical technician. When he completed his training there, he went to Charleston, South Carolina, to get trained for overseas duty. He boarded the U.S. HERMITAGE with 9,000 other soldiers at Newport News, Virginia. They went through the Panama Canal and then to the South Pacific Theatre. Thirty-six ships were in the convoy, which included destroyers, aircraft carriers, submarines and troop ships. When they hit enemy waters, the entire convoy practiced zigzag patterns over the seas to avoid being zeroed in by the enemy.

They landed on January 31, 1943, in Brisbane, Australia after 36 days en route. After a short stay at Camp Doomben, he was sent to Sidney, Australia, for six months of hospital duty. He had been assigned to the 174th Station Hospital in Australia where they set up camp in the midst of a thick jungle near the ocean on Milne Bay, New Guinea. He served in the New Guinea Campaign in the Asiatic Southwest Pacific under his commander, General Douglas McArthur.

Hospital huts were crude and had been made by the natives. Roofs were made of coconut tree leaves. Coconuts often fell through the roofs. The sides were open. The framework was constructed of poles from native trees and nails were not used; strips of tree bark held it all together.

That was where Osterbuhr would make his home for a while - at a makeshift hospital which consisted of 12 ward huts that had 42 beds in each. The staff spent their time caring for victims of jungle diseases; dinghy fevers, spinal meningitis, malaria and epileptics, to name a few. He gave shots and medications and performed duties much like nurse's do, he said.

Osterbuhr was in charge of Ward Hut #10. It was next to a ward that contained shell shock patients. A ward that was indeed a sad place to witness. Other ward huts contained wounded combat soldiers who had made it to this place they called a field hospital.

For the first three months, he worked the day shift. Later on he worked the night shift, which was in total darkness from 7 p.m. to 7 a.m., 7 days a week, for the next 9 months. "It was cooler at nights," he said. He slept on cots that were also made by the natives. The cots had to always be covered by mosquito nets.

Japanese snipers were constantly in the trees and jungles trying to pick off what they could. Osterbuhr said they were not supposed to shoot into field hospitals, but "They did it anyway. We lost a lot of guys by these snipers." Snipers would tie themselves to branches up in the trees. That way, should they get shot, they wouldn't fall down. If they were only wounded, they could still keep shooting, he said.

Wild pigs ran all over the camp and hospital. Clothes were washed in the ocean on rocks along the beach. It rained every day and the ground was always soggy. Water squished in their shoes daily. Trees were so thick the sunlight didn't hit the ground very much. The heat and high humidity made it an undesirable place to be

Osterbuhr contracted a common infection known as jungle rot. It affected his toes, toenails, fingers and fingernails. The nails came off and then would grow back again. Ten different times this happened in the jungle and once more after he returned home. The doctors didn't know how to treat it at the time.

One day Major Saither, a doctor in the hospital, recommended Osterbuhr to leave the jungle area due to his poor condition. He checked in the 118th General Hospital as a patient, about 20 miles further back from enemy lines from where he had been for about a year. They then put him on ship a called the USAT MAUI, which was headed for San Francisco in the good old USA. He spent some time in Lettermen General Hospital and transferred to Winter General Hospital in Topeka, Kansas, for six weeks.

He received his medical discharge in November of 1944, with his hands and feet in bandages. After being back in a dry climate, his wounds from jungle rot healed. It took a while but that was the only cure back then, he said.

He was awarded the Asiatic Pacific Theatre Ribbon, the Bronze star and Good Conduct Ribbon.

He went back to his hometown of Hildreth and worked for a farmer about a year. He then got married and moved to Hastings. He says he is proud to have served his country. "It was my duty," he concluded.

PAVELKA, BERNARD F.

This WW II veteran is from Hastings entered the service in October of 1942 at Fort Crook, Nebraska. He was assigned to the 31st Army-Anti Aircraft Artillery Brigade, which was under the 9th Airforce, 5th Army. He remembers "blood and guts," Patton very well. He said that General George Patton did have a lot of guts, but "it was our blood." Pavelka obtained the rank of Corporal.

Pavelka recalls the scariest part of the war which he was involved in was the air raids when he landed in Oran, Africa. He was a truck driver and transported troops. When he wasn't doing that he was a chauffeur for Brigadier Generals like Hewett and Chappan. Hewett, at the time was about 60 years old, slim and active. He liked to swim in the ocean and didn't care how fast Pavelka drove. Chappan called his driver, Pavelke, and seemed to always want Pavelka to take his picture with his helmet on while standing by the jeep holding a canteen of water. He sent them all home to his wife. Chappan was a "worry" type person. Chappan was opposite of Hewett because he would always control Pavelka's fast driving and instructed him not to drive too fast.

Being a chauffeur was not always fun. He would have to wait and then wait some more; often five hours would pass while the Generals were in a meeting discussing where and when to attack next.

His part time job did have its advantages. He was able to meet General Eisenhower when he was in Algeria, east of Tunis, Africa. He was also there when Eisenhower was in Reims, France and Rhineland, Germany. He comments that Eisenhower's chauffeur was Kay Summersby, a divorcee and former fashion model for the House of Worth in Paris. She was tall, slim and of course very pretty.

Pavelka was stationed in many different places: Oran, Africa, Tunnesia, Algeria, Sardina, Corsica, Rome, Italy, Reims, France and Rhineland, Germany and finally Belgium before going back to France and home. He was discharged in November of 1945.

PETTIT, NEAL

This WW II aviator is from Lincoln. He was a navigator with the 448th Bombardment Group, Army Air Corp, flying out of Seething, England during the European Theatre Campaign. Lt. Pettit has quite a story to tell. Since his wife of 45 plus years passed away, he began to open up to his children concerning his experiences. Picking through the many letters the two had written back and forth almost daily during the war, they were able to record much of the history of his experiences. Pettit and his wife, Yvonne, were not yet married when he was in service. After his return, they were married as soon as the arrangements could be made. He is glad he was able to come home in one piece so he could marry his wartime sweetheart.

What Pettit and his children have is a book in itself. Being a navigator on the B-24s, he kept a daily log. He has recorded each mission he flew on and what happened in great detail. His kids and grandkids will forever; know what he did for his country and that's wonderful. As Vickie, Scott and Tracy refer to as, "each description creates celluloid-like images of their Dad's story, reflected by experience."

Pettit is quick to point out that each veteran may have his own account of what took place on a particular mission. There may be as many stories about that mission as there are veterans, everyone seeing it a little differently. I would have to agree as while I sit and write various stories down from other veterans who were in the same place at the same time, I too see things that one veteran forgot and the other remembered. I thank Lt. Pettit for pointing that out. In action, a lot of different things take place, simultaneously. One may have seen something the other did not. And the fact that it has been over 50 years later, people tend to forget things that happened that long ago as Lt. Pettit will agree with. He verified much of his story with other comrades who were with him to be certain it would have few errors. In my attempt to do a little editing, I hope I don't mess it up for him.

His story unfolded as he left the United States on October 22, 1944, and landed in Liverpool, England on November 3, 1944. After settling in with his group he began his service with the 712th Bomb Squadron, later the 714th Bomb Squadron of the 448th Bomb Group.

His first mission took place on November 26. His last took place on April 25, 1945 after his plane went down, of which you will read about later in his story. Note that almost all the missions he was on, 26 of them were flown in temperatures of sometimes 50 degrees below zero, always very cold. They would usually leave the base at around 5:00 a.m. and reach an altitude of over 20,000 feet normally. They carried 6 bombs often weighing 1,000 pounds each. On other occasions they carried 500-pound bombs, 8 of them and perhaps a couple cluster of 500-pound incendiary clusters too. M-17's, another 500 pound bomb would also be aboard sometimes. The type of bombs carried depended on what the target would be. Often they would dribble out maybe 52, 100 pound M47 bombs for a given situation. Loads varied and I will attempt to make note of this later. For Pettit, the missions began November 26, 1944 and concluded his April 4, 1945.

Mission #1 was targeted at Bielefield, Germany; a rail viaduct had to be taken out. This first mission he said was not too bad. They did receive some flak over the target area but "we were so inexperienced-we didn't think too much about it."

Mission #2 was over Offenberg, Germany to do some damage on a rail marshalling yard. They had a very close call that could have been fatal. They were flying on the left wing of a plane that had been very badly shot up on a previous mission. They had some new crew members. In keeping with the style of flying a very tight formation, this plane kept falling further and further back from his position as they approached the target area. Pettit's pilot, Lt. James Shafter got on the radio and informed the plane that if he did not get back into formation he was going to move up and fill that spot which they did. Soon the pilot of the other plane decided he better take his advice and get back into position and attempted to fly back in where he had dropped out of now filled in by Pettit's crew. The pilot of the plane nearly hit Pettit's plane. If Shafter would not have pulled the plane up at the last minute allowing the other plane to slide under he would have hit them.

They were flying at a very high altitude heavily loaded with bombs. Under those conditions the B-24 is very unstable. Pettit's plane stalled and fell off on the left wing and headed straight down in a left wing spin. By the time the co-pilot, John Paxson, was able to pull it back they had dropped 10,000 feet and were headed in the opposite direction. They were within minutes of their target so there was nothing to do but get rid of the bombs and head home.

Mission #3 was a target at Koblenz, Germany, another rail marshalling yard. They received some flak and a few holes in the plane, one in the engine cowling but made it home without serious problems.

Mission #4 was to hit another rail marshalling yard at Bongen, Germany. Temperatures ranged from 23 to 31 degrees below zero. This run took place during the worst part of the Battle of the Bulge when air support was badly needed by the ground troops. Pettit recalls that the morning of December 19 was terribly foggy with visibility only about 100 yards on the runway. This kind of weather makes planes react differently as the lift from airflow over the wings is at its very worst. The only thing a pilot could do is point the thing down the runway, stand on the brakes, open the throttle and turn it loose. The only thing they could see was the runway lights along side just off the wing's tips. The goal was to keep the plane lined up between those lights and get up enough flying speed so they could clear the runway.

Then, climbing up through ten thousand feet of clouds caused severe icing problems on the wings. Bear in mind that another plane is just 30 seconds ahead of you and another is 30 seconds behind you. Everyone has to play strict attention to the rules. One plane that took off directly behind Pettits plane was never heard from again.

They formed their formation and journeyed on to the target. They hit flak sooner than expected because they were unaware the Germans had advanced so much further in the Bulge than was reported.

After dumping their load they headed back home when more problems arose. They could not land on the base they normally would have. They were diverted to Barnstaple instead. The nose wheel failed to function so now they had to land it without a nose wheel. The pilot always landed the plane very smoothly but this time when he applied the brakes the nose came down to far. "Nose gear landing can be dangerous," Pettit said. The co-pilot, knowing something was amiss, shut the entire plane down hitting the crash switch. The plane slid about a hundred yards down the runway on its nose and came to a stop with the end of the props only inches from the end of the runway. Amazingly, the prop did not touch the ground. A bunch of guys came out and stood on the tail section bringing the nose up, kicked the nose wheel down and it was taxied off the runway so others could land. They were later informed that this particular B-24 was the only plane capable of landing that way. The only damage it had was a hole in the bottom of the nose where it skidded down the runway. It was all repaired and was ready for flight once more.

Pettit later said that he must have been the only one who saw the red flashing light from the tower. It didn't dawn on him at the time that this meant they were being rejected permission to land. However, if they had tried to pull up at this stage they never would have made it. There had been another plane in the runway at the time but it must have gotten out of the way.

Mission #5 took place on Christmas Eve Day. Destined for Euskirchen, Germany, a rail marshalling yard was to be blown up. This was the longest air raid the Air Force ever launched against Germany, Pettit said. After several days of being grounded because of the weather, all repairs on the planes were complete. On December 24th, at dawn, it was bright and clear. Everything the allies had they threw at the Germans that day. Over 2,000 bombers from the 8th Air Force with more coming from the English and southern bases did major damage that day.

Over the target area it was heavy flak into and out. They received a few holes but one plane in formation was not so lucky. It was hit and caught on fire and eventually lost a wing.

Pettit wrote Yvonne that day informing her that they had delivered a lot of Christmas presents to the Germans but he didn't think they appreciated them too much. It seems they all blew up about the time they got to their destination he said with a grin.

On a personal note, Pettit stated that he doesn't recall if it was this mission or not but when they landed a 100-pound bomb was found still in the bomb bay area that was still hanging in the hanger. The safety wire had been pulled from the fuse, which means it was fully armed. Any little jolt could have set it off. The engineer was to always check after the drop assuring that all bombs in the area was empty but this time he had missed seeing it.

The story around the air bases was that if a new crew made through five missions, you had a 50/50 chance of finishing the rest of your tour. Thirty-five missions were required. Pettit wonders how he even finished five. The casualty rate at the time was high but not as high as it was in the beginning. He sees now statistically it didn't get any better for the next 22 missions he would fly on.

Mission #6 was flown on Christmas Day, 1944, to Waxweiler, Germany, to hit a road junction and warehouse on the outskirts of town. There was again some flak, they were hit and managed to get an 18-inch hole in their rudder with some other minor damages. When they got back, landing conditions were very poor with bad weather but everything worked out well and they landed safely.

Mission #7 was to be at Euskirchen, Germany striking a rail and highway viaduct. It was 31 degrees below zero. It went letter perfect with no problems.

Mission #8 was 8 miles north of Koblenz, Germany striking another rail and highway viaduct. It to went well with little flak and no other problems.

In between the 8th and the 9th mission, Lt. Pettit was asked to ride along with another crew on a mission and it too went very well. It would not count as a mission however it was in his log.

Mission #9 was to take out a rail track and tunnel near Pirmasens, Germany. They experienced a fair amount of flak on this trip and had a dozen or more holes in the plane from enemy aircraft fire. They managed to return to base okay.

Mission #10 was to take out another rail and highway intersection near Achem, Germany. When the squadron left the base, one plane lost all its power and the crew bailed out and landed in England. Over the target area there was more flak and they lost another plane and several planes were badly damaged. Pettit and the crew he was with came out okay.

Mission #11 was to Worms, Germany where a rail suspension bridge was to be destroyed by the bombers. "This was a bad one," Pettit recalls. They were bombing a bridge over the Rhine River. It was not a clear day so bombs were supposed to be dropped using instruments. When Pettits crew made the turn to approach the bombing area, the clouds suddenly ended and they could see the target area plainly. They demolished the bridge but the lead pilot took a right turn immediately after the bombs were dropped and all the rest of them were supposed to follow the leader. Their orders were to fly straight after unloading the bombs and then turn. Turning too quickly with no cloud cover made them a good target for flak gunners down below. They were using 105 mm. instead of the normal 88-mm. guns. Because of this error by the leader, one plane of the nine in the squadron was shot down with a wing blown off. Three others made emergency landings at the closest friendly airfield on the continent.

When they arrived home, only about 3 of the 9 landed. It was getting dark with a ceiling of only about 500 feet and visibility was only about 300 yards. "We were like a bunch of tired birds looking for a place to roost," he said about the ordeal.

Of the 30 planes the 448th put over the target area that day, at least a dozen were damaged, several quite badly. Pettit's plane had about a dozen holes in it, some rather large.

Mission #12 was at Sieger, Germany, a rail marshalling yard. Temps dropped to 53 degrees below zero this trip. They had no flak or enemy fighters to contend with but one of the superchargers on one engine went out. They were able to deliver the bombs anyway. With the supercharger out, it meant the plane would burn more fuel than normal. They dropped the bombs and headed to the nearest friendly base at St. Trowne, Belgium. The weather was not good with poor visibility. The tower, using radar, guided them perfectly down the runway. The airfield had belonged to the Germans and was quite nice with bunkers with a flat thick concrete ceiling and a strong tile roof over that. They could sleep on stretchers, which were a chunk of canvas between two poles. They were laid over utility pipes in the attic leading to the hospital about two feet off the floor. The setup had been used by the hospital for draping blankets while the blood dried he said.

The base was covered with allied and German aircraft littering the airfield. Most of the aircraft was still sitting where they had been shot down.

Their plane was quickly repaired and they again were on their way. A colonel requested a ride back to London. The pilot put him in the waist section of the plane. As soon as they got off the ground they again hit fog. They didn't see the ground again until they landed at their home base. The crew all wore throat mikes and headphones and was able to communicate with each other. The colonel didn't have one. One of the crew commented the colonel didn't look very good. The colonel was scared to death.

When they landed the colonel commented he never wanted to ride one of those planes again and found it hard to believe how these guys did this sometimes day after day. He patted the ground when he got off. What he didn't know was that the crew was also somewhat worried that trip.

Mission #13 was to Oshabruck, Germany taking out a communications installation. Weather was a problem. They were supposed to drop their 12-500 pound bombs at 10,000 feet but had to climb back to 20,000 and drop them by instrument. They never found out if they hit the target or not. Some scattered flak but those shooting at them didn't know where they were any more than the crew did he said.

Mission #14 was bad Pettit states. Flying to Halle, Germany to do some damage on a rail sorting siding, the trip turned out to be a very close call. It was an extremely long flight, almost nine hours, with over half of it at high altitude and they had to use oxygen. It was a long flight over enemy territory. That morning they loaded 20-20 pound bombs and 2,700 gallons of fuel and the supercharger was acting up again in one of the engines.

When they came over the target they had only about 700 gallons of fuel left. They weren't too concerned because they had gotten rid of the bomb load and were going down hill. The fuel would go much farther than it did trying to reach their drop zone. They thought they could land at St. Trowne again but radio conversations said no, fighting was going on there again and the airstrip was a mess. They had to go to Brussels to land in Belgium. That was almost too far. Pettit gave his pilot the heading for Brussels. The air base was way on the other side of the country but they left the formation and headed for it. Fuel gauges on the plane were nothing more than sight gauges giving one a visual view of the remaining fuel. The sight gauges registered at the bottom. The radio operator got on the radio looking for help and contacted a British Spitfire base after transmitting a "Mayday." The base informed them that their base was merely a 3,000-foot steel mesh runway, not long enough for a bomber like a B-24 to land on. The crew was desperate and informed the base it would do just fine. The base said to go for it and they would help them line up with the runway by sending up a British Spitfire to guide them in.

One of the crew spotted the Spitfire and the pilot followed it in. By this time there had been no fuel in the sight gauges to be seen for the last 20 minutes. As they landed, one engine caught on fire from being run on a very lean mixture of fuel and it was overheated. This type of fire pilots could keep revving the engine and cool it down which the pilot did.

The runway, made of steel mats was hard on the tires when the pilot stood on the brakes. By the time they stopped sliding, one side was flat enough they would create a bump when they turned.

They landed safely and inspected the fuel tanks to see just how much was left. Walt Petrovich, the radioman, crawled out on top of the wings and took a close look. With a flashlight, he lit up the inside of the tanks. The funnel-shaped tanks were nearly bone-dry. The tank in the left wing had only about a six-inch puddle in the bottom of the tank. The one on the right was a little bigger than the size of a dinner plate. A tanker was brought to their plane to refuel it. Pettit believes the English had some Frenchmen or locals working for them. What happened next really created a ruckus with the plane's crew. It was 5:00 p.m., the workers quitting time. They refused to refuel the plane and informed the crew they would have to wait until morning. "I couldn't believe this could happen at this point and time. We never forgot it," he said.

The crew went into town that night and looked it over. The pubs were busy in spite of the war or perhaps because of the war, Pettit isn't sure. One pub had "live" music consisting of a drum, accordion, and some type of large horn resembling a saxophone. People wore wooden shoes. Pettit brought some wooden shoes home later along with some Belgium coins.

The 8th Air Force put them up for the night and a tanker showed up in the morning to refuel their plane. They took off for home base in spite of the short runway, which was not designed for a B-24 even without its bomb load.

Mission #15 headed for Augsburg, Germany, dropping bombs on a rail station. It was a long mission but went rather smoothly. The crew wished they would have all be as good as this one.

Mission #16 was to take out a synthetic oil and gas refinery at Magdeburg, Germany. Flak was heavy, one hole in the waist measured about a foot and a half in diameter. Several small holes were also found in the waist and the tail section but none caused any severe damage and luckily no one was injured.

While on this run they were attacked by a ME-262 jet fighter coming directly out of the sun and headed on to their formation. It focused on a plane above and to the right of the lead bomber in the formation. It took a direct hit into the cockpit. The B-24's nose went up and then slid straight down first and knocked the tail off another plane below them. Both planes immediately went down. Lt. James Guynes was flying the B-24 that was hit in the nose. He was one of two crew members who cleared the falling bomber when they bailed out. Unfortunately he died shortly after being captured by the German military due to complications of serious injuries. He had lost an arm and a leg. Pettit helped Lt. Guynes oldest sister find the long lost information about the fate of Lt. Guynes.

Mission #17 was an air strike on an oil refinery at Harburg, Germany. Very accurate flak was encountered, #2 engine was shot out over the target. Fortunately it was a short mission, not very long over enemy territory and managed to take the plane back to Seething. Pettit notes the B-24's could take a lot of abuse before they wouldn't fly anymore thank heaven.

Mission #18, Rheine, Germany, where a rail marshalling yard needed some attention. It was another short trip; they took some flak but no problems, at least for the crew Pettit was with. Two other planes were lost. No one ever knew what happened to them.

Mission #19 was a trip with no problems to Kiel, Germany, striking a gas and rubber incendiary, submarine yards and pens. This trip appeared to be a multiple choice to this author.

Mission #20 also was a good trip with no problems. It went to Hanover, Germany, (where this authors father came from in 1925.) The mission was to blow up a tank factory or at least do some damage to it.

Mission #21 was a different sort of run. This time they carried 312-20 pound fragmentation bombs designed too much damage to whatever happened to be sitting around the airfield at Ahlhorn, Germany. Jets, ME-262's and the barracks resided here. It was easy, too easy Pettit stated.

Mission #22 marked the end of the good times. Just when things started looking better, instead it rapidly deteriorated. Carrying 52-100 pound bombs, they headed for Kitzingen Airfield, Germany. The bomb bay area contained vertical posts, racks, with places to hang bombs one above the other. Large bombs were hung one to a station and smaller ones in a cluster. The number in the clusters depended upon the size of the bombs. One hundred-pound bombs hung in clusters of 3.

Bomb release was controlled electronically by the intervolameter, an instrument in the nose compartment of the plane near where Pettit rode. The device could be set to release all stations at once or string them out at any desired interval. Each station had a little red light on the panel. When one station was released, the light would go out. If a station failed to release electronically, they could be opened mechanically by pushing a lever. On this trip the intervolameter failed completely. When Pettit pushed the lever, all the bombs released and dropped at once. Pettit explains how bombs function:

The detonating fuse was in the nose of the bomb. It consisted of a charge of powder about the size of a large thimble that fired like a shell when the primer was struck by a pin. There was a little propeller just under the head of the pin that held a little horse shoe collar around the stem of the pin so it could not be accidentally driven into the primer. The propeller was kept from spinning itself and releasing the collar by a wire called the arming wire. One end of the arming wire was fastened to the bombing rack and the other end was put through a hole in the propeller.

Under normal release, the bombs fell away from the arming wires, releasing the propeller to spin as the bomb fell, which then unscrewed a keeper that held the collar in place. Once the collar was gone the bomb would nose into its target driving the pin into the primer, setting off the small charge that ignited the bomb. The delay in loosening the collar allowed the bombs to be a "safe" distance from the plane before they were armed for explosion.

This time, however, when Pettit pushed the lever, the bombs dropped from the racks but for some reason continued hanging in the bomb bay doors. In doing so, they managed to jam the control cables for the rudders making the plane very difficult to control. Since the bombs had been released from the racks, the safety wires were all pulled and we suddenly had 52 live 100 pound bombs armed and laying in every which way in the bomb bay with little propellers spinning like a bunch of windmills Pettit said.

One of the waist gunners walked out over the catwalk over the open bomb bay to work at dislodging the bombs. The catwalk is about 12-15 feet long, very narrow and offered no handholds other than the now empty bomb racks. He kicked and lifted the bombs out of the open bay until the key bombs released and the whole mess was gone without incident. WOW!

While all this was going on, some ME-262s were attacking their formation. Fortunately the bombers escort, the P-51s, challenged them. Other than scaring the "hell out of us," they received no damage.

Mission #23, to Munater, Germany, where another rail marshalling yard was to be the target. Heavy flak, their #1 engine was hit and they had to feather the prop and shut it down. A German 88-mm. shell, almost 4 inches in diameter, had made a direct hit on the plane.

The waist of the plane had a door in the floor and the shell struck the latch on the door, a very solid spot, and took it completely off. It then cut the control cables to the rudder once again making the plane very difficult to fly. Then it went through the left side just ahead of the horizontal stabilizer.

Flak shells had an "altitude" fuse; set by the Germans just prior to firing, set at an altitude the Germans guess the planes were flying. When the shell arrives at this preset altitude, it explodes throwing flak over a wide area in hopes to hit a plane directly or to distribute the flak so maybe a plane would fly directly into it Pettit said.

The artillery shells had a contact fuse, which exploded upon impact. In this case it failed to work properly. If it would have, it would have wiped out everything behind the bomb bay and would have likely blown off the tail of the plane. This shell exploded a little late going a short distance above and behind them before it exploded. Since everything blows "up and out" it did them no further damage with the exception of a few flak holes, of which one was pretty large.

Since they had lost #1 engine they found it hard to keep up with the formation. A lone plane is a sitting duck for German fighters. They called for "Little Bear," the code name for the escort planes. They informed them they were wounded and alone and very much in need of them. Almost immediately they had a P-51 sitting just off each wing tip waging their wings at us and giving us the thumbs up. What a relief!

Mission #24 was not any better. Bear in mind now that at this time the crew was flying every day without a break. It was March 24, 1945 and some paratroopers now needed supplies. This time they were armed with 5,000 pounds of supplies, shells, guns and first aid equipment. It was 8 degrees above zero for a change, a heat wave compared to usually being below zero.

When they arrived back on base from mission #23, they found the base was restricted. No one could go off the base. A high degree of secrecy was felt all around. Later they learned why. The allies were going to cross the mighty Rhine River the morning of the 24th. Only a few selected bomber crews were selected to fly the B-24s dropping supplies into the area. Pettit's crew was chosen along with a total of 240 B-24s. Twenty-three of them would be taking part from their base at Seething, England.

The strategy was to fly at tree top level and just before reaching the drop zone pull up to 300 feet allowing just enough altitude for the chutes to open. Then back to treetop level on the way out. The reason for flying so low was to give the enemy the least amount of time to bear their guns down on them.

They were told to fly low, and low they did. Pettit said at one location they flew between a church steeple and a smokestack.

Of the 240 planes that left on this mission, 20 were lost, 6 or 7 being from Seething where Pettit was from. Some of the planes were shot up so bad they couldn't land so their crews bailed out over England.

Pettit recalls that the plane he was on was leading the three other planes. After the drop, another pilot, Lt. McCluhan, contacted Pettit's pilot informing him that he had no hydraulics left and had very serious damage to the controllers. Their radio compass, engine instruments and several other details didn't work and he was looking for someone to follow back to base. Though it was difficult for Lt. McCluhan to keep them in sight, Lt. Shafter, Pettit's pilot made it as easy as he could. Shafter landed his plane and looked for McCluhan. They could see him coming veering to the right. Shafter was still sitting on the runway because of damage to the nose wheel of his plane. As they watched McCluhan approach, off course, co-pilot Lt. Paxson gave the engines full throttle and got out of McCluhans way. If he would not have, it would have been a full collision other than just a wing tip as it turned out. No one was injured.

Later, in checking over their plane for damages, they noted many bullet holes made by enemy machine guns and rifles. Something had hit a life raft near the rear of the plane and set it on fire. It was thrown out of the plane at the time. They found a bullet hole directly through the fuselage from one side to the other directly in line where Lt. Walt Peterson usually sat at the radio. Apparently when he had left to close the bomb bay doors after dropping supplies when the bullet came ripping through. The plane was in a steep banking turn at the time they were fired upon noted by the angle of the holes.

Mission #25 they were attacked again by enemy jet fighters and had some flak. They went to Brunswick, Germany and dropped 12-500 pound bombs on a rail marshalling yard. No planes were lost and they had only minor damage. After the previous mission, this one seemed like a "milk run." Pettit said.

Mission #26 had a primary target at Parchin, Germany. The name of the plane was "Miss B-Havin." They were shot down before arriving at the target by ME-262s. This is a story by itself. Here is what it was like from start to finish. This is what men like Pettit had to endure so we could be free.

On the morning of April 4, 1945, Pettit was laying in his bunk at the base asleep. When the orderly would come in and quietly awaken those who were to fly that day, everyone would hear him open the door. Most would pretend to be fast asleep, or act like they didn't hear him, especially when he came to your bunk and informed you, "you're flying today." It didn't do any good to cover your head or pretend to be asleep. The orderly was looking for you and you would be on the next mission. There was nothing you could do about it.

This particular morning the orderly showed up at 1:15 a.m. He went to Pettit's bunk, turned the blanket back and directed his flashlight in his face. Then he would announce, "Lt. Pettit, are you awake? Sir, you are flying today." Briefing was at 2 a.m. The orderly also told him they would be loading 2,700 gallons of fuel. Pettit knew then that it would be a long mission.

He got up; dressed, picked up some letters he had written the night before, took a long look at Yvonne's picture and headed for the mess hall after first stopping at the latrine. Breakfast consisted of powdered eggs with marmalade and toast and of course, strong coffee. No matter how much you needed the coffee, one was careful not to drink too much because getting rid of coffee on the plane wasn't easy. A flight would often take 10 hours. There were no fancy restroom facilities on board. And with bulky clothing, one would tend to avoid having to relieve himself. There was what is known as a "pilot's tube" toward the rear of the plane. This was nothing more than a funnel shoved into a rubber hose that projected through the side of the plane and was apt to freeze up.

After breakfast, trucks picked them up at the mess hall and headed for the long trip to the flight line. First everyone had to assemble in the briefing room behind closed doors. No one was allowed to leave until it was over. The focal point in the room was a large map covered by a curtain at the front of the room. Pins were strategically placed on the map with a ribbon placed through them outlining their flight path. As soon as the curtain was pulled, everyone knew where they would be going on that mission.

This morning what the ribbon described was "unnerving" as Pettit calls it. A long flight over water to Berlin where most of the fighters of the Germans were still concentrated. It would be a long ways home if anything did go wrong. They were instructed that if it did, to try to find a neutral country or as far back from the front lines as possible if they could. There was a lot of trouble with civilians beating and killing downed American airmen, especially in the area near Berlin. As a navigator, he had special maps to pick up and received special information as well as the pilot and co-pilot.

After the briefing they had to go to the equipment room and pick up their equipment and get dressed for the trip. Over their long johns, they wore their heated suits, which was designed much like an electric blanket. The helmet snapped to the jacket, the jacket snapped to the bib type pants and bulky gloves and the pants snapped to the shoes. Each snap built part of a circuit that when completed, plugged into the side of the airplane. It was a serious concern when the wiring in the entire suit failed. Over the suit they wore a heavy coat, pants, and sheepskin lined rubber boots. Added to that they wore goggles, throat mike, oxygen mask and a parachute harness. "A guy was really bundled up and loaded down by the time he went to the flight line," he said.

They left at 5:05 a.m. with over 1,000 planes destined for Berlin. The flight went smoothly until a German ME-262 fighter attacked them.

It was an hour and thirty-five minutes from when they took off that everyone was in formation at 10,000 feet. Once over that altitude they used their oxygen masks. They then flew over the North Sea for another hour and thirty-three minutes while climbing to 20,000 feet. They crossed over into Germany just north of the Elb River, 50 miles northwest of the city of Hamburg. They passed over to the right of the city and they could see British Lancaster bombers taking a beating from the flak. Smoke rose to the altitude Pettit and rest were flying at. They crossed the IP, Initial Point, a predetermined spot four miles or more in the air the Bomber squadron flies over while making a turn to get all of the groups in trail of each other. The outside of the turn has to hurry a little, while the inside might have to slow down. To close ranks, pilots swung their planes wide and if they were behind they could cut a corner there. As Pettit's plane completed the wing IP word came over the radio, "bandits in the area. As the planes all assembled for the bombing run which by now was only about 10 minutes away, it was important that all planes fly straight and level regardless of what action was taken against them. If the mission was to be successful, they had to get a good bomb pattern on the target.

In the 10 minutes that followed, they were not too concerned. The gunners had spotted the bandits. Two of these enemy fighters were zeroing in on Pettit's plane at about the 4 o'clock position, a little lower than they were coming straight at them. The gunners were giving them everything they had.

Pettit saw another plane just to their left blow in half, Lt. Mains' plane, but they didn't have time to watch it as they had been hit too. A fire was blazing in the nose wheel compartment only a couple feet from his feet and legs. The bombardier came with a fire extinguisher, as there were none in the nose compartment. He was not able to put the fire out. Pettit informed the pilot via his mike but there was no familiar click and he could not communicate. He pulled off his glove from his left hand and tried to tamper with the mike and get it working. He discovered the radio had been destroyed. Both engines on the right side were out and the wing was on fire. No doubt, gas was feeding the fire as the severely damaged wing housed fuel tanks.

The fire at Pettit's feet grew steadily worse. He had informed the crew that if anything like this ever happened they were to follow him. He would now be their leader. With no radio, he turned to the nose turret to get Bill Kaiser's attention. The door was closed and only opened when the turret was pointed straight ahead. Bill was tracking the enemy with his gun. Pettit took hold of the door handle and as the turret reached 12 o'clock position, it opened up. Bill turned around very upset with Pettit shutting him down. Pettit just pointed to the fire on the floor, it was too noisy to talk or even shout and be heard. Bill's eyes got real big and he came out of the turret.

What happened in these few seconds are vividly burned in Pettit's mind he said. Even after 50 some years, he hasn't forgotten but admits, that others who are familiar with this type of situation can fill in the gaps.

The escape door on a B-24 is the same door that opened to let the nose wheel out when the landing gear is down. To open it, in case of emergency, there was a red lever about six inches long on the center front underside of Pettit's table where he conducted his navigating. All he had to do was push down on the lever and it pulled the hinge pins to these two doors and then they were supposed to drop off the plane. He reached down among the flames and pushed the lever, nothing happened. He sat down and scooted onto the door, still nothing. He was moving directly into the fire. His heavy clothing protected him well, except for his left hand that was now, ungloved. His face and the top of the oxygen mask and the helmet also were now exposed to the fire.

Everyone has often heard the saying, "it's always the last thing you try that works," Pettit said. Time was running out and he would make one last try at opening those doors. He raised his feet as high as he could with those big ugly flying boots and brought them down as hard as he could on the doors. It worked; he was out. He hadn't unplugged his oxygen hose, electric suit cord or earphones from the plane. It made no difference now; he was on his way down in the wild blue yonder.

He remembered one was supposed to free fall to a low altitude before pulling the ripcord on the chute. They were at 22,000 feet. He didn't remember the rules however, and pulled the ripcord, but nothing happened. He was wearing a chest type of chute, easy to get at. A parachute has a little spring loaded chute, called a pilot chute, that is supposed to pop out, open, and drag the rest out behind it. He pulled that business out; the chute opened and when it did he simply tossed it into the air.

He then realized he had been negligent in adjusting his harness, especially where it fit in the crotch area. "I paid my dues," he said. Pain combined with fear, he got the dry heaves. Being up so high, the lack of oxygen didn't help the matter either. He remembered then that he opened his chute a little too soon. Looking at his watch it was 09:27. Later he learned that his plane had crashed at 09:30. By looking at his watch, maybe when he landed on the ground he would enter that time in his logbook, which was still on the plane, he added.

As he looked around, the clear sky, the quietness, "It was scary," he says. About 15,000 feet below him the sky was about 90% overcast. It took him about 10 minutes to descend to that point and about 3 minutes to get through it. When he broke through the clouds he figured he was about 3,000 feet off the ground, he could see everything clearly. As he drifted along a dirt road, he could see a wagon pulled by two scraggly white mules and a very old man and young boy sitting on the seat. They were completely unaware he was drifting above them.

He was jolted real well when he landed in a pasture. Luckily, he received no injuries from it. Now he would have other things on his mind than looking at his watch. A brisk wind added to his dilemma and the chute wanted to drag him. First he tried to crawl fast enough to catch up with the chute and pull on some shroud lines to collapse the thing. The ground was very hard but some cattle had made tracks in mud some time or another and he managed to place a heel in these cow tracks and finally able to stop. The pain in his burnt hand now was excruciating from trying to hold on to the chute, which was still full-blown. Little by little he was able to lunge at the lines and eventually dumped the chute.

He stood up, unhooked the chute and looked around. He saw a stand of trees and not a soul in sight. He grabbed the chute and headed for them. He tore off some material off the chute and made bandages for his hands. He knew his face was burnt but couldn't see the extent of it. He didn't know that the very next day his eyes would be swollen shut. He went ahead and hid the chute and decided it best to put his 45 pistol in it too. He no more than did this and a group of people were coming toward him. He was relieved to see that none of them were carrying a pitchfork or a club. He soon figured out they were Polish slave workers. One of them insinuated that if he had a pistol he wanted it. It didn't take them long to find it in the chute. Then they, along with Pettit headed for the road where he had seen the white mules and wagon shortly before. They motioned for him to follow. He couldn't speak their language.

It was only about a mile or two to a small village. Local authorities took over from there. He was taken to a private home and questioned but he couldn't communicate with them or they with him. "Even if I could have, I wouldn't have let them know it," he stated.

An old lady, who perhaps lived in the house came out with a bowl of what Pettit thought was butter and applied it to his burns. He thought it must have been butter because of the salt in it because it really stung when it hit his burnt flesh. She then reapplied the silk from his chute forming a bandage over his hands.

It took some time for them to figure out what to do with him. Based on what happened the next day, he assumed they were in communication with military authorities. Eventually he

185

was taken out in the street and an old man, whom he assumed was a civilian policemen was on a bicycle carrying a rifle, motioned down the street and motioned for him to get going. He was not aggressive but insistent. Pettit recalled what he had been instructed at the briefing concerning civilians so close to Berlin, hoping he would not be exposed to any of them.

Soon he found himself with a guard who marched him down a dirt road that turned out to be nothing more than a trail into a forest. It seemed now the forest was closing in on him. They came to a large log along the path and Pettit sat down on it too rest. He was in agonizing pain because of his burns. The guard, he could tell, didn't appreciate him sitting down. Pettit told him if he was going to shoot him, do it and get it over with. He felt he was not going to walk to a place of his choosing. Lucky for me, Pettit said, he didn't understand him.

The guard decided to let him rest a few minutes but looked at his watch every few minutes. After about 15 minutes the guard began making signs for him to get going but he was still not mean about it. Pettit finally got up and started down the road again which led to a narrow brick highway and they continued heading down it.

"It's strange what the mind will retain after 50 years," Pettit stated. When they were on the brick road, he remembers turning left. They were only on it for a short while and they came upon another road, which joined it from the right. Waiting at this corner was another guard with Walt Petersen, the radioman from his crew. He only had one shoe. It was common to lose a shoe when the chute opened. He joined Pettit on the rest of the trip cracking statements like, "we're not in Kansas anymore." Both Petersen and Pettit had the same dream of going home and getting married as soon as they got home. Eventually, they did, within days of each other with children born about a year later.

But for now, they must follow their new leaders. A car came down the road what looked like about a 1930 Plymouth coup. It was pulling a flat bed trailer with some kind of burner on it that was burning pine wood chips. A flexible tube; two or three inches in diameter ran all the way up to the engine. The car was running on whatever gas was generated by the wood chips. Pettit realized now that their efforts bombing the refiners must have done some good. Rarely did they know how successful they had been.

A German officer jumped out of the car and began asking questions in broken English they could barely understand. He had other information about other airmen shot down that morning and he was trying to put it all together. He was trying to figure the puzzle out as to which prisoners were members of the same crew and what plane they flew on. The officer had one name in mind and tended to focus on it and was trying to find him. He asked several times about a Lieutenant Major and Pettit kept telling him that our Air Force had lieutenants and majors but no lieutenant majors. In reality, the plane crew did have a Lt. Major along with them that day working as a co-pilot. He was a substitute when the regular co-pilot was ill and in the hospital. They later found out that Lt. Major had hit his head when he exited the plane and his chute didn't open. This was probably why the officer wanted to know which plane he had bailed out of. One has to wonder how they could tell what had happened to him after he had fallen four miles and hit the ground at such a tremendous speed Pettit remarked.

The German officer continued with his interrogations. Pettit noted a vest this guy wore was different and unique. It was covered from top to bottom with three or four rows of pouches each filled with colored pencils. It looked like he had at least a hundred of them or more. Pettit and Walt concluded he must have been an intelligence officer probably involved in mapping and used the pens as some sort of color code. He is not certain however but that could have been possible.

The German officer seemed to be in a hurry. After he obtained little or no information from his captives he was rather disturbed. He stomped back to his car and left. Pettit and Walt continued on their way.

The pain in Pettits hands was becoming unbearable. With many layers of clothes on, he was getting rather warm too. He got the idea that perhaps the silk on his wounds was shutting the air out so he removed his makeshift bandages. Looking at the burns he saw no blisters. It was worse than that. The skin just rolled up in hard ridges along the side of his wrists and fingers and whenever they were touched or rubbed against something, it was pain. He solved the problem by biting the ridges off with his front teeth as they walked along. The burns continued up his wrist to the wool cuffs on the coat he was wearing. Looking at the cuff, it looked normal but crumbled when he touched them. The collar was the same all due to the intense heat from the fire.

The road soon intersected with the German highway known as the Autobahn. As they turned the corner to begin a long walk on the Autobahn, he noted a sign, which named the next town. He translated that into being about 20 miles away. Later he learned, at a reunion in Texas in 1990; the name of the town was Ludwigslust. Miraculously they made it there at the time.

Upon arrival in this town, they were loaded up in trucks and taken to the other side of town and then they had to walk again. Pettit believes they were hauled through town so they wouldn't be exposed to civilians there. As they walked to a pine forest they noted at both sides of the highway there were holes dug about two feet in diameter and about four feet deep with dirt piled up around them. Personnel used them when bombers like the planes Pettit was on would strafe the highway. They would quickly jump into these holes and avoid the bomb fragments.

About a mile from the forest was a German airbase snuggled into the trees. The only clearing was the runway. Even the planes were parked in the trees. After seeing this Pettit doesn't remember what happened next. He knows the Germans dressed his wounds with some sort of crepe paper looking bandages and applied something that took a lot of the pain away. His face was bandaged with only peepholes for his eyes to see out. His eyelids must have blistered he said because by morning they were swollen shut. His right hand, even though he still had the heavy glove on when he bailed out through the fire, also had third degree burns. He had used it to reach down in the flames to pull the release handle for the emergency escape hatch. Pettit admits as he wrote this documentation in April of 1995, fatigue, shock and fifty years played games with his memory that time.

They were placed in a cell, which Pettit describes as being only about 8-9 feet square; no windows, just a little peephole in the door about an inch across. No furniture except an iron cot with wires fastened to the sides with springs attached. They had no bedding and Pettit felt alone, frightened and in great pain from his wounds. He was told there would not be any food served until the next morning when the mess hall opened up. When they brought it, it was nothing more than a broth of some sort with a chunk of black hard bread about the size of his fist. He soaked it in the broth to soften it. He still has the big aluminum spoon with the swastika on the handle. Meals were served only once or twice a day and always the same menu.

In this prison like environment were other airmen who had been captured. Charlie Cupp was already there. He was the sole survivor of a plane that was blown in half mentioned earlier. He had landed in the town of Ludwigslust. Also the crew waist gunner, Virgil Beall, had arrived about the same time Pettit did, but not with him.

The Germans took three or four of their prisoners into town three nights in a row hoping to load them on a train destined for POW camp farther north. Our Air Force had worked over the trains and rail yards so much that nothing was moving. As they sat there waiting, guards informed them to be very quiet as many civilians were also in the train station. They were told to not laugh or point their fingers at anything. Pettit, with his sight coming back, saw posters on the wall of the train station depicting the fate of allied airmen coming down by parachute. Civilians with pitchforks and clubs were killing them as they hit the ground.

Upon occasion, Pettit recalls, riding in a cart with hay in the bottom pulled by a mule. A guard was sitting across the wooden seat driving; another was riding in the back with the four other prisoners, including Pettit.

After he had been in Ludwigslust, which was about 100 miles northeast of Berlin, for about a week, they were loaded in a truck. It was a slow lumbering type of vehicle covered like a covered wagon with hard rubber tires. He believes they must have crossed the Elb River on a railroad bridge. Planks had been laid between and beside the rails so trucks could cross it. They arrived at another air base which turned out to be Stendal, about sixty miles west of Berlin and only about five or six miles west of the Elb River.

They were told they would be going to an interrogation center, which were nothing more than a brick house, for questioning. Hangers and German fighter planes were parked on the grounds. Other prisoners were also there, about forty of them. Among them was four of the crew Pettit was with. The pilot, Jim Shafter, nose gunner, Bill Kaiser, Jerry Kearney Jr.,

189

who operated equipment to jam German radar, and the engineer and turret gunner, Dan Graham.

The highest-ranking officer at this place was Colonel Trop Crawford the commanding officer of the 446th Bomb Group, one of the three groups in Pettits combat wing. Crawford should never have been there, but he was. He had been flying in British mosquito coordinating bomb groups. When the German fighters attacked, his plane flew in close to the 446th bomb squadron thinking it would be safer. Pettit doesn't think so, as the Germans would seldom fire at the mosquito because it resembled their own fighters. That was the problem. B-24's thought he was a German fighter and shot both his engines off. That's how he ended up a POW.

This air base was a prime target for the allies; Crawford had confirmed that. One day our P-51 and P-47 fighters made a raid on the base strafing the area real hard trying to do some damage to German planes that were parked there. Fifty-caliber bullets began to ricochet off the concrete flying every which direction. They came through the windows in this brick house they were in. They clutched steam radiators used for heating that lined the walls under the windows. The plaster wall on the opposite side of the room was riddled. Plaster dust was everywhere and the noise resembled a high-powered rifle firing next to your ear. Fortunately no one was injured but like he says, "some toilet paper may have come in handy after it was all over." These air strikes by our own people continued for the next few days. Meals didn't get served and the situation didn't get any better.

Now it was Pettit's turn to be interrogated. They walked him over to another building like the one he had been in, only a few houses from them. He looked up at the roof of one and saw what was left of one our fighters. It had flown into a house. The house had a tile roof and the plane knocked the ridge off the width of the wing span with a deeper gouge made by the fuselage.

"I have always felt the interrogation was subtle but a deliberate act of torture. They removed his bandages as if to doctor his hands and face. They applied something on his wounds that immediately caused excruciating pain. The longer it was there, the worse the pain. He was put in a room with no windows and the door was closed for what seemed like hours. Then someone came in and took him to an office with a major sitting behind the desk. He spoke excellent English. He had attended school in the United States. He asked many questions about the crew, the plane and the targets, which they might have hit. He didn't get any answers that would do him any good. He insinuated that the American Air Force was "a bunch of hired killers from mobs in the big cities." He would not discuss, however, what the Germans had done in many cities of Europe and England they had bombed.

After they "danced" around a while the Major grew tired of it and released Pettit to go to the dispensary for better treatment. A so-called doctor put something on his hands and face that made his wounds feel much better. He wrapped his left hand with more paper bandages. The other wounds were left open as he recalls.

When he got back to "jail," things started happening. Word was that the Americans were heading for the base, which was only a short distance away. The Germans were thinking of evacuating but pondered what to do with the prisoners. Shooting them was considered and orders were given as such. Some prisoners like Shafter, Kaiser and Graham were taken to another POW camp at Barth. Altogether, ten men were sent there.

Pettit and the others were ordered to leave the air base along with two German guards. The plan was that the guards would take them to be liberated with the guards receiving preferential treatment when they were captured. The men were given Red Cross packages and Pettit wondered why they weren't given these before with the food being in such short supply. He questioned the fact that they were going to be liberated too.

They crossed a plowed field what appeared to have been recently planted to rutabagas or something. A small shed and a railroad track ran next to the field. They sought shelter in the shed, all thirty prisoners, with the guards waiting outside the door. It was crowded. The shed appeared to be a barn where horses were kept. It didn't have a door that closed, just an opening. Between the odor of the deluxe floor covering and thirty unwashed bodies huddled together on a warm day, "It was not the same as a room in the Hilton" Pettit comments.

They got water from a small ditch, not a stream, behind the railroad track. During the day the ration of food was dolled out and consumed. Pettit recalls that all the food was put into one pot, boiled and made into a gruel of sorts.

There were a few cigarettes, some in the Red Cross boxes, two in a box. They were placed in a pool; one was lit and passed around so everyone could get a drag off of it. Walt Petersen, always at Pettit's side, got one of the butts about a half-inch long. He placed a straw in it and puffed on one corner until it burned his lips. They could hear the war going on around them.

That night Walt and Pettit sat in the darkness with their backs to a wall. Exhausted, Pettit fell asleep. The next morning Walt shook him to awaken him. From the way he shook him, Pettit says he must have been really out of it. Pettit had been unwrapping his hand and already had several layers unwound and that was the reason Walt had roused him. The hand was really causing trouble now. It was infected and there was nothing that could be done for it.

On the morning of April 13, 1945, gunfire could still be heard the same as the day before. The group was now, you could tell he said, loosing their hopelessness and fatalistic attitudes. Everyone realized they might soon be getting out of this predicament. "We wanted to live," he said.

They could hear the rumblings of armored vehicles in the distance but could not see anything. The usual foot traffic on the railroad tracks was still evident when the Germans were moving away from the advancing Russians and toward the Americans. The Germans had no where to go.

An FW 190 German fighter flew over their location very low. They weren't too concerned as it was doubtful the pilot knew there were Americans by the shed and they all stood there watching him. It flew over a dense patch of forest between the shack and the road. As it flew over a clearing, about a quarter mile from them, it was fired upon. They could see the shell bursts. Pettit doesn't think they shot him down however. Soon a tank appeared from the trees, more tanks and armored vehicles. Someone took a white rag on a stick and walked out to the column. Soon an ambulance also was on the scene. The first thing they heard was the fact President Roosevelt had died, April 12, 1945. It was not until years later; that Pettit learned the group had camped by the shack that night and had started back from the front the next day. Three or four of them were taken by the ambulance for treatment to a field hospital that had been set up at Stendal, only 2-3 miles away.

The room at the field hospital was quite large with a bed, chair and a small table that held the medical supplies. The medic or doctor told Pettit to lay on the bed but he preferred sitting in the chair. He insisted he lay down and informed him, "this is going to be a ripe one, I can smell it," the medic stated. When he cut the bandage with his scissors, Pettit knew what he meant. He immediately was given a shot of Penicillin in the rump; his rotting hand was cleaned, then soaked, salved and bandaged. For the next two weeks he would receive a penicillin shot every four hours as part of the daily routine.

Later, in the night, Pettit, along with others who were taken to a hospital in Hanover, Germany, about 150-200 miles away, traveled all night totally in black out conditions. Although the United States had pretty well been through the area, it was not secure. A roadblock could be present at any time they were told. Fortunately, the trip went without incident. The ground troops had done a good job.

It was well after daylight when they arrived in Hanover, a large city, with 10-15 story buildings, stood as hollow shells or lay in ruin. The once wide streets were piled with rubble from fallen structures. The German hospital, which the Americans had taken over, had not been destroyed. Pettit was wheeled into this hospital on a narrow gurney and parked in the hall where doctors and attendants were rushing around. He laid there for what seemed to be a very long time. A Salvation Army person came and visited with him. She informed him he could send a short cablegram home telling his family he was safe. He did, addressing it to his wife to be, Yvonne, and his parents. "What a great feeling of relief," he said. His family had already been informed that he was MIA, missing in action.

He thinks what happened next must have been a moral booster. Some officer came up to him with his "Purple Heart" and a document stating how and where he earned it. He had no place to put it, but remembers it showed up with the rest of his personal belongings including the spoon he had taken to eat the so called soup.

Then he finally got his turn to visit the doctors. In a one pound Folgers coffee can there were strips of gauze covered with a substance that looked like Vaseline. It had been poured over the gauze hot and allowed to cool. His hand was laid completely flat and covered with these saturated strips. Then it was covered with a shredded substance that looked like cotton waste. When they finished wrapping his hand, it was the size of a football. He was still getting shots in his rump. His right hand was also bandaged somewhat but nothing like the left. His face was healing well and the doctor confirmed that he was lucky to have gotten proper treatment when he did.

Now treated, he boarded an ambulance to go to an airport in Paderborn, Germany, for a flight back to England. Paderborn, unlike Hanover, did not have bombed out buildings still standing. Everything was totally flattened. He was told the Germans had put up stiff resistance here so the American lined up their tanks around it and shelled it into submission rather than send combat soldiers in to try to make it one building at a time. No mercy was shown on this town.

Many POW had to go through a "delousing" time. Pettit was no different. He recalls it probably took place after he got back to England. As your turn came around you stripped your clothes and left them. Then you went into a room and you were dusted well by a couple of guys spraying you with this powder with some kind of blower. Then you had to take a hot shower and were given new clothes. Where the Purple Heart and spoon was at this time, he doesn't know. They showed up again later.

He wrote Yvonne and his parents from the hospital in England, via a "V" letter informing them he was back in England and should be coming home soon. "Soon, would be longer than I thought," he said.

A doctor would come in and see him a couple times a day, unwrap his hand to see how it was doing. The doctor was quick to let Pettit know that taking care of his hand was his business, not Pettits. He did not need Pettit telling him what to do!

Pettit contacted his base by telephone informing them of what had taken place, giving them the status of other crewmembers, which were standard operations. What Pettit could never figure out was the fact that back home his parents received a message from the War Department on the 21st of April, he was still MIA. The military knew very well on the 15th, he had been liberated.

On he 18th, he had received a letter from Yvonne informing him that on Friday the 13th, was her lucky day. She had gotten a pay raise. It brightened his day. Now all of his belongings, including her picture, toothbrush and shaving kit were with him.

The doctor took off his bandages on the 17th and he informed Yvonne that everything was healing well with only scabs now on his eyebrows and no scars would present. His left hand was healing, but still a little tender. He still had to soak it about 30 minutes a day in Epson salts water three times a day. He was given a soft rubber ball to squeeze to regain movement in his hand and fingers. His knuckles would crack and bleed but it had to be done.

On the 20th, a buddy, John Paxton, came to visit Pettit bringing along five letters from Yvonne and one from her mother. The visit from him, along with the letters and the pictures, "were the best thing that could have happened to me," he said.

On January 14-15th, Pettit had written Yvonne telling her how much he loved her and asked her if she would accept an engagement ring. He didn't get an answer until February 16, over a month later. Her answer was, "I would love to have your ring. What did you think I would say?" She was probably thinking, what took him so long Pettit said. Pettit had saved a couple hundred dollars and sent her a blank check to buy the ring with.

On April 1, he got a two-day pass form the hospital to go back to his base. He was given a key to go to the MIA room where things were stored to be shipped back home that belonged to these unfortunate individuals. There he found more clothes. He went to the post office and picked up 21 letters from Yvonne dated from April 1st to the 23rd, five more from home and six or eight others.

At the base he visited with the squadron navigator, the boss, and he asked Pettit if he would like a picture of his plane after it had been hit and left the formation. A person, whose specific job it was to take pictures, had one and Pettit now has it.

On March 20th, Pettit received word from Yvonne that their pending wedding was now official. The engagement notice was published in the Lincoln paper. He was floating on cloud nine, anxious to get home and marry his sweetheart. He rested with the knowledge too that he didn't have to fly anymore. But nothing is ever that simple he says. It wasn't until May 8th he received his shipping orders.

It was VE Day, Victory in Europe; the war had ended. The lights in the heart of London were turned on for the first time in four years. Piccadilly and Circuit streets were full of excitement. This area is like Times Square is to New York. He was to report to the Red Cross there. The city was absolutely wild! It took a few more days and finally he was leaving for San Antonio, Texas where he would have leave. Pettit didn't want to go there. He wanted to go to Nebraska. They changed his destination to Fort Leavenworth instead. Unfortunately, he would have to wait longer if he wanted to go to Kansas. He told them to leave it the way it was then and he would go to Texas. But no, it was now to late for that. He would have to wait.

On around the 17th of May, he was told a ship was leaving for the states. When they read the list of men's names off, no one bothered to look back at the order. He just answered, "Hear," grabbed his duffel bag and the bus heading for the ship. He left England on the 18th. When he was on the ship, for the third day, his name came over the loud speaker for him to report to the office. When he got there they had a copy of the shipping orders for the group he was with and then they informed him he was not supposed to be on this particular ship at all. "For once, I wasn't intimidated at all," he said. He asked an officer who far outranked him, if he was going to turn the ship around and take him back realizing this gesture could have gotten him into lots of trouble. But, the officer went along with him considering its humor and told him, "that would be all."

The ship was a Norwegian luxury liner turned over to the United States and was converted to a troop ship like many were in those days. It had over 4,000 passengers aboard, several times the number it was designed to carry and all were liberated POW's.

With so many passengers, only about two meals were served a day. But it was good food. They ate at round tables and had their own waiter, which was a switch. The dining room was beautiful and it indeed was a luxury ship.

He doesn't remember arriving at New York harbor in the late afternoon of May 29th. He does recall the short trip by bus to Camp Shanks, New York, in time for the evening meal. T-bone steaks french fries, and all the trimmings, including pie and ice cream. No one dished it up, you just kept going back for more if you wanted to he said.

Then it was a mad dash for a telephone where long lines waited to use one. He called Yvonne and informed her he would be heading to Texas instead of Kansas. He also called his parents and told them when he got to San Antonio he would board a bus and head for Lincoln, Nebraska. ASAP! But after his parents had time to think about the decision, they traveled to San Antonio and picked him up. There was no way they could tell him they would do this and he missed them. He had to go to Fort Sam Houston and do his paperwork. For once the military did something unusual, at least when it came to paperwork. They did it in a hurry and arranged for his leave. He headed for Lincoln and Yvonne. Sindt, was her maiden name.

When Pettit arrived, Yvonne had no idea as to when he would be coming. She was out shopping for the wedding. The bus stopped a half block from her house. She always rode the bus, except for this time; she came home in a taxi. Yvonne saw Pettit and didn't bother to pay the driver, so her mother paid him. Pettit and his future wife had their reunion on the sidewalk west of the house on Sheldon Street. One week later they were married on a Sunday afternoon, June 10th, 1945 in a Presbyterian Church in Lincoln.

Lt. Pettit knows of seven other crewmembers that got of the burning plane that dreadful day. Other planes noted 10 parachutes opening. "We only counted nine," he recalls. It is possible, 2 or 3 of the crewmembers died landing, no one knows. Perhaps their fate will never be known. Civilians or SS officials may have killed them; it was not uncommon later in the war. Wherever they are it is our hope that they rest in peace knowing what they did for our country was not in vain!

And so concludes the life and times of this fine veteran during times of war. Thank you Lt. Pettit, for this fine summary of your experiences, and most of all for helping provide us with the freedom to write about it.

PEIRCE, NORMAN A.

Peirce is a WW II veteran from Red Cloud and he still wonders how his parents coped with having four sons in the war. It must have been hard on them. Two of his brothers served in France. One in the same division as he only after Norman had returned home. Another brother trained for the paratroopers but never had to leave the states. Norman, is the only one who is still among us. He is very active in the local

VFW and American Legion and serves as Chaplain for over 50 years. "I have said the last words at over 114 veterans," he said.

Peirce was with "I" Company, 1st Bn., 180th Regt. 45th "Thunderbird" Division on the Anzio Beachhead south of Rome in early 1944. He served in close combat in a weapons platoon against the Germans who outnumbered them four to one.

On one occasion, he and a buddy were assigned to a listening patrol. Bear in mind that the Germans were only about 100 yards away from the front. Peirce was one of those who had to sneak up to them and try to gain some information. This time, they heard a noise. His buddy whispered to him asking what that was? Peirce told him it was heavy breathing of some Germans who were also on a listening patrol. That was close!

The assault on Anzio beachhead lasted 120 days. 8,972 men died there for freedom. Incidentally, that calculates out at 739 men a day who died in battle. A time, Peirce does not like to recall. After 51 days, where Peirce was involved fighting along side those other soldiers with him, only 7 of his platoon of 51 survived. Peirce was put in a hospital because of injuries he sustained. Besides his Sgt., there were 5 Cherokee Indian boys along with Peirce. Today, only Peirce and his Sgt. Cuano, are still alive at this writing. Peirce finally located Cuano and keeps in contact with him who lives in Massachusetts. Most all the others died within two years after the war of wounds they sustained in battle.

After he returned home, he became involved in a new interest which he has pursued all his life. I wondered if those five Cherokee's didn't play a part it. I called him and he verified my suspicions, they did indeed. Peirce wound up in the hospital during the war and those five young braves came to visit him. He made them a promise, in spite they warned him not to, as white men don't keep promises. But Peirce told them that when he got home he was going to try to do something for them. They smiled, not believing him. They reminded him that short of being the President of the United States, there was little he could do.

Peirce has become a noted historian on the American Indian, a vital part of our nation's history. He has written several books about them, all very interesting. He is keeping his promise, reminding the white men what the American

Indian has been through and how the white men dealt them a raw deal. He has been teaching young and old alike the ways of the American Indian. He knows Indian sign language and at his many speaking engagements concludes with the 23 Psalm speaking with his hands. He especially helps with the Boy Scouts teaching them crafts and focuses on feather art. His artwork is exhibited in 48 states and 29 countries. I would say, he has kept his promise.

He is reminded of the words of Chief Red Cloud, of which his hometown is named after. Speaking of the white man, the great chief stated, "They made us many promises, they kept only one. They promised to take our land and they took it."

Peirce was in the grocery business before the war, sold it, lost a lot of money, but felt obligated to fight for his country. When he returned he started up again and later sold it too because of the stress it was causing. His doctor advised him to sell out or he would end up in the graveyard. He chose a less stressful life as janitor of the school and retired from that job in 1990.

He informed me that for about four years after the war he would have nightmares concerning things he had went through. Then it more or less left him. Now that he retired, he says he has too much time to think about it and the days at war are in his mind again, except for the nightmares. He understands veterans, especially of the Vietnam war, who complain of this. "It's real," he said. Unless one has been through war, one can't imagine what it was like. "You never get over it," he concluded.

QUIMBY, D. M. (BING)

Quimby is from South Sioux City, Nebraska. I received his book in the mail and he put a note in it telling me I should page through the book and pick out what I wanted to use. The name of the book is "One of the Last," an autobiography of the life of Quimby. He calls the portion in the book concerning his life in the service to his country, "The greatest part of the book." He admits, it may not be as interesting as many combat vets can tell but these were his experiences.

Because of his documentation of his ordeal in the armed forces, for informational purposes I will attempt to describe what it was like and what he felt like at the time he was drafted. I will note the trip as well as his return home so the reader can, hopefully, get a picture of what these young men went through. The anxieties of leaving home, some for the first time. The pain of leaving their loved ones. The frustration when one's life is interrupted by war.

Quimby is proud he was one of the last engineers to operate a steam locomotive. Trains were his life, with the exception of his wife Ardyce and his family. He loved them. Beginning as a young locomotive fireman, he watched as the big change was made when the trains were switched from steam to diesel.

Like so many young men, Quimby had a job and a girlfriend when WW II broke out. He didn't want to go. He admits he was scared, and that was not unusual for these young men. He was thinking of marriage and joining the army at $20 a month didn't sound like much money. He went to the local draft board after he got his draft notice. He told them he had just gotten a job as a second class fireman and wanted to be promoted to first class before he went to the army. He didn't think the plan would work; but it did. They gave him a thirty-day deferment.

Now, with thirty days left, he would have to make the best of it, especially with his girl, Ardyce. He was crazy about her, and the more he was around her, the more he realized what a sharp and ambitious girl she was. The couple continued having fun until December 7, 1941, when they heard the news that the Japanese had raided Pearl Harbor. "We knew then, the good life was over." He recalls. He figured he would have to go almost immediately. He was wrong, matter of fact, he later learned, that when war breaks out, the U.S. literally has to prepare millions of people. That takes time and planning. It wasn't until March of 1942 that he received one of those letters thousands of young men did in those years, "Greetings. Your friends and neighbors had selected you to go into the army," he said.

Quimby recalls being shipped out of South Sioux City with about forty other guys, most of them he knew. He was on the first busload bound for entry into WW II. He wondered how many would be returning home again as they waved to the crowd of well wishers, parents, sweethearts and others. Several years later, he learned that two of the forty did not return home.

He said going to the army didn't bother him as much as leaving Ardyce. "I was really feeling low," he said. While the other men felt like partying, he didn't feel like it. He missed his girl.

There was no getting off, so down the rails he rode on the Burlington train number 26 until their arrival in Omaha. From there he went to Beverly, Missouri and then on a bus to Fort Leavenworth, Kansas. By then there were many drunken young men on the bus. Some became a little mouthy and uncontrollable. Army personnel paid them little attention and sent the group to bed in their quarters. At 4 a.m. they were told to dress and get ready for breakfast. One guy noted, "We didn't get up to milk the cows at home that early," the young farm boy declared.

After breakfast, they took physicals, some shots, a written test and were issued clothes. "It seemed odd we were all dressed alike. I had trouble recognizing my old buddies," he said.

When the group was taking their oath to serve their country, three of the men instead of saying "yes," said "no." It was distracting to Quimby and the others. When the oath was finished, the soldier who administered it went to the three men and said they were in the army anyway and if they had a problem with that they should go see the chaplain.

After supper that night, Quimby had some free time. Of course he had to call his girl, Ardyce. That made him extremely lonely. He went to the PX and had a couple 3.2 beers with the boys and then went to bed. He was awakened again at 4 a.m. and told he was on KP duty. Now he had pots and pans to wash. He learned that was a job that was never done. It seemed like the cooks prepared food 24 hours a day. There were always dishes to wash. At 10 p.m. he wondered if he would ever be relieved of his job.

About that time, a soldier came in and ordered him to drop everything because he was shipping out. He went to his quarters, changed clothes and gathered his belongings and loaded on a bus for Kansas City. There, he and a few of his buddies were loaded on a train headed for Los Angeles. It was a real nice train, luxury, it even had a barber shop and showers he said. It was an enjoyable trip he added.

When they arrived in Los Angeles, they were put on another train and headed for Camp San Luis Obispo. He ended up there in the quarter master corps. Like most draftees, they feared getting shot in the infantry. The QMC didn't excite him too much either he said.

Then he was told to put on a mechanic's outfit and then he wished he were in the infantry. "I didn't think I could do much for the war as a mechanic," he said. He later found out that he had scored real well in mechanics, thus the reasoning behind that.

Quimby says he ended up lucky, although he didn't realize it at the time. He didn't have to have the thorough basic training that the others did. It was later, however that basic training was required by all draftees.

He was assigned to a peacetime company on detached service from their battalion, which was headquartered at Fort Halebird, Maryland. The big "A" patch on their sleeves meant they were with the 1st Army. They were sent to the West Coast to repair army vehicles, to bolster the West Coast defenses. He was involved with a group of people that was "As military as it could be," he said. The 20-year veteran first sergeant loved the army and loved his job. To Quimby and the rest of the recruits, "He was about the meanest man we ever knew," he states.

A buck sergeant out of the company gave them some basic training. He ran them over hills, took them on long hikes, and gave them field inspections and other "Boy Scout" stuff Quimby writes. "One has to be in the army awhile to see the value of it all. My mind was still back home with Ardyce."

After three weeks of marching over hills, it was time for a driver's examination. He knew that standing inspection was bad enough let alone getting a truck ready for inspection too, so he deliberately flunked the eye test. That prevented him from getting a military driver's license. They put, "Not fit to drive a military vehicle" on his record, but he got a truck anyway. They packed up their trucks and headed to Los Angeles in a convoy. Some of the time they spent drilling him when they should have been teaching him to drive a truck he said. In Compton, near Los Angeles, they were put in a high school gym where they were ordered to be very careful so nothing was damaged. They set up portable shops in the schoolyard and basic training continued when they were hauled out into the country.

The rifle range was next. Quimby had done some hunting back home but didn't consider himself to be a good shot. He did well and won a cartoon of cigarettes as a prize and finally had something good to write Ardyce about. He said he really didn't shoot that well. It was just the fact that all the other's shot very poorly.

At the rifle range they still used the old war rifles and other WW I equipment. The M-1 rifle was being manufactured but it would take a while to get them to everyone involved.

Quimby didn't like where he was at all and wished he were somewhere else. Perhaps the infantry would have been better he kept thinking. He was now a full-fledged mechanic and a soldier. Unexpected inspections, sometimes at 2 a.m., got to be old stuff. He wasn't happy but then he thought and decided that he wouldn't have been happy anywhere because he had so much at home. Because the West Coast was on alert, passes were hard to come by. They worked seven days a week. He didn't like some of the men. Regular army guys weren't too bad, but some resented the way the army was changing. They didn't like the new type of ROTC officers. To them, they didn't know as much as they did. You could almost see the first sergeant burn, as he had to salute a young college kid with ROTC behind him.

Things improved somewhat when he learned that Ardyce was planning to come and visit him. Wow, that was great. She had a brother in Los Angeles to visit, too. He would have to be on his best behavior or there would be no pass to spend some time with her. Fortunately, it all worked out and they were able to talk, neck and yes, make plans for their wedding day, which would be only a week away.

The Army, fearful of a Japanese attack on the West Coast, would make it difficult to acquire an overnight pass to spend on his honeymoon. He would have to see the CO, which he dreaded to do. The CO would have to give him the pass and fortunately, yet grudgingly, he did. He gave him orders about the fact that he must change his marital status at the company clerk.

He found a Presbyterian chaplain and they were married in a Presbyterian Church. Ardyce had gone to the dime store and picked out a ten-cent ring that she was most proud of. She had registered at the local hotel as his wife, because she felt that would look better as they went in and out of their room together prior to the wedding. A doctor, who had given her the blood test for the license took a liking to her and he and his wife picked them up that day and showed them the sites and then to their beautiful home and lovely garden. They had a Japanese gardener who had been taken away to an internment camp suspected of being involved with the enemy, Japan.

The wedding took place and plenty of buddies even showed up for the event. He offered the organist $10 but she stated, she never charged a soldier more than five. Quimby was glad, because ten was about all he had. A reception was held and after spending only one night together, he would have to return to base and Ardyce had to go back home to her job. Maybe not seeing each other for a long time.

In July of 1942, the soldiers received a pay raise. From $21 per month to a whopping $50 per month. Now that Quimby was married, his wife would receive $25 of it so he found himself $4 ahead. But that was fine. He never went anywhere. He would have a few beers with boys until the money was gone and that would be the end of that. One nice thing was that their letters were now postage free.

After a short while, Quimby was transferred to the head office of the Military Railway Service at St. Paul, Minnesota. He later found out that one of his buddies had arranged it to which he was very glad. He now headed for Camp Claiborne, Louisiana to the 711th Railroad Operating Battalion Engineers and then to Texas to Fort Worth to Alexandria, the closest town to Camp Claiborne.

It didn't take long before the 711th received orders to be shipped overseas. They were the first railway battalion activated during WW II. He eventually found himself standing in Brooklyn, New York, waiting to board a ship to take him overseas. The ship was the USS West Point, originally the USS America, a luxury liner converted into a troop carrier. They were packed in like sardines Quimby recalls. For three weeks they didn't see land. He ate a lot of baked beans and rutabagas, which he didn't care for but it was, eat or go hungry. When he came on to ship he had a quarter in his pocket which he turned into $5 in a crap game. If it hadn't been for the fact he could buy himself a few candy bars, he would have been in bad shape he said. It was boring on the ship with nothing to do but play cards and read.

They were finally informed they would end up in Iran. Aboard an old ship called the HMS Rhona, which was sunk by German subs in November of 1943, loosing 1,200 American men, it was roomy and not as cramped up as they were on the USS West Point. The British manned it and they were served British food.

Finally, on Dec. 12, 1942, they arrived at Khorramshaha, Iran. They marched a couple miles to an area where they were to set up camp. It was nothing more than a muddy field. Here they were to set up their pup tents and wade around in mud half way up to their knees. They griped, but there was nothing they could do. It was wet and clothes were hard to dry out, especially when there was no wood to make a fire to help with the drying process. Wood was worth money. The Natives would carry off crating that accumulated at the docks as fast it arrived. Everyone needed firewood.

The food was not good either. Eating British food didn't agree with him. Mutton stew wasn't too bad but the beans and some sort of bacon with it didn't agree with him. He became sick, not sure if it was the food or some sort of flu. After heaving everything up he had eaten, he felt better in a few days.

During the Hitler days, the Germans moved into Iran, with the permission of the Shah. The German's goal was to modernize the country. They built railroads, buildings and bridges. But just prior to WW II, the British, who controlled most of the Middle East, became concerned that the Germans were building up too much of a stronghold in Iran and Iraq, so they drove them out. The Iranians always liked the Germans, however. Even though they had taken the Shah's money, they had created jobs for the people. They disliked the British and thought all American's were rich so they jacked up prices for everything they figured they would be buying. Beggar's lined the streets everywhere.

Working out of Ahwaz, a town of about 40,000, Quimby worked at the rail yards. He operated trains and the yard switching operations. Later he was an engineer on locomotives traveling around the countryside hauling troops to their destination.

It was February of 1943 when the diesel powered trains came. They used a four-cycle engine of 600 horsepower. Turbocharged they would crank 1000 horsepower Quimby said. Along with the diesel, came the 762 Diesel Shop Battalion to do maintenance on them. Several other battalions were now in Iran performing their duties at the railroad end of the war.

The train Quimby was involved with usually pulled about 70 cars going north and around 100 going south. Northbound trains were the heaviest loaded with all sorts of supplies and war-related materials.

Once loaded, without air brakes, the entire train could back down into the hole where the quarry was located. He hooked on to the cars, made it out but then there was a sharp incline headed downhill after that. He thought if he could hold the train to a creep, he would have it under control at the bottom of the hill holding it with just the brakes on the 1000 HP. diesel.

Upon at least one occasion, Quimby had some anxious moments. They were ordered to pick up about 20 cars loaded with ballast and gravel at the local quarries about two miles south of Andemeshk. Quimby knew his train had no air brakes. He advised the dispatcher of the matter and was told that three other trains had the same excuse. He needed the ballast moved. "I hated to tell him no," Quimby said, so he went ahead knowing it would be risky without a train equipped with air brakes. He was the engineer and would be responsible for getting stopped down a six-mile long hill down into the quarry. He had taken 10 cars out once without air brakes and thought maybe he could that with 20 cars.

He cut off the engine as he entered the quarry and began down into its bottom. He had second thoughts about his decision. The quarry was nothing more than an open pit dug out of gravel and the tracks had been lowered to run along the edge. When the cars were coupled to the engine, one had to be sure that the engine was capable of pulling them out of the pit area. This time, Quimby barely made it.

Once out of the pit, another incline had to be taken to get back to the station. It was too steep for the engine brakes alone and Quimby knew that. But there he was, doing it anyway. He felt if he held the train into a creep, he would still have control at the bottom of the hill. The train continued to pick up speed and faster by the minute. Quimby assumed the worst would happen and that one of his buddies may be coming in on another train loaded with black powder and it would be all over for them all.

He remembered seeing a hand brake sometimes on certain ballast cars. He turned the control over to his buddy, Winey, as he called him. Quimby made his way back and found no cars with a hand brake, unfortunately. But some cars had center dumps, so in a last effort to slow the train down, he opened some gates causing the ballast to fall, which caused the car to drag over it and slowed down the entire train. "It was pretty good braking," he said. At the bottom of the hill he had fifteen of the ballast cars empty and Winey had control of the train.

A lot of fellows felt Quimby should have gotten a medal for his quick thinking but he did not. But one thing for certain, the trains that hauled ballast after that, had air brakes. Quimby had made his point.

Water was an important commodity in this foreign land. Very precious! A water bag holding about three quarts was hardly enough. Soldiers carrying their canteens had hardly enough to get them out of the rail yards on some days when the temperatures in the desert reached 150-160 degrees. Nights often didn't cool down too less than 100 degrees. Sleeping was difficult because of the intense heat and there was no air conditioning at the barracks.

As steam engine trains passed through small towns and villages, the local women would rush out with buckets and pots to collect hot water to wash their clothes with. All that needed to be done was open the injector steam valve and catch some boiling water. Sometimes they would use the water for tea by putting tea leaves in the water in little pots. When the diesel engines would come through town, townsfolk didn't always know the difference. Thinking they could get hot water, there was none. Quimby said they couldn't understand that and would stand there and argue about it.

It has been said that prostitution is the "Oldest Profession." In Iran, it was no different. Quimby is proud he remained faithful but many, including officers and "Men of the cloth," chaplains, did not he says. Though it often struck him odd that these chaplains from virtually every denomination, acted as an ordinary soldier; drinking, talking, singing and chasing loose girls. He couldn't criticize them however, because Quimby did not know what some of these guys had been through in Italy. Even the priests, had to be cheating on somebody he added.

Most of the prostitutes were infected with various types of venereal disease. Ninety percent of them were syphilitic. Battalion doctors gave them frequent examinations. Soldiers were constantly given lectures on VD but it didn't seem to help much he said.

Quimby was aware that young men who in some way or another had avoided the draft were also tempting his wife at home. She was lonely too and was probably getting tired of staying at home all the time. But they had decided to keep themselves for each other, and Quimby, although the temptations were often quite strenuous, he remained faithful to Ardyce.

Quimby and some of his buddies got well acquainted with three of them named, Susie, Mary and Marie. They would board the train and visit other towns as well. These girls were different to some extent and just enjoyed being around them visiting, eating some American food and enjoying the company. They reminded him of some girls in the states he had met over the years.

Later, about a year or so, Quimby said he read in a newspaper where three Persian girls were picked up in Greece as stowaways were trying to get to America. "I knew it had to be them, " he said.

Much of the time Quimby spent operating trains was routine and monotonous. Sometimes, downright dull he said. Up and down the tracks making shipments of most anything connected with the war. A General Motors plant at Andemeshk, made Studebaker and GM parts. They made many of the six by six trucks used in the war. American engineers built roads for them to drive on once the trains unloaded them at certain points. It took thousands of support personnel so those in the infantry had what they needed to win the war.

Sometimes what they received to work with was of very poor quality. A mistake that took place someplace messed the entire chain of delivery. Like once when Quimby received a thousand boxcars, American, by the way, but they came with a drawbar manufactured in Europe, failed to use the proper steel and "they broke like rubber bands" Quimby said and they all had to be replaced by retempering. But day after day they continued hauling trainloads of tanks, artillery pieces, shells, black powder, TNT, gasoline, food and many other items for the war effort. "It gave us a good feeling to know that after the high cost of manufacturing and shipping the material, we were trusted with it on the last leg of the journey." No where in the states, when he returned home, did he haul anything of any higher value than he did during the war, not to even mention the thousands of troops he transported he said.

Quimby also had the opportunity to see the USO shows that were taken over there. Jack Benny paid them a visit once. Benny, he said, wasn't all that funny because of his off color jokes he said.

On January 27, 1944, the German siege of Stalingrad was broken. Though it was good news, as they had a big part in it even though they weren't given much credit, things slowed down after that. No more hustle and bustle of the life they had become accustomed to. There was a change coming. About two to three months before the allied invasion of Normandy on June 6, 1944, the important part of their mission was over. Though they did not really know what was taking place at the time, the high brass left and no more replacements were coming in. Then they shipped out the diesel engines again.

There was a drought in 1944 and Quimby found himself going through dust storms like he had never seen before. Add the misery of the heat and it wasn't a real good time. He watched as a military cemetery got bigger and bigger with sand blowing over the graves.

One night while he and his buddies moved outside to try to get a little more comfortable because of the heat, Quimby found himself having cold chills. He ended up at the medics with his teeth chattering waiting his turn to be seen. He woke up at a hospital where an American nurse asked him if he had a nice sleep. He was unaware he had slept for two days and one night. Doctors told him he had anemic dysentery and also worms.

His buddies came to visit him and happy to announce that he had won a drawing for a free trip to Tel Aviv and he would have to be ready to go in two days. He didn't know whether to feel good or bad, but he wanted to go, he had always hoped to visit the Holy Land. The problem was to get well enough in two days and to be able to leave the hospital. After much begging, he did, but feeling very poorly, he wasn't sure if he had made the right decision. In spite of his health, he did manage to pull it off and enjoyed the trip. Personally, from reading his book, I think the few beers he had probably made him well again.

By July of 1945, the railroads were given back to the Persians and the Iranians. Now it was the matter of going home. He could hardly wait to be back with his wife. But it wasn't until July 23, 1945, because he was one of the last soldiers to board a C-47 plane and start his trek home. Equipped with steel bucket seats, it was joy. "We would have sat on a wire brush" he stated, because they were heading home.

He finally wound up back at Fort Leavenworth where he had originally left and he boarded a train on July 31, 1945 after leaving Iran on July 23. "I felt good about it," he said.

He was now on a Silver Streak Zephyr, which ran from Omaha to Kansas City, and he was getting closer to home. At Omaha, there was only 100 miles left of riding and that was on a Northwestern train to Sioux City. He was the first one off the train he thought and looked all around for his wife. She and his folks were there to meet him. He thought, "Three years and two weeks, is a long time to be away from one's bride." Now he was home, on a short leave, before having to go back to Fort Benning to receive his discharge papers. He had to stay at Fort Benning for another six weeks and it bothered him but now it was almost over. He would soon return home, get a job with the railroad, raise a family and enjoy life. On October 11, 1945, he was discharged.

Quimby did get a job for the railroad again. Men like Quimby found themselves not that welcome. Others were working for the railroad and were bumped back to make room for the veterans returning from war. They often resented that. After being use to much discipline and living in the service, it was not always easy to get back in the groove of civilian life. Quimby had to adjust like so many men who served their country. Without them, we would be without freedom today. Thanks Bing!

REED, COLONEL RALPH

Reed, a WW II veteran, is from Lincoln. I like to refer to him as "Colonel Reed," because that's what he is. He piloted B-17's and B-24's in the European Theatre. He spent 3 long years in the early 1940's and "I was lucky to say the least. Just plain lucky!" He remembers the time very well and he will quickly agree it's something you don't forget.

Reed entered the service, "right off the cultivator," as he says, going into the infantry in 1941. He was another farm boy off to fight a war that he had no control of. He was sent to the Army Air Corp for training instead. He attended UNL under the ROTC program and earned his 2nd Lt. status. He recalls sadly about the rest of his class who were sent to the Philippines. They were all killed or were prisoners of war and never heard from again. Reed continued going to flight school and was sent to the European Theatre. He was based in England. He had the opportunity to listen to Churchill speak to them one day.

Aviators that shot this pilot had the feeling of helplessness when they Often viewed a sight like this. A bomber on fire was usually destined To crash with its occupants either bailing out or went down with it.
Picture courtesy of Co. Ralph Reed of Lincoln.

His first mission was flying into France as the war began to rage there. Troops on the ground needed air support and Reed was there to give it to them if at all possible. On this particular trip, all planes returned but one. "German fighters caught him," Reed recalls.

In the fall he was sent to Africa and then to Iran, to fly more missions. He was co-pilot with Paul Tibbets, a noted pilot of WW II. Tibbets dropped the big bomb on Hiroshima later from his B-29. "Bombers like the B-29 were built in Omaha," he added.

The 88-mm. Anti-craft guns the Germans used were deadly. "They took down a lot of planes," he said. The very tight formations were also something to get used to. If his superiors, like Gen. Curtis Lemay, didn't see paint worn off the wing tips, "we were in trouble." Wing tips were supposed to overlap in these tight formations being advantageous for protection from German fighters. Bombers flying alone were a sitting duck for the German Luftwaffe, fighter planes.

This photo taken by a crewman from Col. Ralph Reed's plane,
Shows a bomber next to him with its wing blown off and
About to detach itself after being hit by enemy fire below.
Picture is courtesy of Col. Ralph Reed.

In the desert airstrips of Iran, dust was a big problem. Engine air filtering systems weren't the best. The B-17 had fighter was after them and if you had good gunners, one could usually fight them off. Flying in formation with other planes, you had a good chance of shooting him down, he said.

He thinks of how much more intense precision flying has become in today's jets. Then flying bombers one was allowed about a 15% margin of error. With the advent of the jet plane, that margin went down to 3%. "I admire those pilots," Reed said.

Reed told of one mission he was sent on to bring four captured pilots back out of Yugoslavia. He did this type of thing four times in 1944. Pilots could be "bought" back by the U.S. government. The Navy furnished the plane. Gold would be obtained from the State Department and flown to where the captives were held. "A whole bunch of gold," he recalls, "was needed to get these boys back home."

As Reed said earlier, he was lucky. He saw many that lost their lives in the air. He considers himself fortunate to have spent 30 years in the armed forces of which 9 were in active duty. He completed his time at SAC, Omaha, working in logistics until 1971 when he retired as a U.S. Air Force Colonel.

He spends a lot of time today working for the Red Cross.

REZAC, SIMONE (JOHN)

Simone Rezac was born in Bee, Nebraska. He now lives in Lincoln. His father was a Village Marshal in Bee. It's interesting to see from the story he sent what life was like for many veterans prior to WW II. I will take exception and make note of it.

He graduated from Seward School in 1937. The following fall, in September, his dad brought him to Denton, Nebraska, to work in the CCC Camp with other young men. He worked planting trees, like many individuals did in those years coming out of the dirty thirties. He says he worked in the fields for five weeks. He was starving to death. Being a big man at 6 foot 2, "I do like to eat," he tells me. At the camp, he knew the cook, who was from his hometown. He asked if he could work in the kitchen hoping to appease his appetite a little. He did, and was able to work there for two years. They paid his father $25 each month to help feed the rest of the family and his father was able to save two checks and buy a milk cow so they would have a little milk to sell, too. "We didn't know we were poor," he said.

After the two years at the camp, he returned home. Then he had to try and find work. He and his three brothers went to Minnesota to pick corn to try and earn a few extra dollars. In November of 1940, a blizzard struck in that area and corn wasn't picked that fall. So while in Minnesota, the brothers all decided to join the Army.

He was in an Army camp in New Jersey when fate dealt its hand. Working in the Signal Corp, one day they put him on KP duty. The head Sergeant at the mess hall asked him if he could help him because one of the cooks was sick. Rezac was the last of the men that the Sergeant interviewed for the cook position. No one else had suited him so far and when the Sergeant found out he had cooked in a CCC Camp, he said, "Thank God." Rezac's days of washing pots and pans were over. After one week of helping the cook, the Captain called him into his office and asked Rezac if he would like to go to school and learn more about cooking and teach other men how. I said, "Okay!" He was made Sergeant for his decision.

The war began December 7, 1941 and by March of 1942, Rezac found himself in a Nevada desert teaching other men how to cook. He then went to a camp in Missouri to teach more men. With 10,000 men in the camp, it took a lot of food. He was introduced to one man who refused to carry a gun. Rezac asked him what he could do. He discovered he came from a long line of bakers from Germany. Rezac said he learned a lot from him and kept him with him throughout the war. He had now became classified as an "Old Sergeant" and no one gave him any lip.

Later he was sent to Sacramento, California to teach men how to cook on the back of a truck in the mountains north of Sacramento. He then moved back to the desert where he fed men who served under General Patton and were preparing for the African Campaign. One night he asked the men what they wanted to eat. They agreed it was apple pie. So he baked 35 pies for that particular group and they ate all of them.

At another base he fed men who were coming back from the South Pacific Campaign. They were a sick bunch he says, "I fed them good," he recalls.

At a base in Texas, he fed men who were loading shells on ships for D-Day. He then went on to Jackson, Mississippi, where he fed 2,500 soldiers for a time prior to being shipped off for the European Theatre from Norfolk, Virginia. He went along with General Patton's tanks and 2100 soldiers, which was headed for a port in France. Their ship was the first to enter France from the south. They unloaded at night and hid out in the hills until pushing on into Germany.

He recalls on the 24th of December 1944, that he asked the Captain if he could attend midnight mass at a local cathedral. The Captain handed him a sub machine gun and told him to take six other well-armed men with him and stay in the back of the church. "That was really something, I'll never forget it," Rezac said.

After the war ended, Rezac was still in France. He met and married a girl in Metz, France. He had orders to stay in France and close a depot that was used during the war by the U.S. When General Patton was killed in a car wreck, Rezac was sent to Luxembourg to help bury Patton.

Rezac was discharged from the service with a Captain's rank at Paris, France. He and his wife had a daughter while in France. His wife gave birth to weak baby because she was undernourished by the hardships she had been through. The baby died three days after it was born.

Previous to their marriage, his wife was one of nine children living in France at that time. The Germans took everything they had. Two of the girls, including his future wife, were forced to work in a German labor camp for four years. She was starving but was fortunate enough to work in the German kitchen so she could get a piece of bread to eat. "She had worse times than I did," Rezac said.

"I was a Sergeant in charge of food. That means a lot when you are hungry and there is no food," he states.

Yes, Rezac admits, he may have had it fairly easy compared to some. But what would have happened to the thousands of men who served their country if not for men like him? Rezac served good food whenever he was given it to prepare. He was often in harm's way. Without men like him, the war would have been worse.

The couple came back to New York in February of 1947, and then moved to Lincoln. They bought a little house and reared four sons. Three out of the four sons are now also veterans. One son served in the Air Force for seven years, of which 18 months were served in Vietnam. The other two sons in the National Guard-one son as a pilot helicopter and the other son as a helicopter repairman.

Rezac, being a fully licensed cook, got a job at Beatrice Foods. Today he still likes preparing food. He sent me a picture of what I assume is one of his grandsons, eating fresh baked filled rolls, which looked mighty tasty.

John Rezac, who once cooked and baked during WW II, now bakes pastry items for his grandson. *Photo courtesy of Rezac.*

ROSE, GERALD D.

This 1st Lt. from Gibbon was in the U.S. Air Force and served from October 6th of 1942 to July 16th of 1945. He was with the 384th Bomb Group, 545th Bomb Squadron, based out of Grafton-Underwood, England where he began his duties as co-pilot and later as pilot of the B-17 bomber. Prior to that, he said he had his first experience in flying with a "Barnstormer" near Lowell, Nebraska as a young lad. It seems to have gotten in his blood.

Rose has written a 32-page book, titled, "Rambling Rose," documenting his time spent in service. I will try to summarize what this veteran did for his country. He's proud to have served and has received the Air Medal and Five Clusters for his service during WW II.

Rose hadn't finished two years of college when he went to night school to learn to qualify to be a pilot. During the war he flew 23 missions as a co-pilot and 12 more as the pilot.

His book begins with the names of the original crew that flew many missions over France, Germany and Holland. I count 35 missions that Rose was a part of; bombing air bases, highways, factories, hydro electric plants, refineries, rail yards, gun positions and lending air support for the ground troops. Rose meticulously recalls some of these missions in detail giving the reader a picture of what really took place while flying over enemy lands. He wrote what it was like.

His original crew consisted of Pilot, Lt. Lloyd Peters, San Diego California, and Rose was the co-pilot. Peters was a deputy sheriff in San Diego County at the time he entered the service. The crew respectfully referred to him as "Pappy. When he returned home he resumed his job in law enforcement only to be killed in an auto accident transporting a prisoner. "He was a great pilot and responsible for our success," Rose said.

The navigator was Lt. Hugh Simpson, from Connecticut, a very able navigator Rose says, many times plotting a course for deep penetration into enemy territory. Often they were battle damaged, low on fuel, alone, but always got back.

The bombardier was Lt. Wm. Rothenberg, from Virginia, who trained and went overseas with the crew but didn't get to go on operational due to medical reasons. Rose feels he would have been an asset if he would have been allowed to join them.

T/Sgt. Wm. P. Hornack, engineer from Maryland was what Rose refers to as a "first rate engineer plus a top-turret gunner. He knew the B-17 from nose to tail, many times making repairs and corrections in flight assuring a successful mission and a safe trip back home.

S/Sgt. John Bridget, a tail gunner from Michigan, they referred to as "Jr." because he was the youngest. He was wounded on mission number five, hit by flak, but returned to finish his tour with as much courage and skill as ever Rose comments.

S/Sgt. Ed Ketchledge, Ball turret from Pennsylvania was a tough ball turret gunner. He never complained and was always alert and ready for anything, Rose said.

T/Sgt. Charles Covell, a radio operator and gunner from Detroit. He was very good with the radio, nervous at first but after being hit by shrapnel and bruised but not wounded, he overcame his nervousness. Rose will always remember the question Covell would always ask during the early, tough raids. "Christ, Rosie, How do they expect us to live through 30 of these?" I am sure many veterans questioned how they could survive their many missions no matter where they were.

T/Sgt. Geo. Palacek, radio and gunner from St. Louis. Rose doesn't know why they were assigned two radio gunners. George was often the lead radio operator while flying with Rose. In another plane and different crew, Palacek and their commanding officer and crew were reported as missing in action over enemy territory.

Sgt. Lowell Hatfield, Indiana also performed his duties well Rose said. He was almost killed when a truck ran over him while he was returning to their plane with his arms full of 50 caliber machine gun barrels.

This was the original crew. "I am proud to have been in one of the best," Rose states.

The last 12 missions of his tour were completed with an alternate crew of which Rose doesn't recall all of their names. They were also very respected, well trained and dedicated Air Force comrades. "You could bet your LIFE on that, and did many times," he said.

Rose enlisted in October of 1942. He had tried for over a year to get into the Aviation Cadet Program and finally was accepted, but then chose to enlist in the Air Corp and waited for some kind of school related to flying.

He was sent to Monterey, California, and issued his clothing and other necessities he would need. He completed his basic training at Bakersfield, California, and was happy he would be able to go to Link Trainer School. In the years to follow, it was very helpful to him he said. While there, he received orders to train for Aviation Cadet. There he could decide what facet of flying he wanted; pilot, navigator or bombardier. He chose pilot. He went to flight school at Ryan Field, Tucson, Arizona and used a Pt. 22 as a trainer plane. He flew his first solo flight after about six hours of instructions. "What a happy day," he recalls.

From there he went to Gardner Army Air Base at Taft, California, and flew B-13 Vultee trainer planes, commonly called "vultee vibrators," because of the extreme vibrations the plane had just before stalling or spinning. He became quite well accustomed to this plane and trained other students as to how great and tough the plane really was.

From there he was sent to Luke Field at Phoenix, Arizona, for advanced single engine training in the North

American AT-6, which was a sweet smooth plane with a 650 horsepower engine, retractable gear and many other goodies. It did have a tendency to ground loop on cross wind landings and had rather tough spin recovery traits.

Finally, on November 3rd, 1943, at a very impressive ceremony, he was given his Wings and 2nd Lt. bars. "One of the greatest days of my life-sure wish my mom and dad could have been there," he said.

After that, Rose was transferred to Randolph Field, Texas, and was given leave to go home. That leave was the first one he had in 13 months. While at home, he and his girl, Mary, decided to go to Kansas City and get married. It happened to be on Armistice Day and all of the county and federal offices were closed. They finally found a sympathetic judge who agreed to come to marry them at a church in Kansas City.

After the wedding, Mary went back to Kearney and Rose went back to Texas to instructor school. He then went back to Gardner Field to start teaching basic flying. It was long and tedious hours in the air, and lots of writing reports and progresses. Soon at this base, he had a chance to go into the 4-engine training in B-17's at Las Vegas. There he met Peters. They began training for the European Theatre operations.

They were sent to Kearney, Nebraska, and were issued their overseas gear. They had some more schooling and prepared to go overseas. Then they went to Camp Kilmer, New Jersey, and boarded a French luxury liner, "Colombie," which had been converted into a troop ship. They joined a convoy of about 100 ships of all types and 16 days later they docked in Glassglow, Scotland. It was impressive to be greeted there by a Scottish bagpipe band, kilts and all. "It made us feel good," he said.

From there, they went on to Stone, England for more schooling before going to Graffton-Underwood Engine. He was sent to school in London to learn the many ways of escape or evading escape when shot down in enemy territory. While there, he had the unpleasant experience of being chased into bomb shelters several nights because of the buzz bombs the Germans were dropping on them.

It was now time for Rose to begin his tour of duty, his first mission. Rose refers to a diary that the engineer, Hornack, kept in those days.

Mission # 1, Chantilly Surseine-ship #917 "Pauline," the 12th of August 1944. The first mission was a big day for Rose and the others who had never been on a mission before. They didn't know whether they should be scared or happy. The fact remained that although they had to go, did they really want to go?

They were awakened at 3 a.m. and they were to eat and be ready for briefing at 4:30 a.m. They were told that the target of the day would be an airfield near Chantilly SurSeine, in France. The temperature at bombing altitude of 20,000 feet was 13 degrees. They were to assemble at 10,000 feet. After briefing they were to pick up their gear, get on their ship, # 917. They had to preflight their guns, turrets and all their oxygen systems. Rose crawled into the cockpit and watched the engines run up. They took and assembled with the other planes as planned at 10,000 feet. It was 7 a.m.

When they sighted the coast of France the order was given to put on their flak suits but Hornack just crawled into his turret with his flak helmet on and started observing for enemy fighters. He saw his first burst of flak, which was a pretty sight to watch, but dangerous if it would have come too close.

They first made a dry run on the target and decided to make another passing over the primary target before going over for the secondary target which was another airfield. "We bombed the hell out of it," Rose recalls. With bombs away, they headed back home. No flak on the way back and the crew was still okay. They landed at 3:30 p.m. with a little flak hole in the fuselage. Time-8 hours-35 minutes.

Mission # 2, Roven Area. August 13, 1944, ship # 106. Rose said he has explained quite well what takes place during the preparation in the first mission so we don't have to go through that again. For this mission they left at 7:30 a.m. with another target, Roven area in France, to bomb bridges and highways to help our troops in France. They headed for the coast and the fireworks began. Flak came fast and surprisingly, accurately, knocking down many of the aircraft. "It was the first time in my life I have experienced seeing a B-17 blow up in mid-air, nothing left, just a puff of a smoke." They saw four others go down in flames and blow up, "what a sight." A sight they never will forget. They saw a man bail out; his chute was on fire. "These things sink into your mind and are very hard to remove," he said. Then it was "bombs away," words they welcomed so they could get out of the area.

Their troubles were not over. Number 3 engine had been acting up and was no longer running. The turbo amplifier went out. The radio operator couldn't find the spare so the engineer went back and switched them around so the engine could give enough power to get away from the target area. After a while they lost the engine again and feathered it, landing on three engines safe and sound. They received only two flak holes that time. Time-5 hours-30 minutes.

Mission # 3 Stuttgart, Germany, August 14, 1944, ship # 135G. Three days now in a row they had a mission. After briefing they were to head for a chemical refinery near Stuttgart. Crossing the French Coast they didn't receive the flak that had been predicted. Reaching the IP, Initial Point, they made their first run, which was as usual, a dry run. The second run, they dropped their bombs and headed home. Flak was meager but very accurate but they lucked out with no holes in their ship when they landed. They recalled flying over the beautiful Swiss Alps. If they had any trouble and had to abandon their ship, they hoped to do so in the land of the Swiss. Time 8 hours-10 minutes.

After a few days of rest and a 45-hour pass, they were ready to fly again

Mission # 4, Anklam, Germany, August 25, 1944 ship # 521, "The Saint." This target was an airfield in Germany that was very important to the Germans. They made the run, dropped their bombs and encountered light flak. A combat wing behind them was hit by 2 ME 210's and the Germans got one B-17. Fortunately the crew had bailed out. They could see that one of the crewmembers had his chute on fire and he was done for. It hurts, Rose says, when you see a buddy in trouble and there's not a thing you can do about it. All you can do is watch and wait and hope you aren't next. They were fortunate to land this trip with a flakhole and no trouble at all. Time-8 hours.

Mission # 5-Gelsenkirchen, Germany, August 26, 1944. Ship # 309, "Lady of Victory." The target this day was a synthetic oil plant in Gelsenkirchen, a city located in the Rhur Valley, better known as "Flak valley," to some airmen. As they reached the IP, flak was really coming up, "just like a black cloud. Flak hit their ship and made a rumpling noise. "That

really makes your heart jump and your Adam's apple drop."
You bite your lips wondering if it was going to hit your engine or
gas tank and explode-then you could say, "you've had it." Men
would hold a service or mass right by their guns. Every burst of
flak you see had a red center, then that "rump." A sound was
heard on the interphone, "I'm hit." "I'll never forget that," Rose
said. Right away you wonder, how bad? Then Rose lost #3
engine to flak and lost their formation and dropped way behind.
The first run at the target was no good but they dropped their
bombs anyway, they couldn't try it again, and blew the highway
all to hell.

**This picture shows the intensity of flak and the many
bombers that filled the
Skies during WW II , European Theatre.** *Photo Courtesy of
Col. Ralph Reed.*

Finally out of enemy territory, the engineer inspected the
damages and found the tail gunner hurt so he patched him up.
Flak had gone through his arm then hit his side. By the time
Bridget was treated they landed. The engineer, in cases such

as this, shot up a red flare as a signal they have wounded aboard. Whiskey at the interrogation room fixed everyone else up again. Jr. Bridget was taken to the hospital and was awarded the Purple Heart. The ship was shot full of holes. A 4-inch diameter hole in the tailgunner's compartment was right in line with Bridget's head. Fortunately he was leaning forward at the time and it missed his head. Ten days later Bridget healed and was back in his position manning the tail. Time-6 hours-20 minutes.

Mission # 6, Ludwigshaven-September 4,1944-ship #518, "Damn Yankee." Assigned to another ship, bomber, the Damn Yankee had a wonderful record and no abortions except a turn back due to mechanical failures. The ground crew was terrific. The target this day was a chemical plant in the city of Ludwigshaven. It was very important to the Germans and must be destroyed. At the briefing, they were warned to expect intense flak. However, they encountered very little. They dropped their bombs and headed home with only very few flak holes. Time 7 hours-50 minutes.

Mission #7 Ludwigshaven September 8, 1944, ship # 518, "Damn Yankee." It was back to Ludwigshaven with orders to hit them hard and give them a staggering blow. As they reached the drop zone they got some flak and it was quite accurate. There was that "whopping" sound again that tended to makes ones blood tingle. Two ships were down and burned. Aircraft can totally burn at 28,000 feet. "It's one of those things, you know, now you see it, now you don't." They dropped their bombs and headed home. A piece of flak went through the waist gunners ammo box and hit his flaksuit but didn't hurt him. The ship was full of holes but they landed safely with everyone okay. Time 8 hours-40 minutes.

Mission # 8, Ludwigshaven, Germany, ship # 518, "Damn Yankee," once again. By now Rose says, the Germans were really "PO'Ed" at them, and moved more flak guns in from Mannhein across the river. There was enough without them moving in more. "Oh well, we'll just sweat it out," was the comment at the time. When they arrived over the target area, it was covered with heavy overcast. They couldn't bomb it, as the orders were they had to visually see it. They bombed Mannhein instead. The flak over this city was not bad, as they had moved their guns in the Ludwigshaven area, all the better for the airmen. With bombs away, the fighter support was excellent and they landed safely. Time-8 hours-20 minutes.

Mission # 9, Sendelfingen, Germany, September 10, 1944, ship # 518, "Damn Yankee." They were briefed over a target south of Stuttgart, which was Sendelfingen. This was an airfield also of utmost importance to the Germans and had to be knocked out. The weather was clear and seeing the target would be no problem. They received a little flak when they made the dry run. When they conducted the second run, flak got real heavy. The engineer was hit on the back of the head and jammed against the gun sight. He wasn't injured however. The second run wasn't any good either so they tried for a third. This time a piece of flak went through the engineer's legs and hit the door, a very close call. The waist gunner got a big hole through his ammo box and hit his flak suit. Then the fireworks began. Engine #3 was down. They lost formation and called for fighter support. Two P-51's perched on each wing. The bombs were dropped and, thanks to the navigator, they made it back to base in one piece. The co-pilot left the cowflaps selector on and they had no brakes. The ship was full of holes. Time-7 hours-45 minutes.

Mission # 10, Merseburg, Germany-September 13, 1944, ship # 430. The target was a synthetic oil plant near Merseberg. This was a rough target and the crew was sweating it out. Weather was good, good visibility for bombing but not good for them. As soon as they got over the Rhine River it began, the ship had flak holes already. As they reached the drop zone, flak was unbearable. The fighter escort did a very good job but every burst of flak bumped the ship hard.

At the 5:00 position, they saw one ship go down. It exploded and nothing was left but dust. No chutes were seen; that crew had had it. At 1:00, another ship went down in flames. Rose and his crew were flying 125 mph., too slow, all at once a burst of flak at #4 engine throwing the right wing up and stalled the left one out. The crew was able to feather #4 engine and pulled out. The engineer fired red and yellow flares to call for fighter support. Two P-51's quickly came for escort. The navigator conducted his job and they headed for home. The co-pilot checked the brakes and cowl flaps. They discovered #2 engine had it's hydraulics shot out so it was kept closed. Tires and wheels were okay and they landed safely and no one was hurt. The pilot and co-pilot were credited for pulling the plane out after they had fallen 5,000 feet. The radio operator was hit in the bottom but didn't break the skin. He didn't qualify for the Purple Heart. Time 9 hours-0 minutes.

"This was, in my opinion, one of our most dangerous missions. We had been under a deadly flak barrage." Rose said. When flak hit the right wing, flipping the aircraft on it's side, they started falling. He released the bombs, which helped, not having that extra weight, and they were able to regain control. At the time, they were about 600 miles into German territory, damaged and alone, a very dangerous situation. Rose recalls they were lucky no enemy fighters found them.

Mission # 11, Findhoven, Holland-September 17, 1944. Ship-"Damn Yankee." After the Merseburg trip, the crew was still pretty shaken up, but they had to be ready to go. This trip was to support the ground troops, flying low at 16,000 feet. Six ships were sent on the mission. They released their load at the drop zone and began turning back. They were loaded with 57-pound fragmentation bombs to be dropped at intervals of 150 feet. This means the bombing run was three miles long or a little better. "A long time to spit your load out," Rose said. They bombed a wooded area suspected of concealing tanks and other motorized armor.

Because of the bursts of flak, the other planes were led off course and one of his buddies was shot down. When he examined his chute, it had 18 holes in it but safely landed and was okay. They saw two enemy fighters, possibly, ME-110's, but they didn't attack. Time-4 hours-15minutes.

Mission # 12-Hamm, Germany, September 19, 1944. Ship-"Damn Yankee," # 518. After a few days of rest the crew was ready to go again. Rose recalls it was very cold. Using their heated suits, they depleted the batteries. They had to hand crank engine #3 to get enough electricity to start the other three engines.

The target this time was the Marshalling Yards at Hamm. They didn't expect much trouble. They did experience a little flak again, which can always mean trouble. When they got over the drop zone, the weather was so bad they couldn't drop any bombs. They headed back to base. Rose said the base was "Old Buckingham," where Jimmy Stewart of Hollywood was the C.O. Time-8 hours-0 minutes.

Mission # 13, Frankfort, Germany-September 25, 1944, Ship-"Damn Yankee," # 518. The target was a factory that made wheels and axles for railroad cars in Frankfort. The mission was predicted to be rough, enemy fighters could be everywhere. Flak, on this mission wasn't as bad as usual except when they approached the target area. Then the Germans opened up with 105 and 155 mm. guns. A ship ahead of them had his tail blown off and spun to the ground. No chutes were seen. Further down on the bomb run, another plane behind them blew up in a cloud of dust. Those that see these horrifying scenes, feel quite small, "about an inch high," as Hornack relates. "You want to reach out and help these guys but there isn't a thing you can do," he adds. Rose wasn't on this mission for some reason and no time was submitted.

Mission # 14, Osnabruck, German, September 26, 1944, Ship-"Damn Yankee." # 518. The mission was to hit an aero engine works in Onnabruck. Another important manufacturing plant for the Germans and had to be taken out. Rose was with them again and the crew was very happy. A substitute co-pilot they had with them on Mission #13, proved not to be the best, Hornack said.

At the drop zone, the flak was intense and very accurate. With bomb bay doors open on the bomb run, they sweated it out. A ship at 5:00 position was in flames, 4 chutes opened with one on fire. The one on fire didn't have a chance. In situations such as this the crew only has one thing in mind, drop the bombs and get out. When the bomb bay doors close, "it's music in your ears," he said. Then came the favorite turn when they move off target and head home. When they landed there were a few holes in the outboard wing. When on the ground, a shot of whiskey hit the spot. Time-6 hours-30 minutes.

Mission # 15-Cologne-September 27, 1944, Ship # 106. The mission was a Ford plant located at Cologne, which was another important plant that had to be taken out. After briefing, the crew carried their guns to the plane. Then tragedy struck. A truck hit the waist gunner, Lowell Hatfield, on the perimeter track. He was hurt very badly, two fractured legs, fractured skull and other injuries. They took him to the hospital. They were given another waist gunner by the name of Lucky Gates and they took off. Unable to hit the Ford plant, they chose a secondary target, a Marshalling yard near the city of Munster. They encountered little flak, with only a few flak holes in the aircraft. Upon arrival back to the base they learned that Hatfield was in critical condition and not expected to live. No time noted.

Rose comments that Hatfield was transferred to a major hospital some miles from the group. A few weeks later, the crew paid him a visit. He had been unconscious for about three weeks. When they entered his room, he did not know any of them. He did know what positions they functioned in the plane, just couldn't recall their names. "He was one hell of a mess," Rose says, with casts all over him, ropes, pulleys and bags of all kinds for traction purposes. Several weeks later they visited him again. This time he knew their hometowns, but still not their names. Later he was shipped home, never to fly again. Rose flew to his hometown of Mishawaka, Indiana, in 1953 to visit him.

Mission # 16, Munster, Germany-September 30, 1944, ship-"Damn Yankee' # 518. The target was a steel plant and Marshalling yard near the city of Munster. There was intense flak as they got over the target area but not very accurate. No ships were seen going down by them. Again it was bombs away and headed back home with only a few holes. "The Damn Yankee brought us back safely again with all the crew O.K." Time-6 hours-5 minutes.

Mission # 17, Cologne, Germany-October 2, 1944, Ship "Damn Yankee," # 518. Hornack says he met a cute little blonde just prior to this flight but doesn't comment on it. He had a 48-hour pass and did say, "I had a pretty good time."

They were to head for the Ford plant again which was primarily hitting the rail yards. Flak was intense over the Rhur Valley. They got into formation and headed out, not really knowing again, what was in store for them. Ahead of them they could see rockets and 10/10 flak at the target site. They were shooting heavy stuff at them. "When this stuff hits, you jolly well had it," he said. You really sweat the situation out. They saw one plane go down in flames and no chutes and it went down and down, into the ground. At 6:00, another plane exploded in mid air and nothing left but dust. "Your heart beats faster and faster, you moisten your lips, but again, there's nothing you can do but hope you aren't next," Rose said. Bandits were reported in the area. The crew was all on alert, watching for the enemy fighters. Thank God, they didn't see any. Flak was thicker than ever, the bomb run seemed to last a lifetime and for some, took a life. Then it's Bombs away, and they headed back home to the sack. "We worship those boys in those P-51's, P-47's and P-38's. We feel safer with them around," Hornack said. Safe back at the base, they were relieved. Time-7 hours-40 minutes.

Mission # 19- Cologne, Germany, October 5, 1944, Ship "Big Dog," # 661. They were briefed to hit the Marshalling yards at Cologne. They were to take the Damn Yankee again but when they tried to start #4 engine; the starter had frozen, so they had to take the spare plane, the "Big Dog." They had no trouble until they reached the drop zone, or the IP. Flak was terrible, with rocket trails filling the skies. All at once flak hit engine #2, making it lose all it's oil hitting the oil cooler. The pilot feathered engine #3 by mistake and then tried to feather #2, but it was too late. The prop went up to 2800 and was windmilling. They were only half way on their run. Rose dropped the bombs near Dursleday blowing the little town to hell. One ship near them went down, the crew not having a chance to bail out. They lost formation and headed back alone. The engineer fired flares for fighter support. The vibration was so great that the left side of the nose had a big crack in it and shook the left gear down. The crankshaft snapped and was turning freely. The engineer hand cranked up the left gear and they limped home. The navigator again took them back. They could see the English Channel. The pilot and co-pilot tried to shake off the prop by diving and stalling but failed to do so. The engine was real hot by then and you could smell it in the cockpit. The crew sweated it out. When approaching the base they expected the prop to fly off while landing, but for same strange reason it did not. That was a load off their minds. The ship was shot full of holes but they were once again, all okay.

Rose comments he recalls this mission very well. His brother, Lee, a P-47 pilot from France had dropped in for a visit. It was cause for celebration so prior to this mission, Rose, his brother and another P-47 pilot asked for a stand-down status so they could go out for a while and it was granted. "We made the liquor shortage even more so," he writes. Rose returned back to the base in the wee hours of the morning only to be awakened at 4: 00 a.m. for the mission. He reminded his superior he was on stand-down status, which should have meant he didn't have to go on this mission. The OD's response was, "You were stood-down, out of the sack and into the flak, earn your flight pay."

After breakfast and several coffees all went fine until they were flying well into Germany. Rose looked at the gauges. Flying in close formation, pilots don't look at the panels that much under those conditions, flying wing tip to wingtip. Rose noticed the oil pressure was falling fast in engine #2. Because the pilot and co-pilot are on different radio frequencies, Rose held up two fingers. The pilot misread them and thought he had three fingers up and feathered #3. By the time he got back to #2, all the oil had been lost and it was now impossible to feather it out. Rose said it seemed to take forever to get back to the base flying only at 100 knots/hour, crippled and not knowing if the prop would separate upon landing due to the excessive vibration. Time-6 hours-25 minutes.

Mission # 20, Strausland-October 6, 1944, Ship "Damn Yankee" # 518. A synthetic oil refinery was next on the list of missions. It was supposed to be a rough target and was a long hop getting over to Stettin, Germany. It was a very clear day flying in formation over the North Sea. A lot of fighter support joined them. "They hugged us close, nice," Hornack says, about those P-51's and P-47's. Over the Baltic Sea, ships in the waters shot at some planes ahead of them down below. They moved the Yankee off to the side. When their group crossed over into Germany, the ball turret operator spotted about 100 German planes on the field below. Another 20 on another, but they didn't come up. No flak or enemy fighters yet either. Their primary target was closed in so they chose an alternate, an electric power plant in Strausland. They dropped the bombs and still no flak. Looking down at the target, it was pretty much up in smoke. They headed back home and found no flak holes and no one was hurt. They hoped for more missions like this.

Rose notes that their ball turret operator spent 7 hours in the cramped turret. "He had a lot of pride in his position, as did all the crew," he said. Time- 8 hours-40 minutes.

Mission # 21, Ruhland, Germany-October 7, 1944, Ship-Damn Yankee, # 518. Deep in the heart of Germany was an oil refinery that needed some attention. They were told to expect a lot of flak. Over Osnabruck it began, thick flak, and accurate 10/10's. One plane, the Dark Angel was hit and turned back. "They were throwing everything they had at us. You bite your

229

lips and then chew your tongue sweating it out. If you are chewing gum, the more flak, the harder you chew," Hornak writes. Finally arriving at the bombing run, the flak didn't let up. One of the other planes was knocked out of formation and he started to turn back. It was the last they heard of them. Fighters were now reported in the area. Ship #294, flying at their left wing was hit and fell out of formation. The ship, "Scotty," was the pride of the 545th. As it fell they could see it had a large hole in #2 gas tank. "You could have stuck your head in it," he said. That was the last they heard from that aircraft too.

With intense flak, the crew was able to drop their load and headed back home. Another ship was knocked down over Munster. One wing was blown off, caught on fire and spun to the ground. Again, no chutes were noted. Again, all you can do is stand there with your mouth wide open, helpless. It was rough seeing your buddies go down. It made you down in the dumps and your heart was about down to your knees. They once again arrived safely back to base. But as the crew notes, "This was no milk run." Time 9 hours-20-minutes.

Mission # 22-Schweinfurt-October, 1944, ship # 518. After a couple of day's rest, the crew was not yet ready to make another run. But, they had no choice. This time it was a FW plant at Schweinfurt. The crew remembers the last trip they made to this place. Only one ship returned. The sweat begun even before they had taken off. When they arrived over the zone, they were the first to get there along with their fighter escort. To their amazement, not much flak was encountered over the drop zone. What a relief. They dropped the bombs and headed back home. This mission, one they feared probably the most, "Was a milk run," Hornack comments. Personally, "I felt we wouldn't get back," he adds. Time 8 hours-15 minutes.

Mission #23-Coblenz, Germany-October 11, 1944, Ship #518. The first target was to hit the Marshalling yards in the city of Cologne. The secondary target, the marshalling yards at Coblenz. The "Damn Yankee," was roaring to go. When they arrived, they received some flak, mostly 88-mm. It was very accurate however. They hit the rail yards at Coblenz and then went safely home again. Time-7 hours-10 minutes.

Mission # 24-Cologne, Germany-October 17, 1944, ship #518. They were to hit the marshalling yards again. With quite a bit of flak they managed to avoid, they dropped their bombs and turned away and landed back home safely.

Rose says this was the last mission he flew while in the European Theatre Operation. He had the honor of flying with one of the most dedicated bunch of guys that he ever met during his military career. After the crew was formed in Salt Lake City, they met again at Dyersburg, Tennessee to start that phase of training. They were all very respectful of each other and considered each one to be a professional at his position in the plane. Rose would have liked to stay with them but the CO felt he should have a crew of his own because of all the combat experience he had. He did fly 8-10 more missions with his old buddies and "You can bet, we kept close watch of each other," he said.

Rose had piloted the old reliable plane, the "Damn Yankee," for almost all the rest of his missions except the last one he recalls. "We were proud of her, our crew and our squadron," he said. Rose flew twelve more missions as the pilot. The longest time clocked in at 11 hours on a mission to Merseburg, Germany, which was a long time to sit in a plane.

Merseburg, Rose says, was the most dangerous part of Germany of all the missions. The area was heavily fortified with 1,600 anti-aircraft batteries in the 40 square mile area surrounding the town. Flak guns consisted of 88's, 105's and 155's that bore down on them every flight. Several times Rose witnessed 36 B-17's disappear ahead of their group into a black cloud made of entirely smoke from flak bursts. His thoughts were "My God we have to go into that too!"

On Mission #10, Rose feels that was the closest they ever came to being shot down. "I will never forget it," he said.

He remembers another mission heading for the rail yards at Hamn, Germany. Although he didn't consider it to be a real tough mission, one flak burst on your plane in a vital spot could have easily completed your mission. About two thirds of the way across the channel, #2 engine started gushing oil out of the air breather. Rose immediately feathered it, but with a full load of bombs and still heavy with gas, it was hard to keep the plane in formation so he had to abort the mission and headed back to base. Normally they would unload the bombs before returning to base if they chose too, but after a couple of hours burning up fuel, they landed with the bombs still in the racks.

"Thought we might make a presentation to the "Krauts" another day," he said.

Rose flew his last mission December 4, 1944, his 35th mission. The last one "you always sweat out," he said. In the Damn Yankee, he was about to take off and "Bang" it blew a tire. His last mission and thought it might be scrubbed. But the tower quickly advised him that all the gear would be transferred to another plane and he should take off and try to catch up with the rest of the group. Rose managed to do that. Dropped the bombs and headed back to the base.

When he got out of the plane, Rose said he knelt down on the ground and kissed it. While walking back to the truck for interrogation, he popped his chute he had carried with him on every mission. Sure enough, it worked. After his meeting he went to his tent and found a cablegram from home informing him of the arrival of his daughter, Mary Lee, and that mother and child were doing fine.

"It's hard to explain my feelings knowing everything was apparently okay at home and not having to be shot at anymore," he said. He had been saving some cigars for the occasion and passed them around to his buddies. After a few drinks with his friends; he returned to his quarters for the best rest he had in two years, as he put it. On his way back to the tent, "I stopped at a little clearing in the English woods, got on my knees again and thanked God for taking care of me and my family," he humbly stated.

As he looks back on his tour of duty he realizes once again that it was just that, a duty to do and the urge to get at it. He doesn't recall any particular fear, it was always there but he feels that perhaps being a hardened veteran made fear easier to accept.

In late November of 1944 he recalls attending a meeting in the group headquarters where he was asked to be stay in the regular Air Force. The war in the Pacific was still raging at its height and most ex bomber pilots were being transferred to B-29 bomber planes. Although he was not looking forward to any more combat, it was the name of the game, he said. It turned out; he was needed to be an instructor and finished his tour as air-sea operations in Biloxi, Mississippi, until he was discharged in July of 1945.

In June of 1990, Rose received a letter from Chuck Covell, the radio gunner with the crew. Covell reminds Rose of another incident that took place one time. They were carrying 100-pound fragmentation bombs with instantaneous nose fuses. Somewhere along the channel, they checked to make sure the bomb doors opened properly. They did, but when they tried to close them again, a motor burned out and smoke filled the radio room "scaring the hell out of him" as he put it.

On their way to France to support the ground troops with air support, the bombs were their contribution to the retreating Germans. Flying at 20,000 feet with unlimited visibility, Covell joined Hatfield in the waist section as he always did. The flak was heavy and the planes were falling like leaves, maybe exaggerated a little he adds. But if you lose one plane out of 100, it's too many, and to the guys, if one plane goes down, it may as well be 100. He looked out the side window and saw one B-17 in flames to their right about 1000 feet away, burning with all four engines still running. Flames were streaming back from the wing, melting the skin from the fuselage and trailing behind the tail surfaces.

The cockpit seemed intact but it was hopeless for the survivors. One guy bailed out of the waist door. He pulled the rip cord about a hundred feet from the plane, it opened beautifully but the heat was too intense that close to the plane and instantly it was one flash, aflame. He fell to his death like a rock. Covell wondered, "Is that going to happen to us?" A second crewmember did the same thing and fell to his death. The plane was by now a huge black cloud and when the bombs went off inside the plane, it vaporized. One engine was falling away from the smoke-nothing else fell.

As he writes this to Rose he reminds him of his comment, "Christ, how do they expect us to survive thirty of these?" Survive they did and lived through many exciting missions he concluded.

Rose received other letters from his buddies retelling the many experiences they had. Men like Jr. the tail gunner who also notes that it was a wonder they returned home alive. He still asks, "How did we survive?"

You may have noticed the ship; Rose and the crew used "Damn Yankee" quite a bit. It was interesting to read that on October 23, 1944, when another crew was flying the plane, it was crashed landed and had to undergo extensive repairs. The plane had just been taken out of the repair shop after running into a flock of pigeons.

George Holms was skipper at the time when he forgot to put the landing gear down. It landed on its belly but the crew was all fine. Later, Holms was awarded the "fur lined piss pot" for his error. Spare planes were used until the Yankee was again in flying condition.

Following is a little information about the B-17 and what it was like. The plane was equipped with 97 bombs I am told. When they started the engines they began from left to right. The plane vibrated while warming the engines. When a green flare could be seen from the control tower, it was time to take off. The waist gunner, tail gunner and the ball turret gunner would be up in the radio compartment at takeoff. As dark low clouds often hung over the airstrip, airmen often asked themselves, "What am I doing here!"

The oldest man in the crew was Peters, at the age of 26. They were for the most part, young men, in their prime, ready to die for their country.

On each mission, planes carry what they call "chaff" on the floor, in boxes. It is nothing more than thin strips of aluminum foil, in bundles. When approaching enemy radar, this is tossed out to confuse radar. On a cloudy day, it worked great, as they couldn't be visually sighted either.

The temperature outside was often 50 degrees below zero. At 28,000 feet, oxygen is needed via a mask. Turret gunners would sometimes rip these lines off swinging around in their turrets causing big problems.

While on a mission it has been said that the sky was crowded with planes. Both bombers and fighters who escorted them stretched out for miles transporting their deadly cargo. Crewmembers remark they couldn't see from that height as to what damage they actually did or how many people they killed. Most had a certain amount of sympathy for what they were instructed to do.

Over the target area they could see guns flashing at them trying to knock them out of the sky. Then, a few seconds later, shells would be bursting all around the many planes, often with devastating results. When a brand new B-17 would get one of its wings blown off and it could be seen spinning towards the earth, you would watch for chutes, and if none would appear, the airmen felt a deep sorrow. Then it would be back across the channel, home, a warm meal, cigarettes and beer, hit the sack and wait until tomorrow or maybe a three day pass to London or off into the wild blue yonder, sweating it out.

SANDAHL, DEAN E.

Sandahl is from Lincoln. I had the pleasure of meeting him in December of 1999 when the 106th Division had their mini reunion in Lincoln. Attending were those of that Division who had fought in the Battle of the Bulge. It was most interesting visiting with these veterans.

Sandahl, like a lot of Nebraska veterans went to Fort Crook, Nebraska early in 1944 where he passed his physical examination. From there he was sent to Fort Leavenworth, Kansas for induction. Then he went to Camp Roberts, California for 17 weeks of Infantry Communications Basic Training.

At Camp Atterbury, Indiana, he joined the 106th Division. By then it was early fall of 1944. He was assigned to the 1st Platoon of Company B, 422nd Infantry Regiment. Finally he found himself at Pier 90, in New York City and boarded the British ship the H.M.S. Acquitania. He was bunked in the hold of the ship near the propellers, which was in the second deck below the water level. It was very noisy, muggy and hot. He was seasick most of the trip in the 7-8 days it took to cross the Atlantic while zigzagging to avoid enemy subs to Glasgow, Scotland.

Trains transported him to Southhampton to board a ship crossing the English Channel. They crossed it at night and loaded on an LST, a landing ship tank, with front drop unloading ramp. They beached at LeHavre, France but the water was quite deep and with heavy packs it was a struggle to wade ashore. He helped a Lt. that stepped in a deep hole and went under.

Now ashore they marched inland several miles to bivouac and to the assembly point. Trucks of the "Red Ball Express," as they were known, transported them toward the front lines. It was a long rough ride to Brussels, Belgium. They stopped briefly there. Some of the men jumped out of the truck and visited a bakery and bought some bread. They almost didn't make it back in time because the trucks were leaving. Sandahl grabbed the tailgate of the truck on the run.

They arrived at St. Vith, Belgium, where the Division Headquarters and the Command Post were located. They were to replace 2nd Division troops in holding actions with no enemy activity apparent. They were informed that the front was all quiet and it was time to have a picnic. It had snowed and the scenery was beautiful as they moved into position the first part of December of 44. A few patrols were sent out but there was no activity on the enemy side of the lines.

The men lived in log and earth covered dugouts that were relatively shell proof between the 3rd and 4th row of pillboxes in the old Seigfried line. The 422nd Regiment Command Post was in an old pillbox constructed of concrete that had not been destroyed. This was part of the Maginot-Seigfried line of defensive positions of pillboxes and Anti-tank, "jacks" or obstructions. This section was rough terrain in the Ardennes Forest of the Belgium-German border.

Sandahl was quartered in a dugout with his Lt. Fred Koenig, Sgt. Waffle and the Company Medic. Sandahl was responsible for the unit communications network, which consisted primarily of sound-power telephones to all positions connected with wire strung in the trees and on the ground. (No cell phones here.) Enemy shelling raised havoc with the wire and they repaired many breaks and/or ran new wire under sniper fire. Snipers always seemed to be zeroed in on the open spaces in the woods with their harassing burp guns.

Enemy shelling was increasing and the front lines near Sandahl's position were once again coming to life.

Supplies for the company came from LeHavre quite a distance away. Fresh water was out of the question so the men had to melt snow to drink. Fuel for cooking was also running low along with vehicles and ammunition. Food was also dwindling as they waited for supplies. Ammunition was beginning to be rationed. The artillery was limited to 9 rounds of 105-mm. ammo per day. During one period of shelling, the Battalion Command Post took a direct hit. Lt. Col. Kent, the Battalion Commander, was killed. "Kent truly was a soldiers leader. He carried his M-1 rifle and walked the front to visit outposts every day. He always had time to chat," Sandahl said.

The Commanding Executive, 1st Lt. William Brice, a West Pointer was killed by a sniper bullet right between the eyes. Sandahl said Brice loved to polish the silver bar on his helmet. This proved to be fatal as the shiny bar made a good target for the sniper. The same day, Sandahl saw his first dead German.

The patrols reported an increase in German activity. They could see the town of Prum by now. Enemy shelling was also increasing. They captured two young very frightened German soldier boys. They were moved to the rear of the group. Sandahl often wonders what became of them after what was soon to take place. Attacks were increasing by ground troops. The men held their position under heavy artillery fire. It was difficult to keep the phone lines in tack. Repair and maintenance was conducted at night. Sandahl was recommended for the Silver Star for his bravery in trying to keep the lines repaired but the recommendation was lost, as were many field promotions, he said. He was supposed to have been promoted to Sergeant, too, but it never took place. He did receive the Bronze Star and Purple Heart, however.

Fighting had become more intense and the word came that the supplies had been cut off. Germans who had broken through the lines north of their Division by bridging the tank traps with heavy timbers surrounded them. The order came to retreat and "Get out the best we could," Sandahl said.

The men had relayed word back to Division Headquarters several days earlier that they could hear tanks moving into the area opposite to their front each night. HQ "pooh-poohed" the idea, as did the higher echelon. The men knew it was true because they had also received word that the 106th Division Headquarters had moved to St. Vith.

Sandahl recalls loading up on a few extra pancakes at the mess tent the morning as they prepared to move out. The retreat was orderly, in a northern direction, roughly parallel to the front line cross-country through rough wooded areas. They bivouacked the night of the December 18th in a small wooded area just outside Schoenburg, Germany. They were under orders to fight their way through this town the next morning and that they had a chance of making it. Tanks could be seen and the officers informed the men they were British tanks and that no one should worry about them. When the 88's started firing at them they soon discovered that these tanks were not British but brand new German Royal Tiger Tanks complete with big diesel engines running each track with immense armor. The bazookas the men fired back at them wouldn't faze them. Several German infantrymen were killed however before the men found themselves surrounded by 5 tanks in a flooding open area with haystacks across the valley. Men who tried to take cover were being picked off one at a time by the 88-mm. guns on the tanks. The aid men, with his Red Cross markings, went to help a fellow soldier and were blown to bits. The men tried to move up the valley in the water but they were pinned down. Sandahl was nicked in the shoulder by shrapnel or a bullet, he doesn't know what and then was knocked down by a burst of a shell that wounded Lt. Koenig in the leg. Sandahl's eardrum was damaged and he was knocked unconscious by the concussion of the shell. When he came to, he saw every one around surrendering with white flags and their hands above their heads. He smashed his rifle and threw away the bolt into the water and used the gun as a crutch to hobble out with the rest.

They now were POW's. As they made their way to wherever they were to be taken, they crossed a stream where Sandahl filled his canteen. A few yards from where he filled it, he noted a dead cow and horse floating in the water. He emptied his canteen and filled it again upstream and put a couple extra atabrin, water purification tablets, into the canteen. "It tasted good," he said.

The men were hastily searched by the very young German soldiers, probably Hitler youth and marched back to the town of Schoenburg and corralled in a cattle yard. The wounded were loaded on tanks and taken away. "There must have been several thousand men captured with many wounded or killed," he said. It was the entire 1st Battalion, 422nd Infantry Regiment plus a bunch of stragglers, he added.

The Germans used aged guards, 60-70+ years old, Austrian Volkguards they were, that marched the men to their POW camp. The first day, December 19th, they were marched to Prum, about 30 km. There they were bedded down in straw like cattle in an old bombed out university building without any windows he recalls. They were given no food either and it was very cold. The second day they were given a cup of warm ersatz tea and marched to Gerolstein, a total of 80 kilometers. There they were loaded into the infamous 40 X 8 boxcars designed for 40 men or eight horses. But the Germans squeezed in 67 men and locked the doors in the car Sandahl was in. The train traveled through what could have been Cologne and Koblenz where they could see all the bomb damage through cracks in the car sideboards. They had also noted the cars were not marked with a Red Cross on the top as regulations of the International Red Cross called for. A plane of ours could have easily bombed them and added to their problems. The railroad tracks were damaged, as the train had to zigzag around repairs.

Finally they arrived in Limburg where they were supposed to go to Stalag 12-A. Sandahl said that it apparently was already full so the Germans left them locked up in the cars with no privacy. The car was so crowded they couldn't all sit down at one time, let alone lie down and sleep. The men relieved themselves in their steel helmets and dumped them out through the cracks. Later they would have to eat from the same helmet.

On the night of December 23, the RAF bombed the area intended to do some damage to the railyard. The men later learned that Stalag 12-A was also bombed. Fortunately, they weren't locked up there. Some box cars sustained direct hits, too, with many men killed. Miraculously, the car Sandahl was in was "shredded like a sieve, but no was wounded," he said. The next morning they were allowed to leave the car to relieve themselves.

Christmas Eve they moved out by rail and rode all night until they arrived at Bad Orb, Germany, at noon Christmas Day. There they were unloaded and marched about 3 miles up a mountain to Stalag IX-B. They were the first American POW's to arrive at this former Hitler Youth Camp which was complete with wall murals with Nazi propaganda to encourage propagation of the "Pure Aryan Race." This was the place where healthy Germans, and other captive citizens, girls, were brought to mate with handpicked German soldiers on leave from their army duties. Hence the term, Hitler Youth, for this new super generation of Nazi's.

The barracks were generally cold and gray with few windows and only inside toilets for night use, which consisted of a 6-inch hole in the floor with a honey pit below! The barracks were in long rows with a cold water washroom between 2 barracks. The outside latrine was a deep open pit with long "benches," on all four sides. The wire enclosure was 2 rows of barbed wire fences with 15-20 feet between the fences. Guardhouses were on the fence and corners and also on the sides. Sandahl was in Barracks 43 A, closest to the outdoor latrine.

One of the Germans in command was a Corporal who was an America citizen and owned a business in Chicago. He had returned home to visit his parents before WW II and was conscripted into the army. He had even sang in the church choir and was sympathetic to the cause of the American prisoners, at least as much as he could be.

The men were locked in their barracks at night and rousted in the morning at the crack of dawn when the head count was taken. They were given a small cup of warm ersatz tea and waited until noon to receive some watery soup of some sorts. It had little or no meat unless they found a dead cat, dog, horse or cow somewhere Sandahl said. The soup was made with a few beets; carrot or turnip tops with little or no seasoning and was usually cold when they got it. One of the men, by twisting the cook's arm, got a horse leg to gnaw on one time. The evening meal was a small loaf of black German bread that tasted like half sawdust. Six to ten men shared this little loaf. They would take turns carving the bread so the one carving had the last choice. The men were always hungry. They would make lists of candy bars they dreamed of. They had the list to over 100 different kinds.

Two Chaplains were also with the men. One was a Catholic and the other a Methodist. Two medical officers, one dentist and several medics were also on hand. They had regular church services, Bible classes and discussion groups. Favorite hymns like; the captive men sang "Blest Be the Tie That Binds, Rock of Ages, In the Garden". Psalm 121 was most fitting for where they were. Some Sunday mornings they would have as high as seven baptisms. Men could attend quiz shows and also talent shows the men put together to pass the time. Sandahl remembers a Negro boy who sang, "Danny Boy." Another Negro was quite a comic. He had been in an East Coast, U.S.A. prison camp. Sandahl said his only spoon was one he whittled from a flat stick of wood to use with his GI helmet for a bowl.

On Sunday, January 28th, the men were all rousted out of the barracks and lined up in the yard with several machine guns surrounding them. The ultimatum was given to produce the person, or persons, who had killed a cook in the kitchen. Apparently someone had tried to steal some food and they had been caught. After several hours of searching, some bloody clothes were found in a bunk and two GI's were taken and undoubtedly executed. "This was truly a Black Sunday," Sandahl said.

The "one a month" showers were a farce. They were ordered to undress and then they were given some sand grit soap and the cold water was turned on. When their bodies were all soaped up, they shut the water off. Then they would say, "Alus Kaput," or meaning the water supply was broken. It was nothing more than more psychological warfare. Wiping the grimy soap off without a towel and putting on their dirty clothes was bad for morale. They were able to wash their own underwear and hang it out on the fence to dry but often it was stolen. Toothpaste and toilet articles had all been taken away from them. Cigarettes were scarce but they were a medium of barter exchange. Each compound had its own wheeler dealer trader tycoon. They were no doubt in cahoots with the Germans to acquire some of their merchandise in trade. They only received one Red Cross parcel while imprisoned there. They were shared with others, as the quota of one per man was not met.

Occasionally, the men would see American planes fly over and a few new German jets. Once P-47's strafed the camp as they were dog-fighting the Krauts over the camp. The men hit the floor. A 50-caliber bullet went through the bunk where Sandahl had been laying just minutes before. Three men were killed and the horses that were bringing up Red Cross parcels were also killed. Later, they had horsemeat in their soup. The Red Cross parcels burned up with the wagon.

February was nice and mild. The men would stand outside as much as possible trying to get some sun. But, weak as they were, standing on the south side of the barracks, men would often pass out while standing in the sun.

Work details were used to cut wood away from the camp and one could earn extra food, thicker soup. Also details were used for the honey wagon dipping the waste out of the cesspools with a rope and bucket. The buckets would be dumped into a tank wagon on wheels and pushed by the men to the field and dumped.

The men dreamed of food and liberation. Girls weren't thought of much. For 3 months they had not seen a female. The men who suffered most were the married ones, especially those with expectant wives, not knowing anything. The men were allowed to write one card per month. Towards the end of the captivity, food became better with more potatoes being in the menu.

What the men needed most was a positive mental attitude with hope for the future. Sandahl said he saw strong, healthy men simply give up with no will to live. They would be dead in a week.

The medics imprisoned with them worked wonders with little or no medicine. An epidemic of spinal meningitis broke out in the camp just a few days before they were liberated. Sandahl doubts if he, himself, would have lived another month. He lost a pound a day during the three and a half months that he was captive. In the 105 days, his belt that once fit comfortably around his waist now could be wrapped around him twice and buckled. He estimated he weighed less than 90 pounds.

During Holy Week, they could hear heavy fighting in the valley and on the plains below. The German guards gathered the men together and told them liberation for them was imminent and for their own safety they should stay put and not leave the area. The guards took off and the fighting in the distance came to a lull.

On Easter Sunday morning, April 1, 1945, the men awoke to see an American flag raised at 6 a.m. on the clock tower of the compound. By 8 a.m. the German officials had given up and advance units of the 44th Infantry Division greeted the men. A Sherman tank approached the small gate that was built for small German cars and trucks. The tank paused, revved up its engine and proceeded to push the fence with heavy timbers and bounced over. It circled the barracks with antennae whipping and the GI's shouted and were crying for joy. The first one out of the tank was a six-foot plus Major with pearl handled revolvers on each hip. Blood was on his tanker jacket. He, along with the other GI's who rescued them, "looked like supermen to us poor emaciated POW's," Sandahl stated.

Ambulances and food were brought in by 10 a.m. Men were taken to the hospital and men were given huge chocolate candy bars, which proved to be a mistake to consume. Their bodies were not used to eating them and they became "sick as dogs," he said.

242

A few days later the men left the camp and went down the mountain to Bad Orb. German citizens were afraid of them. They gave them good bread and orange marmalade from Red Cross parcels that had been meant for them previously. The men, too tired to walk, had caught rides on M-8, 6 wheel trucks, loaded with cases of wine, cognac and whatever else men would be delighted with.

They had left Stalag IX-B the morning of April 7, 1945 and were trucked to delousing stations and showers near the Hanau airfield. The chemical DDT was used. Clothes were all replaced and they were flown to Collimeers, France, on a C-47 that circled the Eiffel tower in Paris enroute. They were processed at Camp Lucky Strike and loaded on the ship USS General Richardson, a troop ship for a two-week leisurely convoy trip back home leaving LeHavre, France.

The men were treated like walking wounded with no duties. Officers from the Air Force even conducted KP, kitchen duties for them. Sandahl and the rest of the men arrived home before VE Day and spent 60 days on temporary duty at home. The "Grand Old Lady in New York harbor never looked better. We kissed the ground of the good old U.S.A.," he concluded.

Sandahl was discharged on December 8, 1945, at Fort Logan, Colorado. He chose to stay in the reserves.

SEKORA, EDWARD D.

Sekora is from Grand Island. His story was obtained by the efforts of his nephew Craig Buescher, of Deweese, and his son Brian who conducted the interview. Brian, while at UNL, visited with his great uncle as part of a history assignment. Sekora served in WW II in the European Theatre. He was there during the Battle of the Bulge, the largest military battle in the history of the U.S. Army. It also proved to be one of the most significant events of the Second World War era.

Buescher, during the interview, learned what perhaps history books cannot always tell. One has to talk to someone who was actually there, he said.

Sekora was a Staff Sgt. in the 255th Medium Maintenance Company at the time. He was not at the front lines, but very near. He saw the results of the battle and was there when these results were obtained. Here is what Buescher learned during this interview.

Around 77,000 Americans were killed, injured or captured during the Battle of the Bulge. Many are still alive today. Germany was now in a position of having to fight a defensive war. From the time of D-Day, June 6, 1944, Sekora followed the war as it pushed into Germany. The Allies had attacked German occupied Normandy, France. Now they were running for the lives from the quick moving Allied forces that hit the beaches treading on German occupied lands. It would take the Allies six months to liberate France and make its way to the German border.

On December 16, 1944 Sekora and the 255th Maintenance Company stopped at Eupen, Belgium. During the two months before the attack in the Bulge, few shots were fired; both sides avoided irritating each other even though soldiers were well within rifle range of each other. The fact was that most soldiers who were in the Ardennes at this time were better off than those fighting at some of the other battles.

Hitler was depressed with the fact the Allies had made it into France and the liberation of it. However, he wanted to make one last attempt in winning the war. In this one last attempt, Hitler, along with his Chief of Operations, Colonel Jodi, devised a plan with two premises. One was to catch the enemy by complete surprise. Two make sure the weather would not be favorable for the Allied planes to be in the air. They devised a plan of attack in the region of the Ardennes. Germany had never lost a battle their before, dating back to 1870 and fighting two battles their after that, in 1914 and 1940. Hitler saw no reason they could not do it again. He felt the Allies were the weakest in the Ardennes and also would sooner attack the inexperienced Americans than the more experienced British elsewhere. He postponed the attack date twice, finally settling on December 16, 1944. In spite of his Generals attempting to discourage him, Hitler refused to listen committing to either total victory or total defeat.

German had prepared for the battle very well. The Allies weren't expecting an attack and the Germans had assembled 410,000 men, 2,600 military pieces and 1,400 tanks. They had cut off all radio communications to keep the event as secret as possible. They moved their troops at night covering up the noise of the ground troops by their aircraft flying overhead.

The Allies were not ready for this attack although they suspected it could take place. The Allied forces by now assumed that the Germans figured there was no way they could win the war and they would not initiate any major attack. One American Colonel tried to explain and convince the staff that Hitler was going to attack in the Ardennes, but he was ignored. Instead, he was sent for some R & R to Paris for a few days.

The Allies also underestimated Germany's ability to produce the materials needed to fight the war, thinking they had destroyed most of the manufacturing plants by the fall of 1944. Germany, during the four months before the attack had produced a million tons of ammunition, three quarters of a million rifles, 100,000 machine guns, 9,000 mortars and 9,000 heavy artillery pieces. Also, they produced over 3,000 single engine fighter planes during this time. They were getting prepared.

On 16 December 16, the Germans made their move. Located on several fronts the Germans produced an artillery barrage that lasted nearly an hour. Because the Germans miscalculated, most of the American Divisions did not endure a great number of casualties as a result of this initial attack. The Germans had attacked directly in the center of the Allied forces and our forces were able to hold them back.

Further south, the Allied forces weren't doing so well. With a mighty artillery barrage, the Germans managed to penetrate into the Ardennes 60 miles before they were stopped. It took the Allied 3rd Army of General Patton to eventually stop the advance on December 18th. By December 26, Patton broke through the city of Bastogne. The Allied 101st Airborne division held the city starting December 18, but by the 22nd, the Germans had them surrounded and were asking the 101st to surrender. At this time, our General McAuliffe told the Germans to more or less, "go to hell," they had no plans of surrender and continued to hold the city. When Patton made it to Bastogne, the Battle of Bulge was more or less reduced to this city. The German attack on the Ardennes had failed.

Fighting continued in the Bulge throughout December and early January but by then it was apparent the Germans were backing out. Then the skies cleared off so that by January 21-23, the Allied planes could bomb again creating a great blow to the Germans. They lost vast numbers of men and equipment. The Germans began taking out their best troops first leaving the 2nd and 3rd string to slow the quickly advancing Allies. By January 28, the Germans had been pushed back to their original positions. The battle had officially ended for the Germans. It was an utter failure for them.

What went wrong for the Germans? By this time Adolph Hitler was no longer mentally competent to order the attack. He even had some his Generals try to assassinate him already in July of 1944. He had made several illogical actions in the fall of 1944 proving his state of mind was deteriorated. The attack on the Ardennes was entirely too ambitious and not realistic, his Generals knew that. His plan really never had a chance when he underestimated the firepower his army would have to encounter. Hitler had assumed the Allies would give up, but they did not. He did not realize the Americans were such a viable force to resist his attack.

Sekora recalls the situation well. First the weather, one of the coldest winters on record. The American soldiers were not well equipped for such cold weather and suffered immensely, he said. Snow, ice and slush underfoot and a drizzle sleet falling. Sleet would fall down your neck with no way to keep it out. "You just hunched up and tried to keep the wind and the wet out the best way you could," he said.

Gloves were too short and checking the guns every now and then, soon got wet then froze. Feet were soaked inside of a half-hour of walking. "We had no overshoes and my shoes leaked like a sieve," he added.

The weather had its affects on equipment as well. Roads, either snow or mud, made them slick and movement was difficult. A shortage of antifreeze produced that problem. Without clear weather the Air Force was not able to support the ground troops. "Air superiority was insignificant in the Battle of the Bulge until later," Sekora said.

Basic necessities, food and shelter made life almost unbearable at times. No warm place to sleep, some soldiers dug three-foot deep foxholes to sleep in but they were neither warm nor comfortable. Fires could not be started to keep warm because the smoke would give away their positions and draw enemy artillery fire. With food in short supply, soldiers had to endure extreme cold with near empty stomachs.

The battle at the Bulge also had its psychological effects on the men. The ground shook with artillery fire day and night. Soldiers lived in constant fear of being killed or wounded. They had to deal with the fact their friends were being killed beside them. "At an age of only 20-21 years, this was extremely difficult to endure," Sekora said.

Sekora told of one of his friends by the name of Anton Hubble who never that made it back. Hubble and Sekora had gone to the same church in the Deweese area. They shared the same birthday of November 15, 1920. Hubble was a special friend. Throughout the Campaign in Europe, Sekora and Hubble kept in contact by their letters. The last letter Sekora wrote was returned. On it was written, "Deceased, 9 November 1944." Hubble had died in the same forest Sekora was in during the Bulge battle.

It is no wonder; men like Sekora find it hard to talk about what books portray as often a "glorious battle." It was not glorious for those who fought in it. It was hard for Sekora to talk about and the Battle of the Bulge has had a lasting effect on the men who fought it, Brian Buescher stated.

"A first hand eye witness like Staff Sergeant Edward D. Sekora can try to help us understand the humanity behind the statistics," Buescher concludes.

SMITH, JACK D.

From Kearney, Smith was a Master Sgt. in the Army fighting in Korea with the 24th Division Medical Battalion. He was a Medical Supply Sgt. He was involved in 5 Campaigns and has the Battle Stars to verify it. Along with those he also has the Bronze Star, Korean Presidential Citation and Good Conduct Medal. He entered the service in September of 1947 and performed his duties until September of 1951 when he was discharged. His stories could be many, he said, but he chooses not to tell about them. He feels good about serving his country he added.

SMITH, ROBERT

Smith was born and raised in Nebraska and considers himself a Nebraska Veteran. With family and friends living here he has "fond memories of the place I call home," he said. His niece had sent him a Lincoln Star newspaper where I was once featured in concerning this book. Smith was kind in sending me his story.

He enlisted in the Army Specialized Training Program, ASTRP, "pronounced Asstrap," he said, "cause that was the case." You were in a sense, trapped. He had completed one quarter of college and celebrated his 18th birthday during the quarter. He knew his number would be coming up so he was off to Fort Leavenworth, Kansas for training on December 20, 1943. His life was interrupted and even messed up Christmas and New Years when the army sent him to Fort Benning, Georgia for infantry training.

At Fort Benning there was an area known as Harmony Church, which had been a POW area at one time. But the army decided the quarters were inadequate for the POW's and moved them out to make room for trainees like Smith. These lovely tar paper rectangular buildings had double deck bunks along one side of the structure and three more at each end and two on the side where the doors were open. In the middle of the building was the central heating unit, a potbellied stove. When it was fired up, those on the sides would be too hot and those on the ends could see their breath.

After two and half months training in this place of mud and misery he indeed felt trapped. He was sent to Fort Bragg, North Carolina to join the 100th Infantry Division, and completed his training there. Then he left for his all expense paid trip to Europe as a member of the 2nd Platoon, Company B, 398th Infantry Regiment.

His job was lead scout for the squad. This gave him the opportunity to see the territory first hand and meet the inhabitants. Some, of course, were tourists from another country and frequently objected to men like Smith taking over their accommodations. I suspect he's smiling as he wrote this.

By December 20, 1944, his platoon had the strength of 13 men and one officer. It had started with 42 with 14 other men and one officer already acting as replacements. On this day, his platoon was a reserve for the Company. The Company came under mortar fire and hit the dirt. Since forward movement was essential they moved out in single file. After a few minutes word came that two people ahead had been injured and contact broken with the rest of the Company. Small arms fire could be heard up ahead but due to the terrain and wooded area, it was uncertain where it was coming from.

Smith, along with another Pfc. Pete Smith, was ordered to work themselves back down the hill to acquire instructions from the commander on what to do next. Attempting to do this, they encountered a German flanking patrol. The two signaled to the rest of the men that the enemy was in sight but it was too late. Smith was carrying a BAR, Browning Automatic Rifle, and the other Smith, an M-1 rifle. Trying to return fire, the BAR jammed. Pete was in the brush not having a clear field of fire. A potato masher grenade exploded between them and within moments, two Germans, who appeared to be 15 feet tall, aimed their 200-mm. Schmeiser automatic rifles at them. They were only about six feet away from them. Though the height of these men is exaggerated, they seemed that big especially with those large caliber rifles. Now they were POW's, and quickly taken into custody joining about 12 other men. Although the company had seen their signal, they were unable to respond and render them any assistance.

They were taken to the rear headquarters and questioned. The answers the Germans received were, name, rank and serial number. They were taken by vehicle to a compound in Zweibrucken, or known as Du Ponts, or two bridges.

The building they were put in at this compound was a prefabricated type with floor supports that had collapsed. It was unheated and had no beds. They were to sleep on the floor. For meals, they were given rye bread, inedible, at least the first day. By the second day it was tolerable and by the fifth day they looked forward to it as mom's apple pie he said.

Christmas and New Years was spent at the compound. Little as he liked the holidays at Fort Leavenworth, he likes it less here. Then on about the 4th or 5th of January, along with about 75 other POW's they were marched to Kaiserslautern. The local citizens were not too receptive of the men because; the airbase there had been bombed by our Air Corp. The citizens displayed their anger by spitting on them and throwing an occasional rock.

Soon they were loaded on the standard 40 X 8 boxcars, 40 men or 8 horses, not very comfortable. Having about 35 men per train car, the sanitary facilities consisted of a bucket in one corner. No seats, blankets or other comforts were available. The train stopped twice and they were allowed off the train once a day. They were given a piece of bread at one stop and some thin soup at another.

After three days they arrived at Villingen, their first regular prison camp or Stalag. Accommodations were a little better here than at Zweibrucken, but nothing to write home about. There were three levels of shelves, which occupied three of the four walls of the building. They were each about 6 ½ feet wide and about 3 feet between levels. About 70 men were put in each room that measured 20 X 30 feet.

Food here consisted of thin soup with few solids; a potato and some bread usually rye bread. They were allowed to go outside three times a day to the latrine and exercise once a day.

Each person had one thin blanket and no pillows. No shower or laundry facilities were provided. As one can imagine, after a time, everyone was becoming a little "gamy" he said.

In other parts of the POW camp were also British and Russian prisoners. Upon one occasion in the Russian barracks, they refused to come out for a head count. A dog was sent in to force them out. The dog however, was killed and thrown out. They could see the other prisoners but there was no intercamp communications.

They were moved from Villingen, which was near the Swiss border to Stalag III-A at Luckenwalde, Germany, about 40 miles south of Berlin. The same "travel agent" was used as before for this trip with all the same luxuries. This prison was much more established than the others were. Beds were wooden double deck bunks in groups of six, with wooden slats rising slightly at one end provided support. Straw filled burlap pads were the mattresses and each person had a blanket.

Smith estimates there were about 120 bunks in the room he was in. A board divided the bunks that were three in length and two feet wide with common posts supporting the head and foot of each bunk.

When they arrived at this new site, their welcoming included being deloused and they could take a shower. An overcoat was issued to them and a warm, billed cap. Their clothing was all stamped with the letters, KGF, which stood for Kreigs Gefangnen, or war prisoner.

Food, too, was slightly improved. In addition to 200 grams of bread a day they would have either soup or a boiled potato. Once a week they were given a pat of margarine, a teaspoon of sugar and occasionally a slice of salami or some other sausage.

A ceramic stove in the center of the room provided heat. The Germans provided enough wood to burn about three hours a day. A few bed slats were burned but they found them to be irreplaceable so few more were burned.

In about a month they were moved again to another location at Magdeburg. They found out later that those going there ended up working in a brickyard. There "travel agent" was not around so the men were invited to hike to this new location. They began at 9 a.m. and got there by dusk.

Smith looked the situation over as they arrived in this little town only about three blocks long and a block wide. He stepped outside the file onto the sidewalk and no one said anything. He stepped back in the ranks and said to Pete, "let's get the hell out of here." They both got on the sidewalk and walked along with the rest until they got a corner and turned leaving the rest continue on the march straight ahead.

In the darkness they hurried up the road and out of the village. As they scurried away someone shouted, "zwie mannen," which meant "two men." Their absence had been discovered but neither of the two was aware of a search effort. They continued on to a shed that was used for storing machinery. It was the only building around and it had a storage loft. They broke into the building and spent the night there. The next day they developed a phase two of their plan to escape. They decided they should go east and meet the Russians who were probably much closer to them now than the Americans. Bare in mind, they had no compass or map and in all actuality, had no idea where they were. During this planning they consumed the rations given to them for the trip to Magdeburg.

That evening they started for the eastern front. After walking about two hours they heard someone say, "Halt!" It wasn't Pete or Smith. They complied with the request and as the flashlight a man shone in their faces made them squint, when they saw the black uniforms and the lightning bolts on their collars, they knew they had walked right into a German SS training camp. "Lucky us," Smith said.

They were searched, questioned extensively and fed. The German SS troops thought it was hilarious they had escaped from the Wehrmacht. They asked them about their treatment at the prison camp. The camp commandant stated, "you should be better cared for than you have described.

Someone in authority should be made aware of conditions." He placed a call to Berlin and made an appointment for Pete and I to tell our story.

The next day we went in the back of a covered truck to Berlin. A Dutch member of the German SS who spoke excellent English was their guard. His mother had an apartment in Berlin and she happened to be gone to Amsterdam. The guard invited the men, if they agreed not to try to escape, to stay at this apartment with him. They quickly agreed.

That night was a social event. The son had came home, friends came over and refreshments were served and records were played. Duke Ellington's "Mood Indigo," was played and still is a favorite of Smith's. Twice those night air raid sirens went off and each time they would go to the basement for about a half an hour and come back up again.

The next morning they toured Berlin via the subway with their guard. In the afternoon they spoke with the Colonel in the German Army. Each of them was interviewed alone. After Smith had complained about the conditions and lack of Red Cross packages, he was told the rations were the same as the German civilians received and that the Red Cross packages would be distributed if the Allies would stop bombing the railroads. At the close of the interview he offered Smith a Chesterfield cigarette, from a Red Cross package.

The colonel informed the guard that the prisoners should not stay in civilian quarters but they should be placed in a jail in Berlin. The next day they went by train back to the area of the German SS camp to await return to Wehrmacht control. They had dinner with the camp Commandant one day, horsemeat, though they didn't know it. Allied aircraft had killed the animal and the meat salvaged for human consumption.

In three days they were back at Stalag III-A. For escaping they were given six days in confinement with only bread and water. This was a compound within the camp, which was basically a jail. Two men cells with barred doors and windows. Between the cells were ceramic stoves to heat the building.

The jail was operated by French prisoners and the prisoners would sneak them soup and potatoes so they ate better than they would have in the regular camp. Another prisoner in the jail was an English soldier. He gave them a tin of bully beef, which was delicious. He had obtained it from a

British Red Cross package. He was awaiting transfer to a criminal prison for assaulting a German officer. He had been on a work detail guarded by a civilian.

When their six days were up they were put back in the regular prison camp compound. All of the prisoners were new, having been moved from near the Polish border area due to Russian advances. A few days passed and their Red Cross packages started coming. The two men felt that maybe it was due to their efforts.

After another two weeks the Germans wanted two people to go to a work camp. Smith and Pete were chosen, out of 800 prisoners at the camp by now. They figured it was another reward for escaping. They were taken to a food warehouse about 35 miles from Luckenwalde to a town called Juterbog. The warehouse had an eight-foot high fence with barbed wire on the top. Their first assignment was to clean a warehouse that was used for root crops like carrots and beets, etc. They put a bag of onion underneath a pile of dirt they had cleaned out of the warehouse in a wheelbarrow. They took it to a place near the fence, covered it with dirt in hopes they could use the onions for trading as they were valuable for that purpose. Other prisoners smuggled carrots, salami, potatoes and other foods in. They wanted to stockpile more but the wheelbarrow broke down and couldn't continue to finish that job. Around 75 American prisoners were at this camp at the time.

Now they had snacks to eat during the day. Canned meat was on hand so with his "10 in 1" can opener on his dog chain, they opened the cans of meat very neatly. They would open a can, take a few bites and put it back on the shelf. Prisoners were searched for the can opener but no one ever found it.

Smith remembers a civilian supervisor by the name of Herman who didn't really care if any work got done or not. Smith wanted to learn some German so in about a span of a month, he was able to carry on a limited conversation thanks to Herman who taught him.

The Germans still used horses on the eastern front. Straw was also shipped to these locations for them. Smith had to load bales of straw on the railhead for loading. A German civilian was supervising that detail. He was not a happy guy and was quite unpleasant to be around. Especially when a bale fell down and knocked him off the wagon, he became more unpleasant Smith said.

While on one of the straw hauling days, an armed guard and Smith got into it. Smith admits he provoked it when he tried to catch a chicken. It really provoked the guard more when Smith informed the guard that he could leave at any time. He could show him how. Smith grabbed his rifle off his shoulder leaving him defenseless. Then it dawned on him that was probably a dumb thing to do so he handed the rifle back to him and turned away. The guard shouted at him a lot but probably figured he would get in trouble for shooting a prisoner who was not trying to get away.

Cookies were also stored in one of the warehouses behind locked doors. The two figured out how to remove the lock and stole a box of cookies. On their first attempt a German civilian interrupted them, as they were about to leave. Pete started berating the guy loudly in English and they both walked out with the cookies. Later in the afternoon they were searched but the two had hidden the cookies in a hay barn. Almost every night they were taken out of their barracks because of air raids. They would head for the trenches near the hay barn and grab a few cookies while they were out there. Every evening after work they were searched but not when they returned from the air raid shelter.

Pete was placed in the prison bakery. Life was improving with Red Cross packages, rations and what they could steal, and they no longer were constantly hungry.

On the evening of April 22, 1945, they could hear the artillery fire and bombs exploding in the distance. Several planes were seen flying over with Russian markings. On the 23rd, guards informed the POW's they were leaving for Bavaria and marched them out of the warehouse area. The men could see that the Germans were making preparations to destroy the warehouses.

They had been marching for three days when they heard a guard say, "the Americans are about two kilometers ahead. Go to them." Smith and Pete assisted other POW's with hurt feet who were bringing up the rear. An American GI rode up to them on a motorcycle and inquired, "Where the hell have you guys been?" They were back in American hands near Halle, Germany.

During the time they were prisoners, none of their parents knew where they were or what happened to them. They had been listed as "missing in action," until they returned to U.S. control. Smith said in the book of the 100th Infantry Division's "The Story of the Century," still has them as missing in action.

Smith states that the four months he spent as a POW has effected his entire life. "Daily I am affected by it," he said. John Peter, (Pete) Smith, remains his closest friend. Robert met his wife when he was on a special leave afforded to POW's and his discharge date was also determined by that fact. As an ex-POW he does receive some added benefits which he very much appreciates.

But, on a sad and yet humorous note, his favorite bureaucratic story, in 1948 Congress decided that since the POW's had not been fed by the U.S. while they were imprisoned, they should receive $1 a day for the days they were POW captives. Each POW had to fill out a form which stated the dates, etc. It also asked if they had ever escaped. Smith reported the two days he was free at the time so the government deducted $2 from his check.

A year later Congress again decided to change the rules. Now if a person was a prisoner for 60 or more days it was prima facie evidence that he had been mistreated and the imprisoning nation should pay him $1 per day. This time the Germans deducted the $2. Result: Escaping for two days, cost him $4.

That's what it was like for guys like Smith. Another story to remind us the high cost of freedom!

STOKES, EARL, (BILL)

Stokes chaired a committee for the 50th Anniversary Celebration and at that time compiled stories and memorabilia concerning WW II. When I visited with him, he stated that those veterans, "deserved some recognition for their part in the preservation of freedom."

Bill was deferred twice from service to help his dad on the farm. All his friends were being drafted for the Korean War and he felt he had to join too. With out consulting with his parents, he went to the draft board on his own and asked them why he hadn't been drafted like his friends. They told him it was because of his farm deferment. He told them to draft him and they did. He never did tell his folks.

In January of 1951 he went to Fort Omaha and was sworn in along with other draftees from Antelope County. In a short time he made friends with Robert Miller of Clearwater. He had a serial number right next to Stokes so they found themselves together quite often. From there they went to Fort Riley, Kansas and were processed into different units. It is with sadness he notes that Miller was put into the 7th Infantry and Stokes was placed in the 746th Engineers Heavy Shop Company and sent to Granite City, Illinois for more training. In a matter of few short weeks, Stokes received a letter from his mother saying that Robert Miller was killed in Korea. He was an only child of Guy Miller of Clearwater. Stokes visits his buddy's grave at least once a year at Clearwater.

Stokes wound up in Thule, Greenland at an air base working on heavy equipment. He was involved in Operation Blue Jay, a secret operation that involved listening devices to monitor Russian radio communications. He spent his time in service there until he returned home in January of 1953.

Stokes missed the service for a time and the new friends he had made. Men who joined the service during times of war never know for sure where they would end up. Stokes could have been with him his buddy Miller when he was killed but fate had it that he wasn't there. When they were drafted they were put where they were told and fortunately for some that they didn't have to go through the horrors of war like so many did. But at the same time they supported those who did in some way or another.

STONE, JACK

Stone is a WW II veteran from Lincoln. He served in the European Theatre with the 101st Division of the U.S. Army. He was with a temporary regimental combat team. A division normally consists of three regiments; he belonged to a fourth regiment. He told me that it was a unit by itself.

He was drafted into the Army and his country took him where he was most needed at the time. He began his tour of duty on June 6, 1943. He was a rifleman who earned three battle stars and he went through hell during the notorious Battle of the Bulge. Yet, he states, "It was a privilege to serve my country."

Stone is glad he was in the generation he was in. "A truly fabulous and courageous generation. I'm proud to be an American," he proudly proclaims. At the time, all his friends and classmates were in the service. Every home in the neighborhood had a close relative involved in the war, no one complained, "We were all in the same boat, WW II was everyone's war," he said.

He began his story at the Battle of the Bulge. It was in the dead of winter and his feet and hands were frostbitten when he was heading back to the rear area with a wounded comrade. With his wounded buddy's arm around his neck, they were trying to get medical attention for him. They thought they were alone. Suddenly a man dressed in white appeared. Stone thought he was an American medic because there was a Red Cross on his sleeve. Because there was no one else around, he summoned for the man in white to come help him. He refused, instead, motioned for Stone to come towards him. Since his buddy going into shock, Stone cursed at the medic and shouted at him to help. Stone could hardly walk himself, his feet only shuffled on the frozen snow. It was early in the morning with heavy overcast skies, and at 50 yards from the man he still thought the man was an American. But when he refused to meet him, he wondered if the man was an American. At 10 yards, Stone, in the gloomy haze, saw a visor on the man's field cap. "I knew then he was a German," he said.

Behind the man was a house. Stone peered over towards it and saw men looking out of every window. They were German men who belonged to a German Ski Patrol. There was nothing he could do about the situation that he found himself in. His hands were clenched shut by the cold; he couldn't even open them to grab a weapon if he wanted too. "I just thought we were dead," he remembered.

Finally the man in white took two steps towards him and low and behold helped Stone carry his buddy into the house with the help of two other Germans who came out. They were put into an empty building and guarded. The wounded man, now in shock, was taken into another room. Stone never saw him again and Stone was left alone with his captors.

Stone said that the German in white was no doubt a medic. He asked Stone if he would take off his shoes so he could look at his frostbitten feet and Stone could not because of his frostbitten hands. The German took his boots off for him.

Then he asked Stone if he had any cigarettes. Fortunately, he had received six packs of Raleigh the day before. He didn't smoke, but they were used to trade with a lot of the time so he kept them with him. Stone told him they were in his pocket. The man pulled them out, unwrapped the pack and took one out and smoked it. Stone offered him the whole pack but the man said, "no-no," as if that wasn't necessary.

The German proceeded to remove the socks from Stone's cold feet. He applied some black looking grease, which appeared to be axle grease on his feet and put a dry pair of wool socks back on him and kept his wet socks. Stone appreciated the dry warm socks.

By now another German soldier had come into the room wanting a cigarette too. The kindly man in white, who we will now refer to as a medic, told the soldier it wasn't right to take his cigarettes. The thoughtless soldier did it anyway. Stone worried that if the soldier would have been caught with the American cigarettes on him that the officials would have questioned where he had gotten them.

Stone was now a POW. For the next five days, he journeyed to what he believes may have been their division headquarters. An unfriendly Gestapo soldier interrogated him while outside a raging blizzard was taking place. The rough soldier asked for Stone's name, rank and serial number, which he gave him. The German wanted to know where he was when he was captured. Stone told him he had no idea because being a private, no one informed him where he was going. The German didn't believe him. He then asked how long ago he was captured and Stone told him, about 10 days.

This infuriated the tough German. He had a leather dice cup on his desk which he threw at Stone. He got on a field phone, asked a bunch of questions and was mad as heck Stone recalls. He slammed the phone down, and to Stone's amazement, he apologized for losing his temper. He told Stone that it infuriated him when there was inefficiency among the troops. Ten days was too long ago for a proper interrogation. Questions pertaining to where he was would no longer be of much value. He was upset because Stone was not questioned during the 10 days after his capture. It was really only about 5 days, but he believed Stone.

The interrogator continued asking which unit he was from. "I don't believe I am suppose to tell you that," Stone said.

He didn't like that answer and asked him how much punishment he could take. Stone, replied, "Not very much." He was sent outside with a guard to stand in the frigid cold, blizzard and all. After about 10 minutes the guard jerked him back inside.

Then he was quizzed, "Did you ever kill any Germans?" He didn't think so. "Why were you shooting at us," was the next question. Stone answered, "Because you were shooting at me. It was kill or be killed!" Then, "Were you mad at us?" the German asked. Stone answered, "No, but you probably weren't mad at me either." The German asked, "What are you doing here?" Stone stated, "I was drafted - I had no choice and I'm only 18, they didn't tell me anything as to where I would be going" he answered.

Stone was dismissed. He felt that he had given the Germans something to ponder. He was put in a cellar. It was dark and there was straw on the floor. To his surprise there were other prisoners in the cellar. It was crowded and he nudged one soldier to scoot over to give him some room to sit. The voice beside him asked, "Is that you Stoney?" Stone peered through the darkness and recognized an acquaintance by the name of George Frenchick. It was soldier from Minnesota, whom he had become acquainted with earlier. Frenchy was his nickname, and belonged to the same company as Stone. "We were wiped out," Frenchy informed Stone. The German Ski Patrol, who had captured Stone, had wiped out Frenchy's company by circling the company and had captured or killed everyone.

For about two more days they were marched to a town called Prum. The U.S. Air Force had bombed the dickens out of the place so they moved on to Kiel, which was way up north. They were loaded into little boxcars with about 40+ other men. The boxcars were so crowded that you couldn't sit down. There were no toilet facilities and when you had to go, you just went where you stood. For three days they traveled the noisy train without food or water and the train never stopped to let them get off and relax. The train also was carrying German tanks on flat cars. The boxcars were disguised as Red Cross cars in hopes the Allies wouldn't bomb the trains. When they arrived in Kiel, they could tell that the U.S. had heavily bombed that city also.

The prisoners were given a choice: they could either reload on a boxcar or walk 150 miles to Frankfurt. Stone chose to walk. It would have been suicide on the train with no food or water. If they walked, they would perhaps at least receive a morsel of bread from farmers along the way. They would get to sleep in half way warm barns at night and on the trains sleep was out of the question.

They finally arrived at a town called Badorb. A large prison camp was there with several thousand POW's like himself. He recalls when the 7th Cavalry liberated them. "The 7th Cavalry was the same one that General Custer lead in the days of Custers last stand" he said. They were shut up in the barracks at night and they were not allowed to peak out of the door or the Germans would shoot them. Then the prisoners started hearing heavy shelling by guns that could shoot 10 miles. They didn't think too much about it until they were able to identify other shells capable only of firing at 5 miles. Someone was closing in. The sound of an American tank was the next sound they heard. You could always tell the difference between a German and American tank Stone told me.

Then, he didn't know if he was hearing things, but he thought he heard the voice of an American. His barracks were right next to the barbwire gate where everyone went in and out. He peeked out the door and saw an armored vehicle with an American soldier who was at the gate talking to the guard. The American was trying to tell him to open the gate but the guard would not. He heard the American say, "You dumb SOB," he then started his vehicle and drove through the gate. Stone knew now their day of liberation had arrived. "We all hollered and yelled" he said. In the back of a vehicle there were boxes full of rations that were quickly dispersed to the men. About an hour later, the POW's were taken out.

Stone said his rescuers were non-combat Army Government troops detailed to pick up the POW's after the Germans had been cleared out of the camp. Some medics told them to bring the sick and wounded first and the rest would be loaded later. Stone was one of the last soldiers to get on a truck destined for a camp that had showers and clean clothes. "We were full of lice so they treated us all with DDT and burned our clothes," he recalls.

After they had been cleaned up, they were loaded on a C-47 and flown to France where they were treated at a big hospital. For two more weeks they were treated and some were brought back to health. Their stomachs had shrunk up so bad that food had to be given to them a little at a time, six times a day. To begin with, they had a soft-boiled egg and a half slice of milk toast was all they could handle. "At first, we would be hungry every three hours, until our stomachs stretched out again. We were not used to food," he added.

After a while their menu was gradually broadened to eat regular food again. Dysentery was widespread among the POW's. Their stomachs couldn't handle food that was too rich or greasy. After spending six long months with little food like Stone did, it took a while to get everything back into sync, he said.

Unlike some German POW camps where the Red Cross was allowed in with food and medical supplies, Stone never saw the Red Cross. When he was captured he weighed around 163 pounds. Two weeks after he was in the hospital, they weighed him at 106. "I was fortunate," he stated.

They were eventually loaded on a luxury liner called the SS Argentina and taken back to the states.

Being captured was devastating Stone said, but perhaps the alternative would have been worse. Perhaps the Lord had a plan for him and the others. If they would have been able to fight, they might have been killed.

Stone credits his survival to the fact that he helped take care of Frenchy the entire trip as a POW. "It helped me to take my mind off myself," he said. Stone and Frenchick kept in contact after they returned home by writing letters. Frenchick wound up being a college professor and always thought of Stone as his hero. He always told Stone, "You saved my life!" Frenchick died about five years ago. Stone misses his correspondence.

Stone worked on the railroad as a conductor for 42 years with the CB&Q. He and his wife still live in Lincoln.

TAYLOR, KENNETH W.

Taylor's story comes from a cousin of his, Catherine Wilkin, of Lincoln. Wilken is a writer and recorded this story first on a tape recorder, then into a hard copy, which she graciously sent to me. I thank her very much for doing that. When Taylor's family learned this book was being written they persuaded Kenneth to tell his story. This, by the way, was not unusual, as many stories that have been locked up for over 50 years in some cases, now finally are being recorded. Without individuals like Catherine Wilken, Perhaps many of these stories in this book would have gone untold.

Taylor graduated from St. Edward High School in 1943. WW II had already had a head start on him. He intended to enlist into the Air Cadet program. He loved flying ever since he was five years old. When planes would fly over his home, he would stand there and watch them until they disappeared.

Things don't always work out as we plan. This was the case with Taylor. He went to Omaha and passed everything except the physical. He went back home until May of 1944 and enlisted into the Navy. They took him and he boarded a troop train headed for Minneapolis and from there to Camp Farragut, Idaho, where he conducted his boot camp training for six weeks. After that he was given a 15 day leave to go home and then back to Farragut to train to be a gunners mate. He graduated from that school in December of 1944. He reported to Treasure Island, California, across the bay at San Francisco. He had been informed earlier that upon graduation he would be sent to overseas duty.

He was assigned to a troop ship, USS Admiral Kuntz, at San Francisco. Along with 5,000 other young men like him, he was amazed at the size of this ship. Being a farm kid from Nebraska, "I've never seen anything like that before," he said.

The ship sailed for Pearl Harbor, then on to the island of Ulithi, taking about 30 days to make the trip. Mealtime was quite different than at home he recalls. The chow line seemed like to last forever. If you wanted to eat at noon you better line up after breakfast or you would miss it. He and some other didn't like that routine so they decided there must be a better way. They took crates of potatoes and onions and got some guys who worked in the mess hall to bring them loaves of bread under their coats.

They were going to eat raw potato and onion sandwiches for the next 30 days rather than have to wait in the long chow lines. They bought candy bars at the ship's store and, along with those sandwiches, got along quite well.

At Ulithi, he was transferred to the USS George in January of 1945. They were in and out of Guam convoying ships up to Okinawa and Iwo Jima. They also were on anti-submarine duty.

Officials on the ship didn't realize he had been trained as a gunner's mate so they assigned Taylor to the galley. "I never peeled so many potatoes in all my life," he commented. But after about a week, the Chief Gunners Mate, Gallagher was his name, sought Taylor out and inquired of him if he had graduated from gunner's school. Taylor admitted he did and he was quickly transferred to the Ordinance Division or, O Division. He now would service and work on 20 mm. buns on the ship.

Soon he found himself servicing and maintaining other weaponry. The total armament on the ship consisted of 3-inch 50's, 1.1, and 10 20-millimeter guns. Also aboard were two depth charge racks on the fantail of the ship along with six K-guns, which fired depth charges over the side of the ship at enemy submarines. With the ever present saltwater from the sea, keeping these guns in working order was a challenge. By the time you had dismantled and cleaned the last one, it was timed to start over again. Guns, covered with salt water spray, "it was a continuous job," he said.

Taylor said one time while they were providing convoy escort, a mine was spotted floating around in the ocean. They were sent out to destroy it. The ship sailed past the mine with everyone shooting at it and missing it. The Captain swung the ship around so they could get a closer shot at it. With the mine directly in front of him only about 100 yards away, Taylor squeezed the trigger letting one burst fly. He missed so he shot another burst, which hit the floating 300-pound bomb. Shrapnel flew everywhere, even hitting the ship from that far away. An Executive Officer happened to be climbing up a ladder to the bridge when it exploded. It scared him so bad he fell off and skinned his shins. Talk was he put in for the Purple Heart.

Next the ship anchored at Iwo Jima where they were issued Thompson submarine guns. Word was, the Japanese had been swimming out to ships with explosives strapped to their bodies to blow them up. One night, one of the younger kids aboard the ship thought he saw something in the water and let loose with his Thompson. That incident made everyone a little nervous Taylor said.

While at Okinawa, Taylor saw the ship, Pennsylvania, which had been damaged by Kamikaze planes. The main purpose they were there was to watch for these suicide Japanese planes referred to as Kamikaze's. In April, Taylor was along when the ship picked up three B-29 survivors on its way back to Saipan after bombing Japan that didn't make it. They used a whaleboat for rescue purposes. Lowered from the side of the ship it served its purpose. When they tried to get the whaleboat back on the ship the seas became so rough it was impossible. So they just tied the small craft behind the ship and pulled it behind.

Like many sailors, Taylor was among those caught in a typhoon while at sea. The sea was safer than being tied to a dock however. When the typhoon was predicted, every ship that could move was sent out into the Philippine Sea. At sea, the ships were secured by shifting fuel to different tanks and filling the empty tanks with sea water, which made the ship more stable. All hatches were secured the same as when the men manned the battle stations. The ship would steam ahead at slow speed keeping the wind over the stern, the best way to ride a severe storm. Winds can reach 100 knots with swells covering the entire ship.

They rode the storm out but the ship did encounter a 64-degree roll one time. Battle Stations were sounded in this type of emergency situation. Taylor was sitting on a torpedo tube at the time and force pitched him forward nearly knocking him off. He knew he had to hang on to those tubes or he would end up in the sea. He watched the mast of the ship and wondered if it was going to go into the water. If it would have, the ship would have capsized. In seas like that, there would be no way everyone could have been rescued. It was a sight he can't explain. He says, it's like being in a valley, looking up to the top of a hill. Then the next moment, you are on the hill looking down into the valley. "I'll never forget it, " he said.

In August, Japan signed the surrender terms on the ship USS Missouri. Everyone was issued two beers and a Coke to celebrate.

Taylor said that during the island invasion, the island of Truk was most heavily fortified. To invade it would have been suicide for the U.S. troops, so they had bypassed it invading Iwo Jim, Guam, Saipan and Tinian. But after the surrender, USS George was sent to the island of Truk. The General in

Command there came aboard ship dressed in his white dress uniform, with crisp white shorts and jacket trimmed in gold braid. He, along with the garrison at Truk, signed the surrender terms aboard the USS George.

The Japanese had came toward the George on a motor launch on the port side of the ship. Taylor was there manning his 20 mm. guns, aimed right at them. They really weren't sure what these guys were up to, maybe they just wanted to blow up the ship, Taylor said. The Japanese knew the war was over but for men like Taylor, they had to consider the history of their suicide missions in the past. They had to play it safe. Taylor recalls, when the papers were signed, the good feeling that now they could all go home.

The ship then traveled back to the U.S. At San Pedro, in September of 1945, until February of 1946, Taylor spent his time upgrading the armament on the ship. Three-inch guns were replaced with five-inch guns. 1.1's were replaced with 40-mm. quad-40 guns. The ship itself was completely overhauled. When completed, it was taken out for a shake down cruise and weapons were also tested.

They went to Long Beach, California and had a ship's party. "It was quite a celebration," Taylor said.

Upon entering the service, Taylor said his mother wasn't all that upset. But, deep down, he thinks maybe his parents would have been more upset if he had not chosen to enlist. He received his Honorable Discharge at Great Lakes Training Station in Chicago in April of 1946. When he got back home, his dad and he went into town and sat down and had a beer. Beer at that time was only 5 or 10 cents a glass. He remembers a bartender by the name of Andy Hanson who inquired of his dad if Kenneth was old enough to drink. His dad replied, "He's got a uniform on. He's old enough!" This was the first and the last time he was ever able to enjoy a beer with his dad. He died shortly afterward, in the fall of the year.

Taylor could have farmed but he had seen too much of the depression days. He didn't want anything to do with it. So the family had a farm sale in January of 1947. It was located 5 miles east and a mile north of St. Edward. He moved to Lincoln and got a job with Western Electric.

He still wanted to fly so he used his GI Bill to take flying lessons out at the Arrow Airport. He got a private license, then a commercial one, and then he was awarded his instrument rating and instructors rating. "That was going to be my life," he thought at the time. By January of 1949, most of the students he had used up their GI Bill money and being an instructor folded up. He had only one student, Phil Oxley, left at that time. Oxley worked for Grain Dealers Insurance Company. Taylor mentioned to him that he thought he would starve to death that winter with no students to teach. Oxley told him he should apply for a job at the Grain Dealers Insurance Company.

He thought he would just work there temporarily until things picked up in the flying business. He had also done some crop spraying along with instruction. And the insurance company had a plane someone had cracked up so he was in hopes they would buy another and he could be the pilot. It never happened, any of it. He kept working for the company until he retired in May of 1991.

Taylor has no ill feelings concerning the Japanese or the war. The ground troops had it much different than he did, fighting often in hand to hand combat situations he said. He is also aware of the atrocities that the Japanese committed to our POW's. "That was over 50 years ago. I have no prejudice. We did what we had to do. I have no regrets," He stated.

On the ship, they ate well, you had a place to sleep and it wasn't that bad, if you didn't think about what would happen if the ship were sunk. "Then you were done," he concluded.

There are many men like Ken Taylor who served in this way and many others. We are proud of them all. Taylor's family is no different. Catherine Wilkin used her writing skills to write a tribute to Kenneth. The piece can be referred to many thousands of soldiers who went off to the serve their country. She entitles it...

THE COMMON MAN

You will not find him profiled in the Washington Post or The New York Times. There will be no made-for-TV special. NPR will not feature an in-depth-interview.

The world is full of common men and yet, there are never enough. Their birthdays are not remembered in historic text. There are federal holidays. They are born, live and die, just like every other living creature god created. The common man's one defining feature is-he goes forward through his life compelled by an unseen force that even he does not recognize, acknowledge nor understand.

He honors his parents by surviving and thriving despite all the mistakes they make. He honors his school by studying and making a contribution to his society. He honors his country by believing in his heart that he had a duty to fulfill and is bound to this commitment by love, pride and humility. He honors his friends by being a friend in thought, word and deed. There is nothing so great a true friend asks that a true friend will not answer. And there will be nothing asked for in return, no tally kept for a debt owed, or paid. He honors his family by loving, cherishing and protecting his wife; by being the best father through acts of good citizenship, kindness and passing his name down through the generations. His children will grow and mature and in turn honor their father through acts of good citizenship, kindness and passing his name down through the generations. His children want to be with him, content in the simple act of being together through a meal or a ball game or a fishing trip. Their bond is quiet, strong, and can never be severed.

The common man is not perfect for this is not why he was created. Forged in God's image, he is not God, nor God like. He is, simply, man. He will make mistakes. He will fall. He will rise up again in spite of the odds for the spirit of the common man is a kin to the racehorse. His heart is begging, his eyes, sharp, his nature, wild, his focus, pure. You can beat him, but you cannot beat him down. He will rise up again to continue his work, for that is his nature, his reason for being.

We take the common man for granted when he is with us every day, working at tasks, doing his duty, until the day he is gone from our midst and then the cavern appears. A crack in our foundation is created by the loss of this one incredible, common man. There is a wound in our heart that will never truly heal. And it is only then that we know, and it is made painfully clear, and our eyes are opened to the truth, that this one common man whom we depended on, took for granted and loved mightily, is gone. And it is only then that we realize this common man was anything but, and now we know, he is irreplaceable. We are left with a pain so deep that it cannot be explained or talked away. There is no medicine that will numb the ache. Only time will help us through this inevitable part of life's journey. WE now pay the price for the endowment received; the gift of his presence, his laughter, his caring, his persistence and consistence. Only time will help, and for now, that does not seem enough, and there is no comfort. We must be patient and patience fails to come and we curse the world and all its inhabitants, and especially God, while we wait for patience and time, and some days, all we can do is curse, for the waiting is too hard and patience is a universe away and it is in no hurry to come to us, even as we scream.

The common man has not done one extraordinary thing for which history will thank him. He has lived an ordinary life during an ordinary lifetime, but by his very nature, his life turned out to be anything but plain and when his piece is removed from our puzzled existence, we understand how important he was to the complete and whole picture of our life. With him gone, we will move one, but the picture, as we knew it, will never be the same and we will mourn our loss for the rest of our life.

It is imperative that we thank our fathers, grandfathers, uncles, brothers, cousins, neighbors

*and friends; those common men who turned out to
be, not so very common after all. They have kept
themselves going, kept us going, kept our country
going, throughout history and time. Through
uncommon valor, strength and perseverance, they
have prevailed. Not through one act, but through
many acts performed daily, hourly, generation by
generation, one man at a time. One common man.
One incredible, individual, larger than life, common
man.*

*Dedicated to Ken Taylor, and in loving
remembrance of all the common men who served
their country, and their families, and who's debt
can never be repaid.*

Catherine Wilken

Wilkin wrote this for Taylor when he was stricken with cancer
and not expected to live. He beat it and lives today in Lincoln,
Nebraska.

TWEEDLY, STANLEY R.

Tweedly lives in Grand Island. He fought in WW II in
Europe and Africa. He joined the army and planned on possibly
making a career out of it. He was with the 68th Coast Artillery,
Anti-Aircraft unit. He joined the service in September of 1940
and he was the 68th Coast Artillery, Anti-Aircraft Unit. After his
training, it wasn't long and he was fighting in a war.

He started his tour in Italy, "At the boot," as he puts it,
working his way with many other soldiers, to the German
border. His first big battle was near Naples. He was amazed at
the accuracy the Germans could zero in their shelling. "They
could drop a shell wherever they wanted to," he said.

Tweedly was trained to shoot all types of guns. The 90,
40 and 50-caliber guns to name a few. He also was known as
"The Bazooka Man." He remembers batteling it out with tanks.
The little Shermans he said, were no match for the German
Tiger tanks. Seventy-millimeter low velocity shells bounced
right off the Tigers he said. The Tigers were armed with eighty
eight-millimeter guns and were very accurate he added.

269

He sometimes fought with tanks. Sometimes on the ground he placed a log in the tracks of an enemy tank in an attempt to throw the tracks off. He worked with combat engineers helping clean out mine fields with the tank trying to stay one step ahead of the infantry to assure the roads were secure.

Considering all he went through, he considers himself lucky. He remembers many friends of his, "Who weren't so lucky. They were killed," he said.

He remembers how the fighter planes defended twenty-one airfields on the East Coast of Italy. He also recalls when 2,000 planes ran one bombing run to Casino, an observation point for the Germans. The U.S. hated to bomb it because of all the beautiful buildings in the city. "But we had to take it out. Later, we rebuilt it," he said.

Mt. Casino where a furious battle took place when the Germans occupied the mountain. *Photo courtesy of Col. Ralph Reed, Lincoln, Nebraska*

During the war he sent his mother a letter. He told her about the bombings. Excepts from that letter are as follows;

"You get to know, Mom, why millions of dollars are spent every day, why there are high taxes and why the government asks you to buy war bonds and stamps-you get to know this Mom, when you see an enemy bomber blasted out of the sky."

Tweedly was in North Africa at the time he wrote the letter. He goes on to explain what it was like to be in an air raid. He portrays what it was like for a man behind an anti-aircraft gun when he saw dozens of enemy planes come out of the night sky with murder in their gun sights.

"It came at 4:30 in the morning. The clouds were low and it was raining, a bit. This was just right for us. It meant the planes had to dive below the clouds and some of them never pulled out of their dives. They were blasted right out of the air." He continues with a description of an air raid, though, he tells his Mom, is hard to describe.

"The alarm sounds. The gun crew jumps to the guns. Everyone knows just what has to be done and where to do it. The searchlights go on, one by one, and search the skies hurriedly a second or so. Then in one of the beams appears a silver object. It's a bomber and it isn't coming on a friendly visit. Thousands, yes thousands of shells, Mom, suddenly fly into the air. Tracers from smaller guns travel on their course to the plane. Straight and true they travel.

The plane tries it's darndest to get out of the beam of light, but not a chance. The boys know every trick and are always one jump ahead. More planes. Other searchlights pick up one and stay with it. Others take care of others.

All hell breaks loose now as gun crews pour everything they got into the sky. Now the first plane's bomb bay doors open. It's getting ready to drop its load. It comes in on its bomb-run, a straight level course in order to get on its target. Hundreds of shells fly at it, burst all around it and rip into it. But that plane's crew is determined to drop its load of death.

The bomb bay doors are open wide now. But this bomber doesn't drop its load. Its number is up. A shell bursts right under its open bomb bay doors. The plane rocks heavily, then a second later it explodes, and the plane is no more. One less foe to bomb us.

All this happens in less than five minutes. The regiment has gotten its first taste of warfare and its first kill. The boys are on the ball. They get the range on other planes. Tracers crisscross. This time a smaller gun gets the range on a plane and pours shell after shell into it, riddling it from tail to nose. It flies on a second or two, then starts to plunge to the ground.

No. 2 for the fellows, and he didn't have a chance dropping a bomb either.

Then we hear that loud whistle of bomb on its way down. Where it will land no one knows but its coming. No one gives a damn. The crew sticks to its guns. The lights stay on and the bombs fall but the guys fight on. The enemy is determined to drop its bombs and the regiment is determined the enemy won't get away alive.

It's finally over and two-thirds of the enemy planes are down. There's the last one-like a duck hit while in flight, first absorbing the shocks of the shells, then pouring out a black smoke trail, finally plunging to the ground in a mass of flames-the grandest sight."

Corporal Tweedly goes on to say that no two air raids are alike, but the determination of his regiment remains the same and closes his letter with, "Our motto is, 'Keep 'em Falling', and we do."

That's what it takes in a war. A positive attitude that has no option but to win. To defeat the enemy. That's what war is all about. I would imagine some Germans could tell a similar story to their families, as they shot our planes down. But, that's the way it is.

WEYER, MARVIN

Weyer lives by Liberty, Nebraska, near the Kansas border. He grew up in the Wymore area. He served in WW II with the 311th Timberwolves Regiment of the 78th Lightning Division. He was going to business school in Grand Island when he registered for the draft in February of 1942. He was about finished with his schooling when he went to serve his country. He first served as a guard for German prisoners and by October, after his infantry training, he was sent to fight in the European Theatre.

He went to Tongren, Belgium, in December where he and others were to relieve the 28th Division. He then went to the Hurtgen Forest where he encountered his first combat. He was a green corporal carrying a heavy Browning automatic Rifle. The regiment waited there for two days when the rest of the 78th got there to make the big push.

"A" Company, which Weyer was with, was picked to be a decoy. They were supposed to occupy a hill on the backside of the Germans. The hill was very steep and snow covered. The Germans opened up on them with everything they had. The U.S. Platoons were supposed to have scouted the area out but something had gone wrong. Either they failed to scout it or the Germans moved in right after they scouted it. Weyer never figured out what happened. American soldiers were being killed or wounded all around them. "The Germans chased us around the timber all day," he said.

Towards evening, the German shelling got close enough to do much damage. A guy next to him got hit in the stomach with shrapnel. They called medics and got him hauled away. Weyer remembers the guy saying, "Thanks fellas." Later Weyer learned he had lived through it.

At a front line outpost a few weeks later, while manning a three-man post, the Germans captured Weyer. He wants to clarify the term "front line." He says it wasn't like in WW I when the front consisted of trenches dug in behind barbwire. Here, the front consisted of a series of clumps, outposts where troops took turns watching for Germans. Sitting in damaged pillboxes they had taken over, they watched the enemy still in other pillboxes nearby. Men at these posts would call for mortar fire and try to direct it to take these machine gun pillboxes out. With a four-foot thick concrete in the roof, it was difficult to take them out. Once a hole had been blown in the top, the allies would use them as outposts inching there way to the next one.

Weyer was with one of three guys who were sent to one of these blown out pillboxes. The Germans had sent scouts out, about a dozen of them. Weyer and his two buddies had just gotten to the post at about 5 a.m. so it was still dark and the temperature was 10 degrees below zero, when the Germans attacked. Weyer had a telephone they were to use to direct mortar fire. They used it, at least until the phone went dead.

"One of the Germans got on top of the pill box and started throwing hand grenades down into the pillbox where Weyer and his two buddies were. One buddy was hit. Weir's Browning fired one shot and jammed. The other buddy's M-1 jammed, too. So they started throwing grenades back at the Germans. "We had about a bucket full, throwing them like baseballs," Weyer said. They had no idea if they were hitting anything or not. They just threw them out of the pillbox and hoped they hit something. While the phone was still working they called for mortar fire and got it. It was the only help they got. The men knew they had to get out of the pillbox while it was still dark. If they tried it when it was light out, they would be picked off very easily. They tried but it was no use. As soon as they poked their head out, "Shells were flying off the concrete like stars," he recalls. He remembers wincing, as they hit. "If they, his division, would have sent them any kind of help we could have held them off." But help didn't come and Weyer and his buddy were taken prisoner. He doesn't know what happened to the other guy who was hit by the grenade.

Weyer and his buddy, who's name was Jack Work, were taken back to another German pillbox. A severe and brutal German who he thinks must have been an SS Trooper interrogated Weyer. "I expected to be shot," He thinks the only thing that saved them was the fact the Germans had suffered many casualties too and needed the American to help transport them. He and Work pulled one wounded German on a sled to some town.

The German SS Troopers were mean. When captured, the first thing they did when they captured someone was to strip them of their overshoes and gloves. They took anything the prisoners had on them; food, cigarettes, or whatever they had.

After helping the wounded German, they were walked to a jail at Flammersheim, southwest of Bonn, Germany. Eventually around 150 other prisoners were there. It was literally a jail. It was small and they could not all lie down at one time. "You laid down and bedded like a hog," he said. You couldn't sleep at night because of the fleas and lice, and during the day you would almost go crazy just sitting around. At night, they were used as forced laborers and moved supplies or cleared debris from bombing raids. The work was done in the dark to not risk being seen by allied fighters and bombers, he said.

It was in February when the Americans began shelling Flammersheim. One night Weyer had a close call unloading sacks of barley from a boxcar. One of the guards had a lantern, the wick and oil type. One night he laid it out too long and an airplane came over and spotted it. It didn't take long until the plane made a dive and "laid an egg" by them. With the concussion, there was much shrapnel and frozen dirt. "We were just lucky we were on the other side of the door," he said. The next day they went back to the site that had been bombed and, "Man, the crater, you could have driven a couple cars in it," he added.

Weyer was moved from the POW camp when a couple of other guys became ill with diphtheria. "That helped us get out of there," he said. They were transferred to Stalag VIG, called a hospital camp, where a battalion doctor was present. During the move, Weyer and Work were separated. He never found out what happened to him. He thinks perhaps that he was taken to another POW camp at Bonn, where the Germans were using prisoners to do factory work. The factories in the area of Bonn were all disguised as hospitals to thwart off being bombed. "As far as you could see, were all buildings with red crosses painted on the roofs." Later, someone discovered it was a fake and it was eventually bombed. Many POW's were there and many lost their lives and Weyer wonders if his buddy, Work, was one of them.

Weyer's next move was to a POW camp southeast of Cologne. They were herded on foot on the 20-mile trek. Starving and tired, the POW's literally crawled the final yards to the camp. Many of the prisoners could walk no further. "We were on our hands and knees," he said. The only food they had eaten was a little piece of blood sausage before they left Flammersheim. "We never got anything to eat or drink until the next afternoon." All that was consisted of was something that they called soup which was made out of barley, dehydrated cabbage or rutabagas boiled in water. He lost a lot weight. When he was captured he weighed 135 pounds. When he was liberated in April of 1945, he was down to 95 pounds.

The day of liberation was a joyous occasion. An American tank destroyer unit entered the camp on April 12, 1945, which was the day President Roosevelt died. "It was a happy day," he said, in spite of the death of Roosevelt. POW's were taken to allied hospitals and were treated and fed. "Everything tasted like dessert," he remembers.

Weyer realizes there was a big difference between the German and American POW camps. German POW's were brought over here to work on farms and to do other jobs and were paid for doing those jobs. American POW's were not, and were forced to work at night under adverse conditions. German POW's were fed and clothed quite well. As an American POW in Germany, he wasn't fed much and wore the same clothes from December of 1944 until his release in April of 1945. The Germans got to sleep on mattresses in U.S. camps. Weyer slept on burlap bags sewn together, filled with straw lying directly on bed slats. They were not very comfortable, to say the least.

After the war, Weyer returned home to the farm to join his father and brother. He married Evelyn Paul in May of 1947. They had four children, three sons: Gary, David, Mark, and a daughter Connie.

WOLLER, PAUL V.

Woller was teaching school in Hastings when he was called to serve his country. In June of 1943, he was married, had a son and had his college education. Yet he found himself in the U.S. Army. Because of the education he had, the Army thought it best to utilize his talent in some way or another so they sent him to the University of Tennessee to become an X-ray technician.

He went aboard the Queen Mary, which had been a luxury ship. Woller recalls that it was no longer a luxury liner because it had been converted into a troop ship with little luxury left. En-route to Europe, it zigzagged across the ocean making it more difficult for German submarines to detect it. Everyone knew they were out there, but no one knew exactly where, so precautions like this had to be taken.

The trip took, "too damn long," as he puts it, but they eventually landed in Glasgow, Scotland. Woller was now a member of the U.S. Army Medical Corps and was sent to Southport, England where the 109th Evacuation Hospital was being set up. Strategically located, it took in the first casualties from Normandy. As soon as a location in France would be made secure by the allies, the hospital would be moved there.

Woller recalled the D-Day invasion. Everything was moving that morning with the sky filled with all the fighters, bombers and transport planes; they were all heading south to France. It didn't take long and the aircraft began returning, at least the ones that could. When one would look up at them flying over, "you could see daylight through the holes in the wings and tails," Woller said. Some were limping along on only one engine and others appeared to have twisted tails. Woller, along with others on the ground, wondered how some of these planes made it back at all.

With the hospital put on alert, Woller and everyone else on staff were waiting for the inevitable. At first it seemed like the war wounded were never going to arrive. Then, it seemed like they never were going to stop. Litter after litter of young men, covered with blood, shattered limbs, gaping stomach wounds and missing faces came through the 109th Evacuation Hospital. Forty surgeons, forty nurses and a staff of medics worked tirelessly to save lives, limbs and alleviate pain. In three weeks the hospital had treated 1,163 soldiers.

The 109th was a part of the 3rd Army now in France and was commanded by General George Patton. It had to be mobile, as Patton's army did not stay very long at one place. Another problem was the fact that being with Patton, the hospital itself was often under attack. Woller said they spent a lot of time digging foxholes and keeping their heads covered. "We were always within range of those big enemy guns," he added.

A WC-54 Dodge Ambulance used in every Theatre of WW II and Korea as well. The crew consisted of two Medics and numerous items of equipment were carried with them. It would seat seven men or four men could lie down on litters. Many a veteran owe their life to vehicles like this.
Photo was taken at the Hearland Museum of Military Vehicles Lexington, Nebraska.

Upon one occasion, Woller was visiting with a young German soldier who had also been brought in on a litter. The officer, awaiting treatment, said to Woller, who also spoke

277

German, that he sounded like a "Berliner," because he had a similar dialect.

Woller's brother, Roland, also served in the European Theatre. They managed to get together upon a few occasions while there.

Woller came home in December of 1945, and resumed teaching school again. He will never forget those brave young men who came into the hospital area for treatment. Nor will he forget those who didn't make it to get treatment. Those who did make it home, often arrived minus limbs or forever scared, bearing the marks of men who have seen bitter battle.

He is thankful that he was assigned to a unit that was put there to save lives. Woller and the staff of the 109th, were the first medical people soldiers at the front came into contact with when they were wounded. He says it was great to be able to reassure some of these brave men that they would be okay, even though, sometimes, "I knew it wasn't so."

The U.S. Army Medical Teams performed a great service during this war and all the other wars as well. Without guys like Woller, WW II could have been a whole lot worse. They often served beyond the call of duty.

FILIKN, WAYNE

Filkin resides in Grand Island now but originally he was from Wood River. As a WW II vet, he has seen a lot. He served in the European Theatre replacing men that had been through the Battle of the Bulge, "Anything that happened after that, I was in it," he said.

Filkin was a member of the 92nd Cavalry Reconnaissance, 12th Armored Hellcat Division. By the time the Division was through Bavaria, there was hardly enough left of the territory and its Nazi defenders to stage a gang fight, a newspaper clipping read at the time. In 37 days the Hellcats conquered 22,000 square miles, liberated over 8,000 Allied prisoners, most of who were Americans. They freed 20,000 slave laborers and captured 63,000 German prisoners.

The Hellcats saw their first action in December of 1944 in operations against the Maginot Line. One mission that was highly successful and much needed was the capture of a bridge across the Danube at Dillingen. The news made major headlines at the time. It was over this bridge that the 7th Army poured a ceaseless flow of men and materials across the Danube, which aided in the winning of the war.

Following the capture of the bridge, the Hellcats hit the road again and served as point of the 7th Army's Flying Wedge as it was called. With the Nazis on the run and the 12th Armored on their necks, planes, airfields, factories and prisoners fell to the advance of the Hellcats. The Landberg prison, where Hitler had written, "Mein Kampf," was taken and 3,000 prisoners alone were freed there.

All tolled, in those 37 days, the Hellcats had cut a swathe from the Rhine to Austria. Filkin remembered some of the instances where his life was on the line. He was a tank gunner and operated a half-track vehicle. One day, they were being overrun, or so it appeared. He had to abandon his vehicle and in his haste, didn't have time to grab his gun on his way under the half-track. The shelling was intense, he had to find cover of some kind and the heavy half-track seemed to be the answer.

While he was laying under the heavy vehicle some Germans joined him there. "They had guns," Filkin said. But, it didn't matter, the Germans had one mission in mind and that was to surrender. Filkin had no gun so the armed Germans gave him theirs. "They were just as scared as I was," he stated.

On another occasion, Filkin was with those who discovered a large hole, which was filled with bodies, presumably Jews. Some were still alive. The soldiers pulled them out and gave them some K-rations to eat. The rescued prisoners were grateful.

Filkin had tried to enlist at age 17, but ended up waiting to be drafted at age 18. "It was my duty" he proudly proclaims. His wife Cereta is very proud of him and so is their daughter, Joni Aycock of Central City who sends her dad a card and gift every Veterans Day to honor him. A letter from his wife addressed to me, concludes that her husband is, "One of America's Best!"

WEHRER, CHARLES S.

Wehrer was born and raised in Norfolk and presently lives in Omaha. He attended college and when WW II rolled around, he was asked to serve. He is known as a Professor because he had earned his doctorate degree. He was in the U.S. Army Air Corp serving in the European Theatre and earned the rank of Captain by the end of the war.

He was a commander in charge of a newly formed truck company serving with the 534th Air Service Group. His company soon became recognized as the number one company that had carried the most tonnage and personnel, covered the most miles, carried the most bombs and other firepower in support of aircraft bomb groups. They were often under enemy fire.

Wehrer distinguished himself as a soldier on several occasions in the 4-½ years he served in the military. One of these times was while he was serving at an air base near Oran, Africa. He saved a young officer from dying one day when enemy agents shot him off his motorcycle. Wehrer, took action with his own weapons and fought off 20 men of the enemy and held them down until finally another truck came along to help him. Wehrer himself sustained a bullet through the shoulder.

Later, on March 27, 1944, while stationed with the 2234th Truck Company, 534th Air Service Group, 15th Air Force in Italy, he witnessed a B-24 bomber plane from the 740th bombardment group, crash land near the base. As a Commander, Wehrer took charge and took two enlisted men with him to see if they could render aid. It only took them about 7 minutes to arrive at the scene. Not knowing if the plane would all of a sudden be engulfed in flames, they worked for 3½ hours rescuing the 10 crewmen aboard the plane and saved them all. The pilot had been pinned in the wreckage and the rest of the crew were in shock and had other extensive injuries. With the help of a summoned ambulance crew, all were rescued.

For these acts of bravery and gallantry in action, Wehrer received the Soldiers Medal and the Bronze Star. However, it was not given to him at the time. It took 33 years for the medals to be awarded to him. Finally, on December 6, 1978, he was given his awards at SAC Air Base, 33 years after the fact.

Wehrer also recalls the hunger that often goes along with war. At one air base in Italy, orphans and other children would make their way to the base and beg for something to eat. They were given food because they had been eating dogs and rats Wehrer said. Soon, parents of some of these children also showed up at the base holding their tin cups wanting food too. Entire families wandered around outside the mess hall waiting to eat the garbage.

When the preparations were taking place for the invasion of Italy, he recalls being in a B-24 bomber when two of its engines were shot out by enemy fire. "We prayed a lot, we offered the Lord all sorts of deals," he said. Fortunately, perhaps with the help of the Lord, they landed but not without the help of the base fire department and some foam. They went to church the very next Sunday.

WOMEN IN WAR

Women gained much respect during the war. For the first time in the nation's history, women were accepted into the Armed Forces. The Women's Auxiliary Corps was created on May 14, 1942, as part of the regular Army. Later it was renamed as the Women's Army Corps, WAC. Seventeen thousand members of this elite group of females served overseas.

Other branches of the armed forces followed suit. The Navy created an organization known as the WAVE's. The Coast Guard called their women members SPAR's. The Air Force called their women WAF's. The Marines also had an auxiliary unit. All totaled, over 200,000 women served in the Armed Forces and many of them were decorated for their meritorious service.

Other women who didn't join a branch of the service also contributed very much. After Pearl Harbor was attacked, in less than five months, 750,000 women volunteered for duty in armament plants. That's right, volunteered! For some, their men were gone to war and they simply wanted to help them in some way.

In industry, managers involved in heavy industry doubted them at first and were a little leery of hiring these women. Of the 750,000 who volunteered, only 80,000 became employed at the manufacturing plants but that soon changed. By 1944, 3.5 million women stood side by side with 6 million men on the assembly lines. Their accomplishments were remarkable and astounding.

With the help of women, an entire cargo ship could be built in 17 days flat. They reduced the time it took to make a bomber from 200,000 man-hours to 13,000. In the process they won the coveted Army-Navy "E" pennant for excellence in meeting what seemed impossible, weapons quotas.

Hitler was not impressed however. His propaganda minister would not acknowledge the overwhelming triumphs of the U.S. war production potential. He could not accept this new fact that American "Girl-power," was another one of our nations wartime strengths. Thank you girls!

DEIBLER ROSE, DARLENE

This lady from Creighton knows the pain of war. Her story is rather unique and is very worthy of retelling. She certainly has been through a lot.

For four years, her and her husband, Rev. Russell Deibler, along with some fellow missionaries were held captive in a Japanese prison camp. Their days were spent as forced laborers and suffered separation and deprivation. Her husband died by the hands of their captives. Darlene was also among those lined up against a wall where a Japanese officer with a drawn sword was about to kill her too. For some reason, he withdrew and her life was spared.

The couple had arrived in Batavia, Java in August of 1938. She was a young bride at 21 at the time. She had been married only one year. Her husband had been a veteran missionary who had served in Borneo. When married, they decided to work in the interior of New Guinea.

On December 7, 1941, they heard the news about the Pearl Harbor attack on their radio. Within months the Japanese reached the Netherlands East Indies. Dutch and Australian forces held out as long as they could.

They had an opportunity to leave the islands one day when a Dutch officer informed them that a ship was being made ready to evacuate all foreigners. The missionaries gathered for prayer and when the truck arrived to take them to the ship, none went. They felt their mission was to stay. Ironically, three days later, the ship they would have been on was torpedoed and sunk. Now it would be only a matter of time before the Japanese would be knocking at their door.

The day soon came when Darlene was working in the garden. A Japanese officer stood in front of her with a gun pointing in her face. She and her husband along with other missionaries were rounded up and then later released.

One of them announced that they were Americans. The Japanese officer quickly informed them that the entire American Navy had been sunk. On March 8, 1941, just three months from the day they had heard about Pearl Harbor, the conquest of the Netherlands East Indies was complete. Five days later, the Japanese took the missionary men, including her husband, loaded them in trucks and it was the last anyone saw them.

Darlene was removed from her house in December and interned at Kampili, near the city of Macassar, Indonesia.

By November of 1943 she received word that her husband had died in another section of the camp. He had been dead for three months before she had been informed.

In May of 1944 she was moved to Kempeitai prison in the city of Macassar. She was accused of being a spy and because of her contact with the Allies was sentenced to be beheaded.

She was ordered to write as an officer dictated to her. "Many, many thanks to the Imperial Japanese Army for their goodness in forgiving us our evil deeds against them," she said.

As soon as she signed the document an officer held a sheaf of papers, which was a record of the accusations against her. He drew his finger across his throat, then slapped the sword strapped to his side, indicating it was over for her.

Fate now played a part in her survival. As he drew his sword, some cars pulled up in front of the headquarters. The officer withdrew, then reappeared and released her to a car headed back to Kampili. Upon arrival they found the camp destroyed by the allies so the prisoners were moved deeper into the jungle to crude shelters where they would now live. Eventually they were informed the war was over. Navy planes evacuated the American prisoners to Manila in 1945.

Weighing only 88 pounds she was under a doctor's supervision until she was strong enough to return to the states.

She arrived in Oakland, California and was welcomed by relatives from Creighton. In 1948 she married Gerald Rose who had seen a documentary of Rev. Deibler's trek to Dutch New Guinea. They were married in April of 1948 and began a ministry in New Guinea the following year. They remained there until 1978 when they moved to outback Australia. They plan to continue their missionary work in Australia.

HANNIBAL BEBEE, LEOTA

This woman from North Platte served in WW II with the Women's Army Auxiliary Corp. and took her basic training in Daytona Beach, Florida. The army had taken over a number of estate homes for Army headquarters. She used to drive jeeps on the beach back and forth to different army posts. The area now is well known as the Daytona Beach Race Track.

1942 Willys Jeep, symbolic of WW II. It carried many officers to various locations during the war. *Photo taken at Heartland Museum of Military Vehicles; Lexington, Nebraksa.*

After basic training she was sent to Fort Banks, Massachusetts. She remembers driving the staff cars through the ten-mile tunnel under the Hudson River to Boston.

She served as a telephone operator when she enlisted and expected to be in communications. Instead, she was sent to the motor pool. There she took care of her own vehicles whether it was a jeep or a car.

She kept the motor clean, changed the oil, and checked the filters and tires in the vehicles. But most of all she had to keep the vehicle itself, very clean, the army way.

On Sundays she would drive the chaplain to several different bases to conduct his services. She only had to attend one service so she could enjoy the dances the civilians would often sponsor for those in the army.

She also drove officers from Fort Banks all along the coast of Maine. She said the Atlantic Ocean on this route was very beautiful.

When the Army took over the Women's Auxiliary Corp., she had the choice of going over seas or getting an honorable discharge. She chose the latter because she wanted to get back home and get married. The war was over six months later.

In 1994 she was very happy to have had the privilege of going on the troop train to Omaha for the 50th reunion of VJ Day. The train picked up veterans along the way and at every town people were out with flags, bands and waving at them. The celebration lasted three days. They were in parades, at dinners and watched an air show at Eppley Air Field. The last night they enjoyed an elaborate display of fireworks. "We felt like VIP's," she said.

Bebee is proud of the flag and to have served her country. "It was a privilege," she concluded.

RAYER JONES, RETA E.

She was from Creighton and joined the Naval Reserves, Waves, in January of 1944 and served for 32 months. She trained in various places in the U.S. and served overseas in Tripoli, Africa. She earned the American Theater and Victory Medal.

SPENCER-OSTERBERG, EVA CAROL

Eva is from Kearney and recalls a time when every day on her way to work in 1943, she would pass a poster that read, "Are you the girl with the Star Spangled Banner?" Being a friend of many airmen who had already joined the service, she felt that perhaps joining herself would eliminate having to say "goodbye" to any more. Eva became the first enlistee into the Women's Army Corps after it was changed from the Women's Auxiliary Army Corps. However, she says, there were many more "good-byes" during her enlistment.

She was sworn in at Omaha and was stationed at Fort Des Moines, Iowa, for basic training. The administration school she attended was at Richmond, Kentucky. For a short time she worked at the Station Surgeon's office at Walter Reed Hospital, Washington, D.C. From there she went to Fort Oglethorpe, Georgia for overseas training. She crossed the mighty Atlantic on the Queen Mary and landed at Firth of Forth in northern England.

On a train ride to London she first saw what the ravages of war were like. Many city blocks in London had been demolished. She remembers a little four-year-old girl on the train with her mother. She asked her mother if the girl could have a piece of gum, her mother replied, "she does not know what gum is." Eva, along with other women, received a new slant on the war she said.

Eva was assigned in London to the Historical Division and stayed with it until the fall of 1945 when she mustered out of the WAC. She then stayed in France and Germany for six months as a War Department Civil servant.

In London she had numerous experiences. She noted the V-I rockets, buzzbombs that bombarded England that had zeroed in on London. That was time when air raid warnings meant you had better head for cover.

She was with the first detachment of WAC personnel, which to be assigned to Forward Eschelon Communication Zone, European Theatre, United States Army---ETOUSA. They sailed across the English Channel in a little British ship and landed either at Normandy or Utah Beach, she doesn't recall for sure which one it was. There, they lived in tents, ate in tents if it was raining and their offices where in tents. They landed on the Continent in July of 1944.

In Normandy, Captain Isabel Kane was the commander and Master Sergeant Nancy Carter was her cadre officer. Since they had traveled in trucks from the beach at Valognes, the soldiers along the route at first thought they were all nurses. When they saw the non-commissioned officer stripes on the girls, they threw their helmets in the air and said, "The war must be almost over. Here come the WAC's."

They were invited as a group to go to dances with other units in Normandy. The first was at a finance company and a graves registration unit near Valognes. The building had been a former headquarters for the German Army but had a Red Cross insignia on the roof because one wing was called a "hospital." The Germans knew that the allied airmen would not bomb a building with a Red Cross on top of it.

Once they were trucked to a dance for a Corps of Combat Engineers. They had set up three barrack-like buildings. The officer in charge told them that the men took days to build the first one. When they told the men it was for a dance hall, a lunchroom and a movie hall for the Normandy

WAC's from Valognes, it took one day to put up the next two buildings.

They were later convoyed to Paris in September in trucks on the Red Ball Express as it was called. This trip was a one way round trip for trucks hauling supplies from the coast to the interior. Paris was still considered a combat zone because of the many snipers. Subsequently, the detachment members like Eva; all received two combat area stars in their ETO ribbons.

Eva was awarded the rank of Technical Sergeant Third Class, Tec 3-or Staff Sergeant rating. She stayed in Paris during the remainder of the war and was discharged at Camp Phillip Morris. She then went back to the historical site at St. Germain-en-Laye, Seine-et-Oise, France, until her office was transferred to the I. G. Farben building in Frankfurt, Germany in the spring of 1946.

When Eva was at Philip Morris, one young man from that company came over and showed her a picture that she had given him at a party and asked her if that was she. He had carried her picture through the war in Europe. Eva has no idea what his name was.

While many people believe women received much harassment while serving with the armed forces, Eva says this was not the case. The enlisted men and officers always treated her very well. They were very thoughtful and often quite protective of her and the other women

She returned home on a worn out ship named the Laconia Victory Ship. GI's called it the "La Cognac" because when the cooks boiled eggs for breakfast, the ship would even come to a stop because it would run out of steam. Another ship would have to come along and pipe water into its boiler so they could finish the trip to Boston. They spent Easter Sunday in the Mid Atlantic. They held an "Easter Hat Parade" on board and the soldiers judged the best hats. She and another lady, Ruth McDevitt, took first and second place. When they arrived in Boston they took a train to New York.

Eva keeps in contact with many historians concerning the war days. A friend she met in London, a Texas corporal by the name of Glady Self, still keep in touch. She has done a lot of typing for historians like Colonels, Ganoe, Cole and Marshall who later became a Brigadier General. She typed for Marshall and Westover on the book "Bastogne: The first eight days."

When she returned home she met her husband Myron who also has his story in this book. These two veterans continue to serve. Eva has been commander of Post 52, VFW Post 759, and VFW District 14. Her and Myron serve in the color guard and firing squads at funerals, parades and other functions that need a color guard. 1999 is the sixth year they have headed the Annual World War II Reunion in Kearney. She was awarded the Bronze Star, ETO Ribbon and Good Conduct Medal when she was discharged. She is proud to have served her country!

VAN DEVEER RADOSTI, ELIZABETH BETTY

This woman is from the Creighton area and served in the Navy Wave as Yeoman 3rd Class. She trained in Cedar Falls, Iowa. Later she worked in the Armed Guard Center at Treasure Island in San Francisco, CA., in the receiving and transfer department. The Center put gunners on tankers, transports and supply ships.

"My job was to see that the sailor's records were sent with them to wherever they were transferred." She said it was a busy department but was very interesting and important.

It is noble with reference to the reason she joined the war effort. "I had no brothers and I wanted to help get the war over with," she stated.

When she enlisted she signed up for the duration of the war. She ended up serving her country for 2 years, 4 months and 2 days.

HISTORICAL NOTES
WW II

January 1, 1945 France joined the Allies in full partnership. On January 3, 1945 the Americans counterattack in the Ardennes and the Germans retreat. On the 21st the Allies re-established a line that had been broken by the Battle of the Bulge.

On March 7, 1945 the Americans seized Remagen Bridge over the Rhine and Cologne falls. On the 17th, the bridge collapsed but the allies were beyond it by then and Coblenze was also taken. By the 26th, the entire Allied front was east of the Rhine River. On the 27th Patton's 3rd Army entered Frankfurt.

The story of the Rhine attack centered on one of few bridges that were still intact. They were a little over 1,000 feet long and carried rail traffic only. The bridge was named "The Ludendorff Bridge," named to honor General Erich von Ludendorff, one of Germany's hero's of WW I. He was also a supporter of Hitler's Nazi Party. In history, the bridge goes down as "The Bridge at Remagen."

Remagen was a small picturesque town on the West Bank of the Rhine between Bonn and Coblenz. Bonn lay is about 12 miles north and Coblenz around 23 miles south. The town of Remagen, as well as the entire area, felt the awful touch of war as the U.S. 1st Army pushed its way through and onward.

WW II ended in Europe formally on May 7, 1945 after the new German head of state, Admiral Karl Doenitz agreed to General Eisenhower's demand for an unconditional surrender. The surrender papers were signed at the city of Reims, France at 2:40 a.m. that day.

A few minutes later Eisenhower sent a telegram to his headquarters, which read: The mission of this Allied Force was fulfilled at 3 a.m., local time, on May 7, 1945.

The following day, May 8th, was declared VE Day, Victory in Europe Day. Celebrations began virtually all over the world.

Soon the letter "V" appeared all over Europe as graffiti on walls and whatever else they could write on. The symbol sprang up all over Europe, people would hold up two fingers making a "V". Although no one knows where the symbolic gesture really originated, for those in Europe it meant "Victory," the Nazi's had been defeated.

MEDALS

The Air Medal was first authorized in WW II, and was awarded in the name of the President to recognize single acts of merit or heroism or for meritorious service while participating in aerial flight.

The Silver Star Medal was used in WW I, the third highest award for bravery and is also in the name of the President. It is awarded for gallantry in action against the enemy. Subsequent awards are denoted by an oak leaf worn on the ribbon.

The Bronze Star was first authorized in WW II. Also awarded in the name of the President for heroic or meritorious achievement or service in connection with military operations against an armed enemy. Awards for act of heroism were denoted with a "V" on the ribbon. Awards were also made to recognize single combat zone acts of merit or meritorious service. Subsequent awards are denoted by an oak leaf worn on the ribbon.

The Medal of Honor was first given during the Civil War. It is the highest American military award for battlefield bravery. Awarded by the President in the name of Congress to those members of the armed forces who have distinguished themselves conspicuously by gallantry and intrepidity at the risk of their own lives above and beyond the call of duty.

The Navy Unit Commendation is awarded by the Dept. of the Navy to the U.S. Navy and Marine Corps units for heroism in action against an armed enemy or for extremely meritorious conduct in support of military operations.

POW's

Prisoners held by the Allies: German - 630,000; Italian - 430,000; Japanese - 11,600.

Prisoners held by Germany: French - 765,000; Italian - 550,000; British - 200,000; Yugoslav - 125,000; American - 90,000.

Prisoners held by Japan: British - 108,000; Dutch - 22,000; American - 15,000.

TOLL OF WAR

Killed:	Army & Air Force	234,874
	Navy	36,950
	Marines	19,733
	Coast Guard	574
	Total military killed	292,131

Wounded:	Army & Air Force	565,861
	Navy	37,778
	Marines	67,207
	Coast Guard	432
	Total military wounded	671,278

Merchant Marines; Died as POW's - 37
Missing/presumed dead - 4,780
Killed at sea - 845

Estimated International Costs of WW II.
Battle deaths - 14,904,000
Battle wounded - 25,218,000
Civilian deaths - 38,573,000
Direct economic costs - $1,600.000,000,000

BOMBERS

The long nose of bomber planes were a natural canvas for the imaginative artist. They were usually paid anywhere from $60-$100 for artwork that would usually refer to wives or girlfriends. The name of the plane appeared on it. Nose art was always on the left side of the plane. Official photos, taken from the plane were always taken on the right side of the aircraft so the nose art would show on the plane they were photographing.

The crew, in bombers like the B-29 consisted of 12 men. Aircraft commander, pilot, bombardier, navigator and the flight engineer were officers. The radio operator, radar operator, central fire control gunner, left & right gunners and the tail gunner were enlisted men. Crews were permanent and had trained together.

GRAND ISLAND VETERANS HOME

Thanks to the wonderful efforts of Nancy Klimek, Manager of Recreation and Volunteer Services, I have a nice assortment of stories from our veterans who reside in this home. It is indeed wonderful that the men who served their country have a comfortable place to live when their health and welfare is in jeopardy.

Klimek, along with her staff of activity assistants in the recreation department made the contacts with these veterans asking them if they wanted to be mentioned in this book. Grand Island Northwest High School Sociology students were contacted to assist in this endeavor. I want you all to know that I am very grateful, as I simply did not have the time to interview each and every one myself who wanted to be mentioned. I did meet some of these men however and I thank them for their kindness in contributing.

In an institution such as this, in some cases, guardian consent is needed in order to publish their stories. Klimek and her staff have acquired that consent from all the veterans mentioned. Of the stories they documented, there was only one, at least to my knowledge, who refused to allow the veteran in questions story to be printed.

Klimek informs me that perhaps some of these stories are perhaps not as in depth as one would like. That's okay, I understand completely. I just appreciate the fact that, like she says, "for those veterans, who participated, their stories will not go to the grave as many have already."

Also bear in mind that war is not glamorous. Veterans have scars, emotionally, physically and mentally in some cases. These scars are long lasting, "as is evident at our facility," Klimek said.

The following stories are the collection the volunteers from Grand Island Northwest recorded. The staff at the facility paired the veterans up with their interviewers. Some of the stories are very brief listing of only their military record. I feel that is important as well. They served their country and the public should be extremely grateful. Some of these men simply don't recall all the details and in some cases, wish not too. Age and health problems often affect one's mind.

Klimek informs me that they appreciate the fact this book is being written so more people can appreciate these acts of service and heroism in some cases. Prior to this book the only reference they have on hand is simply the veterans military background. "Their sacrifices yesterday, resulted in freedom today. We hope to continue to interview our veterans to keep their stories alive," she concluded.

I will now attempt to list these veterans beginning with the most recent wars to the WW II vets.

GRANADA CAMPAIGN

JACOBSEN, WILLIAM "Jake"

Jacobsen enlisted in the Marines in January of 1981 the day after his 18th birthday. He was a Corporal during the Granada Campaign. Although he did not see combat during that brief action, he was prepared. He trained as a field radio operator. He qualified as a sharpshooter and was stationed in Japan and Hawaii. He was discharged from the Marines in December of 1983.

He comments, "I was glad to serve my country and would do it again."

VIETNAM

CROSBY, DONALD D.

Crosby is one the veterans I personally visited with in Grand Island. He was in the Army during the Vietnam War but never did get to the country itself. Drafted, he entered the service in November of 1967 and served until February of 1968 when he was discharged. He trained in Fort Lewis, Washington and it was discovered he had some physical problem and was discharged.

He was in long enough to recall some of the good times while with his unit. Every platoon usually had a couple of jokers he says that those guys who more times than not get the entire platoon in trouble. One of them tried to melt shoe polish out of the inside of the can with lighter fluid and started a fire. The rest of the guys got the fire out easily but then this other

291

guy goes and turns on the fire alarm. They all had to answer for that he said.

Another incident he says was when one morning they were all lined in formation and the acting Corporal noticed an officer on the other side of the street in the parking lot. He yelled the platoon to attention at the top of his lungs. The officer across the street simply stated, "Good morning recruits!" The Corporal then inquired to the rest of the guys as to how he knew they were recruits?

It turned out the officer was the Major General in command at Fort Lewis who naturally knew who were the new recruits especially as to how the corporal conducted them. "It was embarrassing," Crosby said, as everyone is suppose to know that one does not yell attention unless the officer is within six paces.

CROWDER, CLIFFORD W.

In March of 1964 Crowder entered the Army and was destined to serve in Vietnam. He gained the rank of Sergeant and served with the 1st Artillery, 173rd Medical Regiment. He was a medic, "so I helped my fellow comrades get well so they could return to their unit," he said.

One of his special memories is when he was stationed at Cameron Bay over the Christmas holiday. Bob Hope came to entertain the troops. Crowder says he was probably the shortest man in the unit and couldn't get a good view of Hope's performance. He says he climbed a telephone pole so he too could see the program.

Among his awards were the Army Unit Citation, Infantry Badge and the Sharpshooter Award.

He enlisted into the service because it was a tradition in the family and felt it was his duty. "I feel proud and honored that I was able to help future generations enjoy their freedom. I hope that young people in the future never have to fight in a war, and that they will always cherish the freedoms that they have," he stated.

He didn't leave the Army until November of 1977. He had re-enlisted twice after the first time he signed up with the Army. He served in the years 1964, 1969-1970 and 1977.

KOREA

BRIDGMON, NORMAN

This veteran entered the Air Force in December of 1950 and wasn't discharged until October of 1953. He trained in the states in the field of electronics and radar mechanics. He learned how to make better radar equipment and feels it was important. Although his expertise was utilized in this country, he fulfilled his duty and made a valuable contribution to the war effort. He feels great that he served his country.

REITER, STANLEY L.

Reiter received the Korean Service Medal for his part in the war. He had entered the service in November of 1950 and was discharged two years later in November of 1952. Reiter was from Kearney prior to now living in Grand Island.

He served as a PFC in the 724th Railroad Battalion in the Army. His primary task included connecting train cars and driving the train to the front lines. He remembers the times he was off duty, the free times, which were most enjoyable he said. He is glad to have served his country.

SCHOLL, ANTON P.

Scholl was drafted into the Army in March of 1951 and continued his tour until March of 1953 when he was discharged. He was 18 years old at the time he entered the service. In Korea he assisted with loading supplies behind the front lines. He said he would always remember landing and being unloaded from the ship that brought him over there. He wondered, "What are we doing here and what are we fighting for?"

STOCKER, WILLARD K.

Stocker entered the Army in April of 1951 serving until March of 1953. He knows what it's like to be in action. He was with the 7th Infantry Division in Korea. His job was one with the recovery of tanks.

293

One particular day Stocker was inside a tank in enemy territory. Three officers were sitting on the top of it. The enemy opened fire and a shell hit beside the tank blowing the officers off unto the ground. Fortunately, they all lived to tell about it.

His worst memories are the horrible conditions they had to work in. Seeing little children freezing and starving because of the war was very horrible.

Another day Stocker will never forget was when one of the men he served with was hit. His legs severed below the hips, he was still alive. Men of the 7th got him quickly to the medical battalion as fast they could he said.

He admits when he returned home that he was somewhat bitter. He was ready to be done with military life. He was awarded the Korean Service Medal, UN Service Medal and three Bronze Stars.

TILLEMANS, JEROME L.

Tillemans served in the Army from April of 1951 until April of 1953 when he was discharged. Originally from Hastings, he served as a cook during the Korean War. He was with the 7th Infantry.

He says he had interesting experiences as cook. One time he somehow lost the firing unit on the stove. His commanding officer inquired as to how he lost it. Tillemans, answered, "it wasn't easy." To that reply the officer jumped on top of the serving table and yelled, "I know it wasn't easy!" We can assume the officer didn't much appreciate Tillemans answer.

He said he feels good about doing his part in service to his country.

WALKER, CLIFFORD E.

Walker served with the Marines, 5th Battalion, 1st Division, and the National Guard. I visited with him in Grand Island when I was there. He later mentioned more details to his interviewer at the Veterans Home.

He served from January of 1948 to April of 1953 and in several of the most popular battles in Korea. He fought at the notorious "Pork Chop Hill," he told me. He was in the signal corps when he first entered the service and later volunteered for combat. He didn't talk about it much but his unit did receive the Presidential Citation for their efforts in 1950. He mentioned the fact, that on more than one occasion the enemy surrounded him and his company. Fortunately, the Army and the Air Force were always able to get them out of tight situation. Many times life in Korea was terrible cold and the living conditions were horrible. He did enjoy his R & R in Hawaii he said.

While in the reserves, he also helped break up riots in Manila during that time of his service life.

He concentrates today on love, and that is indeed an admirable attribute. He told me he loves his family, sports, movies, zoos, animals, and music and loves to sing. "I love my country very much, I love the USA, I'm proud to have served my country but I wouldn't want to do it again," he stated with emphasis.

Walker had triple by pass surgery not long ago. He has traveled around in many of the nation's states and loves to fly. He built his own house and is a lifetime member of the VFW of which he is proud to proclaim. He added that he has been married for 27 years he concluded.

WEIR, ROY E.

Weir was from Butte, Nebraska and entered the Korean War in July of 1952 and stuck it out until he was discharged in July of 1956. He served with the Air Force where sometimes, "I felt like a prisoner of the Air Force," he said. Many veterans I am sure have felt this way knowing there is no way out and you have to stay. There is no choice as many have related to me.

Weir served as an engine mechanic with his primary task to fix fuel and oil leaks. He also changed tires and performed other maintenance on the planes.

Basic training was quite tough, and he was glad to get that over with and get to the work he was trained to do. "The work was really much more fun," he said. "I am proud to have served my country," he concluded.

WW II

AQUIRRE, CRISPIN G.

Aquirre was drafted into the Army in November of 1943. At the time he wasn't pleased about it but now, "I'm glad I was. It's a wonderful thing to serve your country," he said.

Where he served, is not clear. I understand he was in the infantry but where I couldn't find out. He explains his training where he had to clean guns, work in the kitchen etc., and that's about it. According to his records he was discharged in March of 1944 after serving what appears to be about five months in the military.

BASS, CLARENCE A.

Bass was in the Navy from June of 1943 until February of 1946. He served in the South Pacific, enlisting at the age of 17. He was in Guam and Northeast Australia. He operated anti-aircraft guns from his ship. Concerning the war, "It was a unique experience and I got to see the world," he said. He was formerly from Wayne, Nebraska.

BURROWS, DURWARD E.

This veteran entered the Army in January of 1942 and was discharged in November of 1945. He was from Springfield, Nebraska enlisting in the military. He served as a Tech Sgt. and Corporal with perhaps an unusual job. He shoed horses, a farrier, in the animal transport section. "I spent many an hour driving nails in horses feet," he said. He served his time at Fort Robinson, Nebraska, and India, Burma and China. Although he earned the Marksman medal, he said he never had to serve in actual combat.

CERNY, VICTOR N.

Cerny entered the Army in September of 1942 and served until December of 1945. He was a Sergeant in the 34th Division of the Army Air Corps. He attended basic training at Louisville, Kentucky and signed up to be an aircraft mechanic. However, there was no room in the training program so he was transferred to California to wait for an opening. While there, he joined the photo lab to learn how to process aerial photos. This turned out to be his primary task during the war.

At Camp Killmer, New Jersey, he boarded a ship headed for Europe. Two units were scheduled to go overseas, one to England and the other to Italy. By the flip of a coin, his unit "won" a trip to England. The other went to Italy. Later, the ship that went to Italy was hit and everyone was lost. His Colonel made the remark, "that was the luckiest coin toss I ever made."

His ship was the Queen Mary, which landed in Scotland. Then they traveled by train to England to prepare for the D-Day Invasion. Cerny was shipped off to Omaha Beach one week after the invasion took place. While attached to Patton's 3rd Army, "we took pictures of everything," he said.

Every flight leader had pictures of where they were going thanks to guys like Cerny. The army would pick out targets for bombing and then send photo planes to take pictures of the targets. Cerny was on a 338 plane taking these pictures. After the bombers had dropped bombs, he would take photos of the destruction to assure officials the mission was accomplished.

Planes like Cerny's didn't have much protection. They were built to be lighter and faster to avoid dogfights with enemy fighters. They flew at an altitude of 30,000 feet to avoid being shot down.

Working on the ground he recalls being in Nance, France, about 40 miles south of where the Battle of the Bulge was taking place. They had to dig foxholes whenever they stopped. With the ground being frozen it was impossible to dig and provide you much cover he said.

When the war ended he was sent on into Germany to wait orders to go home. He later boarded a ship leaving from Belgium and arrived in New York and met by a boat playing "Sentimental Journey," blaring from it's speakers. At the PX, the first thing he bought was a gallon of milk. He had enough of the powdered stuff. The men were treated to steak dinner while in New Jersey and he was processed to go back home on December 5th 1945.

Cerny felt it was his duty to join the military. "I'm happy I did that. I got to see a lot of Europe, which was a great bonus. I'm glad I was a part of the war effort," he stated.

FISHER, LILBURN

Fisher was in the Navy from May of 44 until July of 44, coming from Webster County, Nebraska. Serving about two months, he never left the states spending his service time in San Diego and Los Anglos area. He recalls learning "real quick to do exactly as you are told," he said. He adds that he had fun with all the rest of the sailors who were also stationed in the area.

GREGORY, BOYD E.

Gregory joined the Navy in July of 1943 and was discharged in March of 1946. While in the South Pacific, he was a 3rd Class Petty Officer at age 18. He worked with communications operating radar equipment. It was his job to report anything he saw on radar.

While in New Guinea, a bomb hit his ship and he survived. He didn't go into the details. He is proud to have served his country. "It was an honor, but we all kind of accepted it as the way it was back then," he stated.

JOHNSON, JEROME U.

Johnson lived in Gage County when he went to war. The year was 1940. Even his dad wanted to go and help fight the war but was told he was too old. "That made him mad," Johnson said.

This story of Johnson's appears as he may have made up for his dad's absence. He served his country from December of 1940 until October of 1945. What he had to endure, as so many did, is indeed admirable.

When the war broke out on December 7th, 1941, he was a Corporal with the 35th Army Division. He was a squad leader with 20 men under him as he fought in Europe. For two years he fought his way to Germany beginning at Normandy on Omaha Beach, the Rhineland and across France and Belgium to Germany ending up at the Russian border.

Johnson admits that at the time, they felt "really big, knowing we had better equipment than they did. We knew it was us, or them, so we did our best in kicking their butts. Even if you were shot and injured, you just kept on going because there was no other alternative," he said.

Johnson, among his hazardous duties was driving ammunition trucks to the front lines. "I was always with 300 yards of the front line," he said. Much of his time was spent marching carrying his backpack, rifle and ammunition, which weighed around 80 pounds. "It was a lot of work marching from one town to the next," he added.

One time they tricked the Germans into thinking a certain town was deserted. Everyone was taken out of this town. The Germans, thinking it was safe for them to go in there, did. "We blew up the whole town," he said.

Other times, the shoe was on the other foot. Johnson lost many of the friends he made with Company C, fighting with them side by side. While fighting vicious battles, 182 of our men died, killed in action on the front lines, he said.

Johnson finds it hard to explain what war is like. "No one enjoys being shot at, fearing every minute, day and night, for your life. Laying down on wet, muddy, cold ground through rain and snows with no place to clean up and no way for a hot meal or hot cup of coffee in the cold. Then the fact, that often there would be no rest or sleep," he stated.

He also is well aware of the people back home who helped the military win the war. People who worked in war plants and other assorted tasks that helped the war effort. "Our people wanted to help get things made to help our boys, to get the war over," he said.

When the war was finally over, "everyone was happy and to see as many boys come as was possible," he added.

Among his medals and awards he has the Gold Star for being in five major battles.

KLEIN, CALVIN C.

Klein was living on the farm where he had wanted to enlist. His father wouldn't let him so when the draft came up, he had no choice but to enter the military. He signed up in September of 1943 and served until March of 1946, performing his duties in the South Pacific. He was in the Army and I assume with the Air Corp because he notes he was a flight engineer on B-24 bombers. He made the necessary repairs at his job and kept an eye on the instrument panel he said. He spent time in China and Luzon acquiring the rank of Sergeant.

"I felt good about serving my country. I felt I was doing my job for the war effort," he said.

KLOPP, IRVING J.

Klopp enlisted in the Navy in September of 1942 and was discharged in January of 1946. He was from Bellevue, Nebraska. He served in the South Pacific for 3 years as Seaman 1st Class attending his duties steering the ships and man the 40 mm. guns that were on it. He feels serving his country, "was the right thing to do."

LYNN, LEWIS M.

Lewis was from Ogallala, Nebraska. He joined the Army in November of 1941 and served until May of 1946 when he was discharged. He served as Corporal in the 65th Fire Squad. He worked as an airplane mechanic and was stationed in Northern Africa. He also conducted his duties in other places like, Trans Jordan, Egypt, Libya, Palestine, Corsica and Italy. He said North Africa was pretty much desert but South Africa was much nicer.

Although he served his country, "War means people killing people, and I really didn't want to be a part of it," he concludes.

MATSON, CLAUS M.

Matson entered the Navy in July of 1944 and was discharged in July of 1946. He lived at Fremont prior to moving to Grand Island. He was a Boatswain 2nd Class performing his duties with the Navy's 7th Fleet in the European Theatre and the South Pacific. He was involved in the invasion of France and also Okinawa and Iwo Jima. He was on a small assault boat that would carry 36 men, which I assume was probably, an LST. He recalls upon at least one occasion that he made nine trips back to the mother ship loading men that were to be taken to the beaches.

He remembers when he was Okinawa how slow the mail service was. Once the men went three months without mail. He also recalls the time when the men were granted liberty, a short leave. Usually, they just chased pretty girls and got a drunk he said.

Bartering with the civilians was done quite frequently. One time he traded a pack of Old Gold cigarettes for a Porter 51 pen. He still has it and still uses it to this day.

He feels it was an honor to serve his country, "It was also my patriotic duty," he adds. Among his awards and medal he has three Battle Stars to go along with the normal accommodations veterans like him were eligible for.

MOODY, ANITA F.

This lady served exactly a year with the Army entering in June of 1945 and was discharged in June of 1946. She is originally from Greeley, Nebraska. I am certain in that year's time this fine lady has seen a lot during the war in the Pacific.

Moody was a 2nd Lieutenant in the Nurse Corps. Being a Registered Nurse, she took care of the sick and wounded in the Philippines. "It was a task of love for me," she humbly admits.

She was on a ship along with 500 other nurses when she met her future husband. Watching the sunset from the Panama Canal, the next thing she knew she was engaged she said.

Serving in the military, "wasn't all fun. It was lots of hard work," she states. With many illness and health problems lurking around in that humid island, she herself once ended up in the hospital with a bad fungus infection.

People often ask her why she felt compelled to join the military she said. "I just felt it was the right thing to do. It was wartime. I am very proud to say that I am a veteran."

Anita, we are proud of you too!

OLSON, HAROLD M.

Olson lived at Minden for many years. In August of 1940, while listening to the radio one day, he heard a recruiter asking for men to serve their country. Having a love for planes, he enlisted in the Air Corps, and became a Staff Sgt. He worked as an airplane mechanic preparing planes for going overseas.

Olson, however, never had to leave the states. He was discharged in November of 1945.

RANDALL, EVERETT E.

Randall joined the Navy in April of 1940 and served with them for the next four years. He served throughout the South Pacific Theatre working as a Chief Pharmacist and a trained Field First Aid medic, who took care of the wounded in the battle zone. He was involved in many island invasions. "I will always remember the friends I made and the ones I lost," he said.

He continued by saying, "God put me on this earth to serve my country and I felt it was my duty to preserve our great nation!" I feel that this man is a true patriot as so many are.

RIGGS, MARY I.

Riggs is originally from Hastings. Entering the Air Force in September of 1943 she drove jeeps. She prides herself that she got to drive the newest jeeps on the market. Her most memorable incidents usually revolved around the conflicts she would have with officers she would drive around. "I didn't like to say 'Sir,'" she said. She was quite short and had to sit on three pillows in order to operate the controls on the jeep properly.

"I did what I could to serve my country and I learned some very important lessons. One was, life is short, and the other is, kindness is humanity's greatest discovery," she concludes.

SCHROEDER, ARMIN W.

This veteran was with the 14th Cavalry during the European Theatre. He drove an armored vehicle, the M8.
The 32nd Squadron of the 14th Cavalry was sent to defend a village in Belgium. He soon found himself right in the middle of the Battle of the Bulge surrounded by German troops. They wound up there by mistake, misreading a map.

A runner came up to them informing the men that the Germans were over running this village. In this town there was mass confusion. He and his Sgt. escaped into a nearby forest and managed to get into what he refers to as "no man's land." They picked up other men that belonged to the 99th Infantry Division while there. They later learned the town they had been in was totally destroyed and half of the remaining men had been captured. Some shrapnel but wasn't too serious hit him. Not serious enough for the Purple Heart, he said.

He also remembers an incident while crossing the Rhine River. The American troops had captured the metal structure and engineers were in the process of repairing it. Troops and tanks apparently couldn't wait until it was 100% secure so they crossed. It collapsed, killing between 40-60 men. "It was a part of war, it had to be done. We don't think of ourselves as heroes," he said.

Another time when he was with a platoon searching out German holdouts and weapons, he found a bag full of German medals. Some dated back to WW I. An Iron Cross was among the bag. He kept them.

"I am proud that I was able to serve my country and that defeated Hitler. I would not have to do it again," he concluded.

WHITING, MELVIN L.

Formerly from Wood River, Nebraska, Whiting was with the 24th Division, Field Artillery in the Army. His task was to get the heavy artillery guns ready to fire. He refers to it as, "getting the powder ready." He also helped in setting up defense perimeters to ward off incoming enemy troops from coming in.

Whiting served his country of which he is very proud of and feels it was something, "that had to be done," he said. He entered the Army in August of 1943 and was discharged in December of 1946. I was unable to learn which Theatre he served in.

WORTMAN, CLEMENT E.

Wortman is originally from Wood River. He joined the Army in August of 1941 and was discharged in February of 1946. He served in the Pacific Theatre landing by air first at Calcutta, India. From there he climbed aboard a truck and traveled some 2,000 miles in a truck convoy down the "Burma Road." The British, Americans and French were training the Chinese to fight. The Chinese were flown "over the hump" and flown back again.

When the war was over, Wortman was one of three men who were left to tear things down when the rest of the truck convoys left. He was a cook and a clerk. Everything left had to be burned or buried with the bulldozer they still had. When everything had been cleaned up the dozer was loaded on a transport plane and flew out with the men. They beat the convoy back to Calcutta he said.

From Calcutta they flew to Pearl Harbor, switched planes and flew to Seattle, Washington. Then it was board a train back to Nebraska. An officer called his name as well as another fellow soldier to step forward. They had been chosen to do the cooking on their trip back home on the train.

The convoy had anchored about 15 miles north off the shore near Fedala. He recalls the gun ships firing round after round upon the shore where the men were to gain access. The ships moved closer and closer to the beach head continuing their firing at the known enemy positions there. The battle became hotter as the ships drew nearer and the men began unloading to "hit the beaches." As men, war materials and vehicles were unloaded a wedge was created that helped the United States to drive further into Africa.

Later he went along to the shore and witnessed the long lines of German POW's that had been captured. He went to Casablanca and visited the scene where the action had taken place. It was a clean and beautiful city but he says he was glad to get out of it.

While on the ship when the shelling was taking place, Muller says he didn't notice the many shells that whizzed by him or were dropped near him. He was kept busy feeding his gun and elated to see the enemy planes fall from the air.

He also served in the Pacific feeding more of the three-inch shells into the anti-aircraft gun he loaded. He served in both oceans and says he was always ready to get back to his job of pumping those shells into the guns that would help defeat enemy "axis bandits," as he puts it.

VFW POST #1151

On September 10th, 1995, some veterans of the Creighton area celebrated the 50th Anniversary of WW II. Earl W. (Bill) Stokes of Creighton, a Korean War era veteran, was very instrumental in making the event a success. He compiled a book, which consists of many stories of the veterans in the area. Photos of the veterans make his scrapbook one of a kind. Stokes was kind enough to send me this book so I could gather some veteran's stories from it.

With permission from the many veterans, which Stokes obtained, some of their stories will now appear in the following pages. Even though some of their stories are brief, they represent people who had their lives disrupted serving our country, and that's admirable. Stokes had many other veterans in his book which were deceased. Those, I regretfully could not write about it. Those stories, as well as hundreds of others will go untold in this book of mine. As I believe I mentioned in prior chapters, if I were to document all those great veterans who are no longer with us, this book would take years to complete.

I also want to express my appreciation to the Creighton News, which published the following articles weekly during the spring and summer of 1995. Most of them are from the area in northeast Nebraska, such as Creighton and Plainview.

ALBRECHT, ARTHUR J.

On March 11, 1942, Albrecht was inducted into the Army at Fort Leavenworth, Kansas. After extensive training there and at California, he was sent overseas in July of 1943, and was bound for the Pacific Theatre. The ship he was on went to the Aleutian Islands first. The island was deserted because the enemy had fled. Then they went to Hawaii for more training.

He boarded another ship heading for the Marshall Islands. He helped fight the Battle of Kwajalein there. After seven weeks he found himself on another ship headed for the Battle of Leyte in the Philippines.

By late March, he went to Okinawa where he fought in one of the biggest battles of the Pacific. He recalls that a Catholic Mass was held aboard the ship. Many of the soldiers would never return after that battle. The troops landed on Easter Sunday, 1945, not really knowing what they would encounter here. By June 22nd, when it was over, they all knew too well.

Japanese shells whined as they sailed over the heads of the infantry. "You were safe from these. The ones to fear were those you could not hear," he said.

Albrecht was in Battery B, Gun Battery of the 31st Field Artillery and was in the middle of the front. Battery A was on one side and Battery C on the other. One morning the Japanese dropped a shell in A Battery, killing and wounding some soldiers. Replacements were brought in to take their places. "Some of them didn't go to far," he said.

Since he was in Field Artillery, he was only a short distance behind the Infantry. "Most of those in the front lines were killed or wounded," he said. After the battle long rows of white crosses marked the resting places of some 13,000 American soldiers on this narrow, 60 mile long island.

After peace was declared he was sent to Korea until November. He walked off the gang plank at the Port of Tacoma, Washington, without a battle scar. He considered himself very fortunate. He was going home.

He received many awards including the Bronze Service Arrowhead, Philippine Liberation Ribbon with two Bronze Stars.

Today, he realizes that now he is in his "twilight" years. His thoughts often go back to his days in the armed forces. The training in the desert, on the battle fields and on the sea. "There were many hard days, but I am proud of all of them," he said.

Someday he hopes to meet the men he served with in the battles. "Next time though, it will be in a far better land," he concluded.

Albrecht lives near Creighton.

AYERS, JOHN H.

Master Sgt. Ayers served 30 months in the South Pacific as a Section Chief in Radio Section 33 Signal Company. He was inducted into the Army at Fort Leavenworth, KS. On February 11, 1942, he was assigned to the 33rd Division.

He was shipped to Kanai in the Hawaiian Islands and later to Finschaven, New Guinea, and then to Luzon in the Philippine Islands. He participated in the capture of Bagio, the summer capital of the Philippines. He also served during the U.S. occupation of Japan.

As a result of his part in the Philippine campaign at Luzon he was awarded the Bronze Star for his meritorious service in organizing and maintaining the divisions radio equipment during this battle. Ayes, it is said in a letter from Adj. General, stated, "Ayers used quick and accurate judgement to remedy and relieve obstacles and difficulties in the system." Many times, radio communications would reach beyond normal distances for the radios. Ayers was able to somehow remedy the situation.

Ayers, formerly from Winnetoon, Nebraska, now lives in Lincoln.

BAIRD, MAX ARLO

Baird entered the Army in August of 1944. In less than a year he was commissioned as a 2nd Lt., and served in the European Theatre from December 6th, 1945 to August 17, 1946. He was a commanding officer of Headquarters Troop of the 24th Squadron, 4th Cavalry Regiment.

In October of 46 he returned home and became a cattle feeder and farmer until he retired in 1990. He lives in Brunswick with his wife Helen.

BARTAK, RAYMOND G.

Bartak is from Brunswick, Nebraska. Bartak enlisted in December of 1941 and was a Master Sgt. in the Air Force. He trained at Tulsa Oklahoma and at Seattle at Boeing's B-29 flight school. He became a flight engineer.

Bartak served in the Pacific Theatre on the island of Guam. He was flight engineer for General Barney M. Giles, Commanding General of the U.S. Strategic Air Force in the Pacific.

Upon returning to the states he became flight engineer for General Muir S. Fairchild when he became Commanding

General of the U.S. Air Force. Bartak relocated sometimes to accommodate the General. Later Bartak was based at Bolling Air Force Base, Washington D.C.

He made an observation flight with General Giles about a month after the bombing of Hiroshima and Nagasaki. He flew a group of Generals to Europe to observe the devastation of the war there.

Bartak left the Air Force in 1949 and returned home.

BECK, A.J.

Before Beck entered the service, former congressman Karl Stefan offered him an appointment to the U.S. Naval Academy at Annapolis, Maryland. His folks refused it saying that three boys in the family in service was enough. Three months later he received his 1-A classification draft notice. He enlisted in the U.S. Naval Air Corps. He learned to fly a trainer plane and went to aircraft engine training at Norman, Oklahoma. He learned the mechanics of Pratt & Whitney engines. He graduated 3rd in a class of 127 and was sent to flight engineering training at Jacksonville, Florida.

In his spare time he took gunnery training. His instructor was the movie star, Alan Ladd. Beck said Ladd was a tough instructor. On weekends he would visit his sister who was a Commissioned Officer at Charleston, South Carolina, and was in charge of six mess halls for the Army, Navy, Marine, Coast Guard and Submarine personnel.

His assignment was with a four-engine transport squadron. His training took them to various places. One time when they were planning to leave the West Coast, a plane load of Senators and Congressmen came aboard. He spotted Congressman Stefan, calling his name. They were able to have a nice visit while Admirals, Captains and Commanders waited and watched..

From California, their first freight trip was hauling Grain Belt beer, Lucky and Camel cigarettes and Zippo lighters to the Pacific Islands. The return trip they brought the wounded back to the states. Some died on the way. Three nurses and 87 wounded men were transported home.

They made several more trips and upon one occasion he was honored to meet Brigadier General James Stewart.

When it was time for his discharge he was offered more training in large aircraft. His folks didn't want him to be in the service any longer. Five of their boys had served their country. They felt they had enough worry. "To this day, I am still scratching in the dirt," he concluded with perhaps a little regret.

CARDER, EVERETT

Carder was in the Army and served with the 22nd Ordinance M.M.Company. He was inducted in October of 1942 and discharged in January of 1946. He took his basic training at Fort Warren, Cheyenne, Wyoming and was transferred to Ord, Auto Mechanic School at Stockton CA.

He left there in May of 1943 and headed for the South Pacific Theatre starting at Neumes, New Caledonia and was assigned to serve in the Solomon Islands. He also went to New George Islands, Manila, Philippines, Kure and Japan.

Carder witnessed the dropping of the atomic bomb on Hiroshima. He was stationed at Kure, Japan, only 45 miles from it.

He presently lives at Plainview, Nebraska.

CARLSON, DALE W.

Carlson served with the Air Corp 51st Troop Carrier Squad in the European Theatre. He was there for 1 year, 6 months and 6 days. He served as cook for the Officers mess. He came back home to Creighton on December 3rd, 1945 with four Bronze Stars.

CRANDALL, VERL J.

Crandall served in the Army 77th Quartermaster Co. in the Asiatic Campaign for 12 months. For 5 months he conducted the duties of clerk typist and figured out food distributions for all the parts of service on the island of Hokkaido, Japan. He had landed in Yokohama Bay in October of 1945.

He was injured when a tank grenade exploded near him in late July of 1945. He suffered wounds to his head and leg while in basic training. The grenade was fired at a tank and "I will always have part of that," he said. Although experiencing will always have part of that," he said. Although experiencing the damage war does, he concludes, "I saw no real hard service overseas. I was lucky I could run a typewriter."

CROXEN, ELDON E.

Croxen joined the service in December of 1942 and served as Infantry Rifleman in the Army. His time overseas was spent in England, Germany and France. He took part in the invasion of Normandy. He earned the Bronze Battle Star and the Purple Heart.

DARLING, GALE L.

Darling is from Hastings and served in the Army Air Force as a Flight Engineer and top turret gunner on a B-17 Flying Fortress. He was with the 384th Bomb Group, 8th Air Force flying out of England, based at Grafton-Underwood, about 60 miles north of London.

Darling said there were many incidents that took place during his days in the bomber on 32 missions. Even in training things got a little frightening at times. One time, while he was still in the United States at Alexandria, Louisiana, the weather was not good which often was the case. That night the training crew were checking instruments with the pilot and co-pilot. The base was closed and they were heading for Little Rock but they had no navigator with them. It was raining hard and a lightening bolt had taken care of the radio. They had no idea of where they were and their fuel was running low. By some miracle the radio started working again and the crew was able to make contact with the Naval Air Station at Memphis, Tennessee. They were sent to Dyersburg, Tennessee. When they landed each engine only had about 20 gallons of fuel left. They just made it.

Darling is a member of VFW Post 1151 at Creighton.

DEMERATH, EDWARD L.

He was drafted in March of 1945 and performed his basic at Fort Leavenworth, Kansas and then he went to Great Lakes, Illinois. He enlisted in the Navy serving in various places in the U.S. on several different vessels and stations. While at San Francisco, he assisted with the decommissioning of the ships when the war was over. He was discharged in July of 1946.

DOERR, KENNETH A.

Doerr spent 23 months in Europe as a court-martial recorder. He would take shorthand at a trial and then transcribe it making five carbon copies. No errors were allowed. He was attached to the 24th Cav. Recon. And the 4th Cav. Regiment in Austria.

Not all of his work was unfortunate. He met a Romanian girl who was displaced at the time. She had worked in a forced labor camp for four and a half years taking the wounded off of the blackout trains coming off the eastern front at night. They began a relationship that ended up in a marriage.

EHRENBERG, WILLIAM G.

This veteran served 12 months in the Pacific Theatre on the island of Saipan. He arrived in the Marianas Islands just a few days before the war ended. Unfortunately, a group of Japanese did not surrender on the island when the war was over. "They made life miserable for us by firing down the hills on us," he recalls. But after three months they finally were forced to surrender and Ehrenberg was there to witness that surrender.

EXON, JAMES

Former Senator James Exon was a Master Sergeant and served in New Guinea, the Philippines and Japan with the 333rd Signal Company of the 54th Troop Carrier Wing.

Sean D. Hamill wrote an article about Exon when he worked with the Medill News Service. The following are excerpts from that writing that were published in what I believe to be the Creighton paper.

Exon was 21 when he entered the service. He left college and his fiancée to sign up in the Army. It was said by those who worked with him that his ability to lead was uncanny, yet he could be like any other guy.

He left for the service in 1941 from Omaha with 300 other enlisted men to take their basic training in California. Before going overseas to the Pacific he received a 10 day furlough. He went home and married his girlfriend, Pat.

After he returned to the base, they left for the Pacific Theatre. He served the next two years in the radio division of the Signal Corp. and was Master Sgt. of it. Dick Wible, a 2nd Lt. who was with Exon said, "You might say he was the executive in charge." The company commander, George Wilson, had handpicked the group. "He, Exon, would be in intimate contact with the men. He would know their problems and experiences and expertise," Wible added.

Exon himself stated, "I was kind of the father confessor." Men leaned on him for counsel others said. Exon had excellent common sense and "unpretentious."

They hopped from island to island, "hopscotching," as Exon called it, as allied forces moved northward from New Guinea to the Japanese mainland. The job of Master Sgt. in the Signal Corp., wasn't one that made use of the army issued rifles they were given. Like government, was non dramatic, though it had an equally important side that had to be taken care of by men like Exon. "A good original mind," like Wible notes, was needed. Exon fit that bill.

Among his duties, Exon had to organize the movement of 120 men in the radio unit. Everything needed to sustain the unit was also made possible by him. Everything from toilet paper to canned soup, he had to make sure it was ready to go on the next C-47 transport planes. His job also forced him to know a little about all three divisions who were there. Exon tried to know a little about everything from being able to decipher radio codes to conducting maintenance on the equipment. His friends said that if he didn't know something, he learned it.

Exon was known as one whom could "scrounge," items that were needed to make the next move. He could talk or bargain his way around, even past a Navy guard at a supply depot his friends said. He was a good talker, already becoming a politician, they added.

Though Exon often had opportunity to smell the stench of death, he never dwelled on it but accepted it and moved on. He didn't have a defense mechanism that was filled with hate that makes war unbearable. He had the idea that one must do what he could to survive and get out of that situation as fast as you can.

"You get a tiny bit used to people throwing bombs and shrapnel at you. It's not pleasant, but you become hardened to it," Exon said.

Exon made it home following the war just in time for Christmas in 1945. He brought back the customary medals that link you with war. He also has three Bronze Stars and Philippine Liberation Ribbon with two Bronze Service Stars.

He didn't share his stories for over 50 years. Then, one Christmas the family was celebrating with their two son-in-laws who had served in the armed forces and he began opening up about some of his experiences. His wife Pat listened with interest because even she had never heard them before.

"Not talking about it, like the hatred and the horror, is just part of war. It was an experience, but you wouldn't want to go through it again," he concluded.

FISHER, BEN

Fisher entered the service in November of 1941 and served for four years. He served on an Infantry Artillery Ship in the Air Corp. His first 15 months were spent on the West Coast as a radio operator defending our shores. Then he went overseas.

For some reason or another there was no convoy when he and the others headed out in the Pacific. His ship was torpedoed and sunk after just two weeks in the water. He bobbed around in the ocean for 30 hours before being rescued. He then spent 12 days in the hospital. He received the Purple Heart. When he was well, he did as many soldiers did, spent their time island hopping to Leyte, Mindoro, Luzon Island and the Philippines.

His job was to keep track of friendly or enemy planes. If it were an enemy, he would alert others to sound the red alert alarm.

"The Golden Gate Bridge sure looked good when I returned," he said.

FOSTER, BOYD

He entered the Army in July of 1942 and trained for the infantry. He was attached to the Air Force, which crossed the Atlantic by convoy in December of 1943. He worked on the ground crew at B-17 bomber base in England under General Eisenhowers command. He spent 26 months there and returned back home aboard a British aircraft carrier.

He and his wife Pat live north of Center, Nebraska.

FRICKE, DONALD

Fricke spent 38 months with the 3rd Marine Battalion, 3rd Marine Regiment and 3rd Marine Division as a Pharmacist Mate First Class. He entered the service in September of 1942, and he trained at Great Lakes, Illinois, at the Hospital Corp. School. He was sent to the Southwest Pacific Bougainvillea, Tulagi. He was discharged in November of 1945.

GANZ, CARL

Although not much information is available on Ganz, he was also a radioman in the U.S. Navy serving in the Aleutian Islands in the Pacific Theatre. He and his wife live at Winnetoon, Nebraska.

GARDNER, EVERETT

Gardner entered the Navy in July of 1942 and took his boot camp training at Great Lakes, Ill. He trained for being Pharmacist Mate at the U.S. Naval Hospital and later to the National Naval Medical Center at Bethesda, MD. and at the U.S. Naval Academy at Annapolis, MD. Then at the U.S. Naval

Training Station at Newport, Rhode Island, he was assigned to the U.S.S. Bennington, CV-20, an aircraft carrier.

During the invasion of Iwo Jima, Okinawa and the bombing of Japan, Gardner was aboard this ship carrying out his duties in the Asiatic Theatre.

An experience he remembers well is going through a typhoon. For 24 hours they had been cruising to attempt to avoid the storm. At daybreak on June 5th, 1945, the storm overtook them. "We were right in the center of it," he said.

Winds reached 90 knots, as high as the instruments aboard could record. Waves were estimated at 40-50 feet high. The ship, battered by the waves, was damaged and buckled a 35 foot section of the flight deck. When the storm subsided the Bennington headed for San Pedro Bay in the Leyte Gulf for 20 days of repairs.

He saw the U.S.S. Franklin take two 500-pound bombs from a Kamikaze plane causing it to go up in smoke. The Franklin was in their group known as Task Force 58. More than 800 men perished that were aboard the Franklin.

Among his medals he received the Asiatic Pacific medal with three stars.

He was discharged in January of 1946 after serving over 42 months with the Navy. He and his wife Barbara retired and live in Creighton.

GREENAMYRE, VERNIE B.

Greenamyre was born in Brunswick in 1921. He graduated from Creighton High School in 1938. He enlisted in the Army at Fort Crook and was commissioned to 2nd Lt. by 1942 and was selected for pilot training. After he received his wings, he left for overseas duty in the European Theatre in December of 1943. Little did he realize at the time, he would be decorated with the Distinguished Flying Cross, four different air medals and the Purple Heart. The POW medal was also something I'm sure he was not counting on.

He was a pilot of P-38's with the 55th Fighter Group and he flew his missions out of England. Like most fighter pilots his job was to escort bombers in deep penetration raids over enemy territory. He was also to do some bombing, dive-bombing and strafing of various enemy fortified areas after the invasion of Europe in June of 1944.

His squadron was the first American planes to fly to Berlin on March 3 and 4 of 1944. It was a daylight-bombing mission where he escorted B-17 bombers.

As I have mentioned in other chapters, pilots would have a name for their plane. He named his the "Margie Dwaine." Margie was in honor of his wife and Dwaine was in honor of a good friend, who was killed by lighting at Lowery Field in Denver shortly after they had both joined the army.

It was on his 48th mission when things really turned around. German ground fire caused his plane to catch on fire as he was strafing and skip bombing inside enemy lines. He was forced to bail out and recalls the jolt when he hit the ground. He knew he had to quickly hide his parachute and headed for some nearby trees but it was too late. He heard the warning shots of the Germans who were running towards him over the hill. He had no choice but to throw his guns down and sit. He ate a candy bar while he was waiting for them. He was a prisoner of war for the next 13 months.

When the allies were able to liberate the POW camps, it was Patton's armored division who did it in May of 1945.

After he returned to the states, Greenamyre became a test pilot for the Air Force. He tested the first multi-engine jet aircraft the Air Force purchased. In the 1950's he resigned his commission and chose to become a civilian and went into the construction and real estate business.

The upper photo is a Clark CA-1 tractor dozer used with the road grader, lower left photo, to build airstrips in remote places during WW II. They, along with the trailer type cement mixer, lower right, were air dropped from transport planes to their locations. *The photos were taken at Heartland Museum, Lexington, Nebraska.*

GROSSKOP, ERNEST W.

This veteran is from Creighton served in the Air Force with the 72nd Bomb Squad. He spent six months in the states and three and a half years overseas in the Pacific Theatre. He is a Pearl Harbor survivor of December 7th, 1941.

Although President Franklin Roosevelt called the day, "a day in infamy," he had no idea what it looked like. Grosskop said. "I remember well the moments prior to and following the Japanese attack." He was stationed at Hickman airfield at the time.

The 19 year-old airman was sitting in his barracks on this Sunday morning. They had just finished eating breakfast and he was writing a letter back home. In those days one could enlist for a 3-year hitch. If you spent one of those years overseas you could go home after two years. He was writing his letter to his folks informing them he would be coming home soon. But plans changed.

As he sat there writing, he heard planes overhead and some explosions. He didn't think too much about it, he just thought it was just another training drill. Then the explosions got a little closer and he got up and looked up. When he saw

317

the red circles on the planes, he knew this was no drill. He wouldn't have time to finish his letter.

The first thing to do was grab his air mask as they had been trained to do. He went inside to get it and headed back out the door when a Japanese plane flew over and began strafing the base. Bullets flew everywhere. He dove under a nearby vehicle that would offer some protection. The barracks that he had eaten in about 30 minutes prior was bombed and gone. The men managed to locate some rifles and began firing at the enemy planes. "They had caught us by surprise," he said.

After the two hours of shelling and bombing, Pearl Harbor was a sight of destruction. But, he said, it could have been worse if the Japanese would have had more correct information. For instance, they bombed a ball field thinking it was a fuel depot. His barracks were never hit but it certainly was "2 hours of terror."

After Pearl Harbor, it was no going home. He spent the rest of his time, three and a half years, in various places in the Pacific; Philippines, Quadal Canal, Okinawa and Palau. He earned himself the Philippine Liberation Ribbon, Asiatic Pacific Theatre Medal, Good Conduct and American Defense Medal.
] Today he is an active member of the Pearl Harbor Survivors Association. His license plate is #096. He is also a life member of VFW Post #1151 of Creighton.

HANSEN, ORVILLE V.

Hansen is the first entry in the WW II veteran's section in Stokes' scrapbook. Hansen entered the service in September of 1941 and took his basic at Fort Leonardwood, Missouri. He then joined the 2nd Division in San Antonio, Texas. He took Airborne training at Randolph Field and Ski training at LaCrosse, Wisconsin, before going overseas. He spent 2 years, 2 months and 2 days fighting in France, Belgium, Germany and Czechoslovakia during the Battle of the Bulge in the European Theatre.

He recalls preparing for the Normandy invasion. They had to waterproof trucks and load cargo on ships. He drove a truck off a LCT, Landing Craft Tank, at 11 a.m. June 7th, 1944.

For his service he received the Purple Heart, Bronze Star, 4 Battle Stars and a Sharp Shooters medal.

HART, WAYNE C.

Hart served 18 months in the U.S. and then went to the European Theatre. He was with the 11th Medical Depot Company in Pantene, Paris, France, and Bremerhaven, Germany. He joined the military in April of 1943 and was discharged in April of 1946.

HASENPFLUG, MARVIN D.

This veteran was a corporal in the U.S. Army Air Corp. and served a cook and baker. He was with the 38th Service Squadron and 13th Air Force from 1942-1945 and served in the South Pacific Campaign.

HASENPFLUG, ODELL

Hasenpflug today lives in Omaha. During WW II he was a Sgt. with the 12th Armored Division. He entered the war in October of 1942 and served in Europe from 1944 to 1946.

HASKIN, JIMMIE O.

Haskin was a Special Vehicle Operator with the Army. He served 14 months in the Philippines. He was in Manila, Philippines, the day they received their independence. He and his wife Lucille, live in Royal, Nebraska.

HASS, EDWARD E.

Hass is from Verdigre, Nebraska. He served with the 91st Infantry, 363rd Regiment, 3rd Battalion 18 months fought in Italy. Eleven of those months were spent in nothing but combat. Hass said he learned very quickly that "the company was our family." The cooks were to serve at least one hot meal a day. This was not always easy. Taking mountain after mountain often looking the Germans directly in the eye, hauling in the food was a problem. Then the mess kits would have to be cleaned up after everyone had eaten and be ready to get ready for the next meal.

Hass remembers one of the major battles, which was at Liveragno. The company was caught in a trap and nearly wiped out. When they got to the Gothic Line, it didn't improve much because it took the company 11 days just to secure the bridge located there. "We lost a lot of men there," he said. He remembers crawling on his belly under fire to help deliver supplies that were needed.

At North Ridge, he saw 150 dead Germans littering the ridge. Hass helped bring back 40 badly wounded Germans. Food and supplies there had to be hauled on mules.

On Christmas Day, 1944, the men wanted roasted turkey and plenty of it. That day, two feet of snow had to be cleared so he and the men with him could even get to the mules. On the way back, a snow bank slid down off a hillside and Hass fell, slid down the hillside on his back and a mule followed him toppling over his legs putting Hass' right knee out of joint.

In April of 1945 the spring offensive had begun. Everyone had the same thought in mind, it won't be long now, will I make it? The company Hass was with was the first to reach Bologna where other divisions joined them and the rat race across the Powder Valley took place. Germans were now surrendering by the hundreds. Hass brought back to the headquarters a German General. The German snipers still took their toll but after 19 days, it was over. The Germans surrendered.

He recalls the shelling that took place by the Germans. If it had not been for the many "duds," shells that failed to explode, "I wouldn't be here," he said.

Hass received two commendations for outstanding duty and the Bronze Star. His division received a Major Commendation and Presidential Citation along with the Regiment receiving a Presidential Citation.

HOLAN, FELIX

Holan enlisted in the Air Corp. in January of 1944 and took his training at Biloxi, Mississippi, at Kessler Air Base. He then went to Texas to aerial gunnery school where he is proud to say he finished with the highest of marksmanship ever acquired at Horlingen, Texas base. Then he went to Edwards Air Base to train for long distance flights and flight engineering. After this he was sent to the Pacific Theatre and landed at the Palau Islands. From there he served bombing targets "wherever we could reach," as he puts it.

During one mission, his plane took a direct hit from a cannon shell but they were able to return to base. They were moved to Guam so they could reach the Marcus and Treek Islands.

When flying into Guam they spotted a hospital ship that had been hit by a Komakasi plane. He knew he had a cousin, George Vondracek on this ship. Fortunately, his cousin survived and Holan visited him in the hospital. He had been wounded with shrapnel from the attack.

They were moved to Okinawa so they could reach and fly missions to Japan. On August 6, Hiroshima was bombed that later ended the war. But on August 9th they flew a mission to Iwakuni Airfield about 20 miles from Hiroshima. The sky was still full of dirt but they could see the destruction of Hiroshima. On their way back to base they noted a large column of black smoke rising on the west-side of the island of Kyushu. Later they found out the second atomic bomb had been dropped on Nagasaki about 15 minutes before they saw the smoke.

"I feel the dropping of the atomic bombs saved thousands of American lives, maybe mine," he said.

Holan returned to the states on December 24, 1945 and landed at Angel Island. He brought back 6 Battle Stars and the Air Medal for bombing Japan from Okinawa. He was discharged January 2, 1946 and returned home.

He and his wife Florence live in Verdigre.

HOPKINS, WILLIAM A.

Hopkins entered the army in November of 1943, and took his basic training at Camp Roberts, California. He then entered the Pacific Theatre landing in Hawaii by August of 1944.

He began serving his hitch as a cook and baker for troops through the replacement depot. He joined the 165th Infantry Regiment, the old fighting 69th of WW I, the 27th Infantry Division.

Upon Japan's surrender he served in Japan during the Army of Occupation as cook and baker in August of 1945.

He was discharged in April of 1946 and he came home to Creighton and worked with Nebraska Public Power District until he retired.

JEDLICKA, OTTO

Captain Jedlicka was in the Army Reserves when he was discharged in April of 1953. He began his service in June of 1941. He served in the Pacific Theatre.

It is equipped with the popular "Quad 50 Caliber Anti-Aircraft Guns on top. One man operated all four guns. *Photo Was taken at the Heartland Museum of Military Vehicles, Lexington, Nebraska*

As a tank commander he served as Platoon commander of the 754th Tank Battalion In Bougainvillea, New Briton and also Luzon. He was an instructor in weapons, communications and map reading. His classes consisted of 125-200 men.

Jedlicka directed and controlled the tactical employment of reconnaissance as well as tank platoons, estimated situations, issued commands and maintained communications with the command post. He coordinated movement with infantry units and had a good deal of knowledge concerning half tracks and medium tanks.

322

In the Northern Solomon's, Bougainvillea, New Briton and the Northern Philippines, Luzon, he was tank unit commander. He received many decorations and citations for his efforts fighting the Japanese. He served five years of active duty and seven more in the reserves.   Now retired, he and his wife live in Verdigre.

JENSEN, HAROLD R.

Jensen entered the military in July of 1942 at Fort Crook, Nebraska. He trained for the medics at Camp Robinson, Arizona. He joined the 363rd Combat Engineers Medical Detachment at Camp Claybourne, Louisiana. He then spent 2 years overseas in the China, Burma, and India Theatre. He helped treat many patients; some of them were soldiers that were going over the hump, the Himalayan Mountains. He was discharged in October of 1945.

JOHNSON, LAWRENCE W. (SWEDE)

Johnson joined the Merchant Marines in 1942 and spent four years with them. As a 17-year-old kid from Nebraska who had never seen a ship before, he learned a lot about them. He notes "they quickly made a Seaman out of me."

He left Savannah, Georgia and headed for a foreign land. Seas were rough and the waves were "enormous" he said, before they landed in Belfast, Ireland. All together he made 11 trips across the oceans traveling by convoy on some occasions. He was aboard troop ships with as many as 150 ships in the convoy. As long as 60 days at sea was common. He would go to Ireland, Scotland, England, and Persian Gulf and through the Suez Canal in his travels. He was on ships that brought locomotives and train cars to the Russians, our allies at the time. He helped transport prisoners back to the U.S. from English ports.

He worked in the kitchens of the ships often. He began as a Messman and went up to a Second Butcher. "I cut a lot of meat and helped feed a tremendous number of people. It was quite an experience," he concluded.

JONES, TRUMAN (TED)

Captain Jones was in the Air Force and recalls D-Day very well. He flew all types of planes including the B-17, B-24 and B-25 bombers. He was also well trained to fly the fighters like the P-51 and P-47. He logged 3,000 hours of flying during his time that he flew both military and non-military planes.

He was a pilot of a "war weary" B-25 bomber. On his 39th mission he and the engineer that was with him, had to bail in heavy flak when his Billy Mitchell bomber was damaged. They landed safely in central Italy. He and the engineer, James Currie, walked 350 miles through German lines as escaped POW's. Because of the rules with the Geneva Convention, he was no longer allowed after that to fly again.

He listened to the radio news of the invasion while flying from Corsica, between the Gold Coast of Africa enroute to Natal, Brazil, another refueling stop before going to the USA. For his service he received the Air Medal with two clusters, Purple Heart and the Parachute Boot Club.

KEHNE, LEWIS F.

He was inducted into the Army in February of 1941, and then went to Fort Riley, Kansas for his basic training and then overseas to Casablanca, Africa. Later he also served in the European, Africa and Mideast Campaigns. He was with the 46th Ordinance MM Company, attached to the 36th Infantry Division.

He saw much action, which earned him the African, European, Middle Eastern Medal with six battle stars and the Bronze Arrowhead. The French government awarded him the French Croix de Guerre with the Silver Star.

After the Battle of the Bulge he repaired equipment from all over he said. He concluded his service as Tech. Sgt.

KELLY, GEORGE L.

He was a Tech Sgt. with the Air Force and he also served as tail gunner in a B-26 bomber with the 17th Bomb Group, 95th

Squad. He was on 52 missions, which included runs in Africa and Italy.

He is credited with one ME and three probables over Tunis. On another occasion his plane hopped by eight German planes of which seven were shot down.

Another time, an engine on the plane was shot out. Flack on another raid hit his sights on his machine gun. In another raid, 23 machine gun bullets were counted that hit the turret gun hood. The gunner came out without a scratch. While bombing Rome, one of the men of the crew took a harmonica along and played "while Rome burned," he said.

While at a rest camp he accidentally broke his leg playing tennis in Africa at the time.

He won the Air Medal with one Silver Oak Leaf and three Bronze Oak Leaves. He also has five Invasion Ribbons.

KIMBLE, MORRIS NEAL

Kimlble is from Brunswick, Nebraska and he served 24 months in Europe as a Personnel Clerk VII at the Corps Headquarters. He entered the service in April of 1941 and completed his tour in September of 1945. He served in battles and campaigns in Normandy, Northern France, Rhineland, Ardennes and Central Europe.

KLOSNER, LEONARD

Klosner was drafted into the army in August of 1941 and served as a Surgical and Medical Technician. He trained at Camp Grant, Illinois. Then he was sent to Camp Crowder, Missouri, and served there for two years. He served briefly in the infirmary and then was placed on permanent cadre. He set up new infirmaries and trained personnel including doctors entering the service.

At Camp Roberts, California, he was in charge of 900 soldiers on a troop train headed for Camp Adair, Oregon. The 70th Infantry Division was formed. In 1944 this Division was moved to Fort Leonardwood, Missouri, where they prepared to be sent to France by way of the Mediterranean Sea.

Now with the 70th Division, Klosner was sent overseas to engage in the war at Alsas Loraine, Bishwhiler, France. He was assigned to set up an aid station and maintain it. One doctor, aid men and a litter squad were on hand. The aid stations were usually located in sight of the front lines.

The Division was now under the rule of General Patton. As the wounded were brought in, their wounds would be redressed, medication would be administered and recorded in their medical records. Then they would be sent back to a collecting station for further treatment. The Division continued to move across the well-known Siegfried line which, consisted of cement bunkers and dragon teeth obstacles.

Their first battle was at Wingen. The infantry had the town surrounded but a group of SS German Troops continued to resist in a school and factory building. Klosner was asked by one of his officers if he could go in and act as an interpreter and ask the Germans if they wanted to surrender or not. After a brief conversation at the end of mainstreet, two litter squads approached carrying two wounded men. They informed Klosner that the SS troops did not honor the Geneva Convention where medical personnel were not to be fired upon in combat. Instead, the SS used the medical insignia worn on the helmets of our men as targets. The litter squads warned Klosner that to go in there would be fatal. Klosner chose not to and went back to the aid station that was set up in an old church. Tanks were called in to destroy the German stronghold.

Klosner remained in the front lines doing his work until VE Day. "The horrors and destruction of lives and surroundings are indescribable" he said.

The 70th Division liberated the POW camp at Limberg, Germany. Klosner was ordered to take charge of identification papers of 3,200 prisoners of war consisting of Russian and Polish prisoners. He also to accompanied them on a troop train to the Elb River for repatriation at Sudenberg near Magdeburg, Germany, with Russian military authorities.

Klosner remained in Germany for a time with the occupation army. He got to see many sights like Hitler's Nest, Dachau and all the devastation.

He returned home in December of 1945 with his Purple Heart and Bronze Star that were among his awards.

KNUTH, EDWIN W.

Knuth entered the Army in September of 1944 and served in the Infantry. He trained at Camp Walters, Texas. He was sent overseas to Europe at that Theatre of operations. He received the Bronze Star for his efforts and returned home in July of 1946.

KUMM, LAWRENCE O.

This veteran was with the 348th Air Service Group as a Postal Clerk. He spent 27 months in the Caribbean area, 11 months in the U.S. and 8 months in the Pacific Theatre. He had entered the service in February of 1942 at Fort Crook, Nebraska.

He was soon sent to Puerto Rico, which was considered a stepping stone for bombers that were in Africa and Europe on bombing missions. Kumm stated that during WW II, "it took 24 men on the ground to keep 1 man in the air."

In the Caribbean Sea, German subs were a real threat. They would sink supply ships forcing men to eat sea rations stored in Puerto Rico. Often as long as three months they would live on these rations.

He was sent to Iwo Jima in April of 1945; two weeks after the 5th Marine Division took the island. Japanese soldiers still lived in caves. Some were found that survived in these caves for up to 44 days. When the Americans found them, some shot themselves rather that be captured. They would refuse to surrender. The island was still being attacked by Japanese air raids, mostly suicide missions.

While there, Kumm handled mail for around 1,200 men in his group, for most of the time he was there. He was discharged in November of 1945.

LAFRANZ, HARRY

Lafranz answered his "call to colors" in April of 1945. He was married at the time like many that were called to serve. He also had two little girls but that didn't stop him from being sent overseas.

The Army assigned him to the 158th Combat Team in the Pacific Theatre. His job, along with others with him, was to search out Japanese officers and men of the Japanese army who refused to surrender. Via an interpreter, they would first

327

try to talk them out from wherever they would find them. If they refused, his orders were to get them out. They also were to locate small arms and bring them to collection point.

After he served his occupational job in Japan he went back home to join his family at Creighton.

LANMAN, ROY E.

From Verdel, Nebraska, Lanman was a quartermaster in the U.S. Army serving from December of 1942 until October of 1945 when he was discharged. He was overseas for one year and seven months with Co. 33 WD 45 at Normandy, Northern France, Rhineland, Ardennes, and Central Europe.

The hardest thing Lanman said he had to deal with was when brother, Robert, was killed in action on March 15, 1945 in the Luzon-Pacific area. Both brothers served their country at the same time fighting in two different Theatres and one never returned.

THE LARSON BOYS

If there was ever a family who gave sons to the service of their country it has to be the Larson family. Anvil Larson and his wife, Katherine, formerly from the Creighton area, had 12 sons and 2 daughters. The ironic thing is the fact that 8 of these brothers served in WW II. Only one of these brothers that served in WWII, James, is still living. Three other brothers, Paul, Elmer and Norman also served in Korea. Elmer is also deceased. Of the 12 boys, only one, Leonard, could not serve.

Though it is bad enough to have a son in some foreign land fighting a war, I can't imagine what it would be like to have eight of them in war at one time. Most of them served in the hottest of places with reference to battle zones. They served as combat men. One son wrote home one time to his mother. "I can't write very well. If I raise my head I might get my ears shot off," he wrote. The brothers served practically all over the world.

Kate was proud of her family. She was proud she had fed them all well so they would be physically fit to serve their country. She believed in "whatever happens, can't be avoided. She longed for the day when they would all be home again. "If your faith is right, you know your boys will be taken care of," she stated to the press back in 1944.

While the boys were in service, Kate would knit sweaters for them. Around 40 sweaters were made with sleeves and 17 without sleeves. She attended Red Cross meetings and worked in a bandage rolling class.

The family lived on a farm. They raised a huge garden for this large family. They would can around 500 quarts of vegetables and fruit. They would grow their own potatoes and whatever else was needed to feed the family.

In the Creighton News, August 16th, 1944, it was said by the state director of selective services that it was a good possibility the Larsons had the most sons in service in the state of Nebraska. Although he wasn't certain, according to what he had heard he said, "It sounds like a lot of them."

LARSON, CARLYLE

Larson served his time in Germany and fought in the notorious battles in the Ardennes, Central Europe and the Rhine Land. He guarded the Remagen Bridge and other pontoon bridges on the Rhine. These were temporary bridges that made it possible for the allies to cross.

LARSON, ROGER F.

Larson was with the 348th Squadron, 99th Bomb Group and the 15th Air Force flying missions in Europe. He flew 51 missions in a B-17 out of Africa and Italy with the Army Air Corp. He flew the first American shuttle run to Plotave, Russia. Among his battles and campaigns were Naples-Foggia, Rome-Arno, Southern France, Normandy, Northern France, the Air Offensive in Europe and Air Combat Balkans. The S/Sgt. was decorated with the Air Medal with 1st, 2nd, 3rd, and 4th Oak Leaf Clusters: European-Africa, Middle Eastern Theater Ribbon with one Silver and two Bronze Battle Stars.

LELAND, GEORGE J.

In the fall of 1943, Leland was drafted into the Army. Little did he know at the time, he would be serving in two wars.

He took his basic training with the 789th Field Artillery Battalion and then he was sent to the Philippines to serve with the 55th F.A. Battalion. He was a Sergeant Major with the Chief Ordnance Depot in Manila as well as 1st Sgt. with the 55th Headquarters Company. He was discharged in May of 1946.

Then in the summer of 1950 he was recalled to serve in Korea. He did not have to leave the states however and served for about a year as 1st Sgt. Of Headquarters Company in Fort Leonardwood, Missouri. This Company trained new recruits for action in Korea.

MACH, LEONARD

Mach was in the Army Infantry in the Pacific Theatre. He was a truck driver stationed at Kabe, Japan. The thing he remembers most is seeing the hunger of the Japanese people. Sometimes he would have to haul the company garbage away. At the dumpsite, the Japanese would be waiting hoping to find a morsel of food that might help sustain them. "They were so hungry they licked the cans out before we could unload them," he said.

For his part in the war he received the Distinguished Unit Badge with two Oak Leaf Clusters, Victory Medal, Asiatic Pacific Service Medal and the Army of Occupation Medal, Japan.

MALISHEWSKI, TONY

This veteran was with the 911th Signal Corp that was attached to the 5th Air Force. He Worked in the Pacific after being trained in the states and wound up being stationed in Australia in the U.S. Headquarters where he served for 28 months.

His unit built airplane hangers, laid runways and delivered messages from the U.S. While there he met friends from the states which he was very glad to see.

McGILL, DANA

McGill had just graduated from veterinary school at Iowa State when he entered the Army in February of 1943. After his basic training at Camp Howse, Texas, he was taken in the

Veterinary Corps and sent to Quartermaster Depot in Fort Worth, Texas. There he spent the next two years inspecting meat, milk and eggs. Later he was sent to Savanna, Georgia, to the Quartermaster Depot until June of 1946 when he was released as Captain.

MILNE, MERLE G.

Milne enlisted in the Army on July 1, 1941 at Fort Crook, Nebraska. He became a part of the 391st Armored Artillery Battalion and served as a tank mechanic. He left the states in September of 43 and arrived in jolly old England and was sent to Omaha beach to work their way into Germany. He participated in the Battle of the Bulge as well as campaigns at Normandy, Northern France, Rhineland, Ardennes and central Europe.

For his efforts he earned himself the Bronze Star and other medals and ribbons. He returned to the U.S. and was discharged in October of 45.

He and his wife Doris live on a farm southwest of Creighton.

MITTEIS, MERLE

Mitteis enlisted in the Navy in November of 1943 at the tender age of 17. He took his training and was sent to the Pacific Theatre serving as radioman at Manus, in the Admiralty Islands. He was also in Leyte, Manila, Tacloban, and the Philippine Islands.

He was discharged in May of 46 and now lives with his wife Donna west of Creighton.

MONTGOMERY, FRANCIS

This veteran entered the Navy in the fall of 1943. He wound up in the Pacific for nearly two years with 20 other Navy men serving as gunners aboard Merchant Marine ships carrying cargo and troops.

They were provided with 20 mm. Guns, which were necessary when entering the war zone. He made four trips across the Pacific and back to the West Coast. He often spent up to 30 days on the water without even seeing land on the longest trip.

He says he is glad he got to see some interesting places like New Guinea, Philippine Islands and Hawaii.

He was discharged in 1946.

MOSER, CLARENCE

Moser refers to himself as "one of the Moser boys." He was one of five Moser boys who served their country during WW II. Clarence entered the service in February of 1941 and was discharged in November of 1945. His brothers were Marion, Francis, Joey and Jim.

Moser served in the Army in the 6th Engineering Division and spent 30 months in the Pacific Theatre. He received awards like the Asiatic Pacific Service Medal, Victory Medal, Philippine Liberation Medal with a Bronze Star and the American Defense Service Medal. He also received the Bronze Service Arrowhead of the 6th Division.

He and his wife Mildred live in Creighton.

MULLER, LEONARD H.

Muller was with the Navy when he joined in March of 1942 and served with them until August of 1945. He conducted his service aboard a troop ship that delivered the ground troops to the Beach head at Fedala, North Africa.

The convoy had anchored about 15 miles north off the shore near Fedala. He recalls the gun ships firing round after round upon the shore where the men were to gain access. The ships moved closer and closer to the beach head continuing their firing at the known enemy positions there. The battle became hotter as the ships drew nearer and the men began unloading to "hit the beaches." As men, war materials and vehicles were unloaded a wedge was created that helped the United States to drive further into Africa.

Later he went along to the shore and witnessed the long lines of German POW's that had been captured. He went to Casablanca and visited the scene where the action had taken place. It was a clean and beautiful city but he says he was glad to get out of it.

332

While on the ship when the shelling was taking place, Muller says he didn't notice the many shells that whizzed by him or were dropped near him. He was kept busy feeding his gun and elated to see the enemy planes fall from the air.

He also served in the Pacific feeding more of the three-inch shells into the anti-aircraft gun he loaded. He served in both oceans and says he was always ready to get back to his job of pumping those shells into the guns that would help defeat enemy "axis bandits," as he puts it.

MULLER, PAUL M.

Muller joined the military after the war was over in October of 1946 and discharged in June of 1947. He was with the Army in Korea and served with the 42nd Engineer Construction Battalion as a construction equipment mechanic. He earned the WW II Victory Medal as well as the Army of Occupation Medal-Japan.

NELSEN, ROBERT

We can call him Sergeant as he served in the Army and worked with artillery. He was inducted in September of 1944, and he soon left for the South Pacific and joined up with the 869th Anti-aircraft Artillery in Hawaii. He transferred to the 5250th Technical Intelligence Company at Tokyo for the occupation of Japan.

His primary function with this group was to locate, secure, analyze and inventory Japanese military weapons and equipment, he said. He noted that some of the military equipment was quite crude and experimental, such a wooden mortar and one-man assault boat. While in Japan he was able to get together with a friend, Don Johnson of Creighton. He was discharged in November of 1946. He and his wife live southwest of Creighton.

PRINTY, MICHAEL G.

In June of 1946, Printy enlisted in the Navy. He served in the supply division aboard ship and was sent to storekeeper school. He had just graduated from St. Ludger School in May and the draft was still in affect. There were four of these boys

333

who decided to enlist. The Navy offered a two year program at the time and they felt it sounded good. While at boot camp in San Diego, California, the draft ended but it was too late.

Printy says he was not regretful he joined when he did. The GI Bill of Rights offered them schooling with tuition, books and $75 a month. He received 36 months of education at Creighton University at Omaha where he attended four years. Following that schooling, he entered the seminary where he studied for the priesthood. Presently he is pastor of St. Patrick's in Jackson and St. Mary's in Hubbard.

He recalls while on the ship while in the Navy how beautiful it was at sea. He got to go to Guam on one occasion. From there he was flown to Shanghai, China. He then wen back to the states by ship in September of 1947. He notes how fortunate he was that he did not have to look the enemy in the eye like so many others did. "God was thanked many times by us all," he said.

He is grateful for his father, George Printy, who served in WW I. He was an example to the Creighton community showing his patriotism he concluded.

RAFF, GORDON H.

Raff served 41 months as a radar operator with Company A, 581st Signal Air Warning Battalion in the Pacific. One incident stands out in his mind as he recalls those days.

He picked up some Japanese planes coming in on his radar. When that happened, Raff notified the plotting center. American planes would then be sent out to attack. At one time the enemy planes were about 50 miles from the base. "I can remember our planes got all the Japanese planes," he said. This shows just how important radar was.

Raff lives in Plainview.

RANDA, MAX F.

Randa was a supply Sgt. in the Signal Corp. He entered the military in May of 1942 and was discharged in November of 1945. He spent his first two years at Camp Crowder, MO. He then served in Europe from March 6 to November 13 of 1945. He was in England, Belgium, France and Holland. He spent VE

Day in Holland and was in France for VJ Day. He has attended reunions with his outfit in California.

RAYER, WILLIAM JR.

Rayer entered the Army in February of 1945 serving in the Infantry, field artillery and MP's. He was sent to the Pacific Theatre and served in Luzon, Philippines and Chinhae, Korea from August of 1945 to December of 1946.

He served as a corporal, battery clerk in the Philippines and supply Sgt. in Korea. He was discharged in December of 1946, after serving 22 months in the armed service.

When he got home he worked for the REA in Creighton for 33 years. He and his wife Betty retired there.

REES, DALE W.

Rees was in the Army Air Corp. and served at the West Coast Training Command where he taught instrument flying in B-17's and B-29's. Pilots who served in WW II may remember him. Planes, of course, were very instrumental in the U.S. winning the war.

RISH, BLAINE L.

Rish was another one who "answered Uncle Sam's call, I want you," he said. He left in February of 1944 and trained in auto mechanics. Then he was sent overseas to the Pacific.

He served in the Army and he was in battles in New Guinea, Luzon, Demortice to Bagio in the Philippines and in Japan on VJ Day.

He has praise for the engineers whom painstakingly constructed roads trying to clear the way over rugged mountains of Philippines as the infantry battled their way to Bagio.

ROHRER, WAYMOND C.

Rohrer is from Hoskins, Nebraska. Rohrer joined the Army Air Force in July of 1941. He attended pilot training schools at San Antonio, Texas, and was transferred to Laughlin Air Field, Del Rio, Texas for B-26 training at Marauder Pilot

School Headquarters. He was later assigned to Post Headquarters as a recorder of 201 individual files for several hundred enlistees.

"I remember working many nights until 10 p.m. to complete shipments of comrades and friends to gunnery school and overseas," he recalls.

His most memorable day was when the war ended. The base was closing and troops who were coming back went to Ellington Field at Houston, Texas, for separation.

ROKAHR, FREDERICK D.

This Naval veteran went to war in June of 1944. He was trained to fight fires and for amphibious work. He was assigned to the U.S.S. Woodford AKA 85 and was part of a small boat's landing crew. The ship was brand new at the time and had just been commissioned.

He was in the Pacific islands like Okinawa, Guam and Saipan when the Japanese surrendered. He was among those occupation troops on the Japanese mainland. He encountered two typhoons, which were memorable. He arrived back in the states at San Diego, California, just in time for New Years Eve on December 31, 1945.

The ship was decommissioned and he became a "plank member" of the Navy, being part of the ship's crew his entire life. By June 6, 1046 he was discharged and went back home.

He and his wife Beulah live in Randolph.

SANDERS, DEAN

Sanders was a Civil Engineer in the U.S. Navy Construction Battalion, better known as the Seabees. He served 37 months with the service of which 33 were spent overseas in Alaska, the Aleutian Islands, Hawaii and Japan.

His battalion was commended for preparing an emergency landing strip for planes in the Aleutians. The strip was necessary because in cases of severe weather, which was frequent, planes needed a place to land when on patrol.

In Japan he was stationed at a base named, Sasebo, a large naval base, just 60 miles from Nagasaki. He, and others, wanted to see the destruction of the bomb but was not allowed to go because of the Japanese snipers who might have refused to surrender.

SAUNDERS, IRVIN B.

Saunders entered the Army in September of 1944. He had some railroad experience so he was able to take a machinist course for 13 weeks at the Union Pacific Railroad shop near Fort Warren, Wyoming. Then he was shipped to Camp Beal, California, and was processed for action in the Pacific Theatre. He trained for jungle warfare in Hawaii and then he headed for Okinawa on a ship. While he was there, the big bomb was dropped on Hiroshima and the war ended.

After seeing the results of war in Okinawa, the rotting decaying bodies and all the devastation, he stated "God bless President Truman for his fortitude to make the decision to drop the bomb, saving millions of lives."

He was sent to Korea with the 13th Combat Engineer Battalion to secure that country and move the Japanese out. He worked with the railroad while he was there.

SAWATZKE, LYLE LANE

Sawatzke was a motor machinist with the Navy and served in the Asiatic-Pacific Theatre. He was on the Submarine Tender Pelias, the USS Triton the Grenadier Sub. 210.

When he was on the Grenadier, it was on her 6th patrol from Fremantle Australia heading for Adaman Seas with a purpose of destroying or investigating enemy shipping. When it was on its way to the Sundra Straits, two freighters of about 3,000 tons each were sighted. Surfacing to gain position for attack, a heavy Japanese Naval bomber dropped two 1,000-pound bombs while the Grenadier was passing at 90 degrees. The ship was badly damaged. The sub lay on the bottom of the ocean all day while men tried to repair it. At night it would surface so repairs could be made on the outside.

One morning, at dawn, several ships were sighted coming in but the sub was unable to emerge beneath the waters. A Japanese Zero plane tried to bomb it and missed a direct hit and the Grenadier shot down the plane. The Grenadier, now with more damage, was about to sink. The

Captain ordered the command no one on a ship likes to hear. "Abandon Ship!" They did and now became POW's of the Japanese. Sawatzke was one of them.

It took the Japanese sailors about an hour to fish the men out of the water. They received horrible treatment as did most captured by the Japanese. Conditions in the prison camps were very bad, he said. He was a prisoner for 32 months. They were liberated in September of 1945. "This was probably the best day of my life," he stated.

By March 4th, 1946 he was discharged. He lives today at Crofton.

SAWYER, ERVIN

Sawyer is from Royal, Nebraska. He was a Sergeant with the Air Force and served 30 months in the South Pacific. He was a sheet metal worker and repaired damaged structures and also B-17 and B-24 bombers. He served in New Guinea and the Philippines. He was in Luzon when the Allies took Luzon, Philippines.

SCHREIER, CLIFFORD L.

Schreier served in the Pacific Campaign with the Army in the infantry. He and his wife live in Verdigre.

SCHWARTZ, JOHN B.

Schwartz served in the Army from December of 1944 to November 30, 1946. He was in the Philippines and trained in chemicals and left the U.S. in May of 45 and headed for Manila. There he joined Company A, 80th Cml. Mtr. Bn., as a replacement.

His most memorable moment was when the bomb was dropped and the war was over. When the war did end, he didn't have enough points to return home so he transferred to the 85th Cml. Mt. Bn. In Manila he conducted engineer service and he operated a road patrol. He finished his tour there and returned home with a Bronze Star among other numerous medals.

He and his wife Leona live on a farm west of Winnetoon, Nebraska.

338

SEDIVY, ROBERT D.

Sedivy served in the Philippines and Japan for 15 months with the infantry. He remembers the training for the Japanese invasion that was to take place. He was taking amphibious training off the coast of Luzon at the time. Then the news came of the Japanese surrender. "The use of the atom bomb saved the lives of many of my comrades, and perhaps my own," he stated. After that he served with the occupation efforts.

SHEFL, JAMES A.

Sgt. Shefl was a Squad Leader for the 46th Armored Infantry Battalion, 5th Armored Division and served 18 months in Europe. He entered the Army in March of 1942 and served until October of 1946. He served as a leader of a 57 mm. anti-tank crew of eight men. He is a veteran of five major battles.

Among his many decorations are the Bronze Star, Purple Heart, Infantry Combat Badge, five Battle Stars and the European Theatre Ribbon with two Silver Stars.

It is without a doubt this man is a veteran who has seen much action, much of it was heroic action.

SLECHTA, ARTHUR G.

Slechta entered the army in January of 1944 and honorable discharged on March of 1946. He served under great generals like Patton with the 3rd Army and Eisenhower in the 1st Army in the 329th Infantry, 83rd Division. He fought in famous battles of the Battle Hedgerous in French, Hurtgen Forest and the Battle of the Bulge.

SORENSEN, LEO R.

He was a S/Sgt. with the 1981st QM Truck Company and served for 34 months in North Africa and Italy. He hauled infantry under General Patton while the trucks were brand new. Later he hauled supplies, gas and bombs for the Air Force. He was awarded the Bronze Star for his heroic and meritorious achievements with military operations against armed enemies.

STELLING, GILBERT H.

Stelling entered the Air Force in July of 1942 and served with the 908 Quartermaster for three years at Coffeyville, Kansas. Later he was transferred to the infantry for six months.

For three months he was on guard duty in Germany with the 4th Division and spent the remaining three months of his time back in the United States waiting for his discharge after the war ended. Since 1948 he attends a reunion each year with friends of his outfit from the war days. They meet at Norfolk.

STOKES, EARL W. (BILL)

Stokes is a Korean Veteran from Creighton, Nebraska. He has been kind enough to contribute many brief stories of veterans he knows are still living. He assembled a scrapbook when the 50th anniversary of WW II was celebrated, compiling newspaper articles. On September 10, 1995, the celebration took place, it was held at the Creighton City Hall. VFW Nebraska State Commander, Max West was the speaker at the celebration. Stokes is a member of VFW Post #1151, which sponsored the event. He said that he asked the VFW members if there were any objections to putting their stories in my book, "Operation Recognition" and he said there were no objections.

As I compile the efforts put forth by Stokes, of which I am very much appreciative, because of the briefness of some of the stories, I will document them one following another as they are put forth in his book.

Stokes was deferred twice when our nation was drafting men for Korea. He was to help on the family farm. He says all his friends and neighbors were drafted and he felt guilty because he hadn't been drafted. He felt especially guilty when one day while picking up potatoes, a brother of a boy who was drafted asked Stokes why he wasn't being drafted. After that incident, he, without his folk's permission, went to the draft board by himself and told them to draft him. "I never did tell my folks," he said.

On January 21, 1951, he was sworn in along with other draftees from Antelope County. He then went to Fort Riley, Kansas and was assigned his unit. Robert Miller of Clearwater and Bill soon became friends because they had serial numbers right next to each other. But, they were soon assigned to different units. Miller was put in the 7th Infantry at Fort Riley, and Stokes was put in as an engineer at Granite City, Illinois. Regretfully, Miller, an only child, was killed in Korea in October of 1951. Stokes visits his grave at Clearwater at least once a year.

SUHR, CARL J.

Suhr was with the Army and went overseas as a replacement, unassigned. Then he became located with the First Cavalry Headquarters in Japan as Postal Clerk. Later, he was in the 271st Field Artillery at Kamakuma. He served with the occupational forces in Japan.

His duties were to pick up mail in Tokyo for the mail clerks. He operated A.P.O. 201 Unit 3 as a post office and sold stamps, mailed packages, registered mail and sold money orders.

He now, along with his wife Lila, reside in Creighton.

SUKUP, MARVIN

Sukup was with the Army and served as a medic in Africa and Italy toward the end of the war. He was a recipient of the Purple Heart for his part in combat. He lives near Winnetoon on a farm with his wife Lois.

SYPEN, HENRY VONDER

For Sypen the war started in May of 1940. He was living in Belgium with his parents. They were refugees. He vividly recalls the Nazi's walking over Belgium. "I survived four years of run and hide," he said. They were liberated in December of 1944, "it was great," he added.

Henry then joined the U.S. Army and served in Germany as an engineer. He had been to France for training and he helped put up two bridges across the Rhine River in Mainz, Germany.

THARNISH, EDWARD H.

Ed was Seaman 3rd Class aboard the Destroyer Escort 104 USS Breeman and conducted underwater searches for German submarines. He served the Navy from December of 1943 until December of 1945.

He recalls on one mission that one of the five destroyers rammed a German submarine. They helped pick up the German survivors. They were then taken to Boston on a ship that Tharnish was on.

He now lives at O'Neill.

THARNISH, ERNEST J.

Tharnish entered the service in 1945. He was with the Army's 33rd Division in the Langayen Gulf in northern Luzon. He was with occupation forces mopping up the Pacific Campaign. He admits his service time was brief but in less than a years time that he spent he saw a lot of sights, like the devastation of Hiroshima and Manila Bay with all the sunken ships sticking out of the water. Only the church was left standing in the town of Bagio. The concentration Camp at Mt. Roko was also completely destroyed. That was a place that no one should have ever been.

THARNISH, PAUL

He graduated from St. Ludgers Academy in 1945 and enlisted in the Navy. After his boot camp, he wound up just outside Memphis, Tennessee at a base and found himself barbering on ship service duty. He was at this enlisted man's barber shop for one and a half months and then he went to the Chief and Officers Shop and was in charge of this shop until he was discharged.

He must have liked it, because when he was discharged he made a career out of the trade he did while in service. For the next 45 years he cut hair for a living.

He is now retired and lives with his wife in Omaha.

342

THARNISH, RAYMOND G.

In the first contingent of WW II, Tharnish left Knox county and trained with the Air Force Technical Schools. He became a maintenance specialist on heavy bombers. He was an engine mechanic for three years and as a preflight and crew chief instructor on B-24 and B-17 bombers.

He was discharged in November of 1945, he now resides in Lincoln.

THOMAS, OSCAR E.

Thomas ended up being a Captain when he volunteered as an officer candidate, VOC, in September of 1942. He was assigned to the "Mule Pack" mountain artillery for basic training. After that he attended Artillery Officer's Candidate School at Fort Sill, Oklahoma. After completing that he was a 2nd Lt. and was assigned as a battery executive officer in the 681st Glider Artillery Battalion of the 17th Airborne Division.

In 1944 he joined the 88th Blue Devil Division in Europe and later commanded Battery C. 338th Field Artillery Battalion. He fought in Rome Arno, the Northern Apennines and the Po Valley Campaigns. The unit fought from the toe of Italy to the Brenner Pass.

Lasting memories consist of things really not of the war itself. He recalls the disastrous soil erosion in North Africa. In Europe it was the other way around where people showed extreme reverence for the care of the land, historic cities and mountains. He got his first taste of the grand opera there as well as eating his first trout and enjoying the music of Vienna.

He especially remembers getting "called down" for shelling to close to the Leaning Tower of Pisa.

At Volterra, he was wounded and received the Purple Heart. Later he received the Bronze Star with 2 Oak Leaf Clusters and the American & European Theatre Ribbons with three Battle Stars. He was also awarded the Victory Medal with four Battle Stars.

He then served with the Army occupation of Germany and married an Italian girl and returned home.

TIMMERMAN, WALTER W.

He was a Sergeant in the U.S. Army, 3rd Division, 7th Infantry. He left for the service in October of 1942. "We didn't know where we were going until we got halfway across the Atlantic," Timmerman said. Then they were informed that they were being the ones to make the Invasion of North Africa at Casablanca. He will never forget climbing down the cargo net on November 8th, 1942, and dropping down onto a landing craft heading for the beachhead at Fedala. A shell hit their craft and knocked out their engine. A buddy of his, sitting across from him was killed.

"I saw shrapnel come out of his chest. I thought, that could have been me," he said.

They continued bobbing around in the water finally getting out and jumping into waist deep water the last 100 yards. "We were under fire all the time," he recalls. The large ship, Joseph Hewes, which they had just gotten of when they jumped on the landing craft, was blown up shortly after that and sank to the bottom of the sea. "It blew up right after we got off," he added.

Timmerman survived and road the Queen Mary back to the states in September of 1945. They played the song, "Sentimental Journey" on the ship. The ship seemed to rock with the waves to the beat of a song; all the way home he said.

He was awarded the Combat Infantry Badge and Invasion Arrowhead with four battle stars.

UHLIR, EDWIN

Uhlir served with the Army and was in the Pacific campaign for 36 months island hopping to seven different islands. The last one of the islands was Luzon when they invaded it. He was a 1st Gunner on a Browning Automatic team with the 40th Division 185th Infantry Company A, 3rd Platoon, 3rd Squad.

He volunteered to join in June of 1941. When war broke out he was automatically in for the four-year hitch before he could be discharged in June of 1945.

When his platoon invaded Luzon, "I saw some action," he said. A Japanese machine gunner squared off with him.

344

While shooting the BAR, Browning Automatic, he shot 140 rounds at the gunner. When the smoke cleared his buddies stated, "Good shooting, Uhlir."

Diseases were common in the Pacific. Uhlir contracted malaria while on the front lines. When well, he spent 33 days on an LST encountering Japanese Zero's when they were about to land on the beach. Thanks to the Navy, they shot down the Zero's.

He earned the Expert Combat Badge, Bronze Star and three Campaign Bronze Stars.

He lives in Battle Creek.

WARREN, MERRITT C.

Lt. Warren was an Engineering Officer with the Navy from July of 1943 to June of 1946. He performed his duties on an LST 602 in the Mediterranean Theatre, which carried troops and tanks to Italy.

His ship was being readied for the Pacific when the war ended. He spent the remaining six months of his time mothballing 700 amphibious ships in the St. Johns River near St. Augustine, Florida.

His best memory of the war days is coming home and seeing the Statue of Liberty, the "Welcome Home" sign the welcoming with whistles and horns of other ships when they entered the harbor at New York.

Warren is a retired District court judge and resides in Creighton.

WATTERS, EARL G.

Watters served 22 months with the Naval Reserves in the Pacific aboard the U.S.S. Cushing. Judging from the typhoon he was in, he may have been in the same one as Gardner.

"I remember riding out a typhoon prior to the Okinawa landing," he said. His ship was 10 miles off the coast of Japan when the big bomb was dropped on Hiroshima. Lt. Watters also lives in Creighton and is the brother-in-law of Everett Gardner,

WEGNER, FREDRICK P.

Wegner served with the 319th Army Postal Unit and was a photographer in the European Theatre. He remembers the many horrors of the war. Starving people, children raiding garbage cans and the look of despair on their faces was a common sight. They were glad to see the Americans liberate them he said.

The incident at Dachau will forever be burned in his memory. He was asked by his C.O. to drive him their just a few days after the death camp was liberated. "Whenever the Holocaust is mentioned, I see hell on earth," he stated.

He sees in his mind the lice, starving people with typhus, skin and bones, filth and signs of carnage. "I smell the odor of the ovens, the piles of trenches of rotting bodies," He asks, "How could one man, Hitler, cause the death of 50 million people?"

In his memory he sees the destruction of towns and the countryside that cost billions to destroy and billions of dollars to rebuild. He and his wife have gone back to Europe three times and have seen the restoration that has taken place. He wonders how the European countries could do all this rebuilding and still provide medical care for their citizens? The U.S., who didn't have restoration costs; still can't provide health care to their people he states.

Wegner remained in the Army Reserves and National Guard until he retired. He completed his career serving in Intelligence and Flight Operations and rose to the rank of Captain.

Among his awards are the Bronze Star, Army commendation, Purple Heart, Eur-Afr-Me with Rhineland, Central Europe and Ardennes Stars, the Eisenhower Unit citation and many others.

WEST, LOYD LEWIS

West joined the Navy in the summer of 1944 and went to boot camp at Great Lakes. He then went to radio operator's school at Madison, Wisconsin. Then he was shipped overseas to the Pacific Theatre. He served on a ship that operated out of Guam and later out of the Samar-Leyte area of the Philippines.

He recalls while in Guam, that the chow line usually had someone from the Philippines constantly watching for the Japanese soldiers up in the hills that were real hungry. They would sometimes try to sneak in the chow line for some food. Americans could not always spot them or pick them out but, "the Philippinos could," he said.

WIES, DON

Wies is also from Creighton. He entered the Army Air Corp. in early 1942 and attended airplane mechanic school at Lincoln Air Base and LOCKLAND P-38 School in California. Then he spent 33 months overseas with the 6th Air Force based with the 48th Headquarters Air Squadron at France Field in the Panama Canal Zone. His part time duty was served in South America, in Columbia, Peru and Ecuador.

He worked as an aircraft mechanic, crew chief, line chief and aerial photographer. His crew escorted Mrs. Eleanor Roosevelt's plane to the parking ramp on her visit to France Field. Bob Hope and his USO Troupe was also there one time. Wies was discharged in December of 1945.

WORTMAN, LEONARD

Wortman entered the Army in February of 1942 and served with the 3467th Ordnance as an automotive mechanic. In April of 1943 he was loaded on a transport ship that took him to such places as New Zealand, Australia, Ceylon, India and eventually disembarked in Iran. The truck-company took over a truck manufacturing plant there.

There he helped assemble thousands of trucks and jeeps for the Russians. By April of 1945, the plant was closed and the men went back to the states. At Fort Hood, Texas, he was trained to serve in a tank recovery unit but the bomb was dropped and the war ended and the men were discharged.

THE KOREAN WAR

On June 25, 1950, the North Korean Army, KPA, crossed the 38th parallel into South Korea. They were planning on taking over the South. It was a case of socialism verses democracy. The South, being democratic and a member of the United Nations, wanted to remain that way. Problem was, the KPA was much to powerful of a force for the Republic of South Korea, ROK. They appealed to the United Nations for help. President Truman quickly took action to do just that, render aid in the form our military equipment and men to help them with the fighting. This action caused the Chinese to become involved helping their ally, the KPA. This made matters worse. The Chinese, with their vast numbers of soldiers, would cause much blood would to be shed.

In the United States, the draft was extended and the military made ready. People wondered if the atomic bomb would again be used. WW II vets were called back into the service. General MacArthur still had troops in Japan but they were unprepared. Truman ordered him to get them ready and head for Korea. At first, very little ammunition was handed out. Four bullets and a hand grenade were it; and were only to be used in case of an attack.

Later, the war escalated. Ammunition was handed out by the case. The infantry proved once again as the worst place to be. North Koreans were ruthless, and killed many American POW's. However, this proved to make American soldiers fight harder. They fought with a rage that many never knew they had within themselves. Many were ordered to fight to the end with no retreat. Foxholes became knee-deep in shell casings. The North Koreans showed much courage, but used poor tactics and were fighting a losing battle.

Meanwhile, China had said that if the Americans crossed the 38th parallel, they would help the North Koreans. When we arrived there, we had to stop. MacArthur didn't like it. We crossed it anyway on October 1st. China offered much resistance but it only lasted a week and their effort crumbled. Soldiers relaxed thinking it was over, but it was not. On October 20th, 100,000 Chinese soldiers shattered one battalion and stopped the 8th Army. More Chinese kept coming; life was cheap to them. By the end of November in 20 below weather, which our troops were not equipped for, Chinese were attacking nearly all around the allies. We were forced to withdraw. The 9th and 38th Division suffered the most casualties in history. Hand to hand combat was frequent. Seven hundred thousand Chinese stood ready to defend at Manchuria. Problem was, the largest weapon they had was mortars. They were high in numbers but low in arsenal. Our airmen flew in uncontested skies very often on their bombing and strafing runs. The weaponry of the Chinese was second rate and not nearly as superior as ours. The Chinese began losing scores of men, perhaps up to a million it has been estimated.

By July of 1951, truce talks were in the making but had poor results. The fighting continued for two more years. The KPA would not sign a truce because of the wishes of their own men who had been captured by the South. These Communist POW's, many of them chose not to return to their homeland. The UN wanted to honor their wishes contending that those who want to be free should be given the opportunity. The KPA wanted them back anyway. Finally when the KPA learned that 27,000 of their men, who had been POW's had escaped by the help of ROK guards, they reluctantly signed the peace treaty on July 27, 1953.

The war caused much destruction and human suffering, as most wars do. More bombs were dropped on North Korea than any other place in history. Civilian casualties were never tallied. Militarily, the UN came up with 350,000 casualties. The KPA and the Chinese casualty figures were estimated at over 1.5 million.

The United States with all its Armed Forces totaled 5.7 million men and women whom were involved. When the dead was tallied up nearly 34,000 brave soldiers, who served in Korea, were dead. Over 103,000 were wounded. The ROK suffered immensely, with 2.5 million of their people now homeless and they estimated around 1 million civilians had died.

The ROK had 400,000 military soldiers involved and the UN had another 800,000 people fighting the war. Numbers were important because the KPA had around 200,000 men, but with the help of the Chinese, they had another million soldiers helping them.

The U.S. spent a lot of money fighting this "police action," as it was called. The United States spent eighteen

349

billion dollars helping the ROK preserve their freedom. The cost
of freedom never has a cheap price tag. When casualties are
involved, the price is very high. But freedom was obtained for
the ROK and their enemies will think twice when they get the
desire to take it over again. They will remember the costs they
also incurred.

A M4A3 "Sherman" Medium Tank used during WW II and the Korean War.
It now sits on display at the Heartland Museum of Military Vehicles at
Lexington, Nebraska. It was equipped with a 76 m.m. gun with a range of
over 9 miles and was able to penetrate four inches of face hardened steel
at 1,000 yard.It weighs 34 ton with a top speed of 28 miles per hour
getting.8 miless per gallon of fuel. Korean War Veteran Al Grams
poses by the tank.

Although the war was never considered a "war," but a
"police action," to the many veterans it was indeed war. There
is no other word for it. Even though war was never declared by
the powers that be, men shooting at one another is war, nothing
else but. America once again stood up to those countries that
have no other objective than to take away freedom. It's what we
stand for in the United States, FREEDOM!

Note: *Some facts and figures were obtained from notes I have kept over the years. Some of the facts were given to me from veterans whom I interviewed.*

DILL, HARRY L.

Harry Dill worked at The Debus Bakery in Hastings at the time he entered the service. His two brothers had served in WW II, now it was his turn. He was very proud to have a chance to serve his country, he said. He had gone to a college and he had wanted to learn to fly and the U.S. Air Force sounded good to him. So in May of 1948, he signed up in Grand Island. He was sent to many different places. Texas, Illinois, Mississippi, France, Florida, Labrador, Washington State, Turkey and ended up in New Jersey where he retired in 1968 after serving for 20 years.

It's interesting to see how fate sometimes works in life. He had orders to go to Korea and they were changed at the last minute and he found himself in Labrador. He had orders to go to Vietnam, and ended up in Turkey.

He was involved with communications; so very often on short notice, he had to leave. His family, though they were often without him, were always proud of him, his wife Shirley tells me.

Dill loved to fly and had his pilot's license before he entered the service. When he was discharged he had worked his way up to the rank to Chief Master Sergeant.

LUCE, GEORGE W. (BILL)

Luce is a veteran of the Korean War and entered the service on September 25, 1950 and was discharged on July 19, 1953. He lives in Lincoln now but lived at Auburn before the war. He knew he was about to be drafted so he enlisted into the U.S. Air Force. He had attended college at Peru State and was working at a construction job at the time.

He reported for duty at Castle Air Force Base, Merced, California which was the home of the 93rd Bombardment Wing, a B-50 Superfortress unit of the 15th Air Force and Strategic Air Command.

351

At Kadena, Okinawa, where he was stationed overseas, he was a gunner aboard Superfortress and flew 24 missions over North Korea. Four times the plane was landed with something on fire. Numerous things cause fires Luce says. A broken propeller shaft, generators, mechanical problems of various sorts and enemy fire. "It gets a little scary," he recalls.

One night the crew was forced to shout the distress call, "Mayday-Mayday," for about 100 miles as they left North Korea. Fortunately they made it back landing in flames. Upon other occasions, North Korean, Russian and Chinese Mig 15's which flew at might, liked to pick up the red glow of the exhaust systems of these bombers and try to shoot them down. When they were over enemy territory, flak was another serious problem, he said.

Perhaps one of the most memorable things that happened to him in service was when General MacArthur was given a parade in New York City on what they called, "MacArthur Day." Luce was a clerk-typist at Mitchell Airfield at the time. He was selected to be a member of the parade group from the base. He wrote a letter to his parent's back home concerning the occasion. He told about the great experience of being involved in that festive parade. The day of the parade they assembled at the base parade grounds at 8 a.m. for inspection. "And I do mean inspected," he stated. At 9 a.m. they were loaded on buses, 20 loads of them, and escorted by 6 police escorts to city limits where more police joined them. By 10:30 a.m. they were at the site where they were to get ready to march. At 11 a.m. they were given a box lunch and then they had to wait. Word was, MacArthur had left his hotel and was coming right behind them. Luce and the rest were in the lead. At 12 noon, it appeared as if all hell broke loose he thought. All the boats on the piers started blowing their horns, whistles and sirens. People started hollering and screaming. Confetti, ticker tape, old business machine cards, torn phone book pages and paper in all forms started coming down from the buildings by the bushels. Then they started to march. You couldn't hear commands because of the noise. All they could do is follow the guy in front of you and hope he knew what he was doing. Luce thinks their marching may have looked pretty bad. "I was never so thrilled in my life, it was something you just can't explain," Luce said about the parade. One cannot believe the enthusiasm that one man, MacArthur, could create. After marching about an hour they made it to Washington Square where the Squadron split in the middle and half went to one side of the street and the other half to the other side of the street. MacArthur then passed between them. "He looked just like his picture" Luce recalls, and said that there really wasn't anything spectacular about actually seeing him, it was the just idea. After he passed, the unit was dismissed. "I was glad I was able to take part in it," he said. This event took place in April of 1951.

Although being shot at in a plane wasn't any joy, Luce, like many of his comrades simply state, "It was a great time."

POST, JOHN ROLLAND

Post lives near Pauline, Nebraska. In January of 1952, Post traveled to Omaha to be inducted into the Army. He was not alone, as many other men were also on their way to Camp Roberts in California where 15,000 men were being trained for the Korean War. After completing his training, he was allowed to go back home for a brief furlough, and he was off to the Far East Command, as it was referred to.

Upon his arrival after a 15-day ship voyage, he arrived in Yokohama, Japan and was assigned to the 24th Division, which had, along with the 1st Cavalry Division, suffered many casualties. He was to be a replacement. Fortunately, he and others were assigned to act as a defense force should the Russians decide to invade Japan. "We were overjoyed with this assignment," he said.

Instead of having to go to the Korean front, they were sent to the 19th Infantry Regiment that was stationed at Camp Haugen, a few miles north of the fishing port of Hachinoe. Here he became a jeep driver and traveled around a lot in the area of northern Honshu. Later he received more amphibious training and did make a landing and lived for two months on Mt. Fugi. He was also trained in Aerial Photography Interpretation during the winter of 1952-53. He was also in Tokyo where they had what they called a heavy snow, only about 2 inches. While on maneuvers at Honshu, snow on the level laid 8-10 foot deep, quite a contrast to Tokyo.

In the spring of 1953 when riots broke out at the POW camp at Hoge, off the southern tip of Korea, Communist Korean POW's rioted and took over the camp. They even captured an

American General who happened to be at the wrong place at the wrong time. One of our airborne divisions was sent with rifles with bayonets and grenades to restore order and rescue the general.

Post said there were four categories of POW's during the Korean War. The Communist Korean's, who rioted at Hoge was one. Another was the Anti-Communist POW's who did not want to ever return to North Korea. The Chinese people, when they entered the war, had thousands of Chinese captured and were also POW's now. They also had both sides, some never wanting to go back to China and some that did. They all were kept in assorted camps and separated as to how they felt about returning to their homeland.

Post soon was assigned with the 19th Regiment, to help guard men of our own at Masaua Air Base. Their orders were to keep our men in designated areas ready for boarding on planes that would airlift them to Korea. The "Flying boxcar planes," would leave at intervals of 30 minutes loaded with our troops. When this task was completed, he went back to Camp Haugen and in a few days he boarded a train and headed for Tokyo. Vehicles were loaded on flat cars and drivers were told to stay with their vehicles. They didn't enjoy this. Trains were still pulled by steam locomotive and the smoke flying over the cars was pretty bad at times.

He and about a dozen others were told to board a ship. They did, of course, not having any idea where they were going. This anticipation led to several speculations. Some thought they were heading to the front, others thought Vietnam. "Rumors were rampant," he said.

The amphibious training would be put to use. As they came near an island, they had to climb down the cargo nets onto landing crafts that would take them to the beachhead. The beach was silent. They met a convoy of trucks there who informed the men they were at Cheju Island. Home to about 94,000 Republic of Korea troops who were being trained. Also on the island were about 15,000 anti-Communist Chinese POW's which he and the others were to guard now. Koreans had been doing the guarding up to this point.

Soon after, when the battle lines became more and more stable, peace negotiations began among the powers that be. The question of territory was settled quite easily, Post said.

354

Problems arose when questions arose concerning the POW's and where they should go. "That prolonged the war," he said.

The Communists insisted their people had to go back where they came from whether they liked or not. The U.S. and the South Koreans would not go along with that idea. Soon, Sygemen Rhee, released the anti-Communist POW's who were held on the mainland of Korea. The Chinese POW's were being held both those who wanted to stay and those who wanted to go back, on Cheju Island. The two groups were separated with one group on one side of the island and the other group on the other. It was there; that Post was put on guard duty.

Sleep here was hard to come by Post said. Meals were served at given times and food was scarce. Often they would get up out of bed and go eat because they were working shifts that were 4 hours on and 8 hours off. Their sleeping quarters had been set up at the end of the runway at the air base, which also was a disturbing problem when planes would come in and out. "C 47's sounded like they were coming right through our tent," he said.

The prisoners were kept in large compounds, 5,000 in each. The compounds had 10 enclosures, 5 on one side and another 5 on the other. A lane ran through the center. During daylight hours, guards were posted at the gates of the enclosures to let prisoners in and out for their various details. At night they were locked and the guards were withdrawn. Guards were on duty at night but at other locations.

Two tall barbwire fences surrounded the compounds with a fire lane between them. A machine gun was fixed to fire down the lane if anything moved in it. It was not needed however, at least while Post was there. Guard towers were also located at intervals. Post often would perform his duties in one of these. Lighter machine guns were located in these towers along with other small arms weaponry.

In addition to the three large compounds that held 5,000 men each, a hospital compound was also on the grounds. One day while Post was in a guard tower he noted a truck pull in with a POW in the back. Blood was literally running out of the tailgate of the truck he said. The POW had been working at the motor pool that day repairing a truck tire when it blew up injuring him. He was placed in the hospital. Post never found out how he ended up. Guards never had contact with their prisoners.

Rice was cooked and brought into the prisoners in galvanized buckets and wired to poles on the grounds. An organization called, K-MAG, Korean Military Advisory Group, took care of the prisoners and looked after their needs.

Life as a guard was usually "hum-drum" as he calls it. Except one day when the word came that 94,000 Republic of Korea, ROK, soldiers were coming to release the prisoners men like Post were guarding. Everyone was on alert while looking out toward the sea. He saw a naval destroyer stationed there just in case the ROK tried anything. With less than a thousand men to defend the camp with 15,000 prisoners, "It began to look like we were in it pretty deep," he stated.

Common sense told them the incident would not take place however. South Korea, or the ROK, existed only by the might and power of the United States. If they were to attack American soldiers, serious repercussions would have taken place for certain. "But in war, common sense can't always be depended on," he adds. One morning they saw landing crafts hit the beach with a tank company along with it. "They were a welcomed sight," he said about those who came to help defend the camp.

Life went on and nothing happened, the attack never materialized. But having the tank-company, war ships and ammunition issued certainly meant it was expected. "It is still a mystery," he said.

Sanitation was a problem at this POW camp as it was at many. There were flies by the millions he tells me. This made the environment unbelievably unsanitary. The Air Force would even fly over and spray pesticides but it did little good. They had to sleep with mosquito netting or the flies wouldn't let them sleep. People began acquiring dysentery. Most ended up in the hospital and finally were given drugs of some sort to remedy the situation. The command suffered along with the privates. When it came time to go to the latrine, there was always a waiting line, which often became a time of who was going to be first.

It soon became apparent that the war was going to be over. The Chinese POW's were informed they did not have to go back to their homeland if they didn't want to. Instead they would be transported to Taiwan or Formosa. These POW's were strong anti-Communists. They had even gone so far as to tattoo anti-Communist slogans on their bodies. If they would have had to go back the Communists would most certainly would have tortured or killed them for their anti-Communist actions. Post said he was sympathetic for some of these men. No doubt they had families in China and never would see them again. It had to bother many of them.

When the official word came down that the war was over, it was just like the military to roust them out of a nice sleep and call them to attention in front of the barracks and announce it. Everyone knew it anyway he said. They were indeed glad the shooting had stopped and they prepared to leave the camp.

The prisoners were all given new uniforms and each had their individual picture taken. Only non-commissioned men were doing this and it took considerable time with 15,000 POW's. Pens were constructed on landing craft and ships as well. Guards were also in the pens with the POW's. The POW's looked sharp with their new uniforms he said. Better than the American soldiers in their tattered apparel.

It took about a day to sail to Inchon, South Korea. There the POW's were unloaded and interviewed by their former Communist masters. After that they continued their journey to Taiwan. "It was the last we saw of them," Post said. Perhaps these former POW's are still there, he added.

POW camps were given to the Koreans Post believes. They were of little value except for miles of barbwire he said.

Post was with an advance party, which was going to Koge, a small island near the southern tip of Korea. The POW camp was now empty but was guarded by a trigger-happy combat unit. "We didn't feel too safe around them," he said, and was glad, after conducting more training so that they could leave. He was trained now to be a member of the Intelligence and Reconnaissance Platoon, a part of HQ and the 19th Infantry Division that made up the 24th Division.

It wasn't long until he received his orders to go home. He recalls that the journey to Pusan was one with very rough seas. "I thought we all going to die enroute," he said. Later he boarded a larger ship and eventually made the trip back to his base at Camp Haugen. He got to see some sights while traveling through Japan on a train. He saw Hiroshima and with the destruction of the WW II bombs still quite evident. Finally he boarded the ship for an 18-day cruise heading for Seattle, Washington. Then he went on a train to Camp Carson, Colorado where he received his discharge papers. He said goodbye to the friends he had made and headed home and was thankful to be alive after being in Korea during the war.

SCHEIBEL, NORMAN

Scheibel lives in Campbell, Nebraska. I guess I have known him most of my life. He and his wife farm just west of town. From the contents in his story I would say he is glad to be alive after his duties in Korea.

The Korean War had been in progress just over a year when Scheibel received his "Greetings from the United States Army." He took his physical in November of 1951. After passing it, he was inducted in February of 1952 and spent 16 weeks at Fort Knox, Kentucky. He hoped that his training would keep him alive in Korea.

He had been told the news that two of his friends in the Campbell area, Bob Genereux and Jack Koch, who were already in Korea, had been reported as missing in action. The news left him with some feelings of anxiety wondering what his fate might be.

After completing his basic training, he was destined for Korea. Names starting with R, S, and T, were assigned for the Far East Command. He was given a 10-day pass to come home. He helped his dad harvest wheat. All too soon the furlough was over. He boarded a plane in Grand Island and was flown to Camp Stoman, California.

He was assigned to the USS Migs and was bound for Japan for a two-week cruise full of seasickness and typhoons. It was far removed from being a "peaceful Pacific Ocean," as he had been told.

One day, while standing on the deck during the first week out at sea, spray was flying in their faces. The men thought it was nothing more than sea sprays. Someone replied, "damn, that's not sea spray that's puke!" The men quickly made their way to the bow of the ship where the air was much fresher.

They arrived at Yokohama, Japan, hopped on a train for Gifu, Japan where they were sent to CBR, Chemical, Biological and Radiological Warfare school for two weeks of training. He thought it was hot in Nebraska in August, but it was nothing like Japan in August with its hot and steamy air. Fans did little to move the air. After he completed his training he and the rest of the men boarded a train headed for Sasebo, Japan. Hiroshima was pointed out along the way. One could still see the masses of twisted steel beams hanging like wet spaghetti remaining much the same as it had immediately after the bomb was dropped 7 years prior. As evening approached, the men could see Mount Fuji to the west. It was beautiful with the sun setting. Passing along the route a strange odor filled the air and smelled something like bread baking. They were told it was rice bread baking and it carried a little different odor than wheat flour would.

They arrived in Sasebo, on the southeastern edge of Japan, about dark. They visited with some colored service men that were returning home from duty in Korea. One said, "You are heading for the Land of Morning Calm. You will think it's the morning calm when Joe Chink blows his bugle and starts coming at you," the man said.

Scheibel also learned that these Orientals that they would be fighting would often lay down forming a human bridge over consentina wire, and just keep coming and coming. "Believe me, that news put a real big lump in my stomach," he said.

The men were then ordered to load on a flat decked ship, similar to an LST boat of WW II. They were on their way for a two-hour trip across the Strait of Japan, to Pusan, Korea. They were told to not talk and not to smoking. "Believe me, no one had a desire to talk anyway," he said. The sea was calm, looked like a mirror, and really quite beautiful, he added.

They arrived in a replacement depot known as Repo Depo, for a day or two. "You know the Army, hurry up and wait." He remembered the odor when the Koreans the next morning took their sticks and honey buckets and cleaned out the human waste from the military latrines.

They were loaded on a very small miserable train that moved quite slow and took the uncomfortable trip to Ch'unch'on, just south of the 38th Parallel in Central Korea. As they passed through Seoul, Scheibel began to witness the first evidence of war. The city was in complete ruins and there were holes in the buildings the size of large round hay bales. Broken windows and rubble were everywhere. Refugees seemed to have nowhere to go, but the business of war went on as usual. Military truck drivers seemed to hit every muddy water hole they could splashing the filth on the Korean civilians.

After about a-days-ride, around 600 men arrived in Ch'unch'on, and were assigned to different units. Scheibel, and 3 or 4 others, were assigned to the 73rd Tank Battalion, and considered themselves lucky. All the rest were assigned to the infantry.

They moved farther north in a truck convoy up the Ch'unch'on Valley near Hill #1062. Battalion headquarters were set up there. His duties those first few weeks were to post guards at the gate. Scheibel was assigned a jeep and ordered to deliver supplies to the front. Toward the north, the sky was constantly lit up with shelling. The sound of machine guns chattering could be heard off in the distance. Upon several occasions they were ordered to set up a perimeter around the Headquarters area in case of an attack, but none ever developed.

The M-29 "Weasel" used for the most part in Korea but also used some in WW II. It had the ability to go virtually anywhere. Today it rests at the Heartland Museum; Lexington, Nebraska.

Part of Scheibel's duties was to haul food up to the front lines. By then the temperatures were sub zero with winter fast approaching. The windshield on the jeep could not be placed in the up position to break the wind because it might have caused a reflection from the sun that the enemy could have seen. When he arrived on this occasion, there had just been a skirmish with the enemy. Scheibel had to haul one wounded man back to a main road intersection where an ambulance would meet him. Ambulances were not to go up on the line. The soldier had half of one foot blown off; and Scheibel drove with one hand while the other hand held onto the stretcher.

Scheibel stayed at the front for days at time. He was surprised the bunkers were as warm as they were. But, with so many men sleeping in them, "we were like rats sleeping in a nest," he said. One time, he happened to be in the latrine when he heard the whine of what he thought was enemy artillery overhead. He ran for the bunker only to be informed that "that was outgoing mail, don't worry, go back to your business."

The company would only stay in one area about 5-6 weeks. One time, in preparation to move, tents had been taken down but they were told to find a place to sleep for the night. Scheibel and his buddy laid out their sleeping bags on some ammunition boxes, and slept in full dress with their rifles beside them. The next morning their faces had been covered by snow and the temps were around zero. They scrambled to get to the mess hall for some hot coffee and food. On the way, he noticed someone had left an M-2 Carbine rifle lying around. He picked it up and kept it with him the duration of the time he was in Korea.

The order was given to move out, jeeps first, tanks to follow. After traveling a distance, the tanks were told to take the lead. He recalls that as the M-48 tanks passed him in the jeep, the engine heat from their cherry red mufflers blew over them "It felt so good after driving with our windshields down," he said.

The 7th Infantry pulled back. The 73rd supported the 7th or the ROC Division. During that time Thanksgiving was celebrated. The cooks even had turkey dinners for the troops with all the trimmings, including pumpkin pie sitting right in the middle of the potatoes and gravy.

The winter was supposed to have been one of the warmer winters in the past decade. "It got only to 23 degrees below zero," he comments. But, there was very little wind. Guards on duty could only take it about an hour and then they had to be relieved. Normally guards were on two-hour shifts.

Tents frequently caught on fire from oil burning stoves getting over-heated by a build up of soot. When someone was to awaken, it was done gently, by grabbing a foot and gently shook him, calling his name. Everyone slept with loaded rifles.

One time Scheibel and some other men were told to go up to the 31st or 32nd Infantry Regiment HQ. As they arrived mortar rounds began coming in. A Sgt. shouted to them "get that damn jeep out of here." Scheibel bailed out over the back seat while the jeep sped off. No one was injured he said.

During this time, Scheibel was assigned to drive a jeep for a South Korean Lt. Driving at around 20 miles per hour, the trip seemed to last forever. They came across a truck that had been stopped by some MP's. The truck was loaded with "naughty girls" who were trying to escape from beneath the tied down tarp. The MP's were beating on them with their rifle butts trying to keep them contained in the truck.

They finally came upon a village where the Lt. invited Scheibel to come with him. Scheibel, not knowing what he was doing, told him he would stay with the jeep. About an hour later the Lt. returned but it was getting dark. They had to drive back using their "cat eye's", an iron shield with two little slits in them that was placed over the headlight allowing only a minimum of light to shine on the road.

Each time the battalion moved; it was towards the west. Shortly after Christmas, Scheibel was assigned to a Recon Tank Battalion. In their small M-24 tanks, a crew of five was to sit on top of a hill and radio back to HQ just to see that everything worked. He recalls the first time he radioed HQ and waited for the reply. Someone had turned the volume wide open. He jerked his head back so fast he thought he busted his skull as it hit against the steel interior. The M 24's were also used to "hit and run," go out and look and get back.

In January 1953, he went to Tokyo for some R & R, rest and recuperation. He took a train to Ch'unch'on. He and his buddy were sitting there watching some Ethiopians who were sitting ahead of them. They were setting by an open window, singing and were peeling an apple with a 12-inch knife. His buddy asked him to ask these fellows to close the window for it was very cold, 21 degrees below zero. When he saw the big knives, Scheibel quickly told his buddy, "if you want the windows closed, you tell them." The two spent the rest of the trip with a blanket over their heads to keep warm. At

Ch'unch'on, they put up tents with the order to not turn the fire up, as they would run out of fuel. But someone did, and they did run out of fuel. The next morning, icicles were hanging in the tent.

At the airport they boarded the flying boxcars to Japan. It definitely was not first class accommodations he says. After arriving in Tokyo, a friend of his buddy who was in the Air Force, advised them to eat at the Air Force complex. "Talk about food. It was like eating at the Hilton. All "real" food," he said.

Scheibel rode a taxi to see the sights. If one took a Japanese taxi the cost was 80 yen. If the vehicle were American made it would cost 100 yen; 360 yen equaled a dollar in those days. So it was quite inexpensive to get around he said. He visited the Emperors Palace and the Ernie Pyle Theatre. Temperatures reached about 65 during the day and near freezing at night. It seemed like summer after Korea he said. The five days that they were there were all too short and then they had to go back to Korea and more cold weather.

He was then back on the front. Recon tanks were sent three or four times up on the line to sit right beside a searchlight house. Four men manned the light to illuminate the enemy trenches. He had been assured the work was dangerous. "Joe likes the light, he can see what he is doing," was the comment.

Several days later they could hear the Corsairs bombing the enemy. They were close enough to be able to tell what kind of bombs the planes were carrying when it left the plane. If the bomb fell straight, it was a straight explosive bomb. If the bomb tumbled, it was napalm. The ground trembled as the bombs landed.

The sound of the Quad 50's could be heard. There were four machine guns, 50 caliber, mounted on the top of a half-track. One man fired them all. Every fifth round was a tracer, great fireworks he said, as the guns chattered during the night. By the time our forces got done bombing and strafing the hill, there weren't enough trees left to make a fence post. "I've paid money to see air shows since then, but this was the only one President Truman paid me to see," Scheibel said.

Back again at the searchlight, Joe Chink decided they had enough of that light and dropped mortars on them until the bunkers were nothing but dust. Two or three of the men had been killed and Scheibel wondered, "was that $45 a month extra combat pay really worth it?"

By the summer the troops started getting newer equipment instead of the old WW II stuff that had been using. But sometimes newer was not always better Scheibel said. The trucks with their new automatic transmission were not well liked by their drivers who wished they had the old straight stick back.

Scheibel received his second stripe now as a Corporal. His guard duties were reduced and a lot of the time he was placed on CQ, Charge of Quarters, duty. He sat at a desk and took radio messages. He was on duty when the Cease-Fire Truce was signed.

The war was officially over on July 27, 1953. "I had the privilege of announcing, "Now hear this, Now hear this. P'anmunjom, (north of Seoul on the North/South Korean border) has announced that a truce has been signed. If that is true, the War is officially over." But, Scheibel said, they were cautioned to wait on the celebrating until they knew for sure.

Surprisingly, after the war ceased, the company inspections increased. One time a One Star General and a Captain came around to inspect. The Captain was nicknamed, "Captain El Screamo," as he delighted in screaming at everyone. Scheibel heard him scream for someone to give him a knife. "I thought the crazy SOB was going to cut someone's throat," he said. After the men broke formation, he saw the soldier in question with his unshaven whiskers and his Corporal stripes hanging by the threads like the ears of a cocker spaniel dog. He had been demoted on the spot.

The rest of the time for Scheibel in Korea was quite mild. At times he would operate a M-39 Personnel Carrier. They were much more fun to drive than a tank he says. Everyone was glad the war was over. Soldiers were once again laughing and having fun.

One night he dreamed he was actually home. Everything was so real. But when he awoke and opened his eyes he could still see the tent seams in the ceiling. "DAMN!" he said.

Around the 1st of September the big day arrived. They were going home. They were sent to Inchon where they were supposed to wait. Then were loaded on LST carriers and transported to the USS Brewster for their 10-day voyage home. No typhoons that time he said.

Having a couple of stripes didn't mean dittily squat on the ship. Everyone had to assume duties. Scheibel had the "pleasure" of working in the scullery, where he and others scalded dinner trays. The room was like a sauna. When the work was done they could go up to the deck and cool off with the sea breezes drying their clothing which also was soaked from the work in the scullery. This proved to have a negative affect on him. He contracted bronchitis and had to go to sick bay for 72 hours. When he returned to the scullery, he learned that the ship had been doing some rolling with the high waves and all the glassware had slide off the tables and broke. Now they would use metal, even tin cans for use the rest of the trip, he said.

The ship had been divided into two sections. One for the returning tour of duty men, like Scheibel. The other was reserved for the returning American POW's, about 1,200 plus of them. They were not to be bothered or visited with at that time. But when they docked fairly early in the morning at San Francisco, a POW happened to be standing next to him. Scheibel commented at the Golden Gate Bridge was certainly a good sight to see. The POW replied with a complete lack of expression, "Yeah, I guess." His ordeal as a prisoner was no doubt horrifying, as most were whom the Orientals captured.

Back in the states they went to Fort Carson, Colorado and were given 30-day furloughs. Then they had to return back to the base for the final 30 days. The final 30 days were a complete waste of time. "We just put in our time, that's the way the army is run," he commented.

One day while in formation, the Duty Sgt. called him out of formation. The rest of the men were dismissed. Scheibel, thought, "what have I done now!" After the rest of the men left, the Sgt., smiled and stated he was Bob James from Franklin which is only about 25 miles southwest of where Scheibel lived. James told him to look him up in about 10 days, which he did. James gave him a clearance paper, which allowed him to miss morning formation and go to the head of the line at chow times. Then he put him in the Forwarding Address Office where he was to work only 2-3 hours a day. "The last month was a piece of cake. It was nice to know a fellow Nebraskan," he said.

He was released from the Army on November 19, 1953. While driving through Kansas he ran into a bad snowstorm. He had to spend the night along the way and was able to return to Campbell the next day.

"I wouldn't take a million dollars for what I had seen and done in Korea. Nor would I go back to Korea for a million dollars," he concluded.

SIEBRASS, HARLAN

It was late in 1952 when this Korean veteran from Blue Hill found himself at Camp Chaffer, Arkansas for training. Eight weeks of basic and eight more weeks of light artillery training was what the government required of him before sending him to Korea. By Christmas time, he had his orders. What a present! Out of 200 men who had trained at the camp, 160 were sent to the Far East, Korea and Siebrass was one of them. Soon from Pudget Sound, he boarded a ship, the General J.H. Macre. At sea they ran into a terrible storm which lasted for three days. Most every one of the 3,000 men aboard became seasick. The single stacker ship took 13 days to arrive in Yokohoma, Japan. A day later they departed for Inchon Harbor.

In the middle of the night they climbed down rope ladders on the side of the ship while carrying their M-1 rifles and a duffel bag and jumped into a landing craft in sub zero weather. The harbor spray was icy cold when it hit your face. "It was the coldest night of my life, compounded by fear and wondering what the future would hold," he recalls.

Siebrass was a replacement for the 45th Infantry Division. He rode a slow freight train to Chunckon where the track ended. Then on to 6X6 trucks another 40 miles north over the Skyline. The drive resembled the Rocky Mountains to the Punch Bowl he said.

Upon arrival he was a replacement for the 160th Field Artillery Battalion - Charlie Company, a 105-mm. Howitzer unit. They were in direct support of the 279th Infantry Regiment. Later on in the summer, they also supported a Philippine and Turkish regiment. "They were excellent fighting units," he stated.

The Korean winter was harsh and hard he recalls. They wore Mickey Mouse insulated rubber boots with many layers of clothing and a fur lined parka and over a period of time the cold penetrated through it all. They also had to wear steel helmets that were a nuisance, but a necessity. Korea had it all when it comes to weather. The winters were severely cold and the summers were stifling hot. There were mosquitoes, monsoon torrential rains, and the ever-present stench of human waste in the spring and summer months and a rat infestation that was out of control added to their discomfort.

The President and the news media called the Korean War, a "Police Action." Soldiers joked about it, saying they should have been issued a policeman's badge. "We called it an all out war," Siebrass stated. A forgotten war where over 50,000 Americans died with well over 100,000 wounded. And 8,177 still considered missing in action. The war totaled 7,140 men who were POW's, with 2,701 of them dying as such. "What a tragedy!" he says shaking his head.

When on the front lines, Siebrass said they always moved under cover of darkness. He refers to "Smoke Valley" where smoke pots concealed their position as the enemy held the high ground. He remembers Sand Bag Castle, where the infantry trencher was only 20 yards apart at one point. He remembers hills, 812, 654, Christmas Hill, Artillery Valley and Heartbreak Ridge. "Our Saber jets did a masterful job of keeping the airways clear of Russian MIG fighters," he said. They seemed to come on Sundays. "We didn't know what day it was. We knew when it was Sunday, that was the day we were given out little yellow malaria pill each week."

Siebrass said that the bulk of his fighting was at night using mortars and artillery. It seemed like the worse the weather got, the better the Chinese liked to attack. "Their numbers were horrendous!" As spring came, the Communist offensive attacks increased. From July 13 to July 20, 1953, the "Battle of Kumsong River Salient" took place. The Chinese attacked with a huge six-division assault. They blasted a hole to the left flank of where Siebrass and his unit were located. They went approximately 20 miles toward the south before being stopped or driven back or decimated by our forces he said.

On July 14, 1953, the American 555, (triple nickel) field artillery battalion in the Punch Bowl area was overrun losing over 300 men. They were attached to Siebrass's division. It was one of the worst concentrated losses of the war. "I had some friends in that unit," he sadly recalls.

Near the end of the war Siebrass said they used a lot of white phosphorus shells in continuous fire. The enemy called it "running fire," as it would burn a hole clear through a person on contact.

Siebrass said that more artillery rounds were fired in Korea in a 155-mile front than in the entirety of WW II. Serbia's and his battery would fire 3,000 rounds into the enemy lines.

He remembers the advent of the helicopter. Seeing them fly over with the wounded strapped on one side of the bubble heading for a M.A.S.H. unit, "caught our attention." And yet, to this day, for guys like Siebrass, the sound of a chopper quickly turns their thoughts back to Korea.

The front became strangely silent on July 27, 1953 at approximately 9 p.m. They had been through a terrible barrage of mortar fire and artillery exchange that day, on both sides, up until the last few minutes. "I really didn't think it would end at this time," he said.

His unit withdrew backwards about 3-4 miles and again dug in their howitzers. Siebrass was Chief of Section in command of their guns. It contained six guns in their Charlie Battery, six more in Able and Baker battery's making a total of 18 guns in their 160th Field Artillery Battalion. The Chinese and the North Koreans also withdrew backwards creating a demilitarized zone about two and a half miles wide, the entire width of Korea. But as long as they were there, they remained on 100% alert.

Prisoners of Wars were exchanged at Ascom City, a tent city. Only 21 Americans failed to be repatriated and "we were quickly labeled as turncoats by the press," Siebrass said. These men did not want to return to their country. We can assume that they felt that our government had let them down.

The 155-mile front was, and still is, the most highly fortified military position in the entire world, he said.

On the brighter side, Siebrass notes, after the war ended, they were privileged to see Bob Hope and Marilyn Monroe at a Christmas show. Actress Debbie Reynolds was also there to visit the troops. Those times were nice. You could get out of your steel helmet, shave, take a shower and be a long ways from the front line. Food was just "okay", 'c rations' were plentiful at the time but no one appreciated the "green liver." "It wasn't our favorite," he said.

After spending two winters on this God forsaken peninsula, Siebrass was happy when he was part of the first selected combat units to leave Korea after the cease-fire. The 2nd Division relieved their position and his division returned to Inchon harbor heading back to America. "I was ready to leave," he stated.

A national television network filmed their departure. Those at home had seen them on TV on the Sunday night 6 p.m. news.

Heading back to the states, they went through the Panama Canal and 36 days after leaving Korea, they docked at New York City the Saturday before Easter Sunday, in April of 1954. On Easter Sunday they attended church services and in the afternoon attended a ballgame between the New York Yankees and Washington Senators. Mickey Mantle hit a nice triple that day deep in center field. Siebrass, along with others from his unit were sitting in the bleaches directly on the first base side of home plate. In the 5th inning, they were introduced to the crowd as the retiring 45 Division Thunderbirds. They received a thunderous standing ovation that lasted 2-3 minutes. "I'll never forget it. It sounded like a World Series roar," he said.

Four days later, on a Thursday at 12 noon, 800 of the Division paraded carrying the M-1 rifle on their right shoulder down 5th Avenue. A huge amount of ticker tape floated down from the tall office skyscrapers. Bands played patriotic marching music. "It is with pride I remember we were being honored by 2 million New Yorkers," he said.

But that isn't all he remembers. He also thought of his fallen comrades, his buddies and his friends, those missing in action. They represented all the Korean War veterans that day in the parade. "Even though some refer to Korea as the "forgotten war," New York City certainly honored us on that very sunny warm day in mid April of 1954," Siebrass concluded.

SMITH, JACK D.

Smith is from Kearney and was a Master Sgt. in the Army fighting in Korea with the 24th Division Medical Battalion. He was a Medical Supply Sgt. He was involved in 5 campaigns and has the Battle Stars to verify it. Along with those he also has the Bronze Star, Korean Presidential Citation and Good Conduct Medal. He entered the service in September of 1947 and performed his duties until September of 1951 when he was discharged. His stories could be many, he said, but he chooses not to tell about them. He feels good about serving his country he concluded.

TILLEMANS, JEROME

I interviewed Tillemans while in Grand Island visiting other veterans. He resides at the Grand Island Veterans Home. He served in Korea and was a member of the Army 7th Cavalry, 17th Regiment, while performing his duty in Korea from 1951 to 1953. He knew he was to be drafted so he volunteered and left his construction work for a time.

Tillemans said he was wounded but not in service. It seems that while he was in South Dakota one time, a gas station was being held up. He felt the Sheriff, who had arrived, needed help. In the process, Tillemans was wounded and the Sheriff was killed.

While in Korea, he said he saw a lot of action and lost track of his decorations. "I saw more action than I wanted too," he said. He spent a lot of his time in the northern part of Korea. It seemed difficult for him to clarify the details and I refused to pursue them. He, like many veterans, have the right to not visit about their experiences during times of war.

His concluding statement is profound however. I asked him how he felt about serving his country. His reply was simply, "If you don't serve it, you won't have it!"

THE WAR IN VIETNAM

While most people tend to believe the war in Vietnam began perhaps earlier than 1961, and it did officially ended in 1975. For many Americans, the war will never end. We still have those "missing in action," and possibly some still imprisoned and presumed dead. As you may have already read, or will yet read, in the chapter entitled "The Wall," American service men already lost their lives as early as 1957. More followed in 1959.

In April of 1965, news reporters reacted to Washington leaders that America was once again at war, with North Vietnam. This was similar to the situation in Korea where the communist north wanted control of the democratic south. America was once again called upon to help defend the freedom of South Vietnam. Prior to April, 3,500 Marines had already been sent over to Da Nang to establish a new base at Phu Bai, 40 some miles north of Da Nang. By April 20th, nearly 9,000 Marines and 10 UH-34 helicopters defended the base. In May, the U.S. Army also became involved. By the end of May, the number of American soldiers blossomed to nearly 47,000. They dug in to fight a war; it was evident at that time.

Along with soldiers came the materials of war. Supplies began pouring into South Vietnam. By December, over a million tons of cargo had been shipped. Manufacturers of war materials in the U.S. began pouring out helicopters, jeeps, clothing, helmets, guns, ammunition, boots and raincoats to name a few. Television networks began laying in phone lines to Vietnam to more adequately cover the news there.

The war brought out protestors to the point that as early as Easter weekend, 15,000 of them protested on the White lawn. Nevada's marriage business grew by leaps and bounds performing "quickie" marriages to avoid the draft. While in Vietnam, President Johnson declared all of Vietnam a combat zone.

The war continued to escalate. Not having declared war, American forces were limited as to what they could and could not do veterans tell me. Often, they could only fire-if fired upon. The government continued holding back never really allowing America to win this war. This brought about bitter resentments both from the military and the bulk of American patriots. Most continue to have these resentments to this day.

Many veterans who did return home, in later years suffered from what is referred to as, "Agent Orange," which is a dreaded illness induced by the spraying of deadly herbicides in the jungles of Vietnam. Many were soaked as planes flew over. Not thinking it was dangerous, and not being able to do anything about it anyway, they did nothing, while deadly toxins seeped into their bodies. In my work with the Hastings Tribune, I had the honor and also experienced the sadness of interviewing two of these men near my home. Some of these veterans who returned home, married, only to find that children they fathered were deformed, retarded or still born. The two I interviewed, regrettably, are both dead. Agent Orange killed them, although the Government still wants to deny the fact. The war of the 60's and 70's continues to kill 30 some years after the fact.

Other veterans of the war have been institutionalized. Some in prisons, others in veterans hospitals and nursing homes. Most will never again be well or free. The war has left its mark on them forever.

When the war was supposedly over, in 1975, nearly 3.4 million men and women had served during this era of war in Vietnam. Over 361,000 casualties were reported with nearly 47,000 of them dead. Deaths exceeded the Korean War by around 13,000 people. Men and women, who never again would return home alive to reunite with their families and loved ones. They will never be forgotten.

BERTRAND, GALE

Bertrand was from Upland, Nebraska, when Uncle Sam told him he was to join the armed service. He entered the Army in March of 1969 and was finally discharged in March of 1971. He was sent to Vietnam and was assigned to the Americal Division, 1st of the 46th, of the 196th Infantry Division.

After his training in the infantry, he fought in the jungles of Vietnam for five months before he, like many, were carried out on a stretcher. At the time he was in the area of Chuli, he was fighting, eating and sleeping in the field usually six days a week. One night in three weeks he would stay at his Firebase LZ Professional, as it was called. The rest of his time was spent in the field, where the action was.

Gale Bertrand takes a break from fighting in
Vietnam to write a letter home.
Photo is compliments of his mother,
Milrae Bertrand House of Upland, Nebraska

One night, just after dark, Bertrand was with four other men that found them a place to sleep for the night. The man on watch was a new guy and in the darkness didn't see the up and coming catastrophe that was about to take place. At the time, unbeknown to the men, they had camped in an area that was a Viet Cong, VC, training area. It was referred to as "Sapper Training," where the enemy trained the VC, Viet Cong, how to infiltrate places like Bertrand and the others were in that night. Their mission was to sneak in and kill as many as one could.

Bertrand said none of the men were asleep yet, just lying on the ground talking. They heard a "thud," like something hit the ground. They raised themselves up to have a look just as the first hand grenade one VC had tossed in exploded. Then a second grenade immediately followed. "I remember the first one, it blew me clear in the air, then the second one went off," he said. He was hit by both.

"I was one of the 'lucky' ones," Bertrand stated. The guy laying next to him, on his right, was killed instantly. The guy at his left, was hit in the head quite severely, and lived, but suffered brain damage. The other two received only minor shrapnel wounds.

373

A Purple Heart, a Bronze Star for Valor, and a Bronze Service Star probably wasn't worth the loss of his legs. Bertrand suffered for about one half hour before a medivac chopper that was called in to transport the dead and wounded finally arrived. He remembers well when they arrived. It was starting to mist; he could feel it on his face. His rescuers hastily threw the men into the chopper not realizing the extent of his wounds. They threw Bertrand in first; two guys grabbed his arms, another two grabbing his feet. When his feet were picked up and pulled on, the pain was excruciating. "If I would have had a rifle I would have shot them both," he said. Also, when he landed after being literally blown in the air, one of his arms was also broken when he hit the ground.

There is not that much room in a chopper. Bertrand was laid in first after they put him on a stretcher. Two of the other guys were lying on top of him. Only Bertrand's arm stuck out he said. When they realized the extent of his injuries, they got him situated so he could be a little more comfortable.

On the way back, it was pouring rain. If it had been raining like that when the chopper was called out to rescue the men, they would not have come Bertrand said. This aircraft doesn't perform well in the rain and they possibly would not have left the base in a pouring rain, and he would have died. He had lost so much blood already; he was indeed lucky he lived through it. In the chopper, one tourniquet came loose, and blood again gushed from his wounds.

Bertrand had lost both legs by the grenades. His left leg is gone six inches below the knee. His right leg is missing eight inches below his hip. He still carries large pieces of shrapnel in his body. "I can feel it, they didn't even bother to take it out," he said.

He was taken to Chuli where he would spend about a week while doctors attempted to stabilize him. Then he was transported to Cameron Bay for a couple days, then to Tokyo for the next 30 days.

I remember well the anxiety the family had to endure during this time. Not knowing if he was near death or not. His parents who lived in Upland, along with his brothers and sisters also in the area, had received the news Gale had been injured in battle from the Franklin county Sheriff who had informed them, Gale said. He was still in Chuli when his family learned of his injuries. Then there was no news for a time until Gale was able to call home, which he did. The family and many friends were relieved to know he was alive and really quite well, with the exception that he had lost his legs. We all hated the war more than ever after that, hitting closer to home.

After his stay in a hospital in Tokyo, he was flown to Fitzsimmons Army Medical Center in Denver where his family met him at the airport getting off the plane. All his family was there. His older brother Leon remembers it very well. Gale was brought into the airport on a Red Cross transport plane. When Gale was carried off the plane and saw his family, the first words he said was to his mother, Milrae. "Mom, I made it!"

"There were a lot of days, we just didn't know if he was going to make it," Leon stated. It was a touching moment when we could see him getting off that plane. "We're lucky, we still got him," he added.

Gale was in the hospital for a 13-month stay before he could go home. Leon said he adjusted very well accepting his injuries. His girlfriend, Cinda, had waited for him, stuck with him, and the two were later married. "Lot of girls wouldn't have stuck with him, with the condition he was in. We're proud of her and Gale both," Leon concluded.

Gale lives in Kearney today and has a fine family consisting of his wife Cinda and 3 boys and 1 girl. He has a successful cabinet business with a multitude of friends in the area. I am proud to know him!

In the stories of the WW II veterans, you will find a story about Richard A. House, who served in the Pacific Theatre on submarines. It is interesting to note he is now a part of Gale's family. Gale lost his father, Bernard, a number of years ago due to illness. House had also lost his mate by death. Being the father of Gale's wife, Richard and Milrae had known each other for years. Both being alone, they decided to marry. Gale now can consider Richard House his stepfather and his father in law. Richard and Milrae live in Upland and are two of the finest people I know.

BROWN, LARRY

Larry Brown is a Vietnam veteran from Lincoln. He served in the Southeast Asia war in 1968-1969 in the Central Highlands with the 101st Airborne Division, Infantry. He was involved in an operation called Nevada Eagle, around the end of

February of 1969. The entire company was choppered in for a re-supply to the nearest fire support base called Spear before preparing for the next operation that was called Kentucky Jumper.

Brown related to me how most of the guys in his company felt about the clerks who worked in the rear area. "They had all the hot meals and cold beer. I would have traded places with them anytime," he said. Upon one occasion, Brown and several other men finished the re-supply detail in record time one day hoping to allow them more time at the local pub to indulge in ice cold 3.2 beer. On the way to the pub they found out they were needed for a sandbag detail. Even knowing that would take the rest of the day, they volunteered.

They were told to report to supply and check out their weapons as well as ammunition and report to the pickup area to be transported to bunkers that needed repair. Upon arrival, they found the bunkers full of water and full of rats. Both elements had to go. Sandbags were to be filled in case of incoming enemy rounds. Then all hell broke loose with incoming mortar and rockets bombarding the bunkers.

Just before they took a direct hit, Brown and two others jumped into the closest bunker. The next thing Brown remembers is a medic pouring water on him to the point of Brown thinking he was being drowned. He came to, and ended up with a slight concussion. One of the other guys had a broken arm and collar bone. The third guy ended up without a scratch.

The point Brown wishes to make is this. It's in a form of apology for not thinking much of the clerks. Here was an instance where the clerks had to put up with enemy fire similar to those in the field that did it each and every day. From that day on, "I learned it wasn't safe anyplace in Vietnam. From that day on I never criticized the clerks in the rear," he concludes.

Personally, I have heard this type of scenario before. Infantry soldiers, perhaps a little envious of those who seem to have it made in the rear. The pay was probably the same and some enjoyed more of the little luxuries that were available at the time. Not always did it mean it was the safest place to be either. In times of war, there are few safe refuges and fewer enjoy being where they are assigned. Most would rather be home.

BUNGER, WILLIAM D.

After he received his draft notice, Bunger enlisted in the Army in August of 1966. He took his basic training at Fort Polk, Louisiana, for two months. He then went to Fort Ustis, Virginia for helicopter training. In the early spring of 1967 he went to Fort Sill, Oklahoma, where the 243rd Aviation Company was formed. He went through another four months of training and flew with the aircraft to California. There the Chinook Helicopters were placed on an aircraft carrier, Crotan, and they were off to Vietnam. Bunger spent from October of 1967 until October of 1968 serving as flight engineer on a CH 47 Chinook. He spent eight months in the Central Highlands and four months in the Mekong Delta. Most missions were to re-supply the ground troops and artillery units. All flights were combat flights.

William D. Bunger receives the Army Accomodation Medal for Valor and the Air Medal from his Aviation Brigade Commander in Vietnam. Laterv he received the Bronze Star s well as other citations for his actions.
Photo is compliments of Bunger, which he gave to me probably over 30 years ago.

377

A few weeks after Tet, Vietnamese New Year, he was flying supplies to fire bases around Dak To. While flying over Kontum on the way back to Pleiku, they noticed a lot of activity and distress calls on the radio. They landed at Camp Halloway, Pleiku, and shut down the choppers and then heard the news concerning the siege of Kontum. At around 8 p.m. that night, officers went around the flight barracks asking for volunteers to man four CH 47's, for a troop extraction from Kontum. Bunger volunteered. By 10 p.m. they were all flight ready, four ships and five men per ship.

When it was approaching 11 p.m. the Command was having problems with the order to extract. By 12 p.m. the requirement for extraction was down to two choppers. Each chopper could carry 30-32 troops. Only a maximum of 64 men could be taken out and hundreds, if not thousands of men were there. Some had gotten out by vehicle and hundreds of Americans had already been killed in this action.

By 1 p.m., the two choppers were still ready awaiting orders. The crew was strapped in the seat, "good to go." By 1:30 p.m. the order was given to go with only number 1 helicopter going and Bunger was in it. Number two wasn't needed because there weren't that many survivors left that needed extracting and one bird holding 32 men, could do it.

Bunger flew with the crew and it took only 30 minutes to get there and extract the survivors. Not a crewmember was hit but the helicopter was ventilated. The chopper was smoking but made it back safely to base. Fifteen men were walking of the thirty that was evacuated. Two of the men who had appeared to be wounded were dead when they landed back at the base. Some of the others were seriously wounded.

These brave men had been huddled in an area the size of a swimming pool. The chopper had to land right in the middle of them. When they landed, artillery launched flares from miles away plus there was the close in air support by F-4's and Cobra's. "It was the brightest, noisiest goddamn place I've ever been," Bunger recalls. For actions such as this, he was awarded the Army Accommodation Medal with V-Device for Valor. He also has the Bronze Star and others.

Bunger logged 2,000 hours of flight time while in Vietnam. "I could tell you 2,000 stories," he said. He chooses not to elaborate on more incidents than the one above. "Those of us who were actually in combat seem to endlessly try to explain those experiences to people who were not in combat. Give it up. They will never know, they couldn't understand anyway, but we will never forget," he stated.

He does tell me about his feelings concerning the war. "Those in charge, politicians, Generals, etc. should all be charged with war crimes and stand trial. What the U.S. serviceman was subject to in Vietnam was criminal," he said.

Meanwhile, the general public looked at the Vietnam vet with disappointment and often looked down on them when they should have taken their rage out on the "powers that be," he added.

There have been endless stories of Vietnam soldiers and their behavior. "All men sin, but they sin more in war. Trouble is it goes along with the rules of engagement. The rules are made by those who don't have to do the engaging," he said.

Bunger feels the Vietnam War had three effects on the men who served. Number one is, you were killed. Number two; it destroyed you mentally and physically. Or, number three; it made you stronger and more capable. The percentages of each don't matter. It mattered only to the veterans of Vietnam and which situation they found themselves in, he said. "By the way. At times you had little control of which of the three you were in," he added.

When standing watch one night with a group of others, Bunger says sometimes one saw things that actually weren't there. His aircraft was grounded for repairs for two days one time. He and the other E-5's were ordered to guard the perimeter during the night. Twenty guys, with a jeep and two way radios. Bunger said he was on the west-side of this base camp where there were 5-6 bunkers connected with a zigzag trench. Claymore mines were in front along with sharp barbed wire. The helicopter refuel pad was located just outside the perimeter.

Bunger was armed with his 45-Automatic and his M-16. This incident took place at Camp Halloway at Pleiku. The camp was either mortared or rocketed on a nightly basis. At about 2 or 3 a.m. he was called to one of the bunkers. In the starlight someone had observed movement outside the perimeter about a hundred meters out near the refueling pad.

When an occasion like this was observed, men like Bunger had to call the hierarchy to acquire permission to open fire on suspected movement, other than if they were attacked, when no permission was required. But this time permission was needed. Bunger said he called in and was told to wait and observed the activity for two minutes. If the activity persisted, he was to fire one round at the movement and report the results. Two minutes passed and the man at watch agreed there was definitely movement. Bunger picked up the M-79 grenade launcher, set his sights at 100 meters and fired one round. Movement ceased. At daylight they discovered he had blown a fire extinguisher to bits and the refuel pad had a large hole in it.

Bunger said that at the time they all agreed that there was movement. The fire extinguisher, quite large, is what appeared to be moving. "Try it sometime" he said. Pick out something in the dark of night; stare at it long enough and it does appear to move. That was the case there.

"Time has proven we don't learn from other peoples mistakes, only our own. The best we can hope for is to make the best decision based on sound judgement and be responsible for that action," he said.

Bunger is a personal friend of mine and our friendship goes back to when were little kids. We went to the same church, attended the same church functions together, our parents were best friends and visited at each other's homes often. Knowing he was a brave but somewhat of a daring young man, I worried about him while he was in Vietnam. He knew how to take of himself but for many others, that fact didn't always save them. For Bill, he was perhaps lucky. Being in the air for 2,000 hours, he was a target many times where the enemy could easily see the chopper which he was in. He knows what it's like to be shot at and also knows the effects of having to shoot back. He has my utmost respect and I am proud to call him my friend.

Bill could never seem to get flying out of his blood. Today he serves area farmers with his successful flying service of which he has piloted for many years. I recall one time he told me that he still gets a "high" out of flying. Only now he is seated in a spray plane with his enemy the weeds and bugs.

His aerial flying expertise is something to behold. He is still quite daring and he has a lot of guts, so to speak. I love to watch as he dives down to "attack" the enemy. His planes are equipped with the latest in technology. One can tell he loves his work. He also loves to fly over our house at the crack of dawn to make sure I am out of bed.

He also is a farmer and pioneers some of the latest farming techniques in the area. His wife Kris supports him 100%. Their son Andy is presently going to college and is also a pilot like his Dad. They live on a farm south of Hildreth.

Bunger, like a lot of Vietnam vets, had to come to grips with the ravages of war. He did, not forgetting, but living with it. He is proof it can be done! I am very proud to know this man and his family.

CARLSON, BRUCE

Carlson lives in Lexington and spends much of his time volunteering at the Heartland Museum of Military Vehicle. He is a Vietnam veteran who piloted the "Huey" helicopters there. "Uncle Sam bought me a helicopter and taught me how to fly it," he says with a grin.

This pilot has Three Distinguished Flying Crosses for serving as a rescue pilot. When he entered the service, he admits, "I was just a kid." He entered the service in January of 1968. He was shot down five times. Now at reunions, his buddies tell him it was six, but he doesn't recall the sixth one.

He related to me the details about an incident when he was shot down and the Huey exploded when it hit the ground, but he survived. He remembers being in the cockpit and looking at a "wall of fire" and waiting to die. Miraculously, he did get out and survived. The rest of the crew had already left the area. But by the time Carlson made it out, the enemy was right there and he had a pistol shootout with one of them, the NVA, North Vietnamese Army. Carlson won, he's still here.

While in Vietnam, "I flew every day on hunt and kill missions," he said. He defines that statement as he was the hunter and his wingmen on each side of him were the killers.

Not that he wants to boast about his flight time in Vietnam but he comments on the fact, "it was sure different than WW II airmen." During WW II, airmen would only have to fly around 30-35 combat missions. If they each lasted ten hours, that would come up to 300-350 hours of combat flight time. In Vietnam it was different. Guys like Carlson flew up to 1,500 hours in a year's time that they spent in combat. Flying each and every day, the hours added up in a hurry he said. Every pilot flew at least 1,000 hours he added.

When Carlson finished his Vietnam assignment he carried off one Purple Heart but said he could have had a lot more if he had wanted them. He also has a collection of other medals he earned while flying in Vietnam.

Sometime in the year 2000, Carlson plans to have his book published that will be titled, "Red Bird Down." It is a story about his life in Vietnam. I look forward to purchasing a copy because it will be packed full of hair raising experiences he encountered as he, "Red Bird" flew his missions.

Vietnam Veteran Bruce Carlson with the Heartland Museum, Lexington, Nebraska, poses with the popular Bell UH-1 "Huey" Helicopter used extensively in Vietnam. Carlson flew one of These on many missions while conducting his service in Vietnam.

Vietnam Veteran Bruce Carlson with the Heartland Museum,
Lexington, Nebraska, holds a 2.75 inch Rocket with folding
Fins used Vietnam. These rockets were fired from the
Huey Gunships at the enemy.

Vietnam Veteran, Bruce Carlson, poses with the M-113 at
the Heartland Museum at Lexington, Nebraska. Troops
generally rode on the top with their equipment inside.
It was armed with a 50-caliber or an M-60 machine gun.
It was used in Vietnam.

COUGHTRY, LESTER

This veteran of the Vietnam War, is a poet. He is from Norfolk. He sent me a collection of his poems that he wants published in this book. He served in Vietnam in 1967-68. He entitles his work as, "Let Me Die A Free Man." He was a Private First Class in the Marines. Through his poetry, he gives a clear image of what it was like serving in Vietnam. The following poem, **Let Me Die a Free Man** was written in 1967 and won the Freedom Foundation Award.

A soldier walks through fields of rice,
And longs for home so warm and nice.
His feet are oh so sore and how they ache,
The poor soldier whose heart is about to break.
While at home the coward cries, "Peace in all the world,"
But in Vietnam our flag is unfurled.
The coward burns his body that all will hear,
Or runs to hide his foolish fear.

There do I wish that I might someday be,
In order to make the world free.
Freedom is so very sweet,
But so bitter is the taste of retreat.
And would not you like I rather die for a free land,
Than to live under communistic iron hand?

In 1776, "Freedom," we cried,
After many brave young boys had died.
Once again with foreign rule we are faced,
Let not our country be disgraced.
They may be powerfully strong,
But they are also very wrong.
So let us meet them like an iron hand,
And "LET ME DIE A FREE MAN."

He wrote another poem in 1967, about the Marine who was bound for Vietnam;

For Vietnam I am prepared,
But to go there I am scared.
For myself, I am not afraid to die,

384

But I'd not want those at home to weep and cry.

Over there I'll go and fight,
To aid Vietnam in her plight.
I am destined to be a Marine,
For in it my future I have seen.

Although I wanted it at the start,
I know from my love I soon must part.
She's about the sweetest girl I know,
And if I die it would hurt her so.

To forget me she promised she would,
But myself I know she never could.
So to thee my love I'll say "Adieu,"
And someday soon I'll come home to you.

The next poem he wrote in 1968 entitled, **"Echo 2-3."**

Through the rice paddies we do tread,
Wishing that we were home in bed.
Dodging bullets, sidestepping boobytraps,
And at night fearing to nap.
Men who fight to be free,
Those are the men of Echo 2-3

These men fight, each with a gun,
They fight a battle that must be won.
At night we set upon sand dune,
Hoping the war will be over soon.
A name we have, much feared by the V.C.
It is the name of Echo 2-3.

For freedom we do strive,
Hoping to return home alive.
In the field both day and night,
Though tired we be, we still will fight.
These brave men fight to be free.
These are the men of Echo 2-3.

385

The next poem, also written in 1968, is entitled, **"Men Who Fight the Wrong,"**

I've seen some good men die,
For these I've seen other men cry.
These men were brave, these men were strong,
These men fought what they felt was wrong.

Over here they're soon forgot,
But at home there is forever the thought,
Of how they were killed by Charlie Cong,
As they fought what they felt, what they felt was wrong.

But as men die and at home folks cry,
These men are brave, these men are strong.
And they continue to fight what they feel is wrong.

The final poem has more special significance. This poem was written at the request of a friend shortly before he was severely wounded in a firefight. It was also written in 1968. He titles it, "A Candle of my Thoughts."

As I sit by the flickering candle light,
And think of the battles we must fight,
Of all the men who will stumble and fall
As they bravely answer their country's call.
As they charge across the open field
And to the enemy's fire refuse to yield.
Of how we'll march in the sweltering sun
And of home so very far away.

And how we'd love to be there today.
I sit here with a sigh and a frown
As the candle slowly dies down.

Thank you L/CPL Lester Coughtry.

THE HAGEL BROTHERS

Chuck and Tom Hagel are well known in Nebraska. They are fourth generation Nebraskan's. Chuck, is a United States Senator who now resides in Washington D.C. Tom is a part time judge and law professor in Dayton, Ohio. He was born in Ainsworth. Chuck was born in North Platte. Both of them graduated from Bonaventure High School in Columbus. They were called to serve their country during a time of war. A war they fought in Vietnam that has left its scars on these two men, forever. Chuck was 21 and Tom was 19, young men ready to lay down their life when their country called them.

According to regulations, brothers are not supposed to serve in the same place at the same time I am told. It was by accident that the Hagel brothers ended up fighting side by side in Vietnam both members of the U.S. Army's 9th Infantry Division. It may have been they were destined to be together.

In 1999, both brothers returned to Vietnam, walking over the same ground that both had acquired their many wounds 31 years prior. Tom was concerned about opening up old wounds, wanting to put them behind him but they headed on to Vietnam anyway to see the opening of the new American consulate in Ho Chi Minh City, known as Saigon until the communist takeover in 1975. U.S. and Vietnamese officials arranged for the Hagels and other Americans to tour some of the battlefields where they had fought so many years ago.

It all came back to them, that dreadful year of 1968 when each day they wondered if it would be their last. "It was a tough 12 months," Chuck recalls. "You saw people killed and maimed, something that lives with and is down deep in you," he added. He knew the trip would be an emotional one.

They recalled the day their patrol was trying to pick their way through the dark stinking jungle. The brothers were often asked to walk, "point," and they were used to walking in front of the patrol of 50 men. Just minutes before they had to cross a small stream, the Captain had them change positions and someone else had been assigned to walk the point position. Point was a dangerous thing to have to be assigned too. Many veterans of Vietnam have mentioned that this position held a high degree of responsibility having to watch for booby traps attached to trip wires discharging high explosives. The constant threat of snipers was also a common concern. One had to be very alert.

As these men began to cross this stream, one soldier hit something with his foot. It was not something he wanted to hit as this one led to a trip wire connected to a huge 50 pound mine the VC, Viet Cong, had planted there for just this purpose, get some of these American GI's who were in pursuit of them. The mine exploded with a noise that would burst ones eardrums. Some soldiers, nearest the bomb were simply evaporated. Others were missing legs and arms, with bones protruding out of their almost lifeless bodies as they lay there screaming. The stream turned to blood, which no doubt resembled the Nile River where Moses once changed the water into blood. Tom witnessed the entire ordeal then his thoughts quickly turned to, "where's Chuck?"

Tom found his older brother lying on the ground his eyes were staring towards space while blood was gushing out of his chest. Quickly Tom applied a compress bandage and slowed it down somewhat but blood continued oozing out from it. The medavac choppers would have to come soon. Tom soon discovered he too was wounded. A piece of shrapnel was stuck in his left arm and was also bleeding profusely. As the remaining men with their machetes chopped a place down for the chopper to land, about half of the men were either killed or seriously wounded. They would be removed from the area first.

The brothers were taken to a hospital and healed. When they were well enough they were order to the field again and continued to fight with numerous other "close calls." On another trip they were to check out a village in search for the enemy. This time they had some Armored Personnel Carriers, APC's, and were returning from the village where they had found no one. The enemy had been watching and when it appeared as if they could get the last APC visible to them, they opened up. Mines had been planted where the APC's were crawling along. One went off under the one Chuck and Tom was in. Along with the horrendous blast, it burst into flames. Chuck was on fire, his left side burning, his facial oils were beginning to fry with the intense heat, his eardrums were broken from the explosion. His brother Tom was unconscious. Chuck knew he had to get Tom off the vehicle for fear the ammunition aboard would also explode. With all his might he drug his, what seemed lifeless brother, out of the APC and off to the ground. They hid behind the vehicle as the VC began using their machine guns. The VC was eventually contained and the men found each either in a makeshift field hospital on what was a rubber plantation.

Perhaps the brothers were meant to be together. Each had saved each other's life. Chuck received two Purple Hearts and Bronze Stars. Tom received three Purple Hearts and two Bronze Stars, after he was wounded three times. Twice they both had been wounded at the same time, but perhaps their feelings about the war are world's apart.

Tom is a staunch Democrat, always known for disagreeing with his Republican brother, Chuck. Tom, when he returned home, took to the bottle for a brief time. Chuck chose seclusion for a short time. Both had to heal. Tom says he was disillusioned by the war, angered with the waste, the misery and the lives lost. When Tom entered the war, he believed in it. Not anymore! Chuck, on the other hand still believes the war was a noble effort, but was prosecuted in a very irresponsible way.

"I still believe the United States was right to fight communism in Southeast Asia. But in democracy, a major war effort succeeds only if the public supports it. During the Vietnam War, the American public was confused. Our political leaders misrepresented our actions and the reasons for them. The American government lost the trust and confidence of the American people. Public opinion became so poisoned and divided that it became impossible to succeed in Vietnam. As Colin Powell has said, before you commit the armed forces, you must commit the nation. We did not do that in Vietnam," Chuck Hagel said in his Veterans Day address to his fellow Nebraskan's on November 5, 1999.

When the brothers were in Vietnam in 1999, they thanked God that they were not in that situation again as they were in 1968. At the time, Chuck said, they were half sick from the heat, the humidity, the smells and relentless pressures of carrying out the ugly business of war. Death lurked in the jungle, on the rivers and roads, in the rice paddies and villages. "Mortality haunted us everywhere, we did what we had to do to survive," he stated.

The experience however, gave Chuck an even greater respect for the men and women who serve our country in uniform. "Most Americans do not realize the burdens borne by our service people and their families, the quiet hero's of freedom. Civilized society needs to be reminded of the price these quiet heroes pay to preserve the way of life we take for granted," he stated.

One must think about it all in a positive way. I like what Senator Hagel stated when he proclaimed these words. "You don't escape from an experience like war without scars, but you can make a negative experience work for you. You can allow it to give new purpose to your life. You can use it to sharpen you sense of responsibility. It can help you see the impact of what you do, and what you are capable of doing," he concluded.

JOHNSON, WAYNE L.

Johnson is a veteran of Vietnam. He spent almost all his time in the field while he was there. As a combat infantry soldier, he knows what it was like. He served in 1969-1970 with the RTO Delta Co. 2/35th Infantry, 4th Division as a Sergeant.

In order to elaborate on his experiences, Johnson pens them down in the form of a poem he wrote this back in the 80's. At the urging of his friends, it was published in the Clay County News on Memorial Day 1992. It certainly bears repeating. It reads as follows:

My Vietnam Remembered

I remember the cold of Ft. Lewis and boarding the plane.
I remember thinking will I ever see home again.
I remember feeling proud and brave,
leaving for Vietnam, a country we could save.

I remember our landing at Cam Rahn Bay,
we were ready to fight the Cong and the NVA.
I remember the heat, the smell, and hot white sands,
the paddies, the bamboo, and the jungles of the Highlands.

I remember the Chur Prongs and all the killing,
the smoke, the blood, the insects, it's still so chilling.
The blue lines, the mountains, and valleys so vast,

these all remain somewhere in my distant past.

I remember the Ia Drang Valley, Kontum,
and Dak To,
It seemed there were always new places to go.
Ambushes, LP's, 105,s and LZ's like Penny,
they all had names but I've forgotten many.

I remember tigers, snakes, and those slimy leeches,
claymores, trip flares, and our C.O.'s speeches.
The friends you made, you'll have for life.
Back then, they meant more than family or wife.

I remember the firefights, the screams and the cries,
seeing the tears from grown men's eyes.
Killing a "Dink" felt good at the time.
We look back now for the reason or rhyme.

I remember the DEROS and the freedom plane.
Everyone knew we would never be the same.
We killed and we died for very little gain.
I guess we were all a little insane.

Coming back to the world was the real surprise,
but no one took time to look deep in our eyes.
I remember the wounds that never deserved a "Purple
Heart"
I remember that day and all my bad feelings start.

I remember the homecoming and hugging my wife,
"Nam" took its toll on her and her life.
I remember too clear the year of 1969,
will God ever pass us into the "Great Divine?"

I remember the "Wall" and all my fears,
my thoughts, my pride, through all my tears.
"Dear Lord take care of each and every one of them."
We went over as boys, but we came back as men.

The war is long over, but memories will always remain.
Combat will change you; you'll never be the same.

The soldier in me still cries out at night.
Will we ever know if we were wrong or right?

So, my friend, when you go to bed tonight,
say a little prayer for my buddies and me.
We lived; we fought, and died through a year of hell,
to keep our great country Proud and Free!

Thank you Sgt. Johnson. Wow! I am at a loss for words as I read the above. I have a lump in my throat, and you know what? I'm glad about that and I hope you feel the same.

Johnson also sent another writing of his that is perhaps a summary of all Vietnam veterans. A college student had posted a request on an Internet newsgroup asking for personal narratives from guys like Johnson, addressing the question, "What is a Vietnam Veteran?" This is what Johnson wrote back to this fellow by the name of Adam. When the tears leave my eyes, I will begin to write his reply.... Here it is.

What is a Vietnam Veteran?

Vietnam veterans are men and women. We are dead or alive, whole or maimed, sane or haunted. We grew from our experiences, or we were destroyed by them, or we struggle to find some place in between. We lived through hell, or we had a pleasant, if scary, adventure. We were Army, Navy, Marines, Air Force, Red Cross and civilians of all sorts. Some of us enlisted to fight for God and Country and some were drafted. Some were gung-ho, and some went kicking and screaming.

Like veterans of all wars we lived a tad bit-or a great bit-closer to death than most people like to think about. If Vietnam vets differ from others, perhaps it is primarily in the fact that many of us never saw the enemy, or recognized, him or her. We heard gunfire and mortar fire, but rarely looked into the enemy's eyes. Those who did, like folks who encounter close combat anywhere and anytime, are often haunted for life by those eyes, those sounds, those electric fears, that ran between ourselves, our enemies, and the likelihood of death for one of us. Or we get hard, callused, and tough. All in a day's work. Life's a bitch, then you die! But most of us remember, and get twitchy, worried, and sad.

We are crazies dressed in cammo, wide-eyed, wary, homeless and drunk. We are Brooks Brothers suit wearers, doing deals downtown. We are housewives, grandmothers and church deacons. We are college professors engaged in the rational pursuit of the truth about the history of politics or culture of the Vietnam experience. And we are sleepless. Often sleepless.

We pushed paper, we pushed shovels. We drove jeeps, operated bulldozers, built bridges, we toted machine guns through dense brush, deep paddy, and thorn scrub. We lived on buffalo milk, fish heads and rice or C-rations. Or steaks or Budweiser. We did our time in high mountains drenched by endless monsoon rains, or on the dry plains, or on muddy rivers, or at the most beautiful beaches in the world.

We wore berets, bandanas, flop hats, and steel pots. Flak jackets, canvas, rash and rot. We ate cloroquine and got malaria anyway. We got shots constantly, but have diseases nobody can diagnose. We spent our nights on cots, or shivering in foxholes filled with waist high water, or lying still on cold ground, our eyes imagining Charlie behind every bamboo blade. Or we slept in hotel beds in Saigon, or barracks in Thailand or in cramped ship berths at sea.

We feared we would die, or we feared we would kill. We simply feared, and often we still do. We hate the war, or believe it was the best thing that every happened to us. We blame Uncle Sam or Uncle Ho and their minions and secretaries and apologists for every wart or cough or tic of an eye. We wonder if Agent Orange got us.

Mostly, and this I believe with all my heart, mostly, we wish we had not been so alone. Some of us went with units, but many, probably most of us, were civilians one day, jerked up out of "the world" shaved, barked at, insulted, humiliated, de-egoized, and taught to kill, to fix

393

radios, to drive trucks. *We went, put in our time, and were equally ungraciously plucked out of the morass and placed back in the real world. But now we smoked dope, shot skag, or drank heavily. Our wives or husbands seemed distant and strange. Our friends wanted to know if we shot anybody.*

And life went on, had been going on, as if we hadn't been there, as if Vietnam was a topic of political conversation or college protest or news copy, not a matter of life and death for tens of thousands.

Vietnam vets are people just like you. We served our country, proudly or reluctantly or ambivalently. What makes us different--what makes us Vietnam vets--is something we understand, but we are afraid nobody else will. But we appreciate your asking.

Vietnam vets are white, black, beige and shades of gray, but in comparison with our numbers in the "real world" we were more likely black. Our ancestors came from Africa, from Europe, and China. Or they crossed the Bering Sea Land Bridge in the ice age and formed the nations of American Indians, built pyramids in Mexico, or farmed acres of corn on the banks of Chesapeake Bay. We had names like, Rodriguez, and Stein, and Smith and Kowalski. We were Americans, Australians, Canadians and Koreans, most Vietnam veterans are Vietnamese.

We were farmers, students, mechanics, steelworkers, nurses, and priests when the call came that changed us all forever. We had dreams and plans, and they all had to change, or wait. We were daughters and sons, lovers and poets, beatniks and philosophers, convicts and lawyers. We are rich and poor, but mostly poor. We were educated or not, mostly not. We grew up in slums, in shacks, in duplexes and bungalows and houseboats, and hooch's, and ranches. We were cowards and heroes. Sometimes we were cowards one moment and heroes the next.

Many of us have never seen Vietnam. We waited at home for those we loved. And for some of us our worst fears were realized. For others our loved ones came back, but never would be the same.

We came home and marched in protest marches, sucked in tear gas and shrieked our anger and horror for all to hear. Or we sat alone in small rooms, in VA hospital wards, in places where only the crazy ever go. We are Republicans, Democrats, Socialists and Confucians and Buddhists and Atheists--though as usually is the case even the atheists among us sometimes prayed to get out of there alive.

We are hungry and we are sated, full of life or clinging to death. We are injured and we are curers, despairing and hopeful, loved or lost. We got too old too quickly, but some of us have never grown up. We want, desperately, to go back, to heal wounds, and revisit the sites of our horror. Or we want never to see that place again, to bury it, its memories, its meaning. We want to forget and we wish we could remember.

Despite our differences we have so much in common. There are few of us who don't know how to cry, though we often do it alone, when nobody will ask, "what's wrong?" We're afraid we might have to answer.

Adam, if you want to know what a Vietnam veteran is, get in your car next weekend, or cage a friend with a car to drive you. Go to Washington. Go to the Wall. It's going to be Veteran's Day weekend. There will be hundreds there, no thousands. Watch them. Listen to them. I'll be there. Come touch the Wall with us. Rejoice a bit. No, cry a lot. I will. I'm a Vietnam Veteran, and after 30 years, I think I am beginning to understand what that means.

After reading Johnson's reply, I am certain he knows what it means. I have heard it said many times that Vietnam vets seem to be different from other vets. Why is that, they ask? Johnson has a reply for that question too. I will summarize it.

These are thoughts of Don R. Catherall, a Ph.D. in psychology and co-founder and executive director of the Phoenix Institute in Chicago, which specializes in treating trauma survivors of all ages. He has counseled Vietnam vets suffering from post-traumatic stress disorder and has been an advisor to the Department Of Veteran Affairs. He himself was a combat marine soldier in 1967-68. He authored *Back From the Brink*, Bantum Books, 1992, a family guide to overcoming traumatic stress.

Catherall believes Vietnam vets are less likely to blindly accept orders and perceptions of others. They are perhaps more likely to measure others by their reliability, i.e., is this someone with whom I could share a foxhole? They are less hung up on appearances, less likely fooled, and have had enough bull---- thrown at them that they may see through it a little better than others.

Catherall says that all Vietnam vets share a sadness and a brotherhood that is rare. It may not be active most of the time, but they are able to connect in a way that goes very deep. Think about the guys hugging at the Wall. The same thing the current men's movement is trying to achieve.

Many of the vets have violent tempers and seek adrenaline-rush-type activities. Some are workaholics and are maintaining but still sitting on explosive energy.

They know how to take orders and give orders. They have shared their canteens with all classes of people. They have seen death, close up. They have experienced big-time loss. They have faced their fears and found their courage. As a result, they are different in a way that the Indians understood and prized, but which our society does not well understand and often fears Catherall said.

"We have experience of being judge, jury, and executioner. Many of us were free to take life without having to account for our reason. We were all affected by having that incredible power of living through an experience in which there was no law-we were the law," Catherall concludes.

The messages given by Johnson and Catherall are clear. You, the reader, must now think about it. So the next time you run across a veteran who fought in Vietnam, think about what you just read. As I can honestly say, he fought for me! I was at the age to serve in Vietnam myself. Due to serious eye problems, I wasn't good enough. They only take the best. I had to stay home. My hat is off to you, the Vietnam veteran, as well as all veterans. You did what I could not. Thank You!

KERRY, ROBERT J.

Since I was well aware of Nebraska's former Governor Bob Kerry's Vietnam veteran's status, I contacted him. The honorable U.S. Senator from Nebraska sent me a letter along with a copy of his Medal of Honor Citation.

I have always admired our leaders who have "Been through the fire," so to speak. People who have served our country in the armed forces, and now, continue to serve as leaders of our state and nation. My hats off to Senator Kerry, as well as others who have a leadership role in this nation. Senator Kerry indeed, knows what freedom costs.

Senator Kerry expressed his delight in the making of this book. He stated, "It is important for us to remember and to honor those who served this country and sacrificed themselves on behalf of freedom. I am proud to have had the opportunity to serve my country in a number of capacities throughout the years."

Kerry went on to say that it was a privilege to receive the Medal of Honor Citation. "I accepted knowing that countless acts of unselfish heroism by brave Americans have gone unrecognized." As I procured stories for this book, I found that statement to be most certainly true. He hopes this book will help tell a few of their stories and give them some honor. He wishes me success, and I thank Senator Kerry for your support.

Joseph R. Kerry was a Lieutenant, Junior Grade, U.S. Naval Reserve, Sea, Air, and Land Team, SEAL. He was born in 1943, attended public school in Lincoln and entered the service from Omaha, Nebraska. His Medal of Honor was earned near Nha Trang Bay, Republic of Vietnam, 14 March, 1969.

His citation reads: For conspicuous gallantry and intrepidity at the risk of his life above and beyond the call of duty while serving as SEAL team leader during action against enemy aggressor, (Viet Cong) forces. Acting in response to reliable intelligence, Lt. Kerry led his SEAL team on a mission to capture important members of the enemy's area political cadre known to be located on an island in the Bay of Nha Trang.

In order to surprise the enemy, he and his team scaled a 350-foot sheer cliff to place themselves above the ledge on which the enemy was located. Splitting his team in 2 elements and coordinating both, Lt. Kerry led his men in the treacherous downward descent to the enemy's camp. Just as they neared the end of their descent, intense enemy fire was directed at them. Lt. Kerry received massive injuries from a grenade, which exploded at his feet and threw him backward onto the jagged rocks. Although bleeding profusely and suffering great pain, he displayed outstanding, courage and presence of mind in immediately directing his element's fire into the heart of the enemy camp.

Utilizing his radioman, Lt. Kerry called in the second element's fire support, which caught the confused Viet Cong in a devastating crossfire. After successfully suppressing the enemy's fire, and although immobilized by his multiple wounds, he continued to maintain calm, superlative control as he ordered his team to secure and defend an extraction site.

Lt. Kerry resolutely directed his men, despite his near-unconscious state, until he was eventually evacuated by helicopter. The havoc brought to the enemy by this very successful mission cannot be overestimated. The enemy soldiers who were captured provided critical intelligence to the allied effort. Lt. Kerrey's courageous and inspiring leadership, valiant fighting spirit, and tenacious devotion to duty in the face of almost overwhelming opposition sustain and enhance the finest traditions of the U.S. Naval Service.

MELROY, CHARLES A.

Melroy joined the Army in November of 1964. He served with the 9th Infantry which was attached to the D-3-2/2nd Artillery. He was a mechanic and truck driver. He hauled supplies in Vietnam and operated and maintained electric generators, which supplied electricity to artillery batteries.

The "Mule" as it was called, was designed in WW II but wasn't built until the Vietnam War. It was used to haul cargo and ammunition over rough terrain, places where only a mule could go. The photo, taken at Heartland Museum, Lexington, Nebraska, shows the Mule hauling a 106 m.m. recoilless rifle, a type of huge bazooka.

He feels he accomplished something while serving his country. He was instrumental in getting mine sweepers to finally start dusting the roads that he traveled on twice a day. While delivering important supplies, such as water, the Viet Cong had one particular area they had been using for linear markers with command detonated mines. But it was only after he had a truck blow up from under him that the brass decided they better start using minesweepers.

Melroy came home in the fall of 1967 and had won a Purple Heart, the Vietnam Campaign Medal, the Sharpshooters Medal, M-16, and the Marksman Medal, M-14, for his service in Vietnam. Twice he received shrapnel injuries to his head. He felt his time in the armed services was his duty and obligation. "I'm proud to be an American," he concluded. Melroy lives in Kearney.

REED, CLIFF

Reed was born in North Platte in 1951 and was the second oldest of four boys and two girls. He is proud that he had a father whom, as he puts it, "Taught me responsibility for my actions!" That is an admirable legacy that all fathers should instill upon their young children.

In 1969, on St. Patrick's Day, Reed enlisted in the Marine Corp. By November of that year, he was issued orders to leave for the Republic of Vietnam. Upon arrival, he was assigned to the 3rd CAP (Combined Action Platoon) Group and stationed north of a place called Phu Bai. His group was responsible for the safety and welfare of the people and villages in their area of operations.

The CAP unit consisted of six Marines and a Navy Corpsman. Four or five of the local militia were with them at night. A Sergeant or a Corporal commanded the unit. Reed recalls that once in a while they would get a real "Gung ho" John Wayne type 2nd Lieutenant, someone who thought he was really something. Usually after one or two nights in the jungle they would get a different posting and leave the rest of the men like Reed alone to do their work.

The duties of his group also consisted of training the local and regional militias. They would combine training with daytime patrols and nighttime ambushes. The North Vietnamese would move men and supplies south at night. Reed's job was one of interdiction, to do anything possible to prohibit the NVA from moving southward.

Reed was amazed, and it continues to stand out in his mind that the way the Viet Cong used everything we threw away, against you. They would take an empty tin can; used in containing C-rations that you ate out of today and tomorrow that same tin can became an anti-personnel mine. Unexploded U.S. bombs were taken apart and the TNT inside was used to make satchel charges, booby traps and mines. "The Viet Cong were very ingenious," Reed said. Many had 20-25 years of experience in guerilla warfare under their belts. They knew how to kill the enemy, which were the U.S. service men and women who were there fighting for democracy.

Reed admits, as do most young soldiers, "We were just a bunch of kids who had left home." They had been gone from home about four months and for the most of them, for the first time in their young lives. "We were in a country fighting for what we believed was the right thing," Reed stated. Reed grew up with that instilled in his mind. When your country calls, you go, he added. "This was the way it was for our fathers and that is how it was for us," he continued.

He does not regret going to Vietnam. "I would do it again, in a heart beat." He states. Those experiences he learned while there will last him a lifetime he told me. He didn't miss out on college; he simply went when he returned home. Reed admits, when he did go back to college, he had a whole new attitude towards learning, living and loving.

Combat vets like Reed did learn a great deal. They focused on the positive aspects of the ordeal, became successful and went on with lives. Not that it was always easy, but it is something they had to do. And no, I have not yet had a veteran tell me that they have forgotten the things they had to do in war.

SGT. TUBBY

A Vietnam veteran who lives at the State Penitentiary contacted me after reading in the paper that I was putting together a book about Nebraska veterans. I do not know why he has been incarcerated I can only imagine from communicating with him. He is like many of these veterans who came home from Vietnam who were, and still are, often unappreciated by some. Some did not adjust well when they came home for obvious reasons. What they had to endure both in the field and in society when they came back home was inexcusable. They didn't take orders well, and this in itself, often got them into trouble. I have nothing but respect for them, whoever they are. They did what they were ordered to do and sometimes, after the smoke cleared, they were told they shouldn't have. Vietnam was a confusing, "Police action," which also aided and abetted to their problems and ours as well. Many civilians fail to understand the ferocity of war, let alone a war like Vietnam.

Sgt. Tubby, as he wants to be referred, says by using this name, only his comrades will know who he is. Families of his buddies are to this day, yet unaware of how their sons and brothers died in Vietnam. He was there, he knows, but in order to not open up old wounds, he said he changed the names of these brave men who gave all they had.

I had been wondering why this veteran had been working so hard to get grave markers placed on the veterans graves on the grounds where he now lives. It took him nine years of fighting and with the help of a local veteran's service officer and Vietnam vets there with him, he got the job done. After reading his story, you too will understand as to why it was important to him. This man with two purple hearts, does not wish any veteran to have an unknown or unmarked grave. I will let him tell his story as he related it to me, in his own words...

THE ONES YOU LEAVE BEHIND

About a million years ago, and more than a lifetime, I left part of my soul in Southeast Asia. I was there for the last eight months of action. It was by no means a war. Wars are honorable and the soldiers who fight them are respected and honored and never end up living on the street wiping windows for tips from motorists.

I never dreamed that some twenty years after living in the bush that I would follow the trail and walk right into another ambush, prison. But that is where I find myself at this point in my life.

After begging for about three months to be sent to Vietnam, for reasons that no longer matter now but seemed to matter too much back then, I was attached to a company of the 101st Airborne. You know, the crazy ones that are the first in and the last out. My task was to disarm enemy booby-traps and set up some of our own when we left an area. "Special weapons and tactics," it was called long before the cops adopted the name but not the attitude we had.

Our main barracks were located in the outskirts of Saigon, but we seldom were there. Every time there was going to be a push, either theirs, or ours we were sent out in the bush. We checked for hidden tricks the VC, Viet Cong, used, like hidden tiger pits they would dig and leave for some unsuspecting grunt to fall into. The pits consisted of anything from bamboo shives to the snake we called the "Two step." If this snake bit you, you would take two steps before you die.

402

The mission I will now relive and sweat through is not one that will ever be in the history books. The Heuy, helicopter, we took only had room for eight of us, with our gear and ordinance. One chopper was all that could be cleared to go scout an L-Z near what we were told, was a battalion of Charlie, Viet Cong, headquarters. We landed there in the dark. The friendly bird left us there set to come back and pick us up in two hours, just an hour before dawn.

We split up into two main squads, one being security and the others doing a careful hand an knee search by flashlight of the ground and perimeter making sure there were no dirty tricks places there by Charlie. We also put down some of our own to protect the zone should our units get jumped when landing. We had just started rigging claymore mines and some home made traps, like the standard grenade, "in a can on a string" trick, when I could no longer hear the team to our left. The other team was suppose to be rigging some bamboo shive traps across the trail we had found leading to what everyone thought was the enemy village.

I moved off carefully calling in a low voice for Mack and Nick, but no answer. I had gone about fifty feet when I came across Nick, dead and had been bleeding from his neck. Just beyond was Mack with a bamboo spear through his middle, still standing from where it had sprung up on him pinning him against a hidden bunker trap.

I turned back to my partner, Poncho, and ran right into the black pajama holding an American bayonet. I could barely make him out in the early morning dawn sky. I raised my left hand instinctively as my right went for my .45 on my hip. The thrust of the blade, I later learned had been in one of my buddies, went through my wrist and about nine inches into my forearm. I pulled the trigger on my pistol and nothing happened. It had jammed on the first shell casing. I hit the VC like a tackled dummy on a football field where I had been only a few months before. He went down and I felt the weight of my body push his next breath out of him. As I gasped for air I grabbed the only other thing I could reach, a 12-gauge shotgun I had strapped on my back. It was held tight against the back of my neck by this small little form on the ground.

I yanked the bayonet out of my arm, not feeling the pain that must have accompanied it. I went for the handle with my *right hand and in one motion silenced and stilled the life underneath me.*

I rolled over and watched the blood flowing with each pump of my heart out of my wrist. Then my eyes fell on the lifeless body beside me. In the graying dawn I could see the eyes and long hair of a young woman. I felt shame and relief and terror all at the same moment. I tried to manage my arm, or at least stop the bleeding; I still couldn't feel it. I low crawled over toward to where my partner had been when I left and found him dead. I pulled his handset off his pack and tried to raise someone on the radio. Looking up around the perimeter I could see the forms of others in my unit. Only one, would I ever see again. I was the lone living body in the L-Z. I reported it as such hoping for immediate evac.

But as most things in those last days, instead of one bird with a big red cross on it, I got Peter Dragon and his fiery breath dumped right on my position.

Napalm is a nasty weapon. It's worse when used against the dead. The flames missed my position, but it hit my now dead comrades and suddenly I was a paramedic for the dead, trying hard to save the bodies of my friends. I never did see the chopper land or the Recon team that grabbed me and pulled me back from the flames as they burned the dead. I had only saved one, and that one had taken the lives of my friends. I had pulled her to safety, as if it would do any good now. I had failed to do the same for my friends.

Months later, after a stay in the hospital in Da Nang, I was told by a buddy who had been on the chopper that day and pulled me out of there that his squad had gone back after the fire was out. They had made a safe zone and tried to recover the bodies. They found only bones. They buried them and left no marker. Not knowing these men like I had, they felt no obligation, only to put their bones to rest under the ground.

So when I walked into the line of fire of this walled place where I reside now, I learned that 144 inmates had died here and had been buried up on the hill. I had to do something for those who were veterans. Something I could never do for my buddies back in the bush. I set out to find out who these men were whom their country had forgot. With the help of an able Vietnam service officer of Post #20, which is a group of incarcerated veterans here, pushed hard to help me and win this fight. With the full force of our group we did locate and place 13 *headstones on the graves of those men who served in WW I, WW II, a couple of Buffalo soldiers and one from the Spanish American War. Now I feel I did what I could for the ones I left behind. The debt is paid, the Reaper is satisfied and life goes on, while the spirits rest quietly and they no longer invade my dreams.*

Sgt. Tubby.

There you have his story. I think it commendable that he and the other veterans marked the graves of the fellow veterans. They obtained nine headstones from the Veterans Administration and bought four others themselves and paid for the installation of all of them out of their organization funds. He informs me that each Memorial Day, veterans from Post 3606, Lincoln, honor these men with a rifle salute and the playing of taps at the graves of these veterans, now clearly marked by headstones. An honor they truly deserve!

URBANSKI, RALPH JAMES

This veteran from Kearney joined the U.S. Army in 1970. He was a student in college for two years and was doing construction work on the side. During the Vietnam era, he was drafted but he says he was looking for a job anyway. In March of 1972 he was discharged.

Like many veterans who served during a time when a war was waging in some foreign land, they didn't always get sent there. Upon entering the service he was sent, not to Vietnam, but to Korea. He served with the 1st Cavalry along the DMZ, demilitarized zone. The U.S. military was still defending the borders of Korea and Urbanski served guarding that border. Among his other duties he helped organize flight rosters.

He doesn't tell me much as to what it was like there. He assures me that he was very proud to serve his country. He stated, "How else should you feel? We live in a free country!"

He's right, we do live in a free country. Thanks to guys like Urbanski who helped is some way or another to assure that we remain that way.

THE WALL

The Wall honoring the Vietnam Veterans is indeed a wonderful tribute to the men and women of that era who served in the armed forces. It has been a place of reminiscing and much sadness. A place to recall those who were left behind during this "Police Action," which was never declared as a war. But it was a war for those who fought in it, and for those who lost their loved ones. It was a war Americans will never forget. A war, we hope and pray will never take place again. It was fought during a time when a great nation such as ours became divided like it never has before. The scars still remain today and perhaps they will never heal.

The Fremont Tribune printed a "Salute to Veterans" edition, November 11, 1998 as a special tribute to all veterans. I feel in this portion, pertaining to The Wall is noteworthy at this time. It is an excerpt from an essay about the Vietnam wall.

The date, "1959" is engraved on the upper left-hand corner of the first panel on the east side of this monument. At the lower right hand corner of the first panel of the west side, we find the date "1975." When the memorial was finished in 1982, some people expressed surprise at those dates.

The Vietnam War, they thought, started in either 1964 or 1965 and ended in 1973 with the withdrawal of the troops following the Paris Peace agreement that resulted in Nobel prizes for Henry Kissinger and Le Duc Tho. Thanks to the efforts of the historians, everyone knows that the origins of the conflict go back much earlier in the century.

The truth is, that the 1959 and 1975 do not even begin to encompass the years of grief brought to American families by deaths in the Vietnam War. On line 1 of the first panel on the east-side of The Wall, two of the names are indeed those of soldiers killed in 1959. Chester N. Ovnard, MSGT, Army, from El Reno, Oklahoma and Dale R. Buis, Major, Army, from Pender, Nebraska. Both of these men were killed on July 8, 1959. But they weren't the first Americans to be killed in Vietnam.

Harry G. Cramer was killed nearly two years before, on October 21, 1957. His name doesn't appear on line 1 of the first panel. It does appear on line 78. Cramer was a Captain in the Army from Pennsylvania.

The article concludes, but it is interesting to note that a young man from Pender, Nebraska, was one of the first to die in this bloody war. This reinforces the fact that Nebraskan's don't shirk their duty. They were in the lead to fight for what they felt was right. It was a just war and we must never lose sight of that. Anytime people of the world have their freedom in jeopardy; it is worth fighting for. All the other wars attest to that. Vietnam veterans did that too. They fought an honorable war. It was the politicians of the era that must feel guilty because it was they who wouldn't let them win it!

Jan Scruggs started and directed the job of creating the national Vietnam Memorial Monument. Scruggs, himself was a veteran of Vietnam and was with the U.S. Army's 199th Light Infantry Brigade after graduating from high school. He was also wounded and decorated for gallantry in Vietnam. When he returned from the war he obtained a Masters Degree in counseling from the American University in Washington D.C. It was while he was doing graduate school research on veterans of the war that got the idea for a memorial inscribed with the names of the veterans who gave their lives in Vietnam. Starting with $2,800 of his own money, he succeeded with raising $8 million, all from private sources, to see his dream come true. The memorial was dedicated in November of 1982. Scruggs is to be commended for his efforts.

THE LATTER "WARS."

The Bible declares that there will always be "wars and rumors of wars." This has been the undisputed case throughout the history of the world. America has not been exempt to this fact. After Vietnam, there have been numerous other incidents, which our American military has been called upon to serve their country.

Among these was the invasion of Grenada in 1983. A rivalry between the U.S. and Cuba was once again sparked by a bloody coup in Grenada, which were threatening about 1,000 American medical students there. It turned out to be a way for America to put away with a Marxist regime who were allies to Fidel Castro's Cuba.

President Reagan and the administration became concerned when the Marxist government allowed Cuba to gain too much influence in Grenada. A military airport was constructed along with Cuba military engineers. The Sandinista government of Nicaragua also was involved with Castro. By October of 1983, the Grenadian Army seized power with severe violence being the result. Towards the end of the month, the U.S. invaded Grenada with 1,200 troops who were met by much resistance. More troops were summoned as the numbers increased to 7,000. The enemy either surrendered or ran as our troops searched the mountains for those attempting to flee. America quickly regained control of the island. By mid December, our troops went home.

The brief war had its costs leaving at least 19 United States servicemen dead. Grenada and Cuba combined lost about 80 of their soldiers with hundreds wounded. It would not be considered America's first go around with Cuba. The "Bay of Pigs," skirmish, could also be considered a brief war in 1961. Whatever the case, Grenada was considered our first military victory since before Vietnam.

In April of 1986, the U.S. again found itself defending on foreign soil. This time it was to be in Libya, a North African nation, where only about two dozen American fighter and bomber planes performed a brief air raid, only a matter of minutes, in the Libyan cities of Tripoli and Benghazi. Libya's dictator, Muammar Qaddafi, had his headquarters in one of the bombing targets. Some of his family was wounded in the air strike. Two of our planes and pilots were lost performing their duties.

The reasoning for the attack began when terrorists, suspected to be from Libya, bombed a nightclub in West Berlin where numerous American service men and women often went. Two of our service men were killed and another 50 or so wounded.

Prior to that, back in 1979, when President Carter was the leader of our nation, Libyan terrorists destroyed our embassy in Tripoli. Later, in 1981, when President Reagan was our leader, now had to combat the regime of Qaddafi. Iranian revolutionists gained control over our embassy in Teheran and 52 Americans were held hostage. They were held for 444 days until they were released when Reagan became President.

In July of 1990, it could be plainly seen that Iraqi forces were building up their military in the Iraqi desert threatening to invade Kuwait. By August, they had done so. General Norman Schwarzkopf was summoned to command our forces in Iraq, which was to perhaps combat the fourth largest army in the world. Concern was expressed at briefings, about our interests in the defense of Saudi Arabia and other Gulf oilfields. The plan became a reality to remove the invading Iraqi army from Kuwait. An air base was used in Saudi Arabia and the American military was sent to the Middle East.

President Bush referred to Iraqi leader, Saddam Hussein, as being much like Hitler of WW II, wanting to control the world. Saddam had much military might and weapons of warfare that included deadly chemicals and biological weaponry. He was making weapons of mass destruction. He was ruthless and was willing to deploy whatever it took to sustain his appetite for power. He was also not a man in power that could be trusted.

Atrocities were being committed in Kuwait with thousands being killed or maimed. Pregnant mothers were bayoneted. Cigarettes pushed into their eyes blinded people. Babies in incubators were taken out and left to die at hospitals in Kuwait.

During December, 1990, and January of 1991, American troops along with all the war materials needed were deployed for the Gulf area. Americans, via their television sets could view the war each night on the evening news. They could watch as Skud missiles from Iraq came into Israel. We could watch film

409

footage from the seats of our pilots as their air strikes were performed hitting specific targets. We watched as their guided missiles entered directly into the doors of some buildings. We viewed suffering and death, witnessing thousands of human beings very much concerned about their very life. We sat in awe as we watched in our recliners while our service men fought to preserve freedom.

The war didn't last long. By the first part of June, a victory parade was held in Washington. With any war, it creates massive destruction and costly in human lives. But America, once more, we defended the helpless so freedom could be won. That's what America is all about.

America continues to support those who are less fortunate than most of us. Age-old ethnic hatreds began to blossom in Bosnia. Ethnic boundaries were beginning to become obscure. Extreme nationalists seemed to make it their business to define the three ethnic groups. Very much like what sparked the First World War again was pouring gas on a fire in what used to be Yugoslavia, which was created during WW I.

Three ethnic peoples, the Serbs, Croats and Muslims began fighting among themselves. All had histories if conflict, but few died, until 1992, when everything changed. A civil war raged. Hundreds of thousands were already dead or injured and there were around two million refugees. They hated one another. Perhaps it could even be labeled a religious war. The Serbs are Orthodox Christians. The Croats, Roman Catholic and the Muslims had been converted over to Islam many years ago. Atrocities were again being committed in this region of the world and America felt compassion to try to help settle it.

This book is not intended to be a history book. The history of this war goes back for hundreds of years. When communism collapsed in Europe in 1989, free elections were held in Yugoslavia. In 1990, the republic of Bosnia held elections voting on largely ethnic lines for nationalist parties. The Muslim Party of Democratic Action held the most seats. The Serbian Democratic Party was second and the Bosnian branch of the Croatian Democratic Union won the least.

Disputes that no doubt went back hundreds, if not thousands of years resurfaced. America was once again called upon to restore peace.

The "Humve" which replaced the ever-popular jeep in our nations wars. The Humve was used in recent wars such as Desert Storm in Saudi Arabia. Referred to as a utility vehicle that also carried a 50-caliber machine gun on its top. *Photo taken at the Heartland Museum of Military Vehicles at Lexington, Nebraska.*

The popular Bradley Fighting Vehicle used in the Desert Storm War. It was named after General Omar Bradley from WW II. The tank first appeared in 1978 and has an all aluminum body. *Picture taken at the Heartland Museum of Military Vehicles at Lexington, Nebraska.*

411

BRANDFAS, RICK

Brandfas entered the Navy after the Vietnam War was over. He was a student and thought the GI Bill sounded like a good deal. He joined in September of 1975, spent four years and was discharged in September of 1979 and still is a member of the Army National Guard. Most of his time was spent aboard the U.S.S. Nimitz, as "Storekeeper," in charge of supplies, as he refers to his job.

He liked the Nimitz; it had plenty of room and a nice bunch of guys to work with. The big carrier would sometimes have 4,000 sailors aboard. "It was not a cruise ship," he said. Sometimes, there wasn't a dull moment like when a helicopter tried to land on its deck and didn't quite make it. It had some sort of transmission problems and it went overboard. Personnel had to use a crane to try to retrieve it.

During the Saudi War, he attempted to volunteer to go because he was knowledge about chemicals but it didn't work out. He spent some time in Fort Riley, Kansas, filling in for those who did go overseas.

At the time I visited with him, he resided in Lincoln. Brandfas felt he didn't have much to offer for this book but, like I told him, he served his country during a time when things could have been tough. He was there and that's important to me. I asked him how he felt about serving his country. He said with a grin, "I must like it, I'm still doing it."

DANIELS, MARC

Daniels is from Lincoln and served in the U.S. Navy from 1984-1988 spending most of his time on the aircraft carrier USS Nimitz and USS Teddy Roosevelt as Plane Captain, aviation machinist mate. He was there during two-hostage crises and two terrorist attacks that took place in the Middle East. Situations when he often didn't know for sure what was going to happen next. The carriers were often put on alert and prepared for the worst.

In the summer of 1985, a TWA passenger plane was highjacked and flown to Beirut and hostages were taken. The

Nimitz was on alert, chasing the plane's movement from one point to the next as it landed in various mid east airports.

Daniels was serving on the night shift when a mysterious helicopter landed on the deck of the Nimitz one night. The movie, "Delta Force," could have been based on this incident. Although parts of the movie were fictionalized, Daniels says the Delta Force was real and there were whispers as these guys in the helicopter being it. The Nimitz was not shown in the film. The flight deck had been cleared prior to the landing but Daniels sat and watched it all.

Ten men exited the helicopter that had some bullet holes in it. They were not heavily armed and had no military equipment. A stretcher was removed from the helicopter with what appeared to be a Catholic priest on it. The priest was taken to sick bay where he remained sealed in for two days. The pilot of the helicopter stood watch by the helicopter for the entire time. Daniels, who was standing watch, was informed by this pilot, "This helicopter does not exist!" After about 2-3 days aboard the ship they left and Daniels said it was never seen again. It was only days later when the hostages that had been held captive in Beirut were released. The Nimitz had been alert with planes ready for 90 days off the coast of Lebanon.

In the early spring of 1987, when hostage Rev. Terry Waite was to be released only to be recaptured attempted to negotiate with the terrorists. The Nimitz was again on alert with all personnel assigned to general quarters at launch stations. The ordinance department of the ship was bringing up live ammunition. Bombs of various sizes and other ordinance used by fighter planes were prepared for loading on the planes. The pilots were ready to fly, "like kids in a candy store," Daniels said, eager for action. President Reagan had ordered the green light to begin bombing Beirut but in the final hours the plans were cancelled. The military on the ship was depressed, hoping they could use the skills they had trained for, Daniels said.

The incident was "the real thing," Daniels said, with targets designated ready for striking. When the personnel were called to quarters announcing they man their flight stations, it was no drill he added.

At the famous "Wailing Wall" in Israel, Daniels was visiting on leave one time. While there, a car bomb blew up only a couple blocks away from them. But, he says, car bombs were not unusual there at the time. They were as common as firecrackers here he said.

Daniel's family, including his wife's family, comes from a long line of military serving our country. It dates back to the Spanish American War to the present date. I gathered they served in all branches of the military, some losing their lives in battle. One great grand father served in both WW II and I. Another grand father was in WW II and fought in the Battle at Midway in the Pacific. He was proud to be with the renown "Carlson's Raiders," at the tender age of 15. Their fathers served in Vietnam. Daniels is proud of his ancestors who made themselves available to protect our freedom. I would imagine his family is very proud of Marc too as are the rest of us who appreciate the fact there are people out there watching our defense systems.

THE NIELSEN BROTHERS

Two brothers from Minden served in more recent wars. One of them, Michael Nielsen, I am quite close to. He is my son-in-law of whom I am very proud. He served in the U.S. Air Force for 10 years before making the decision to return back home and enter the construction business with his father, Marvin W. Nielsen. It was tough on his family as well as his wife Ruth's family when Michael and his family were far away from home. Those three little grand daughters were missed, I assure you. They were stationed in England for the last four years of his hitch.

Michael is the oldest of the brothers and Kevin is the younger. Michael joined the Air Force in April of 1988. He trained in San Antonio, Texas at Lackland Air Force Base. From there he went to Lowry Air Base in Colorado for another six weeks.

His job was with weapons and much of it was top secret and he had clearance verifying such. He loaded bombs on the new B-1 bombers, which were only three years old at the time. The weapons consisted of what Michael refers to as "chaff and flare" weapons (bombs and missiles). Radar guided missiles were also loaded on the B-1.

He arrived at Ellsworth South Dakota Air Force Base in September of 1988 where he continued the task of loading bombs on the B-1 and also working with the tanker squadron,

C-135's, EC-135's and B-52's. B-52's were being decommissioned at the time. He was a member of the 28th Munitions Maintenance Squadron.

On June 30, 1989, a date I remember quite well, he married my daughter Ruth. He was still based at Ellsworth so he took her back there with him. We missed them and the round trip of 1000 miles wasn't too bad; we just didn't make it often enough.

While there, Michael was given the title of Aircraft Munitions Maintenance Specialist. He was on alert when the Gulf War broke out in August of 1990 and remained on alert through February of 1991 for deployment. He was told by his superiors to "Get his affairs in order."

"It seemed odd to have do something like at Christmas time," Michael said. Later, he learned that if the war had continued another month, he would have had to leave. When they asked for volunteers, Michael was one of them who did. It was expected of them. "My wife was terrified with a one year old baby girl," but she had resigned to accept it knowing such a thing as this could happen when she married him.

While he was still at Ellsworth, the base decided to split the 28th into two squadrons; the 77th AMU and the 37th AMU, Aircraft Maintenance Unit. Michael then became a member of the 37th AMU, working with equipment maintenance, bomb trailers, vehicles, etc. By December of 1993, he was ordered to serve in England at Lakenheath RAF, Royal Air Force Base, an old base used in WW II by many veterans of that era, near Suffolk, England. There he was assigned to the 492nd Fighter Squadron and worked on F-15 Eagle fighter planes. Again, he loaded munitions and whatever was needed for the maintenance of them. The plane was equipped with 20 mm. gattling guns; it could hold 500-pound bombs as well as larger bombs. It could handle 7 long-range missiles, 9 feet long each, capable of 1,000 miles. It was capable of carrying sidewinder missiles for use in air to air combat. Michael worked with 23 different types of bombs and munitions at Lakenheath.

While the heat built up in Bosnia, it also proved an anxious time for family and friends. Michael was sent to Italy for 30 days in February of 1995 and loaded the F-15's headed for Bosnia. He spent two 30-day tours of duty in Italy in the fighter support area.

In 1996, he was sent to Turkey for 90 days again with support teams that were attempting to enforce the no-fly zone over northern Iraq. Turkey was not fun he said. Here, at the base, tensions ran high at times. The Turkish Mafia were to blame he said. They would excite mobs to congregate outside the gate of the base. Michael was shot at upon one occasion. A 10 o'clock curfew had to be enforced. "It wasn't a safe place to be," he added.

He made it back to England and called it quits with the Air Force. "I was glad to have served. We got to travel and my family got to see a lot of England and other neighboring countries and we plan to go back someday," he concluded.

Kevin Ray Nielsen, Michael's little (?) brother, wanted to serve his country too. He joined the Navy in May of 1990. "I wanted an education, and perhaps train for a trade," he said. He took his basic training at Orlando, Florida. He was assigned to the Guided Missile Cruiser, U.S.S. Leyte CG-55. During the years 91-94 he served in the Gulf War aboard his ship attending to his duties serving in the Mediterranean and Persian Gulf. He made Boatswain Mate 3rd Class and worked in maintenance.

In his last cruise in the Persian Gulf area, his ship was assigned to the embargo of Iraq. They were to see to it that nothing out of Iraq could leave by ship to be exported. Navy Seals, aboard 40-foot attack boats launched from the ship would intercept these cargo ships and inspect them. No oil or produce, like dates, was allowed to leave Iraq. Helicopters were also aboard the ship and were deployed during times of seizures of exporting ships and held until they would be shipped off to NATO Forces elsewhere.

"Then, when capturing these ships, they become ours. NATO in turn sold what was on the ship to someone else and the ships are sold too. "We were on alert many times, ready to fire," he said.

He spent time in the Sea off the coast of Italy patrolling the ocean and was prepared on a moment's notice to pick up downed pilots should one get shot down fighting in Bosnia.

In 1994-95 he left the ship to take additional training as a Fire Controlman and made Fire Controlman 3rd Class at Great Lakes, Illinois, near Chicago. He re-enlisted at that time for another four years.

After that training he trained for CIWS, Close in Weapons System. He is presently back on the ship, U.S.S. Lake Erie, CG70 Cruiser, and he protects the ship from incoming missiles and enemy aircraft. He can sit behind a 20-mm. Gattling gun, which has its own radar system capable of searching and tracking missiles or aircraft. The gun has a special cooling system and is capable of firing 4,500 rounds per minute from six air-cooled barrels. "The gun is very proficient in firing and easy to repair and maintain." Kevin is now a troubleshooter for the weapon and is a work center supervisor. He also works with the 50 Caliber machine gun where he participates as a gunner's mate skilled in electronics.

The ship has 365 men aboard and it is subject to daily and periodic inspections, of course. I think we can be secure in knowing that men like Kevin are out there in the world's oceans watching. "We are always alert and battle ready," he said. During a 24-hour period, those on the ship are on duty 12 hours and off 12 hours. The crew is dividing in half so the two shifts can be properly administrated.

Life on a ship is not that bad. "Our health and welfare is good," he said. There is time for recreation, study and entertainment when it doesn't interfere with duties. The meals are adequate and mail comes regular from Carrier ships stationed in the many parts of the world.

Nielsen said the SH 60 Sea Hawk helicopters often have women pilots which has changed somewhat over the years. They do a good job he added.

Ships are designed differently than they used to be. Nielsen's ship is capable of traveling about 30 plus knots. A knot is equal to about 1.1 miles per hour. The unique thing is that the ship can stop traveling at 20 knots, in roughly 850 feet. The ship is 567 feet long in length. After a six months cruise the ship is brought in for a four-month overhaul. Training exercises are continued then as well.

Kevin has already served for 10 years and hopes to remain in the service make Chief Petty Officer, which is a management position. He plans on taking his 1st Class exam very soon. He likes responsibility and personally, I think he will make it. One thing for certain, like he says, "I can say I've been around the world!"

417

SCHMIDT, RICHARD

Schmidt writes me rather a nostalgic letter concerning his patriotism. He grew up near Campbell, Nebraska, practically neighbors to me. I think his letter needs to be shared by the reader. Although he not yet has a military experience to relate, he may have in the future. But presently, he serves in the Air Force based out of Hill Air Force Base, Utah.

He graduated from Campbell High School in 1986 and he has always felt a deep respect for those in the military that fought and sacrificed so much for our beliefs. Every year, while living in his hometown, he watched with awe the annual Memorial Day services that were conducted. "That instilled an enormous sense of pride in me, even as a small child," he said. He still tries to make it home each year to observe the day. "For me, nothing can compare. I believe it had a lot to do with my decision to join the military," he added.

The first two years of his military service he spent in Okinawa, Japan, at the Kadena Air Force Base. That was a long way from home for a young man who was just fresh out of high school. After that he was sent to Hill Air Force Base in Utah and has resided there ever since. He was sent to serve in Saudi Arabia during Desert Shield and Desert Storm.

When he returned to the U.S. he was contacted by a VFW member, Dewaine L'Heureux of Campbell, who asked him if he would like to join the Veterans of Foreign Wars Post 169 in Campbell. "I can't explain how proud I was to sign up," he said. Those whom he watched for so many years, now he would be a part of. "When I was a kid, I dreamed of being able to march down the street in line with the rest of them in black pants, white shirt, and the black VFW hat," he added with pride.

He wonders if he is worthy to belong to such an organization where he now can march side by side with other veterans who, no doubt, have seen the bitter battles of war. Nevertheless, "I have tremendous pride of being a member of VFW Post 169," he concluded.

Airman Schmidt, I would go, as far to say that the VFW Post #169 is very proud of you too!

418

THE HEARTLAND MUSEUM
OF MILITARY VEHICLES

In 1986 four men from Lexington, Nebraska, had a dream. They wanted to preserve historic military vehicles and the Heartland Museum had its beginnings. They combed the state of Nebraska looking for these old military vehicles and began restoration processes. Many were found abandoned in windbreaks across the state simply rusting away. In 1991 they saw the need for a permanent site and obtained the land for the museum. Now on Veteran's Day every year, they drive these old vehicles out of the building and parade them down mainstreet in Lexington transporting the local veterans.

What began as a vision, now has become a reality with over 60 vehicles and other memorabilia available free of charge for the public to view. The main purpose is to bring honor to the many veterans who personally manned the various vehicles located here. Having them restored here also allows all Americans to learn more about the vehicles of war. They rely strictly on contributions to be able to continue to grow and maintain the facility, which is located just north of I-80 at Lexington.

The large building not only houses many of the various pieces but is also being used for a reunion center for veterans. They are presently constructing a "Memorial to the Wounded Veteran" on the grounds. The facility is a place where people can touch, smell and sit in the vehicles on display there. These vehicles may have saved the lives of veterans. Some of their vehicles are rare with only a handful left in the world. Planes like the "Huey" helicopter are now on display as well as jeeps, half-tracks, tanks, ambulances and many other types of vehicles. It is a memorial "from the people to the people," as their brochure reads. The museum is dedicated to continue adding to and the preservation of the many military vehicles used in our nation's wars.

I want to thank them for their assistance by allowing me to take photographs of some of their historic items and also for explaining to me the history behind them. Bruce Carlson, a volunteer there the day I was there, described the many items they have on display. I thank Bruce, the other volunteers, and the board of directors for contributing this historic place to Nebraska this historic place. I was amazed at the work that has been done there.

CONCLUSION

As this book is being concluded, I am reminded of a Biblical passage. It is found in Hebrews 11, the great "Faith" chapter of the Holy Bible. The writer defines the meaning of faith and later in the chapter he tells us of all the great men and women who, through faith, suffered much hardship. I believe a veteran can relate to this. To serve in the Armed Forces, takes a certain amount of faith. Faith in the government and its leaders to whom you serve. In Scripture of course, faith refers to service to our Divine Master. No matter whom you serve, faith is required to do well at the task before you.

When I read about those people of Scripture that practiced this faith, they also suffered and many were killed. They were martyrs. Towards the end of chapter 11, we find where these people of faith, "Conquered kingdoms, enforced justice, received promises, quenched raging fires, escaped the edge of the sword, won strength in weakness, became mighty in war and put foreign armies to flight." That sounds very much like what our war veterans have done. It goes on to say, "Some were tortured, mocking and scourging, and even chains and imprisonment. They were stoned, sawn in two, killed with the sword, destitute, afflicted and ill treated." Reminds me very much of POW's and combat soldiers.

Then a particular verse in Hebrews 11:38, hits the nail on the head. In the Bible it refers to people who fought the good fight of faith who were extraordinary individuals who did the impossible and were not always appreciated. It reads, "Of whom the world was not worthy-wandering over deserts and mountains, and in dens and caves of the earth."

When I see those who take our freedom for granted, burn the flag and conduct themselves in every imaginable non-patriotic way, they are a part of this nation who are not deserving of the freedoms they enjoy. They are the ones who are not worthy of those brave individuals who suffered so much so that they would have the right to whine and protest about their little problems. They don't know what trouble is, compared to those who fought for them.

Our veterans were faithful. They had faith in a nation of whom they served. Usually the nation stood behind them, supported them, as they did in WW II. As the years pass, a new generation of young people were born who never knew war.

They are unaware of what it took to keep this country strong and free. Those individuals, who, through no fault of their own, never living through a time period of war, often fail to realize how they are able to live the way they do. They enjoy the freedoms but fail to honor those who made it possible. They are the ones who are not worthy. This was the purpose of this book, as I have referred to before, to bring about a renewed realization of the cost of freedom! It is my sincere hope, that the reader will discover that realization within the pages of this script. Then, and only then, will it be a success.

BIOGRAPHY

The author, Ivan Schoone, is from Upland and has lived south of this small southcentral Nebraska town all his life. He has had an interest in farming most of his life.

He has, for many years, been a speaker at many Memorial Day Services as well as churches in the area never forgetting the debt he owes to those who suffered and died in our nation's wars.

The love of God and country has stimulated Ivan into writing. In 1996, he wrote his first book, **"Whiteout 96"** which recorded the many stories of those who spent hours trapped in the January 17th, 1996, Nebraska blizzard which temporarily paralyzed people on the roads in much of central Nebraska at the time.

In 1999, he wrote his first spiritual book titled, **"Then God,"** which shows how God has the ability to make something good and often beautiful from a bad situation. The book indicates that God is not done with us yet.

Because of his interest in people and has observed much apathy among some of the people with regard to disrespect for freedom; Ivan saw the need to write **"Operation Recognition,"** which will inform the reader that our freedoms we enjoy were bought with a very high price. When people realize that and cease to take freedom for granted; then will this book be a success. The Veterans of this Nation will again receive the honor that they so richly deserve.

Ivan is a member of the Nebraska Writer's Guild; Lion's Club, and is a columnist and correspondent for a daily newspaper. He loves America and it is his wish that God Almighty will continue to bless it!

To order additional copies of **OPERATION RECOGNITION,** complete the information below.

Ship to: (please print)

Name_____

Address_____

City, State, ZIP_____

Day Phone_____Email_____

_____ copies/**OPERATION RECOGNITION**@$21.95 each $_____
_____ copies/**THEN GOD** @ $12.95 $_____
_____ copies/**WHITEOUT '96** @ $9.95 $_____
                Postage and handling @ $3.00 per book $_____
                              NE residents add 5% tax $_____
                                Total amount enclosed $_____
        Make checks payable to: **Schoone Publishing**
                Send to: Rt. #1, Box 62
                Upland, NE 68981-9723
                     (402) 756-0217
              Email: ivanandpat@gtmc.net

****

To order additional copies of **OPERATION RECOGNITION,** complete the information below.

Ship to: (please print)

Name_____

Address_____

City, State, ZIP_____

Day Phone_____Email_____

_____ copies/**OPERATION RECOGNITION**@$21.95 each $_____
_____ copies/**THEN GOD** @ $12.95 $_____
_____ copies/**WHITEOUT '96** @ $9.95 $_____
                Postage and handling @ $3.00 per book $_____
                              NE residents add 5% tax $_____
                                Total amount enclosed $_____
        Make checks payable to: **Schoone Publishing**
                Send to: Rt. #1, Box 62
                Upland, NE 68981-9723
                     (402) 756-0217
              Email: ivanandpat@gtmc.net